MILITARIZATION

GLOBAL INSECURITIES

A Series Edited by Catherine Besteman and Daniel M. Goldstein

ROBERTO J. GONZÁLEZ   HUGH GUSTERSON   GUSTAAF HOUTMAN   EDITORS

MILITARIZATION

A READER

in collaboration with

Catherine Besteman
Andrew Bickford
Catherine Lutz
Katherine T. McCaffrey
Austin Miller
David H. Price
David Vine

Duke University Press   Durham and London   2019

Printed in the United States of America on acid-free paper ∞
Designed by Courtney Leigh Baker
Typeset in Din and Garamond Premier Pro
by Westchester Publishing Services

Library of Congress Cataloging-in-Publication Data
Names: González, Roberto J. (Roberto Jesús), [date] editor. |
Gusterson, Hugh, editor. | Houtman, Gustaaf, editor.
Title: Militarization : a reader / Roberto J. González, Hugh
Gusterson, and Gustaaf Houtman, editors ; in collaboration
with Catherine Besteman, Andrew Bickford, Catherine Lutz,
Katherine T. McCaffrey, Austin Miller, David H. Price,
David Vine.
Description: Durham : Duke University Press, 2019. |
Series: Global insecurities | Includes bibliographical
references and index.
Identifiers: LCCN 2019008552 (print)
LCCN 2019016268 (ebook)
ISBN 9781478007135 (ebook)
ISBN 9781478005469 (hardcover : alk. paper)
ISBN 9781478006237 (pbk. : alk. paper)
Subjects: LCSH: Militarization. | Militarism. | War.
Classification: LCC U21.2 (ebook) | LCC U21.2 .M558 2019 (print) |
DDC 355.02/13—dc23
LC record available at https://lccn.loc.gov/2019008552

COVER ART: Toy Soldier. Courtesy Pablo Eder/Shutterstock.com.

CONTENTS

SECTION IV. THE EMOTIONAL LIFE OF MILITARISM

SECTION V. RHETORICS OF MILITARISM

SECTION VI. MILITARIZATION, PLACE, AND TERRITORY

SECTION VII. MILITARIZED HUMANITARIANISM

SECTION VIII. MILITARISM AND THE MEDIA

SECTION IX. MILITARIZING KNOWLEDGE

This book is the outcome of an initiative by the Network of Concerned Anthropologists, which has worked since 2007 to oppose the militarization of anthropology and society more broadly.

Militarization: A Reader has twelve sections, each highlighting a theme related to militarization or militarism. A general introduction to the volume (immediately following this note) provides an overview of these subjects and how the twelve sections relate to one another.

Each of the twelve sections contains a brief introduction and several exemplary readings, compiled by a section editor who is an anthropologist specializing in the field. Most selections are abridged versions assembled from excerpts of longer pieces. Original source information can be found at the end of each section introduction. We encourage readers to refer to the original articles for more information and analysis.

A master reference list can be found at the end of the book, incorporating bibliographical references from all of the contributions and section introductions.

Many people helped us plan, prepare, and publish this book, which has been nearly a decade in the making. Austin Miller played a critical organizational role by securing reprint permissions, weaving together bibliographical references, and providing sound editorial advice at crucial moments. Founding members of the Network of Concerned Anthropologists who were not directly involved in this project provided encouragement—most notably, Gregory Feldman, Jean E. Jackson, and Kanhong Lin. Much of the conceptual work for this book came out of a workshop at Brown University's Watson Institute for International and Public Affairs in May 2012, organized by Catherine Lutz. At that event, Cynthia Enloe, Neta Crawford, Gregory Feldman, and others provided interdisciplinary perspectives that added depth to the project. We are especially grateful to Neta Crawford for her incisive ideas and intellectual generosity. Thanks, too, to June Sawyers, who created the index.

This book was supported in part by the San José State University (SJSU) College of Social Sciences, which provided grant funding to help defray the costs of reprint permissions and indexing. Walt Jacobs and Shishir Mathur were instrumental in securing that support. The SJSU Department of Anthropology provided financial and logistical support for preparation of the final manuscript. Special thanks to Agnes Borja, Shannon Gallagher, and Kristen Constanza for their assistance. The George Washington University provided funds for indexing.

We express gratitude to all those contributors who generously allowed us to include their work in this reader. In addition, we appreciate the support of the American Anthropological Association's Ed Liebow (executive director) and Janine McKenna and Chelsea Horton of the association's Permissions Department. Thanks, too, to Karin Beesley and Mary Ann Muller of Taylor and Francis; to John Mecklin (editor-in-chief) and Rachel Bronson (president) of the *Bulletin of the Atomic Scientists*; and Margie Guerra of New York University Press.

We are especially grateful to our colleagues at Duke University Press. Gisela Fosado provided unwavering editorial support and advice, and Jenny Tan expertly answered literally dozens of queries regarding copyrights, reprint permissions, and final manuscript preparation. Ellen Goldlust helped guide the book through its last stages. Without their patient guidance, we would not have succeeded in completing this volume.

FIG. I.0. In the United States, militarization often begins at home, where children are frequently socialized in ways that normalize armed conflict. Toys, books, television programs, video games, and other media not only reflect but also shape social values. Plastic army men were first popularized in the early 1950s and have been in production ever since. Photograph by Roberto J. González.

Roberto J. González and Hugh Gusterson

In the silence of his basement workshop, Peter Cleary delicately sliced away a few thin slivers of plastic from his latest project. Using a razor-sharp cutting knife, the sixty-year-old Cleary—a retired military man—sculptured the last facial features of a twelve-inch-tall human figurine clad in camouflage combat gear.

For years, Cleary had created miniature historical dioramas, usually related to wartime scenarios: a U.S. Civil War campsite; a Paris nightclub from the World War II period; a model of the famous meeting of Franklin D. Roosevelt, Winston Churchill, and Joseph Stalin. Local museums, schools, and churches occasionally displayed Cleary's work.

But his newest project was different.

As he worked late into the night, Cleary's thoughts transported him to another place and time. His head filled with memories of his only child's first birthday, in late November 1985, when he was stationed at Fort Benning, Georgia. That day, he gave his baby boy a G.I. Joe action figure. He hoped that Pete Jr. would enjoy playing with G.I. Joe as much as he had nearly twenty years earlier—and he did. Over the years, G.I. Joe served as a link connecting father and son. By the late 1990s, Pete Sr. and Pete Jr. would even compete with each other to acquire rare and often valuable collectible G.I. Joe action figures and accessories.

Another bond the two shared was a commitment to military service. Following in his father's footsteps, Pete Jr. joined the U.S. Army in 2008 and trained as a cavalry scout. Later, his wife, Beth, said, "Pete was really proud of his grandfather and dad being in the service. He loved the war movies, he loved John Wayne, and he loved G.I. Joe."

In January 2011, Army First Lieutenant Peter Cleary Jr. was deployed to Afghanistan's Khost Province, near the Pakistan border. Just a few months later, on April 3, he was killed when a mortar shell struck while he was on patrol. Pete Jr. died within minutes of the blast.

When he learned that he had lost his only child, Peter Cleary Sr. was stunned, speechless. He descended into the basement workshop and knew that, somehow, he needed to memorialize his son.

So he created a twelve-inch image in his likeness by modifying and customizing a G.I. Joe action figure.

Cleary gathered photos of his son in combat gear, and over the next few weeks he scoured the Internet for websites selling miniature pixelated Army uniforms, tiny patches, even a meticulously crafted helmet replete with a "helmet cam." He later said, "It helped me work through the grief. I wanted to make it as much like him as possible. It was very therapeutic for me to sit there and feel like I was doing something to honor him."

Others were also affected. Some of Pete Jr.'s Army buddies visited his parents. One said admiringly, "You captured his image, Mr. Cleary." Another silently cradled Pete Jr.'s miniature body in the crook of his arm for the better part of an afternoon.

Fast forward to November 30, 2014, the day that would have been Pete Jr.'s thirtieth birthday. Beth and her two sons—seven-year-old Adam and five-year-old Pete III—celebrated Daddy's birthday by doing what they had done for the past three years: visiting the beautifully manicured Dallas–Fort Worth National Cemetery. The young family took flowers, cupcakes, toys, and a can of Bud Light to their father's grave. And there they spent the day. Beth said, "The boys feel really comfortable here, so they just run and play. It's a safe place for us to come as a family." Later, she added, "They both know how much Dad loved G.I. Joe."[1]

Merchandising War

The story of the Cleary family resonates deeply—a triumphant and unusual case in which bonds of love and affection between father and son, between parent and child, are publicly recognized and celebrated.

But from a different perspective, this account illustrates the subtle means by which militaristic values can be designed, manufactured, packaged, and marketed. It also reveals how human connections—including intimate family relationships—can be influenced by the "military-industrial complex," a concept first developed by President (and former World War II commander) Dwight D. Eisenhower. Eisenhower used the term to warn Americans about the growing political influence of the defense industry and the threat it posed to democracy in the United States.

One can only wonder how many thousands of times similar dramas have played out over the years. For more than half a century, the Hasbro toy company has sold G.I. Joe, its plastic doll—or "action figure," to use Hasbro's term—to millions of Americans. (G.I. Joe was introduced in 1964; its creators were motivated to compete with Mattel's wildly popular and lucrative Barbie doll by marketing a new toy to boys.) Its commercial success was due in large part to hundreds of additional accessories, such as uniforms, weapons, vehicles, and battle stations that Hasbro sold to enthusiasts. Today there are dozens of official and unofficial G.I. Joe fan clubs and collectors' clubs, and original action figures and accessories sometimes sell for hundreds of dollars at antique shops and on eBay.

But Hasbro went a step further. In 2003, it franchised G.I. Joe to Paramount Pictures, which then created the blockbuster *G.I. Joe: Rise of the Cobra* (2009). The film was panned by critics, but it was a commercial success, due in part to extensive "tie-ins" with fast-food chains, technology companies, and other corporate sponsors. In 2014, Paramount released a sequel, *G.I. Joe: Retaliation*, which was also a box-office success.

Paramount Pictures was strongly supported by its partnership with the U.S. Department of Defense. As in the case of many Hollywood films (from *Top Gun* to *Iron Man*), the Pentagon lent a great deal of equipment and personnel for the making of the *G.I. Joe* films, including Apache helicopters, Humvees, and even members of the Army's 21st Cavalry Brigade.[2]

According to a report published by the Bloomberg news service, "Pentagon officials and weapon makers say they've found a savvy way to make US military service seem attractive to teenage boys" and more recently girls: by placing the weapons of war on the big screen (Lococo 2007). The synergy of the Paramount-Pentagon partnership was simple but powerful: free high-tech stage props in exchange for a two-hour recruitment advertisement for the military. Weapons manufacturers enjoyed the added benefit of product promotion. Scott Lusk, a spokesman for Lockheed Martin, provided a candid assessment of including F-22 fighter planes in Paramount films: such appearances "help promote the state-of-the-art, high-tech products that are designed, developed and manufactured" by Lockheed Martin for the US military (quoted in Lococo 2007).

Even before its partnership with Paramount, the Pentagon was involved in a symbiotic relationship with toy companies. In an eye-opening report that followed the U.S.-led invasion of Iraq in 2003, the journalist William Hamilton revealed how Mattel, Hasbro, and other companies inspired state-of-the-art weaponry:

"The M-16 rifle is based on something Mattel did," says Glenn Flood, a spokesman for the Pentagon, which is looking to toys and electronic games for parts, prototypes and ideas that can be developed effectively and inexpensively as battlefield tools. Inspiration has come from model planes (reconnaissance drones), "supersoaker" water guns (quick-loading assault weapons), cheap cellular phones for teenagers (video-capable walkie-talkies) and gaming control panels (for unmanned robotic vehicles). . . . Today's troops effectively received basic training as children. (Hamilton 2003)

Given these connections, the G.I. Joe franchise might be described as a massive joint venture of Paramount Pictures, Hasbro, the Pentagon and its contract firms (Boeing, Lockheed Martin, and AM General), fast-food companies, and other firms that benefit from box-office sales, action figure sales, weapon systems sales, junk food sales, and the like.

But such endeavors can be measured in more than dollars and cents. The social and psychological consequences are also important considerations, for people and families sometimes get caught in the crosshairs. Hollywood churns out films that glamorize soldiers, projecting them as archetypical American men whose struggles define the quest to come of age and find meaning in life. Filmmakers routinely submit their scripts to the Pentagon and rewrite them in exchange for access to military hardware and military locations (Fleischer 2004; Koppes and Black 1990).

Militarized cultures also tend to idealize men, masculinity, and patriarchy. In the context of the contemporary United States, it is striking that so many accounts of military families are framed as intergenerational links in which grandfathers, fathers, and sons share common experiences and identities centered on military service—as in the case of the Cleary family highlighted at the beginning of this chapter. Frequently, women are left entirely out of the picture or are portrayed as passive bystanders. As noted in the section of this reader entitled "Gender and Militarism," this gender imbalance does not provide an accurate representation of reality.

Even when women are drawn into militarist narratives, as in the case of the Hollywood film *G.I. Jane* (1997), they are typically portrayed as people who can be just as aggressive and "tough" as their male counterparts. (This has become an important gendered dimension of contemporary militarism in many nation-states, including the United States, extending militarism by promoting active participation in the armed services, including combat roles.) The intersections of militarism, war, and gender are being analyzed by a growing number of social scientists, including anthropologists (Altinay 2004; Davis et al. 2014; Enloe 1983, 2007; Peteet 1992).

Like any cultural product, G.I. Joe reveals much about American society, including the powerful role played by the complex that links the Pentagon, Hollywood, weapons manufacturers, toy companies, and other industries; the mechanisms by which such institutions succeed in diffusing militaristic ideologies widely and effectively; and the disproportionately large effects of these projects on youth. Nick Turse (2008) has gone as far as to call this interconnected system "America's military-industrial-technological-entertainment-academic-media-corporate" complex, expanding on Eisenhower's notion of the military-industrial complex.[3] Apart from the web of corporations and government agencies connected by symbiotic business relationships, and apart from the economics of profitmaking, there is the question of attitudes and values. What are the consequences of a culture industry that produces war films, toys, clothing, video games, and comic books year after year, in lockstep with the Pentagon's military adventures abroad? How can we better understand the long-term effects of what the anthropologist Catherine Lutz (2009b: 23) has called the "military normal"—a condition in which science, entertainment, business, and even high fashion deeply reflect militaristic values?[4] In short, what are the consequences of militarizing culture?

The story of the Cleary family might be viewed as a bittersweet human-interest story with a heartwarming ending. It might even make Americans feel better about fighting wars that create hometown heroes.

But from a more critical perspective, it illustrates how today's U.S. military-industrial complex is powerful and sophisticated enough to infiltrate and mediate intimate social relationships—between parent and child, family and community, civilian and soldier—colonizing the imagination of those who can help it further its own ends.

What makes such situations troubling—even tragic—is that they reveal how in American society heroism, valor, and love are often expressed in the idiom of a military-industrial-entertainment complex whose architects have altogether different motives. We begin with the story of the Cleary family and G.I. Joe because it is in many ways the story of us all.

Defining Militarization

This book is a collection of readings selected to give readers a clearer understanding of militarization—as both a cultural product and a process—across a range of societies. The contributions to this collection were chosen to provide broad anthropological perspectives on the topic. *Militarization: A Reader* is intended to serve two purposes: first, to encourage other anthropologists to begin their own explorations, particularly those who might not otherwise be inclined to do so; and second, to serve as a handbook for researchers and instructors who are already interested in militarization and who are interested in how a distinctly anthropological approach might inform the topic.

This volume was designed as a cross-cultural reader that explores militarization in different cultural contexts, but readers will discover a disproportionate amount of material dedicated to the analysis of militarization in the United States. This was done intentionally for two reasons. First, the United States today accounts for nearly 40 percent of the world's military expenditures every year; and second, the United States is the most studied and leading model of what might be called a militarized society.

Militarization—and militarism—are integral to global society today. These processes can be seen around the world in the growth of standing armies, paramilitaries, and military contractors; the stockpiling of weaponry; burgeoning state surveillance programs; the colonization of research by the national security state; the circulation of militarized imagery in popular culture; and "the tendency to regard military efficiency as the paramount interest of the state."[5] In militarized societies we are always memorializing past wars, planning for future wars, or debating the nature of war, even when we are technically at peace. No one in the world today is untouched by militarization. However, given the enormous range of local experiences of the phenomenon, from the immiserated war refugee from Syria to the suburban American happily watching *Saving Private Ryan* on its flat-panel living room television set, it may be as appropriate to speak of militarisms as of militarism.

Before going any further, we should ask: What exactly is militarism? What is militarization? How are they connected?

The historian Richard H. Kohn defines militarization as a wide-ranging process that codes "the degree to which a society's institutions, policies, behaviors, thought, and values are devoted to military power and shaped by war." He argues that for nearly seventy years, the United States has "experienced a degree of militarization heretofore unknown in American history." What particularly concerns Kohn is the possibility that American militarization will blur into *militarism*, which he defines as "the domination of war values and frameworks in American thinking, public policy, institutions, and society to the point of dominating rather than influencing or simply shaping American foreign relations and domestic life." For Kohn—who served for ten years as the U.S. Air Force's chief historian and has held various academic positions at the U.S. Army War College—militarism is the more acute condition. Kohn's analysis of the post-9/11 era and the subsequent open-ended "war on terror" raises the question of "whether the very character of the American people changes [as a result], with the emphasis on freedom and individualism displaced by obedience, discipline, hierarchy, collectivism, authoritarianism, pessimism, and cynicism" (see Kohn 2009).[6]

It is striking that a scholar with career-long connections to military institutions would issue such a warning, but others who have served the national security state have echoed Kohn's concerns. Andrew Bacevich, a professor of international relations and a Vietnam War veteran who graduated from West Point, argues that "today as never before in their history Americans are enthralled with military power." He warns that "America will surely share the fate of all those who in ages past have looked to war and military power to fulfill their destiny. We will rob future generations of their rightful inheritance. We will wreak havoc abroad. We will endanger our security at home. We will risk the forfeiture of all that we prize" (Bacevich 2005: 1, 255). By observing increases in defense spending (the U.S. military budget rose from $266 billion in 1996 to more than $700 billion in 2017), the constant growth of the U.S. military arsenal, the worldwide expansion of American military bases, a greater propensity for our leaders to use force as a foreign policy tool, and a "new aesthetic of war" manifested through a sanitized "public enthusiasm for the whiz-bang technology of the U.S. military," Bacevich convincingly argues that the rise of American militarism represents a threat to the country's long-term viability.

More recently, Catherine Lutz (2009b: 23) has noted that "the ascendance of the military came about only relatively recently in US history," since America's founders were suspicious of standing armies and used the Constitution as a means of ensuring civilian control over the military. Until World War II, most Americans generally "saw the military as a burden in peacetime and at best very occasionally necessary. . . . [M]iddle class families were reluctant to send their children into a military they saw as a virtual cesspool of vices." Like Kohn and Bacevich, Lutz describes America's most recent phase of militarization as a process that began taking shape seven decades ago as the United States mobilized for World War II and then the Cold War, with its protracted blurring of the boundaries between peace and wartime mobilization. She reminds us that militarization mobilizes a coalition that includes "all of the institutions and groups who benefitted from a large military budget":

Not only weapons manufacturers but companies like Proctor & Gamble and the Disney Corporation came to enjoy and rely on immense military contracts. US universities were drawn up in a concerted government campaign to put much of the nation's scientific talent and university training at the disposal of the military, to the point where 45 percent of all computer science graduate students with federal support get it from the Pentagon, and 25 percent of all scientists and engineers work on military projects. The military-industrial-Congressional-media-entertainment-university complex is a massively entangled system. (Lutz 2009b: 28–29)

In her book *Homefront*—an ethnography of Fayetteville, North Carolina, a town located near one of the largest U.S. military bases in the world—Lutz observes that "there are many places like Fayetteville in America, from its nearly nine hundred other domestic military bases in such towns as Norfolk, Virginia, New London, Connecticut, and Killeen, Texas, to the thousands of places from Seattle, Washington, to Binghamton, New York, where weapons and equipment are made." Whether they are military bases or production facilities, they produce ingrained patterns of local economic dependence. The economy, geography, customs, fashions, forms of entertainment, and even values of the United States have been shaped by military institutions. Lutz notes: "In an important sense, we all inhabit an army camp, mobilized to lend support to the permanent state of war readiness that has been with us since World War II." Militarization truly affects us all, and it may well be the case that U.S. society has become "addicted to war" (Lutz 2001: 3).

Lutz's analysis provides us with a glimpse of what the anthropology of militarization means and how it might differ from other disciplinary analyses. Anthropology, which integrates several subfields, including cultural anthropology, archaeology, and physical anthropology, can offer important insights into processes of militarism and militarization. The discipline combines empirical methods with culturally informed perspectives and can offer a long-term historical perspective stretching back thousands of years. It can provide valuable information about the biological consequences of militarism, both on human bodies and on ecosystems. Finally, its methods include both cross-cultural comparison and ethnographic approaches based on long-term fieldwork and participant observation, which can provide a ground-level view of how militarism is experienced by those who are most affected by it. The combination of these elements can bring a powerful multidimensional approach not found in other disciplines.

A comprehensive review of the anthropology of militarization would include topics beyond the scope of this book, including the anthropology of social conflict, the anthropology of war, and the anthropology of peace and conflict.[7]

Of course, the United States is not the first society to follow a military imperative. Others have also placed a high value on military prowess and war fighting, but at a cost. It will put our analysis of contemporary militarism in broader perspective if we put it in the context of other societies from the historical record who organized themselves around military conquest and martial virtues. Archaeologists and cultural anthropologists have researched the rise and fall of such cultures in various regions of the world. Although there are many differences among them, they hold in common several salient characteristics.

The ancient Greek city-state of Sparta is among the most famous. It was the dominant military power in Greece for nearly three centuries, beginning in approximately 650 B.C. A male citizen's primary obligation was to be a good soldier, and Sparta rose to prominence on the strength of its infantry.

According to Plutarch, Spartan mothers bathed their newborn sons in wine rather than water to test their resilience. Even more remarkable was the extraordinary dominance of the Spartan state and its institutions. Unlike its rival Athens (and many other Greek city-states), Sparta was a society in which children, particularly boys, were separated from their parents at an early age. All boys were required to undergo a lengthy, physically challenging collective upbringing called the *agoge*, supervised by the city-state's most prestigious officers.

By the time they were seven years old, Spartan boys spent part of the day with peers in physical training. Boys were subjected to harsh conditioning: they lived barefoot, were forced to steal crops to supplement their inadequate rations, and improvised their sleeping quarters. Their overseers brutally punished them with beatings if they were recalcitrant or fell short of expectations (Golden 2003: 20).

The Spartans placed little importance on literature, the arts, or commerce. Instead, education focused on strength, discipline, and austerity. The *agoge* made ever greater demands on young Spartans by age twelve, when most Greek boys had completed their schooling.

Boys lived in barracks under constant surveillance from their elders and military officials. They were also faced with frequent ordeals, including massed brawls. According to the historian Mark Golden, "Only those who proved their fitness could eventually earn election to one of the common messes where Spartan males lived from the ages of twenty to thirty and ate their main meal for thirty years more. The *agoge* aimed to instill soldierly virtues: strength, endurance, solidarity" (Golden 2003: 20).

Perhaps it is for this reason that the great Athenian statesman Pericles once noted that Spartan youth had no childhood at all.

A striking effect of this prolonged training was a severed bond between parents and their sons; indeed, Spartan mothers and fathers had no significant role in raising their children: "The boy belonged, effectively, not to his own family but to the state, and the goal was to produce a strong and efficient military machine whose men were loyal only to each other and to Sparta" (Shapiro 2003: 107).

The nomadic peoples of Mongolia were another society that placed great importance on war fighting and military expansion. Prior to the thirteenth century AD, localized raids among different nomadic groups in that region were not unusual, but Genghis Khan managed to either unite or subdue the various groups by 1206. Then he and his descendants led the Mongol confederation on a series of conquests that would lead to the creation of the largest empire the world had ever seen.

The Mongol army was organized in a strict hierarchy, and its fighters were ruthless. As it expanded across Asia (and eventually into Europe), the army laid siege to towns and cities. Those who refused to surrender were often massacred, and surviving soldiers were incorporated into the Mongol military. Genghis Khan earned the loyalty of his growing army by distributing the spoils among his soldiers and by promoting officers based on merit rather than kinship. He demanded absolute allegiance.

These tactical and political strategies were grafted onto the nomadic pastoral culture of the Mongols. According to the historian Stephen Turnbull (2003: 26), "To be a Mongol man was to be a Mongol warrior. There is no word in the Mongol language for 'soldier.' . . . [T]he whole of a Mongol warrior's daily life was a preparation for war. The same techniques that were learnt for survival, for herding or for hunting had direct application in the Mongol campaigns. . . . Mongol society [was] arranged on a war footing."

An essential part of childhood, particularly for boys, included herding and hunting with bow and arrow. These things were commonly done on horseback; consequently, Mongolian men were experts in horsemanship by the time they were conscripted into the army at age fifteen. The Mongol army relied heavily on its cavalry, which allowed it to move, strike, and, if necessary, withdraw from battle quickly.

But perhaps what is most remarkable about thirteenth-century Mongol warfare is the fact that the entire family—and the entire society—was mobilized in support of the Khan's wars of conquest. In the words of the historian John Masson Smith Jr., "The Mongol armies were the Mongol people in arms:

all adult males were soldiers, and all women, children of age to do [*sic*] herding, and animals served as the logistical 'tail' of an army," resulting in a constantly moving "citizens' army" (quoted in Turnbull 2003: 26).

As the Mongol Empire was disintegrating into smaller entities in the 1400s, Aztec society was beginning to take shape on the other side of the world. It offers yet another example of a culture in which warfare was a central part of the identity of a people.

The Aztecs settled on an island in the lagoon of Texcoco, situated in central plateau of Mexico, in the 1340s. Here they established the famed Tenochtitlán, a sophisticated city connected to the mainland by a series of causeways. Some have suggested that the Aztecs served as mercenaries for other indigenous groups in the region before their ascent to imperial power in the late 1400s (Aguilar-Moreno 2007: 100).

Warfare was a defining feature of Aztec life. It was the means by which they established political and economic hegemony over their empire. Warfare also had religious significance, for most of the victims that the Aztecs sacrificed to their gods were captured in battle.

Military service was mandatory for all Aztec men. Commoner families, who made up the majority of the population, prepared their sons for the military by having them do hard physical work and by strictly rationing their food. Such hardships were designed to instill discipline. By the time they were fifteen, boys were required to undergo rigorous military training at an institution called the *telpochcalli*. There the lessons of home were reinforced and expanded: teams of youth were expected to complete public works projects such as the cleaning and repairing of causeways and aqueducts and to carry firewood over long distances. Veteran soldiers trained youth in a series of exercises that eventually culminated in battlefield experience. Experienced soldiers taught novices to shoot arrows, master the use of the *atlatl* (spear thrower), and deftly swing a *maquahuitl* (a sawtoothed sword studded with sharp obsidian blades). According to Eric Wolf (1957: 145–47), "Youths were taken as apprentices to carry supplies and arms for the instructing warrior when he went to war. . . . Eventually, they would be allowed to participate fully in battle and to attempt to capture enemy prisoners for sacrifice."

Mock battles between groups of boys were valued highly in Aztec society. Youth who deviated from telpochcalli training were publicly humiliated. Those who excelled might one day join the ranks of the elite soldiers: the military orders known as the eagles (*cuacuauhtin*) and jaguars (*ocelomeh*). Aztec emperors granted special rights and privileges to the members of the orders: "the right to wear otherwise proscribed jewelry and daily military attire, to dress in cotton and wear sandals in the royal palace, to eat human flesh and drink *octli* (pulque) in public, to keep concubines, and to dine in the royal palaces" (Aguilar-Moreno 2007: 105).

Aztec women were profoundly affected by warfare. Although they were not allowed to become soldiers, women defended their families from external attacks, even if that meant jeopardizing their own lives. But as in any society undergoing constant warfare, women were most directly affected by the reality and the effects of death. Aztec women frequently lost their husbands, brothers, and children in battle, and the burdens of everyday life were heavier as a result.

A range of experiences differentiates Spartan, Mongol, and Aztec societies. At the same time, certain commonalities appear: the dominance of state or empire over personal relationships; child-rearing and educational practices characterized by hard physical training, harsh discipline, and separation from parents; the extraordinary role of military symbols in songs, rituals, and art; a cult of masculinity; and subordination of the family unit to the warfare state.

Militarism has shaped American society, too, though in different ways. In the twenty-first century, militaristic societies generally do not require boys to be physically separated from their families to be transformed into soldiers. Instead, it is more common for the contemporary national security state to reach into all aspects of life. In the contemporary United States, spending on war and defense is generally unquestioned; economic life is tightly tied to the imperatives of war-making, war preparedness, and national "security"; and popular culture is saturated with entertainment—video games, TV programs, films—that glorify and normalize militarism.

War and Human Nature

So many societies have engaged in warfare that it is tempting to ask: Is war a part of human nature? Are militarism and warfare inevitable?

Sociobiologists such as Napoleon Chagnon argue that humans have been hardwired by evolution to wage war, and a poll conducted by Zogby International in 2009 revealed that nearly three out of five Americans agreed that "waging war is a part of human nature" (Chagnon [1968] 1977, 1988; Zogby 2009). However, a great deal of anthropological evidence refutes this assumption.

In 1940, in an article that has stood the test of time, Margaret Mead made a distinction between violence (aggression at the interpersonal level) and warfare (a social institution with norms and rules). Violence is found in all societies; warfare is not. As Mead pointed out, organized armed conflict among rival groups—that is, the institution of warfare—was unknown in some societies, which did not even have a word for it. Mead noted that some contemporary hunting and gathering groups, such as the Inuit of the Arctic region and the Lepchas of the Himalayas, did not engage in war but instead resolved conflicts through other means (Mead 1940). The ethnographic record reveals that humans have been creative when it comes to ending conflicts: mediation, duels, ordeals, games and contests, court systems, and other means have all functioned as alternatives to war.

More recently, others have expanded on Mead's observations. In his book *Beyond War*, the anthropologist Douglas Fry identifies seventy-four "nonwarring" societies, mostly hunter-gatherers such as the Mbuti of the Democratic Republic of Congo and the Semai of the Malay Peninsula. (Many of these societies are not completely free from violence but have used means other than organized armed conflict to settle disputes.) The evidence is clear: warfare is not intrinsic to human nature. Fry (2007: 2) argues that *Homo sapiens* has "a substantial capacity for dealing with conflicts non-violently," suggesting that this might help humanity pave the way toward a future in which warring is less common.

From an evolutionary perspective, war as we know it is a product of a particular form of social organization—stratified state societies—and only emerged with the first states, approximately six thousand years ago. Occupational specialization was a hallmark of these societies, including occupational specialization of full-time military specialists—namely, soldiers. Consequently, prehistoric warfare (small-scale, limited, and episodic) probably emerged after the Neolithic Revolution (about twelve thousand years ago). *Homo sapiens* emerged as a species approximately 200,000 years ago; therefore, humans have waged war for less than 5 percent of their existence as a species. This long-term perspective makes it clear that war is a relatively recent phenomenon. Peace and social cooperation are much more "normal" (in the statistical sense) than war.

Another anthropologist, R. Brian Ferguson (2008: 33–34), has reached similar conclusions. He summarizes his findings in an essay entitled "Ten Points on War" and notes that "Our Species Is Not Biologically Destined for War" and "War Is Not an Inescapable Part of Social Existence." After presenting a devastating critique of those who argue that humans have an innate predisposition to violence, including Napoleon Chagnon, Ferguson systematically outlines the preconditions that make war more likely to occur—namely, sedentary agriculture (which creates settled territory to attack and defend), increased population density, pronounced social hierarchies and occupational specialization, trade (particularly in prestige goods), and rapid ecological transformations.

In other words, Ferguson argues that war is a relatively recent human invention that has spread as humanity has become more agricultural, more organized into hierarchical state societies and expanding empires, and more involved in cross-cultural conquest and trade.

Here Ferguson's arguments converge with those of the distinguished political theorist Charles Tilly, who argues that, over centuries of increasing state centralization, "war made the state, and the state made war" (Tilly 1992: 42). And, as Andrew Bard Schmookler (1994) points out, in an environment where some states devote great resources to war and the preparation for war, there will be pressure on neighboring societies to emulate them to protect themselves. It is worth noting that the general anthropological consensus goes beyond these points: anthropologists tend to agree that war played a crucial role in the evolution of the state and that states evolved as the most efficient and powerful war-making institutions in human history (Cohen 1984; Cohen and Service 1978; Fried 1969; Fried et al. 1968).

Ferguson concludes with a disturbing point: "People have the *capacity* to learn, even to enjoy, war and build it into their social lives and institutions." Furthermore, he argues, "Once a given society is internally adapted for war, making war becomes much easier—a necessity, even, for the reproduction of existing social relations. Commentators have often compared war to a disease, but a more apt analogy is an addiction" (Ferguson 2008: 34, 40).

Now that we have briefly discussed war and militarism in historical cross-cultural perspective, let us consider the complex and evolving relationship between anthropology and militarism.

How War and Militarism Shaped Early Modern Anthropology

Anthropology has been subtly molded by the priorities of the national security state and the exigencies of other peoples' wars, but until recently anthropologists have written little about militarism or international conflict. They have written still less about their own relations with the national security state.

This is ironic given that modern anthropology crystallized in the context of war. In the United States, anthropology emerged as the state sought to understand and administer native populations in the Indian wars (Borneman 1995). In England, Bronisław Malinowski—a Pole and therefore an enemy alien during World War I—devised anthropology's signature methodology of extended participant observation when he was advised, for his own good, to extend his sojourn in the Trobriand Islands for the duration of the war. In 1918, Franz Boas—often called the "father" of American anthropology—was censured from the American Anthropological Association after he publicly decried the secret involvement of anthropologists in espionage in Central America during World War I. The involvement of anthropologists in the war effort during World War II was even more profound (Price 2008).

Anthropologists' choices of field sites and research projects were also often shaped by war. Anthropologists have generally sought to avoid field sites engulfed by war, and in the Cold War anthropologists in Europe and the United States found the territory of the Soviet bloc largely off-limits even as they had easy access to countries controlled by the Western powers.[8] Meanwhile, from World War II through the first decades of the Cold War many U.S. anthropologists were sponsored by the national security state to carry out research on places of interest to the national security state, whereas others learned during the McCarthy years not to ask the wrong kinds of questions about the Cold War order (Lutz 1999; Nader 1997). During World War II, a small number of anthropologists in the United States were also, in one of the more shameful episodes in the discipline's history, involved in the administration of internment camps for Japanese Americans (Starn 1986). Ruth Benedict's classic *The Chrysanthemum and the Sword* ([1946] 1989), a World War II study of Japanese national character, exemplifies ethnographic work commissioned by the national security state. It was followed during the Cold War in the United States by more anthropological studies of national character, by the rise of area studies, and by the emergence of a positivistic approach to cultural description that was favored by government agencies. At the same time, many European anthropologists were employed by colonial governments in Africa and the Middle East to study the cultural practices and structures of social organizations of societies under colonial rule to enhance the ability of the colonial governments to control them.

The World War II generation of anthropologists, their attitudes shaped by the "good war" against fascism, often saw their work for military and intelligence agencies as relatively unproblematic. By the 1960s, a new generation of anthropologists—trained, ironically, thanks to the educational largesse generated by the GI Bill and Cold War boom years—began to question anthropology's private bargains with these government entities. This generation questioned (and, according to their opponents, exaggerated) anthropologists' covert work in the service of counterinsurgency in Latin America and Southeast Asia in the 1960s (Berreman 1968; Jorgensen and Wolf 1970). A few anthropologists who had studied the relationship between war and the evolution of the state in the late 1960s began directing some of their attention to modern warfare.

Anthropology after the 1960s embodied a strong sentiment against war and militarism, and the American Anthropological Association's "Principles of Professional Responsibility" (1971) took a clear stand against the kind of covert anthropological work the national security state had sponsored in the past.

Given the geopolitical context in which anthropology grew to maturity, some striking gaps exist in the targets of the ethnographic gaze during the mid-twentieth century. Anthropologists hardly wrote about nuclear weapons; about the U.S. military bases or colonial aggression in the countries where they did their fieldwork or where they lived; or about colonialism, imperialism, or the Cold War as a cultural system—with a few notable exceptions (Gough 1968). And although the Vietnam War fractured the American Anthropological Association in the late 1960s, anthropologists wrote surprisingly little about Vietnamese culture or about the Vietnam War until the 1990s. Instead, during the mid-twentieth century, most anthropologists struck an informal bargain with political scientists, ceding to them the international state system while taking for themselves the "tribal zone."

Anthropological Work on Militarism after the Cold War

One could make a compelling argument that for much of the Cold War, anthropologists suffered from a kind of myopia. Many were too narrowly focused on traditional cultural forms until militarism, terror, and violence finally began to come into anthropological focus in the 1980s. This change came about partly because communal violence and terror in ethnographic sites such as Sri Lanka and Latin America were becoming impossible to overlook, and partly because theoretical shifts in anthropology in the 1980s authorized the investigation of new subjects, often by a generation of anthropologists who had come of age during or after the Vietnam War. The end of the Cold War also produced new structures of international conflict, stimulating new theoretical and empirical work in response. Numerous anthropologists began documenting and theorizing terror and communal violence in many regions, including Latin America, South Asia, Northern Ireland, and Africa (see, e.g., Feldman 1991; Kapferer 1988; Manz 1988; Sluka 1989; Tambiah 1986; Taussig 1986). These years also saw the publication of compendia on war, violence, and torture (Nordstrom and Martin 1992; Nordstrom and Robben 1995).

During the post–Cold War era, initiated by the fall of the Berlin Wall in 1989 and the subsequent dissolution of the Soviet Union in 1991, there was a boom in anthropological studies of militarization, war, and violence that represented a major ethnographic and theoretical advance. This body of work focused on ethnic violence and genocide; research on war and memory; the phenomenology of violence; nuclear weapons; the impact of U.S. military bases; and last, but not least, American militarism.

Anthropological research on ethnonational violence and genocide emerged as globalization processes eroded the state's old monopoly of legitimate violence from above—through the "transnationalization of military forces" (e.g., via an expanded and more active North Atlantic Treaty Organization)—and from below, as force was increasingly privatized and subcontracted. The old legitimating ideologies of the Cold War were replaced by reinvented ethnonationalisms, and wars took shape in which the stake was identity. Partly because most of these were internal wars that sought to settle the identities of entire populations that contested their place in countries established through conquest and imperialism, 80–90 percent of the casualties were civilian—the exact inverse of the military-civilian casualty ratio at the start of the twentieth century, when most wars were between states rather than within them. Such wars have taken place in the former Yugoslavia, Chechnya, Sri Lanka, Somalia, Rwanda/Burundi, and now, Iraq, Afghanistan, and Syria (Besteman 1996; Bringa 1996; Hayden 1996; Malkki 1995; Mamdani 2002; Tishkov 2004).

The body of work addressing such conflicts is subtle and historically sensitive in its deconstruction of popular deterministic assumptions about ancient hatreds. It is striking that identities that, according to this literature, are manufactured and contingent are nevertheless so powerful in mobilizing populations for mass murder and that when nations fractured in the 1990s and 2000s, they often did so along ethnic lines. It is understandable why this would be the case. Many contemporary nation-states were created in the aftermath of a global history of imperialism during which thousands of more-or-less independent societies were forcibly incorporated into expanding empires, where they were redefined as "ethnic groups" rather than autonomous peoples. Because they did not give their consent, did not disappear or assimilate, and frequently have been exploited and oppressed, it is not surprising that the vast majority of wars around the world today are internal wars between ethnonational groups and central governments rather than wars between nation-states.

In addition to researching ethnonational violence and genocide, anthropologists have conducted studies of war and memory, often bearing witness to suffering endured by communities they study. Especially in Latin America, after two decades marked by widespread torture, death squad activity, and guerrilla insurgency, some anthropologists have sought (often at risk to themselves) to ensure that their writing speaks for the dead and bereaved and does not contribute to the culture of silence that often enabled the killing in the 1980s and 1990s (Binford 1996; Falla 1999; Green 1999; Manz 2004; Nelson 2015; Sanford 2003; Sluka 2000).[9]

Another rich body of anthropological work focuses on the phenomenology of war and violence: how violence works as a set of cultural practices and what it does to people to live in a society wracked by civil war or state-sponsored terror. In societies where fear is "a way of life" (Green 1999), one often finds a range of interrelated phenomena: a disabling uncertainty as to what might get one killed and which neighbors and friends might turn into enemies; a sense that the future has been forever lost; the use of pain and terror to socially disconnect victims; a public culture of silence and denial about atrocities; a pervasive militarization of daily life often lived under surveillance; waves of violence that, taking people out of everyday mundane reality, create a perverse sense of communitas among perpetrators; the sundering of families by death, forced conscription, or eviction; dead, mutilated, and tortured bodies intended by the perpetrators as semiotic messages in a context where victims experience terror and bodily suffering at the very boundaries of representability; and exaggerated ideologies of masculinity among perpetrators and the feminization of male victims, often achieved in part by the rape of "their" women.

In situations of prolonged military occupation and resistance (e.g., in Northern Ireland, the West Bank, and Gaza) such conditions become internalized in processes of cultural reproduction. Prison detention and torture at the hands of security forces can become rites of passage into adulthood among subordinate populations, often effecting shifts in the balance of power between the sexes and the generations in the process (Arextaga 1997; Peteet 1992). In the Occupied Territories, for example, the young men of the Intifada have parlayed beatings and detentions into enhanced authority within communities that formerly accorded greater respect to an older generation. Meanwhile, weapons training and combat are increasingly common teenage and even preteen experiences, especially in parts of Africa (Singer 2005).

A decade that has seen increasing anthropological interest in globalization has also produced more studies exploring the transnational linkages of cultures of violence and terror. For example, at the School of the Americas (now called the Western Hemisphere Institute for Security Cooperation), American military trainers shared techniques with Latin American military officers, many of whom were involved in human rights violations (Gill 2004). If such violations were once legitimated by the U.S. struggle against communism, the organizing frame shifted to the "war on drugs" in the 1990s and the "war on terror" after September 11, 2001. In reference to such conflicts, Carolyn Nordstrom argues that "the whole concept of local wars is largely a fiction," since local wars are enabled by a globalized shadow economy of arms traffickers, diamond smugglers, and even nongovernmental organization workers (Nordstrom 1997: 5). Other anthropologists are probing the connection between wars in the Third World and the recent growth of the new mercenaries or "private military contractors" in the burgeoning military services industry—an industry whose rise is undermining the monopoly on the legitimate use of violence that Max Weber saw as essential to the modern state (Higate 2012; Li 2015b; Singer 2004).

Yet another fruitful area of anthropological research on militarism has focused on U.S. nuclear weapons testing and production. Pacific Islanders and residents of the American Southwest have experienced exceptional suffering, including environmental contamination and high rates of cancer and birth defects (Barker 2003; Johnston 2007; Johnston and Barker 2008; Kuletz 1998; Masco 2006). Nuclear testing has been challenged by antimilitary activists, and several anthropologists have chronicled their efforts (Krasniewicz 1992; Masco 2006). American nuclear weapons laboratories have been the subject of various ethnographic studies focusing on the web of local relationships within which weapons laboratories are embedded and on the dynamics of simulations in nuclear weapons scientists' scientific practices. This ethnographic work has also scrutinized the public discourses that legitimate nuclear weapons (Gusterson 1999b; Masco 2006; McNamara 2001).

The Anthropology of Militarism in the Twenty-First Century

U.S. militarism was almost invisible in anthropology until recent years, despite the fact that the United States accounts for nearly 40 percent of all global military spending and arms sales in the world while stationing half a million troops, contractors, intelligence agents, and their dependents on nearly eight hundred overseas bases in more than seventy countries. Militarism provides a powerful set of processes for structuring the U.S. economy and society, organizing U.S. relationships with allies and adversaries, shaping the flow of information in the public sphere, and molding popular culture.

A growing body of ethnographic work has focused on military bases, both abroad and at home. By now, it is clear that U.S. military bases abroad contaminate the environment and exacerbate inequality and human rights abuses while military bases at home deplete local resource bases, inflect asymmetrical race and gender relations, and create a privileged category of militarized "super-citizens." At the same time, military contracts often have public support because they provide a significant boost to state and local economies, even as they shift resources away from social services (Lutz 2001, 2009b; McCaffrey 2002; McLeish 2015; Vine 2011, 2015).

Less tangible but equally damaging is the way militarist apologetics have distorted U.S. media coverage of international affairs and helped shape a degraded popular culture saturated with racial and nationalist stereotypes, aestheticized destruction, and images of violent hypermasculinity (Bishara 2012; Gibson 1994; Gusterson 1999b; Hammond 2007; Hannerz and Carter 2004; Jeffords 1989; Pedelty 1995; Weber 2006). In this cultural milieu, the toxic combination of a smoldering backlash against national humiliation in Vietnam and the hubris of being the world's only superpower, aggravated by the injuries of 9/11, has produced a virulent militaristic nationalism that threatens both the American way of life and the stability of the international security system (Bacevich 2005; Johnson 2004; Turner 1996). Donald Trump's electoral triumph is connected to his "America first" brand of militant nationalism—he has called for "the greatest military buildup in American history," describes the U.S. military as "the best fighting force in the history of this planet," and has appointed more generals to positions of power than any president in recent history.

In the years following the U.S.-led invasions of Afghanistan and Iraq, the American military began turning to social scientists for help. A few responded by enthusiastically joining the U.S. Army's Human Terrain System (HTS) program, an initiative that embedded researchers with combat brigades beginning in 2007. Most anthropologists responded with deep skepticism, and as counterinsurgency theories and methods regained popularity in U.S. military circles, a number of anthropologists responded with critical analyses (González 2009; Joseph 2011; Kelly et al. 2010; Network of Concerned Anthropologists 2009; Price 2011). By 2008, both the American Anthropological Association and the Society for Applied Anthropology expressed concerns over the ethical problems inherent in such an effort. In 2007, the Executive Board of the American Anthropological Association issued a statement strongly condemning the HTS, noting that the "Board views the HTS project as an unacceptable application of anthropological expertise" (American Anthropological Association 2007).

Unlike during the Vietnam War era, anthropologists conducted a range of studies directly related to the U.S.-led wars in Afghanistan and Iraq (and, more broadly, the so-called war on terror) during the first decade of the twenty-first century: ethnographic interviews with Iraq War veterans who came to oppose the war as well as studies of the challenges facing U.S. combat veterans seeking to reintegrate themselves into civilian life (Gutmann and Lutz 2010; Hautzinger and Scanlan 2013; Wool 2015); accounts of lives under occupation in Iraq,

Afghanistan, Kashmir, and elsewhere (Al-Ali 2007; Aziz 2007; Bhan 2013; Daulitzai 2006; Duschinski 2009; Enloe 2010; Robben 2010; Visweswaran 2013); the development of new technologies of warfare such as drones, virtual wars, and war gaming (Der Derian 2009; Finnström and Whitehead 2013; Gusterson 2016; Sluka 2011; Stroeken 2012); social and psychological studies of the motivations of terrorist groups, as well as the impact on Muslim communities of the "terrorist" label (Atran 2010); studies of the application of law in the "war on terror" (Li 2015a, 2010); an analysis of the transformation of the "war on terror" into a new kind of conflict pitting the United States and its client governments in Central Asia and the Middle East against "tribal" societies (Nordstrom 2004; Richards 2004); research on how the inhabitants of war zones adapt to living under difficult conditions (Finnström 2008; Lubkemann 2008; Măcek 2011; Nordstrom 1997; Tishkov 2004); and studies of situations in which wars have formally ended but political violence or armed conflict continues (Ahmed 2013). It is a telling sign that the U.S. national security state itself has become a subject of anthropological inquiry (Masco 2014; McNamara and Rubenstein 2011). At the same time, military agencies in the United States and beyond (and private military contractors) are increasingly interested in coopting a simplified version of "culture" that can be incorporated into heuristic techniques, computerized algorithms, and predictive modeling software.

Looking further afield, other recent anthropological work on militarism and war focuses on a relatively new phenomenon: the rise of nonstate paramilitary organizations, including gangs and religious extremists, in postwar settings (Burrell 2014; Campbell 2009; Hoffman 2008, 2011b; Moodie 2012; Muehlmann 2014; Zilberg 2011). These groups tend to be transnational, and in many ways neoliberal economic processes (e.g., deregulation of capital controls, increasing international trade) and other globalizing trends (e.g., the Internet and social media) have enabled these organizations—and their ideologies—to thrive.

Anthropologists have recently become interested in analyzing state-sanctioned memorializations of war and violence, as well as the use of new biotechnologies and forensics to identify the dead (Ferrándiz 2013; Wagner 2008). Finally, anthropologists have been tracking new attempts to link humanitarianism, disaster relief, and militarization (de Waal 1998; Fassin and Pandolfi 2010; Forte 2014; Tate 2015).

The anthropology of militarism and war has broadened in scope, but there are numerous topical and geographical areas in need of investigation. For example, there is great potential for future anthropological research into the ways in which "formal" wars often lead to cycles of ever more intractable problems of violence and instability. And there is broad agreement today among regional scholars that many aspects of the U.S.-led invasion and occupation of Iraq— "de-Baathification" policies that put thousands of armed military men out of work; wanton incarceration of thousands of Iraqis (many, if not most, of whom were innocent); inadequate training of Iraqi security forces; U.S. support for a corrupt Shia-led government; importation of massive quantities of weaponry, military vehicles, armaments, and so on—created the conditions by which the self-styled Islamic State in Iraq and Syria (ISIS) was able to rise to power.

Much work also remains to be done on other militarized societies—for example, China, Israel, Saudi Arabia, Russia, France, Indonesia, Myanmar, Egypt, Nigeria, India, Sudan, Pakistan, Venezuela, and the United Kingdom. A better comparative understanding of militarism will surely lead to more sophisticated theoretical frameworks.

Militarism, like capitalism, is a lifeworld with its own escalatory logic that takes different local forms while displaying fundamental underlying unities. Despite these underlying unities, local processes of militarization are invariably rationalized and legitimated as defensive reactions to someone else's militarism from which they therefore differ in moral character. One task for anthropological analysis is to unmask such ideological processes of legitimation. Despite many advances, anthropology still has much theoretical and empirical work to do to illuminate militarism, the source of so much suffering in the world today.

About This Book

We have edited this collection as a primer on militarism, viewed from a broadly anthropological perspective. In other words, we have attempted to approach militarism holistically, historically, and cross-culturally. As we chose the selected readings, we were determined to include work that analyzed militarism in its full social, economic, political, cultural, environmental, and symbolic contexts. Readers should note that nearly all of the selections are edited or excerpted, in some cases very extensively. We encourage interested readers to seek out the original material for more depth and detail. Collectively, we thought carefully about who to ask to edit each of the constituent sections and tried to approach those who have special expertise in that subject area.

Our reader begins with section I, "Militarization and Political Economy." The selections analyze how war and militarism have transformed national economies, and how the global movement of weapons, soldiers, and defense contractors have played a role in redistributing wealth and power.

Section II, "Military Labor," broadly explores the work of warfare—from mercenary labor in West Africa and U.S. soldiers being displaced by robots to sex workers stationed near military bases. A key theme of this section is that military labor is more than just "soldiering." It encompasses a wide range of auxiliary activities.

Section III, "Gender and Militarism," delves deeply into the ways in which concepts of masculinity and femininity are used for wartime mobilization and to justify killing. The selections also call into question cherished assumptions about men's aggression and women's passivity.

Section IV, "The Emotional Life of Militarism," addresses the question of how people in militarized societies grapple emotionally with daily life. What are the structures of feeling, or the political aesthetics that characterize their interactions with others? To what extent does fear (e.g., about a terrorist attack or nuclear war) influence the everyday decisions of a person living in militarized state?

Section V, "Rhetorics of Militarism," analyzes the ways in which words and images are manipulated to make war seem natural and even beneficial, to encourage military action, and to dehumanize enemies. This section also focuses on the ways in which soldiers are transformed into heroes worthy of veneration. In short, it dissects the controlling processes by which symbols can be deployed to stimulate war fever.

Militaristic policies have profoundly altered physical and cultural landscapes. This is the subject of section VI, "Militarization, Place, and Territory." A wide range of activities—nuclear testing, military occupation, the creation of checkpoints and barriers, the construction of military bases, the development of "strategic hamlets" and United Nations refugee camps—have geographically reshaped space and place.

In section VII, "Militarized Humanitarianism," special attention is given to the growing role of the United Nations, nongovernmental agencies, and relief agencies over the past twenty-five years. As this process has unfolded, it has become clear that humanitarian aid has become tightly intertwined with military intervention in many different regions. The selections in this section view these changes through a critical lens.

Section VIII, "Militarism and the Media," explores the complicity of journalists with U.S. military operations while noting that journalists have also made important critical revelations about the U.S. wars in Vietnam, Afghanistan, and Iraq. This section also explores the valorization of warfare by Hollywood and the emergence of the paramilitary hero in popular culture.

Section IX, "Militarizing Knowledge," explores the long-standing relationship between American universities and U.S. military and intelligence agencies. Although popular stereotypes often cast academics as detached, apolitical scientists who inhabit ivory towers, the reality is much different. Over the past century, many university researchers from both the "hard" and the "soft" sciences have conducted their work in close collaboration with the military, particularly during the Cold War.

Section X, "Militarization and the Body," focuses on the many ways in which war and militarism have physically and physiologically transformed humans. More specifically, the selections address the question of how human bodies have been inscribed, altered, damaged, and destroyed by living in a constant state of war readiness. Disciplinary practices, pharmacological innovations, prolonged exposure to traumatic stress—all of these elements and many more have left indelible marks on human bodies and psyches.

Section XI, "Militarism and Technology," explores the aestheticization of military technology and the ideological power of discourses of technical rationality that promises (often mistakenly) victory in war. It is often said of military technology, particularly of nuclear weapons, that "you can't put the genie back in the bottle," but this section gives the striking historical example of Japan's decision to eliminate guns after they were introduced by the Portuguese in the sixteenth century.

The final section, "Alternatives to Militarization," provides a range of ideas for lessening the harmful impact of militarism in the world. The goal is to inspire readers to think creatively about ways to build alternatives to war and militarism. To paraphrase Margaret Mead, if war and militarism are human inventions, then perhaps it is time for us to recognize that they are obsolete.

We hope that this reader will play a role in moving us a step closer to that moment of recognition.

NOTES

The authors wish to thank Catherine Besteman and Katherine McCaffrey for their assistance and advice in preparing this introduction and Gustaaf Houtman for his careful coordination and editorial work. Portions of the introduction are drawn from two of the authors' previous publications: Roberto J. González, *Militarizing Culture: Essays on the Warfare State* (Walnut Creek, CA: Left Coast, 2010), and Hugh Gusterson, "Anthropology and Militarism," *Annual Review of Anthropology* 36 (2007), 155–75.

1. This account is based on actual events: see Marc Ramirez, "Salute to a Son," *Dallas Morning News*, December 18, 2014, accessed January 10, 2016, http://res.dallasnews.com/interactives/gijoe-dad/.

2. Accounts of the U.S. Army's involvement in the *G.I. Joe* movie are in Holman 2009; Sheftick and Pritchartt 2009.

3. Anthropologists employ similar ideas in the edited book *War, Technology, Anthropology* (Stroeken 2012), which includes work on military video games (some of them designed with the cooperation of the U.S. Army) and the aesthetics of war music videos. See also Grossman and DeGaetano 1998.

4. For a typical example of haute couture military chic, see "Military Issue," a photo spread by Mario Testino, in *Vogue*, March 2010, 446–58. Twelve full-page photos feature svelte models wearing khaki and olive drab blouses, coats, hats, shoes, and accessories by Louis Vuitton, Max Mara, Ralph Lauren, and Chloé, among many others. For a discussion of "military chic" in the fashion world, see Enloe 2007.

5. *Oxford English Dictionary*, quoted in Bacevich 2005: 1, 255.

6. Kohn's qualitative analysis focuses on the ways in which political institutions, the U.S. legal system, and shifts in cultural mores have changed in the post–World War II period and the post-9/11 period, in particular. For broadly similar arguments about the progressive militarization of the United States during and after the Cold War, see Masco 2014; Wills 2010.

7. For example, readers interested in the anthropology of war are encouraged to explore Haas 1990; Otterbein 2009; Waterston 2009.

8. A notable exception is Katherine Verdery (1991), who studied nationalism and ethnic identity in Cold War Romania. Andrew Bickford (2011), doing fieldwork at the end of the Cold War, has written about East German soldiers and their shoddy treatment at the hands of the newly unified German state.

9. Such work often builds on and revoices in a more theoretical register an indigenous tradition of *testimonio*—vivid, first-person eyewitness accounts of terror and violence exemplified by Rigoberta Menchú's autobiography.

FIG 1.0. Militarization tends to be deeply embedded in local, regional, and national economies. In 2017, the U.S. Congressional Budget Office reported spending nearly $600 billion on the five military branches. This does not include funding for the Department of Veterans Affairs, the nuclear weapons program, and related budget items. Millions rely on such spending for their livelihoods—not just the 1.3 million active-duty troops, but also civilians such as employees of Oshkosh Defense in Wisconsin. However, federal spending for many nonmilitary purposes creates more jobs per dollar spent. Photograph courtesy Oshkosh Defense.

SECTION I. MILITARIZATION AND POLITICAL ECONOMY

Compiled by CATHERINE LUTZ

Introduction

As an ideology, militarism does a variety of kinds of work, chief among them explaining and legitimating massive economic investments in, and related political and cultural commitments to, war and war preparation. This section includes readings that review several key issues in the political economy of militarization. In each reading, the problem is to explain how militarism shapes economic life, from the class and marriage aspirations of Sri Lankan women to the fortunes of the sports industry in the United States or the mining industry in West Africa. Examining the political economy of militarism means looking at how capitalism and the global flow of arms, soldiers, and military contractors have come to redistribute wealth and shape political life globally. It also means coming to understand why military occupations are so widespread and historically long-lasting in the contemporary world (Visweswaran 2013).

The literature on the political economy of militarism in the United States identifies the mythic status of two popular beliefs. The first is that objective security threats drive levels of military spending, and the second is that the U.S. population has prospered as a result of that spending. This belief is promoted by a media environment structured around the press releases of military and other government officials that inflate threats and celebrate military labor as self-sacrificing. The second narrative about the economic healthfulness of militarism took off most strongly with the aid of an observed correlation between massive federal spending associated with World War II and the end of the Great Depression.

John Bellamy Foster, Hannah Holleman, and Robert McChesney begin the section with a history of U.S. corporations' interest in maintaining a high level of military spending after the end of World War II. They build on an early argument (Baran and Sweezy 1966) that the installation of a massive "peacetime" military in the United States was the result of the desire to absorb extensive surplus production capacity via military production. This was a high-profit and low-risk enterprise in comparison with nonmilitary production and had the added advantage, when that military was widely deployed overseas, of creating a secure international environment for the accumulation of wealth. Research has identified the opportunity costs of government investment in the armaments industry. The siphoning of research and development (R&D) money and scientists to the work of war has resulted in much more effort going into creating baroque warships than efficient fishing vessels or more powerful rocket engines than car motors (Melman 1985). Heidi Garrett-Peltier (2014) has shown how depressed employment rates have been a direct result of outsize military spending in the 2000s.

The next piece in this section includes excerpts from President Dwight D. Eisenhower's famous "Farewell Speech" on the military-industrial complex. In it he observed the installation of a permanently high military budget through the 1950s and compared it with the small peacetime force and government armories when he joined the military in 1911. In the original draft of the speech, he termed this a "military-industrial-congressional complex." William Astore's contribution examines how the military-industrial complex even extends into the U.S. sports industry, which has intensified its celebration of the military—profiting from it, recruiting to it, and using it to support a politics of authoritarianism.

The evolution of capitalism since the last part of the twentieth century has involved both the erosion of the idea of a national economy and the informalization of the labor force, processes that now shape militarized economies worldwide. Informal militarized labor is also on the rise in the form of militias, security guards, and the widespread privatization of military work. In his fieldwork in West Africa, Daniel Hoffman focuses on the labor involved in war-making and argues that it needs to be seen within the context of a larger set of spaces where that labor is alternately deployed and from which its redeployment in war becomes possible. The section ends with excerpts from Carolyn Nordstrom's work, based especially in extensive fieldwork in the war zones of southern Africa. It identifies the special consequences for women of the invisibilization of these processes.

1.1

THE U.S. IMPERIAL TRIANGLE AND MILITARY SPENDING

John Bellamy Foster, Hannah Holleman, and Robert W. McChesney

The United States is unique today among major states in the degree of its reliance on military spending and its determination to stand astride the world, militarily as well as economically. No other country in the post–World War II world has been so globally destructive or inflicted so many war fatalities. Since 2001, acknowledged U.S. national defense spending has increased by almost 60 percent in real dollar terms to a level in 2007 of $553 billion. This is higher than at any point since World War II (though lower than in previous decades as a percentage of gross domestic product). Based on such official figures, the United States is reported by the Stockholm International Peace Research Institute (SIPRI) as accounting for 45 percent of world military expenditures. Yet so gargantuan and labyrinthine are U.S. military expenditures that the above grossly understates their true magnitude, which, as we shall see below, reached $1 trillion in 2007.[1]

Externally, these are necessary expenditures of world empire. Internally, they represent, as Michal Kalecki was the first to suggest, an imperial triangle of state-financed military production, media propaganda, and real/imagined economic-employment effects that has become a deeply entrenched and self-perpetuating feature of the U.S. social order (Kalecki 1972: 96).

Many analysts today view the present growth of U.S. militarism and imperialism as largely divorced from the earlier Cold War history of the United States, which was commonly seen as a response to the threat represented by the Soviet Union. Placed against this backdrop, the current turn to war and war preparation appears to numerous commentators to lack a distinct target, despite concerns about global terrorism, and to be mainly the product of irrational hubris on the part of U.S. leaders. . . .

Such a view . . . downplays the larger historical and structural forces at work that connect the Cold War and post–Cold War imperial eras. In contrast, a more realistic perspective, we believe, can be obtained by looking at the origins of the U.S. "military ascendancy" (as C. Wright Mills termed it) in the early Cold War years and the centrality this has assumed in the constitution of the U.S. empire and economy up to the present (Mills 1956: 198).

The Permanent War Economy and Military Keynesianism

In January 1944, Charles E. Wilson, president of General Electric and executive vice chairman of the War Production Board, delivered a speech to the Army Ordnance Association advocating a permanent war economy. According to the plan Wilson proposed on that occasion, every major corporation should have a "liaison" representative with the military, who would be given a commission as a colonel in the reserve. This would form the basis of a program, to be initiated by the president as commander-in-chief in cooperation with the War and Navy departments, designed to bind corporations and military together into a single, unified armed forces-industrial complex. . . . Wilson went on to indicate that in this plan the part to be played by Congress was restricted to voting for the needed funds.

Wilson . . . was articulating a view that was to characterize the U.S. oligarchy as a whole during the years immediately following World War II. In earlier eras, it had been assumed that there was an economic "guns and butter" trade-off and that military spending had to occur at the expense of other sectors of the economy. However, one of the lessons of the economic expansion in Nazi Germany, followed by the experience of the United States itself in arming for World War II, was that big increases in military spending could act as huge stimulants to the economy. In just six years under the influence of World War II, the U.S. economy expanded by 70 percent, finally recovering from the Great Depression. The early Cold War era thus saw the emergence of what later came to be known as "military Keynesianism": the view that by promoting effective demand and supporting monopoly profits military spending could help place a floor under U.S. capitalism (Cook 1964; Feldman 1989: 149–50; Wilson 1944; "WPB Aide Urges U.S. to Keep War Set-up" 1944).

John Maynard Keynes, in his landmark *General Theory of Employment, Interest and Money*, published in 1936 in the midst of the Depression, argued that the answer to economic stagnation was to promote effective demand through government spending. The bastardized Keynesianism that came to be known as "military Keynesianism" was the view that this was best effected with the fewest negative consequences for big business by focusing on military spending. . . .

In the 1943 essay "The Political Aspects of Full Employment" and in subsequent essays, Kalecki argued that monopoly capital had a deep aversion to increased civilian government spending due to its intrusion on the commodity market and the sphere of private profit, but this did not apply in the same way to military spending, which was seen by the vested interests as adding to rather than crowding out profits. If absorption of the massive economic surplus of large corporate capital through increased government spending was the key to accumulation in post–World War II U.S. capitalism, this was dependent principally on military expenditures, or what Kalecki in 1956 labeled "the armament-imperialist complex." This resulted in a "high degree of utilization" of productive capacity and "counteracted the disrupting influence of the increase in the relative share of accumulation of big business in the national product" (Kalecki 1972: 75–83, 95–97). . . .

Mass communication occupied a central place in this imperial triangle. An essential part of Kalecki's argument was that "the mass communication media, such as the daily press, radio, and television in the United States are largely under the control of the ruling class." As none other than Charles E. (General Electric) Wilson, then defense mobilization director, put it in a speech to the American Newspaper Publishers Association on April 26, 1951, the job of the media was to bring "public opinion, as marshaled by the press," to the support of the permanent war effort. . . . (Kalecki 1972; Cook 1964).

The result by the mid-1950s was a fairly stable militarized economy, in which intertwined imperial, political-economic, and communication factors all served to reinforce the new military-imperial order. Kalecki (1972: 96–97) observed that U.S. trade unions were "part and parcel of the armament-imperialist set-up. Workers in the United States are not duller and trade union leaders are not more reactionary 'by nature' than in other capitalist countries. Rather, the political situation in the United States, is simply, in accordance with the precepts of historical materialism, the unavoidable consequence of economic developments and of characteristics of the superstructure of monopoly capitalism in its advanced stage." . . .

Many of Kalecki's ideas were developed further by Paul Baran and Paul Sweezy in 1966 in *Monopoly Capital*. Baran and Sweezy argued there were at least five political-economic-imperial ends propelling the U.S. oligarchy in the 1950s and '60s toward the creation of a massive military establishment: (1) defending U.S. global hegemony and the empire of capital against external threats in the form of a wave of revolutions erupting throughout the world, simplistically viewed in terms of a monolithic communist threat centered in the Soviet Union; (2) creating an internationally "secure" platform for U.S. corporations to expand and monopolize economic opportunities abroad; (3) forming a government-sponsored research and development sector that would be dominated by big business; (4) generating a more complacent population at home, made less recalcitrant under the nationalistic influence of perpetual war and war preparation; and (5) soaking up the nation's vast surplus productive capacity, thus helping to stave off economic stagnation through the promotion of high-profit, low-risk (to business) military spending. The combined result of such political-economic-imperial factors was the creation of the largest, most deeply entrenched, and persistent "peacetime" war machine that the world had ever seen (Baran and Sweezy 1966: 178–217).

Like Kalecki, Baran and Sweezy argued that the U.S. oligarchy kept a "tight rein on civilian [government] spending," which, they suggested, "had about reached its outer limits" as a percentage of national income "by 1939," but was nonetheless "open-handed with the military." Government pump-priming operations therefore occurred largely through spending on wars and war preparations in the service of empire. The Pentagon naturally made sure that bases and armaments industries were spread around the United States and that numerous corporations profited from military spending, thus maximizing congressional support due to the effects on states and districts (Baran and Sweezy 1966: 159, 161, 177, 208–11). . . .

U.S. militarism was therefore motivated first and foremost by a global geopolitical struggle but was at the same time seen as essentially costless (even beneficial) to the U.S. economy, which could have more guns and more butter, too. It was thus viewed as a win-win solution for the U.S. empire and economy. . . .

As Eisenhower's secretary of defense, Charles Erwin (General Motors) Wilson (best known for having created a major flap by saying, "What is good for General Motors is good for the country"), observed in 1957, the military setup was then so built into the economy as to make it virtually irreversible: "So many Americans are getting a vested interest in it: Properties, business, jobs, employment, votes, opportunities for promotion and advancement, bigger salaries for scientists and all that. . . . If you try to change suddenly you get into trouble" (quoted in Cook 1964: 277, 299). . . .

The need for the gargantuan military-industrial complex that the United States developed in these years was not so much for purposes of economic expansion directly (though military Keynesianism pointed to its stimulating effects) but due to the reality, as Baran and Sweezy emphasized, that the capitalist world order and U.S. hegemony could only be maintained "a while longer," in the face of rising insurgencies throughout the world, through "increasingly direct and massive intervention by American armed forces" (Baran and Sweezy 1966: 205). This entire built-in military system could not be relinquished without relinquishing empire. Indeed, the chief importance of U.S. military power from the early Cold War years to today has been that it is used—either directly, resulting in millions of deaths (counting those who died in the Korean War, the Vietnam War, the Gulf War, the Kosovo War, the Afghanistan and Iraq wars, as well as dozens of lesser conflicts), or indirectly, as a means to intimidate.

The most important leftist analysts of these developments in the 1950s and '60s, Kalecki, Baran, Sweezy, and Magdoff insisted—going against the dominant U.S. Cold War ideology—that the cause of U.S. military spending was capitalist empire rather than the need to contain the Soviet threat. The benefits of military spending to monopoly capital, moreover, guaranteed its continuation, barring a major social upheaval. The decade and a half since the fall of the Soviet Union has confirmed the accuracy of this assessment. The euphoria of the "peace dividend" following the end of the Cold War evaporated almost immediately in the face of new imperial requirements. This was a moment of truth for U.S. capitalism, demonstrating how deeply entrenched were its military-imperial interests. By the end of the 1990s, U.S. military spending, which had been falling, was on its way up again.

Today, in what has been called a "unipolar world," U.S. military spending for purposes of empire is rapidly expanding—to the point that it rivals that of the entire rest of the world put together. When it is recognized that most of the other top ten military-spending nations are U.S. allies or junior partners, it makes the U.S. military ascendancy even more imposing. Only the reality of global empire (and the effects of this on the internal body politic) can explain such an overwhelming destructive power. . . .

The Labyrinth of U.S. Military Spending

The most direct way of measuring the extent of the U.S. commitment to the military-imperialist complex over the post–World War II period is through an examination of U.S. military spending itself. This is not, however, easily accomplished. U.S. military expenditure is a labyrinth presenting numerous dead

TABLE 1.1. Acknowledged versus Actual U.S. Military Spending, 2007 (in billions of dollars)

Acknowledged		Actual	
National defense (OMB)	552.6	National defense (NIPA)	662.2
		Space (50%)	9.1
		Grants to foreign governments (80%)[a]	29.0
		Veterans' benefits	40.0
		Military medical payments[b]	12.1
		Interest attributed to military[c]	250.1
Total	552.6	Total	1002.5

Source: National Income and Product Accounts (NIPA); Office of Management and Budget (OMB), Budget for Fiscal Year 2009, Historical Tables, Tables 3.1, 3.2.20.

a   Grants to foreign governments are conservatively considered here to be 80 percent military. For instance, under the International Affairs portion of the budget, $8 billion was spent in 2007 on international security assistance and $16 billion was spent on international development and humanity assistance, most of which were imperial expenditures.

b   Includes one-third of "Other" government social benefits category (National Income and Product Accounts, Table 3.12), defined by the Bureau of Economic Analysis as consisting "largely of payments to nonprofit institutions, aid to students, and payments for medical services for retired military personnel and their dependents at nonmilitary facilities."

c   Assumes that 80 percent of net interest payments are attributable to the military. This is less than other estimates by major analysts. Robert Higgs of the Independent Institute attributes 91.2 percent of the national debt to the military. In his most recent estimate, James Cypher (2007: 47, 54) uses a figure of 81 percent.

ends. . . . Department of Defense spending . . . is listed as $529.8 billion for 2007, while adding in atomic energy defense activities and defense-related activities brings total national defense (line 050) to $552.6 billion (Brauer 2007: 61–66)

However . . . , it still remains to add to this . . . all or part of: economic grants to foreign governments; space; medical payments to military retirees and dependents at nonmilitary facilities; veterans' benefits; and the net interest payments on the national debt attributable to military spending. . . .

Our figures, provided in table 1.1, show that actual U.S. military spending in 2007 came to $1 trillion. This contrasts with SIPRI's clearly understated estimate (in relation to countries other than the United States, as well) for all of the world's nations in 2007 of $1.3 trillion (Stockholm International Peace Research Institute 2008: 10–11). . . .

Today, fundamental dissent toward the existence of the military-imperial system, no matter how thoughtful or well-informed, is decidedly off-limits, except for periodic ridicule. Ours is decidedly a "military-industrial-media complex" (Soloman 2005).

Nevertheless, the imperial triangle is increasingly confronted with its own contradictions. As Baran and Sweezy foresaw more than four decades ago in *Monopoly Capital*, the U.S. military system faced two major internal obstacles. First, military spending tended to be technologically intensive; hence, its employment-stimulating effect was decreasing. "Ironically," they observed, "the huge military outlays of today may even be contributing substantially to an increase of unemployment: many of the new technologies which are by-products of military research and development are also applicable to civilian production, where they are quite likely to have the effect of raising productivity and reducing the demand for labor." Second, expansion of "weapons of total destruction" and the devastating effects of the use of more powerful weapons, could be expected to generate a growing rebellion against the permanent war economy at all levels of society, as people perceived the dangers of global barbarism (or worse, annihilation) (Baran and Sweezy 1966: 213–17).

Today the enormous weight of Washington's war machine has not prevented it from being stretched to its limits while becoming bogged down in Iraq and Afghanistan. Although still capable of great destruction, the United States is significantly limited in its ability to deploy massive force to achieve its ends whenever and wherever it wishes. . . .

There is no doubt that a society that supports its global position and social order through $1 trillion a year in military spending, most likely far exceeding that of all the other countries in the world put together, unleashing untold destruction on the world, while faced with intractable problems of inequality, economic stagnation, financial crisis, poverty, waste, and environmental de-cline at home, is a society that is ripe for change. It is our task to change it.

NOTES

Editors' note: This is a significantly abridged version of a much longer article published in *Monthly Review*. Readers are encouraged to read the original for a more detailed argument.

   1. The data are from Office of Management and Budget, *Budget for Fiscal Year*, 2009, Historical Tables, table 3.2; Stockholm International Peace Research Institute, *SIPRI Yearbook 2008: Summary*, http://yearbook2008. sipri.org/files/SIPRIYBo8summary .pdf, 10–11; SIPRI, Military Expenditure Database (United States), http://milexdata.sipri .org/result.php4.

I.2

FAREWELL ADDRESS TO THE NATION, JANUARY 17, 1961
Dwight D. Eisenhower

Good evening, my fellow Americans.... Three days from now, after half a century in the service of our country, I shall lay down the responsibilities of office as, in traditional and solemn ceremony, the authority of the Presidency is vested in my successor. This evening I come to you with a message of leave-taking and farewell, and to share a few final thoughts with you, my countrymen....

Throughout America's adventure in free government, our basic purposes have been to keep the peace; to foster progress in human achievement; and to enhance liberty, dignity, and integrity among people and among nations. To strive for less would be unworthy of a free and religious people. Any failure traceable to arrogance, or our lack of comprehension or readiness to sacrifice, would inflict upon us grievous hurt both at home and abroad.

Progress toward these noble goals is persistently threatened by the conflict now engulfing the world. It commands our whole attention, absorbs our very beings. We face a hostile ideology—global in scope, atheistic in character, ruthless in purpose, and insidious in method. Unhappily the danger it poses promises to be of indefi-nite duration. To meet it successfully, there is called for, not so much the emotional and transitory sacrifices of crisis, but rather those which enable us to carry forward steadily, surely, and without complaint the burdens of a prolonged and complex struggle—with liberty at stake. Only thus shall we remain, despite every provoca-tion, on our charted course toward permanent peace and human betterment....

The record of many decades stands as proof that our people and their government have, in the main, understood these truths and have responded to them well, in the face of stress and threat. But threats, new in kind or degree, constantly arise.

A vital element in keeping the peace is our military establishment. Our arms must be mighty, ready for instant action, so that no potential aggressor may be tempted to risk his own destruction.

Our military organization today bears little relation to that known by any of my predecessors in peace time, or, indeed, by the fighting men of World War II or Korea.

Until the latest of our world conflicts, the United States had no armaments industry. American makers of plowshares could, with time and as required, make swords, as well. But now we can no longer risk emergency improvisation of national defense; we have been compelled to create a permanent armaments industry of vast proportions. Added to this, three-and-a-half million men and women are directly engaged in the defense establishment. We annually spend on military security more than the net income of all United States corporations.

This conjunction of an immense military establishment and a large arms industry is new in the American experience. The total influence—economic, political, even spiritual—is felt in every city, every state house, every office of the federal government. We recognize the imperative need for this development. Yet we must not fail to comprehend its grave implications. Our toil, resources, and livelihood are all involved; so is the very structure of our society.

In the councils of government, we must guard against the acquisition of unwarranted influence, whether sought or unsought, by the military-industrial complex. The potential for the disastrous rise of misplaced power exists and will persist.

We must never let the weight of this combination endanger our liberties or democratic processes. We should take nothing for granted. Only an alert and knowledgeable citizenry can compel the proper meshing of the huge industrial and military machinery of defense with our peaceful methods and goals so that security and liberty may prosper together. . . .

Disarmament, with mutual honor and confidence, is a continuing imperative. Together we must learn how to compose differences not with arms but with intellect and decent purpose. Because this need is so sharp and apparent I confess that I lay down my official responsibilities in this field with a definite sense of disappointment. As one who has witnessed the horror and the lingering sadness of war—as one who knows that another war could utterly destroy this civilization, which has been so slowly and painfully built over thousands of years—I wish I could say tonight that a lasting peace is in sight.

Happily, I can say that war has been avoided. Steady progress toward our ultimate goal has been made. But so much remains to be done. As a private citizen, I shall never cease to do what little I can to help the world advance along that road.

THE MILITARIZATION OF SPORTS AND THE REDEFINITION OF PATRIOTISM
William Astore

As long as I can remember, I've been a sports fan. As long as I can remember, I've been interested in the military. Until recently, I experienced those as two separate and distinct worlds. While I was in the military—I served for twenty years as an officer in the U.S. Air Force—I did, of course, play sports. As a young lieutenant, I was in a racquetball tournament at my base in Colorado. At Squadron Officer School in Alabama, I took part in volleyball and flickerball (a bizarre Air Force sport). At the Air Force Academy, I was on a softball team, and when we finally won a game, all of us signed the ball. . . .

Don't misunderstand me. I was never particularly skilled at any sport, but I did thoroughly enjoy playing partly because it was such a welcome break from work—a reprieve from wearing a uniform, saluting, following orders, and all the rest. Sports were sports. Military service was military service. And never the twain shall meet.

Since 9/11, however, sports and the military have become increasingly fused in this country. Professional athletes now consider it perfectly natural to don uniforms that feature camouflage patterns. (They do this, teams say, as a form of "military appreciation.") Indeed, for only $39.99 you, too, can buy your own Major League Baseball–sanctioned camo cap at MLB's official site. And then, of course, you can use that cap in any stadium to shade your eyes as you watch fly-overs, parades, reunions of service members returning from our country's war zones and their families, and a multitude of other increasingly militarized ceremonies that celebrate both veterans and troops in uniform at sports stadiums across what, in the post-9/11 years, has come to be known as "the homeland."

These days, you can hardly miss moments when, for instance, playing fields are covered with gigantic American flags, often unfurled and held either by scores of military personnel or civilian defense contractors. Such ceremonies are invariably touted as natural expressions of patriotism, part of a continual public expression of gratitude for America's "warfighters" and "heroes." These are, in other words, uncontroversial displays of pride, even though a study ordered by Republican Senators John McCain and Jeff Flake revealed that the U.S. taxpayer, via the Pentagon, has regularly forked over tens of millions of dollars ($53 million between 2012 and 2015 alone) to corporate-owned teams to put on just such displays.

Paid patriotism should, of course, be an oxymoron. These days, however, it's anything but, and even when the American taxpayer isn't covering displays like these, the melding of sports and the military should be seen as inappropriate, if not insidious. And I say that as both a lover of sports and a veteran. . . .

NOWADAYS, IT SEEMS as if professional sports simply couldn't occur without some notice of and celebration of the U.S. military, each game being transformed in some way into yet another Memorial Day or Veterans Day lite.

Consider the pro-military hype that surrounded the 2018 Major League Baseball All-Star Game. Not so very long ago, when I watched such games I would be transported to my childhood and my fantasies of becoming the next Nolan Ryan or Carl Yastrzemski.

When I watched the 2018 game, however, I didn't relive my youth; I relived my military career. As a start, the previous night featured a televised home-run derby. Before it even began, about fifty airmen paraded out in camouflage uniforms, setting the stage for everything that would follow. (As they weren't on duty, I couldn't help wondering why they found it appropriate to don such outfits.) Part of T-Mobile's "HatsOff4Heroes" campaign, this mini-parade was justified in the name of raising money to support veterans, but T-Mobile could simply have given the money to charity without any of the militarized hoopla that this involved.

Highlighting the other pre-game ceremonies, the next night was a celebration of Medal of Honor recipients. I have deep respect for such heroes, but what were they doing on a baseball diamond? The ceremony would have been appropriate on, say, Veterans Day in November.

Those same pre-game festivities included a militaristic montage narrated by Bradley Cooper (star of the film *American Sniper*), featuring war scenes and war monuments while highlighting the popular catchphrase "Freedom isn't free." Martial music accompanied the montage, along with a bevy of flag-waving images. It felt like watching a twisted version of the film *Field of Dreams* reshot so that soldiers, not baseball players, emerged early on from those rows of Iowa corn stalks and stepped onto the playing field.

What followed was a "surprise" reunion of an airman, Staff Sergeant Cole Condiff, and his wife and family. Such staged reunions have become a regular aspect of major sporting events—consider this "heart-melting" example from a Milwaukee Brewers game—and are obviously meant to tug at the heartstrings. . . .

In addition, Budweiser used the 2018 game to promote "freedom" beer, again to raise money for veterans and, of course, to burnish its own rep. (Last year, the company was hyping "America" beer.)

And the All-Star game is hardly alone in its militarized celebrations and hoopla. Take the 2017 U.S. Open tennis tournament in New York City, which I happened to watch. With John McEnroe in retirement, tennis is, generally speaking, a quieter sport. Yet before the men's final, a Marine Corps color guard joined a contingent of West Point cadets in a ceremony to remember the victims of 9/11. Naturally, a by now obligatory oversize American flag set the scene . . . , capped by a performance of "God Bless America" and a loud flyover by four combat jets. Admittedly, it was a dramatic way to begin anything—but why, exactly, an international tennis match that happened to feature finalists from Spain and South Africa?

I'M HARDLY THE first to warn about the dangers of mixing sports with the military, especially in corporate-controlled blenders. Early in 2003, prior to the kickoff for the Iraq War (sports metaphor intended), the writer Norman Mailer issued this warning:

> The dire prospect that opens, therefore, is that America is going to become a mega-banana republic where the army will have more and more importance in Americans' lives. . . . [D]emocracy is the special condition—a condition we will be called upon to defend in the coming years. That will be enormously difficult because the combination of the corporation, the military, and the complete investiture of the flag with mass spectator sports has set up a pre-fascistic atmosphere in America already.

More than fourteen years later, that combination—corporations, the military, and mass spectator sports, all wrapped in a gigantic version of the stars and stripes—has increasingly come to define what it means to be an American. Now that the country also has its own self-styled strongman president, enabled by a spineless Congress and an increasingly reactionary judiciary, Mailer's mention of a "pre-fascistic atmosphere" seems prescient.

What started as a post-9/11 drive to get an American public to "thank" the troops endlessly for their service in distant conflicts—stifling criticism of those wars by linking it to ingratitude—has morphed into a new form of national reverence. And much credit goes to professional sports for that transformation.

In conjunction with the military and marketed by corporations, they have reshaped the very practice of patriotism in America.

Today, thanks in part to taxpayer funding, Americans regularly salute grossly oversize flags, celebrate or otherwise "appreciate" the troops (without making the slightest meaningful sacrifice themselves), and applaud the corporate sponsors that pull it all together (and profit from it). Meanwhile, taking a stand (or a knee), being an agent of dissent, protesting against injustice, is increasingly seen as the very definition of what it means to be unpatriotic. Indeed, players with the guts to protest American life as it is are regularly castigated as SOBs by our sports- and military-loving president.

Professional sports owners certainly know that this militarized brand of patriotism sells, while the version embodied in the kinds of controversial stances taken by athletes like the former National Football League quarterback Colin Kaepernick (cashiered by his own league) angers and alienates many fans, ultimately threatening profits.

Meanwhile, the military's bottom line is recruiting new bodies for that All-Volunteer Force while keeping those taxpayer dollars flowing into the Pentagon at increasingly staggering levels. For corporations, you won't be surprised to learn, it's all about profits and reputation.

In the end, it comes down to one thing: who controls the national narrative. Think about it. A set of corporate-military partnerships or, if you prefer, some version of President Dwight D. Eisenhower's old military-industrial complex, has enlisted sports to make militarism look good and normal and even cool. In other words, sports teams now have a powerful set of incentives to appear patriotic, which increasingly means slavishly pro-military. It's getting hard to remember that this country ever had a citizen-soldier tradition as well as sports teams whose athletes actually went almost en masse to serve in war. Consider it paradoxical that militarism is today becoming as American as baseball and apple pie, even as, like so many other citizens, today's athletes vote with their feet to stay out of the military. . . .

Corporate-owned sports teams are now actively colluding with the military to redefine patriotism in ways that work to their mutual advantage. They are complicit in taking a select, jingoistic form of patriotism and weaponizing it to suppress dissent, including against the military-industrial complex and America's never-ending wars.

Driven by corporate agendas and featuring exaggerated military displays, mass-spectator sports are helping to shape what Americans perceive and believe. In stadiums across the nation and on screens held in our hands or dominating our living rooms, we witness fine young men and women in uniform unfurling massive flags on football fields and baseball diamonds, even on tennis courts, as combat jets scream overhead. What we don't see—what is largely kept from us—are the murderous costs of empire: the dead and maimed soldiers, the innocents slaughtered by those same combat jets. . . .

For all the appreciation of the military at sporting events, here's what you're not supposed to appreciate: why we're in our forever wars; the extent to which they've been mismanaged for the past seventeen years; how much people, especially in distant lands, have suffered thanks to them; and who's really profiting from them.

1.4

VIOLENCE, JUST IN TIME
War and Work in Contemporary West Africa
Daniel Hoffman

Violence is hard work.

The intimate bodily violence of small arms and direct physical confrontation, the kind of violence most common in African conflicts today, is a challenge to perform. It is difficult labor under trying conditions. It is demanding, and it is risky. Violence, in this obvious sense, is real work.

But the hard work of violence has another, less obvious meaning, one that has largely escaped anthropologists and other observers of postcolonial spaces. There has been a curious inability, or perhaps unwillingness, to think of violence as literal work, to think of the labor of war as labor.

That is what I set out to do in this article. I do so because the language of labor, employment, gain, compensation, reward, security—the language, in other words, of postmodern work—was very much the language of militia fighters throughout West Africa's Mano River War. Combatants saw themselves as workers as much as they saw themselves as patriots, democrats, youth, and rebels. In fact, these various titles are virtually indistinguishable in the sociopolitical imaginary of the young men who fought this war. I also find it useful to think of the violence of this war as a mode of work because in much of the writing on labor today we see striking parallels to the activities of militia fighters and their relationship to the world economy. . . .

There are, of course, obvious and much remarked on links between West Africa's black market trade in diamonds and weapons and other moving parts of the global economy. That part of the war economy has been much discussed.

Yet very few observers, on the political left or right, think of or speak of West African warriors as a workforce. It is harder to think of the young men who cycle through the region's mines and battlefields as laborers. Sierra Leone and Liberia appear instead as the dark opposite of the bourgeois fantasy of a world made stable through regular employment. But whereas the Mano River region is generally assumed to lie outside the ideal functioning of the world economy, to somehow have fallen off the map of global labor, I want to explore here what we might learn if we think of West African warfare as a logical extension of certain flexible, so-called post-Fordist patterns of accumulation. I want to ask what we might learn when we think of violence as a mode of production. . . .

Learning to Labor

Since at least the early 1970s, work in the resource extraction industries in Sierra Leone and Liberia has been largely piecemeal, informal, and flexible.[1] In Sierra Leone, the All People's Congress government that came to power in 1968 worked to undercut organized labor as a potential political opposition (see Abdullah 2004: 42–44). In Liberia, the union structure was controlled by the same elite Americo-Liberian families whose members held virtually all positions of power within the government and corporations (Liebenow 1987: 75–77). With the exception of more technical, equipment-intensive enterprises such as iron ore and rutile mining, the labor force working in the mines and forests of the region is largely unskilled and casual, making for high turnover and precarious job security. Even in the heavier industries, ineffective unions and the networks of political patronage that are central to organizing labor have kept the workforce unstable enough to prevent it from becoming an effective economic or political force. . . .

The exigencies of mining and harvesting under wartime conditions further destabilized the labor practices of the region's resource economies (along with everything else). The flexible nature of work and social reproduction in the gold and diamond mines became even more improvisational and precarious throughout the 1990s. Increasing numbers of laborers entered the mining sector temporarily, often working in exchange for food, basic medical care, and the "right" to sell whatever they might find at radically low prices to the patrons who supplied them with equipment and support.[2] Mining, timber harvesting, and rubber production, poorly regulated before the war, became increasingly black market and opportunistic as the war eroded the infrastructure of regulation and opened new opportunities for profiteering, increasing both the risk and the rewards of the resource economy. Soldiers and militia fighters (or those subcontracted by them) increasingly cycled through the mines, alternating work on the battlefield and in the pits as control of the mines changed hands (see Gberie 2005: 180–96; Keen 2005; Smillie et al. 2000). Mining and other resource extraction during the war was less an occupation than a fleeting opportunity.

What is important here is not just that the same laboring bodies were deployed for work in the mines, forests, and plantations as were deployed on the battlefield. Even more disturbing is that these different modes of work became so qualitatively similar. In other words, the organizational logic at work in the region was increasingly one of making young men available for "just-in-time" production based on whatever opportunities presented themselves: mining, timber cutting, tapping rubber, or war fighting. As a study in the evolution of labor practices, this was what in other contexts has been called post-Fordism or flexible specialization.

The body of theory loosely referred to as post-Fordism originates with studies of small artisanal workshops in central Italy in the 1970s and 1980s, the French "regulation school" of political economy, and innovations in Japanese outsourcing of factory production. In very broad strokes, post-Fordist theory explores changes in the transition from the mass production of the modern large factory (Fordism) to a mode of production in which producers operate more "flexibly." Smaller workforces with more part-time or occasional workers, greater technological capability, more responsiveness to shifts in the market, an ability to retool quickly to meet changing circumstances and needs—these are the hallmarks of post-Fordism.[3] Gathering intelligence on the state of the market, erecting communications systems that can speed the transfer of that intelligence, and establishing networks that can assemble outsourced bits quickly are the conditions under which a post-Fordist enterprise thrives. Unlike the classic Fordist factory, in post-Fordism specific duties are replaced by multiple, shifting demands, and the single, repetitive task is supplanted by workers charged with innovating on multiple fronts. . . .

In this regime of production, the workday is ill-defined, if not perpetual. Social life outside the factory also becomes the site of necessary labor. The separation between "work" and "non-work" disappears. The activities of the everyday outside of work are not just training for the new demands of labor in this kind of economy; life itself is increasingly about innovating in ways that will be useful on the job. . . .

If theories of factory production are not a perfect fit historically for the resource extraction economies of this part of West Africa, they nevertheless describe a condition of labor that seems very much in keeping with those facing laborers in the Mano River region. As Michael Hardt and Antonio Negri

(2004: 79–91) have argued, after all, since 1968 the logic of post-Fordist production was also the logic of guerrilla warfare the world over.[4]

But what does this look like from the point of view of laborers in this West African version of a post-Fordist economy? It looks like the micro-encounters on the front porch of a small concrete house in Duala, Monrovia, where in the summer of 2005 young men showed up every morning to consult with the Civil Defense Forces (CDF) and Liberians United for Reconciliation and Democracy (LURD) commander named Mohammed.[5] Mohammed's connections in the diamond trade, the nongovernmental organization (NGO) world, and the militias fighting in Ivory Coast made him a conduit for all-important information about the market for labor. The young men who visited Mohammed virtually every day were simply checking in with a patron who might at any time offer them work or food or news from across the border(s). Any day might be the day a young visitor would be told to pack his bags for the mines of Sapo or the battlefields of Ivory Coast. Or he might be told to go and register with the new political party forming across the border in Sierra Leone. He might be told to travel back to Freetown to campaign, or he might be told to vote the People's Movement for Democratic Change ticket as an absentee in Monrovia. Or he might simply be told to have a bite to eat and come back tomorrow; a plan is in the works to reclaim a vehicle stolen during the last Monrovia siege, and at some point soon Mohammed will need boys to help him. Mohammed described these visitors to me as "a reservoir for any cash politician or would-be revolutionary to brainwash and use the second time around, hoping to get what they didn't get from the first war."

Some days would bring young men who hadn't been seen on the veranda in a while, young men returning from the mines or the forest or across the border. They carried with them the latest news, knowing Mohammed would be interested and that news, for Mohammed, was a favor on which one could trade in the future. Information greases the wheels, and when one has it, one shares it with Mohammed, because Mohammed doesn't forget those who bring it to him.

On those days when nothing much comes from these visits, the young men continue on. They stop by other front verandas or find a position on the street to watch and wait. Labor organized in this way exhibits two of what Paolo Virno (2004) describes as the key elements of post-Fordist production: an inability to distinguish paid from unpaid work, and the paramount importance of opportunism.

In the first case, the extension of the requirements of labor into all forms of social existence (into life itself) means that only some of a young man's perpetual "work" will actually be compensated. . . . Laborers in this moment of economic history cannot reliably predict the possibilities of remuneration for their work. The logical connection between the performance of work and compensation for labor has been severed (cf. Comaroff and Comaroff 1999; Simone 2002). There is profit to be reaped from the very existence of young men, but that profit is not tied to the products they might produce. The compensation for their labor has been mystified. . . .

One learns, in this economy, to gamble: to seize opportunities as they present themselves, to quickly react to the unexpected, and to make the most of what chances go flashing by; to innovate, experiment, and bluff. Two-pile systems are a game of chance, but on occasion one is confronted with an opportunity to weight the pile or to smuggle gravel, and the successful workers do. Looting presents constant choices between reporting what one finds to the commander or slipping off into the bush and across the border with an unexpected treasure; treating civilians kindly in the hopes of deferred reward or punishing severely those who do not give up what they should. The opportunist profits when he can make these judgments quickly, a skill that most learn on the job but with which a lucky few are born.

Fumba Kanneh was not necessarily one of the lucky ones, at least not yet. A miner who had worked on both sides of the Sierra Leone-Liberia border, he was stuck in 2005 in Monrovia. Fumba joined LURD as it pushed toward the Liberian capital. He distinguished himself enough that he soon grew close to the LURD leaders Sekou Conneh, and then Ayesha Conneh, serving as one of the Ayesha's bodyguards in the tense period of Monrovia's occupation. When Sekou and Ayesha left the city, Fumba remained behind. His days now were mostly spent on the city streets, moving from point to point. He kept three rooms in the houses or squats of various friends, never quite sure where he might find himself at nightfall or which of his haunts might be overrun or suddenly unwelcoming.

One of Fumba's regular sites was the Duala market and taxi rank. . . . Opportunities large and small passed through the Duala market often enough that it seemed worthwhile to visit and wait. . . .

Fumba found one such opening a year after I sat with him in the Duala market. Lansana Conté, the ailing president of Guinea, faced nationwide strikes. Violent encounters were becoming more frequent in the capital, and for a brief time the future of the Mano River Union's wealthiest member was in doubt. A friend passing through Monrovia told Fumba that Ayesha Conneh was barricading herself on one of Conté's rural farms. She was looking for trusted ex-combatants to defend her and the Guinean regime. Those who made their way to her would have the support of the Guinean government if they succeeded and the pickings of a wealthy country if the government should fall. The next day, Fumba was gone.

THERE ARE TWO upshots to thinking about the work of young men in the wartime Mano River region in terms of post-Fordist modes of production that outweigh the imperfectness of the theoretical fit. One is explicit in the earlier discussion, and the other is implied, but both are worth reiterating here.

First, this framing allows us to think about violence beyond the terms of identity—or, more specifically, beyond the fantasy constructions of an enemy. This was not the driving force in the Mano River War. Those combatants with whom I worked, and others from the various factions with whom I have spoken over the years, showed remarkably little interest in the "others" who were the subject of their violence. If anything, they were sympathetic to the lives and conditions of the belligerents against whom they fought and largely indifferent to the civilians who were the most affected by their actions. One might give serious consideration to principles such as democracy and security, but the flesh-and-blood individual objects of one's war labors were not a preoccupation. The immaterial labor of the imagination was given over to other things.

The second consequence of thinking about militia fighters in this conflict as a certain type of workforce is that it allows us to begin to understand the fungibility of violence. Unlike the common associations of violence with breakdown and destruction, or the association of violence with exclusion and excision, understanding war as a mode of labor allows us to see how the performance of violence can be traded on the market.

The loose-knit, networked mode of organization that characterized virtually all of the war's factions means that even the most coordinated operations were the result of a subcontracted, businesslike arrangement. Whole units could operate largely in the mode of artisanal guilds, clearly identified with one faction or another (or not), but only sometimes acting on explicit orders or according to plans issued from a central military authority. More common were vague pronouncements by figures such as Hinga Norman stating that a given city, town, or village must be seized from the rebels. Various units then worked out for themselves how to complete the task and reap the rewards of success, sometimes collaborating with one another, sometimes competing. Even Taylor's National Patriotic Front of Liberia, arguably the best organized of the region's factions, was described by one of Taylor's former lieutenants as a series of subcontracted outfits: "Taylor would call up a commander and say, 'I want this place, can you do it?' He would say yes, and then Taylor would give him $5,000 . . . and some rice to pay the men and get the job done." Collectives of armed young men allowed themselves to be "hired out" for all manner of work. Units of the CDF were contracted by Lebanese diamond dealers to protect their concessions, or recruited by businessmen in the city to seize property they alleged had been appropriated by rebel sympathizers. Some of this work was done for a fixed price, some for more ambiguous rewards, a share in the profits, or "on spec."

Private Warriors

The market for violence in the Mano River region has only been widely commented on in one relatively narrow sense. No single aspect of the war generated as much international scrutiny as the role played by a small group of expatriate former soldiers hired by the government of Sierra Leone in 1995. Operating at first under the name Executive Outcomes (EO), and later as independent contractors, the handful of white South Africans, black Namibians, and a smattering of non-African nationals are alternately credited with saving Sierra Leone and accused of delaying the peace process; charged with ruthlessly profiteering while committing heinous war crimes and heralded with leading a heroic (if bloody) humanitarian intervention. The EO was profiled in publications from *Soldier of Fortune* to *Harper's*, and EO veterans have appeared in documentaries (*Shadow Company*) and as the inspiration for fictional film characters (*Blood Diamond*).

The EO's role in the conflict was smaller than all this attention would suggest. Certainly, it was less significant than the mobilizations of domestic irregular fighting units with which the EO sometimes collaborated, and less significant than the deployment of Nigerian and other West African peacekeepers. The emphasis on the EO and other private military corporations tends to obscure the ways in which all manner of African security has been privatized (from subcontracting weapons procurement to the private security guards hired by NGOs and African elites) and the ways in which African militaries are increasingly involved in commercial enterprises. Across Africa there exists what a 2002 Justice Africa report (de Waal 2002) calls a "military-commercial complex." In contrast to the military-industrial nexus of war and weapons manufacture, the military-commercial complex develops around "other economically profitable spin-offs from war and militarism" (de Waal 2002: 123). The disproportionate attention garnered by the EO and the figure of the foreign (especially white) mercenary has eclipsed this more pervasive commercialization of violence in Africa. . . .

Executive Outcomes existed in part because of the worldwide political economy of post–Cold War military infrastructure. With the breakup of the Soviet Union, the end of the apartheid state in South Africa, and the downsizing of a number of state armies, soldiers from across the globe found themselves underemployed—and with a very particular skill set. Military post-Fordism meant the downsizing of the fixed army, the outsourcing of traditionally state military functions, and the creation of a mobile pool of labor, available as needed. When the Sierra Leonean regime of Valentine Strasser found itself with military demands that it could not meet from within its own ranks (training, coordination, and technical assistance) it found a corporate partner willing to provide those services.

As with the post-Fordist mode of production more generally, the exact nature of the services the EO was meant to provide was somewhat nebulous. The lines among guarding mining concessions, protecting dignitaries, training state armies, providing tactical planning and support, and developing useful military infrastructure is often blurred. The job description for a military contractor is an ambiguous one. . . . Ambiguous, too, are many of the corporate links connecting security corporations to other corporate partners; the EO was affiliated with a transnational network of corporate partners that included Branch Energy and Heritage Oil, corporations with holdings in natural resource exploitation and transportation, as well as security. . . .

The willingness of non-African governments and international governing bodies (such as the United Nations) to tolerate EO activity in Sierra Leone—and, in some cases, to condone it—springs from a general neoliberal desire to find market solutions to African dilemmas. It reflects a Taylorist emphasis on the efficient management of African crises as technical problems to be solved. African wars like the Mano River War are not widely seen outside the region as political problems. Rather, they are production problems, kinks to be managed (although not necessarily resolved) so that they do not interfere with the extraction of resources. Technical expertise of the kind the EO had for sale fit this demand. The EO could deploy quickly, offering a just-in-time solution to an acute crisis that no government wished to own over the long term. . . .

Still, the preoccupation with the EO and its long-term consequences misses the fact that the real "private warriors" in the Mano River War were the local militias and the Nigerian-led peacekeeping force, the Economic Community of West African States Monitoring Group (ECOMOG). Yet these forces are rarely evaluated as such.

Conclusion: The Political Economy of Dreg

Just-in-time production does not rely on disciplinary regimes to coerce labor into performing its functions. It relies on movement.

The disciplinary society as Michel Foucault formulated it is dependent on institutions that normalize subjects. These are policing regimes that construct ideal subjects (or ideals of subjects). Schools produce students; clinics produce patients; the military produces soldiers; factories produce workers. The strict imposition of discipline is accomplished through the fixing of identities in defined institutional spaces.

In Gilles Deleuze's writings, the modernist project of the disciplinary society gives way to the postmodern society of control. The formation of subjects in the latter is no longer tied to discrete institutions, and discipline in fixed categories is no longer imperative. Movement, rather than the defined identities, is the locus of power in the new mode of governmentality (Deleuze 1995; cf. Hardt and Negri 2000: 22–30).

By the late 1990s in Sierra Leone, the Krio term *dreg* (or *drehg*) had come to describe not only an activity but also a way of being in the world through movement with which many combatants identified. *Dreg* is one of a constellation of terms that name modes of youth labor at the margins of the economy and society: *san san boys* are diggers who sift gravel in the diamond fields in search of stones; *rarray boy* and *savis man dem* describe youth whose activities and modes of survival (especially in the cities) straddle the line between legality and illegality (see Abdullah 2002, 2004: 45–46). A dreg man maneuvers the city in what amounts to a hustle. *Aw di dreg?* (How is the dreg? or How is the hustle?) became for many urban combatants and ex-combatants a slang greeting. *A di go dreg* (I'm off to dreg) became a recognizable expression of parting. In both cases, the implication was that one was on the move and in search of profit; how one found it would be tied to one's speed, wit, bravery, and cunning.

What a political economy of dregging meant was that a population of male youth was constantly available to be put to use for virtually any form of labor. Deployment and employment became virtually indistinguishable as young men took it for granted that economic opportunities were likely to be located "elsewhere" and that to profit would mean to move: move across real and social borders, move through space, move across identities and across legal categories. One needed to be flexible and able to travel; indeed, the mobility of these youth was what qualified them as dreg man dem and what made them attractive as labor.

So, too, did their capacity for violence. It was not innately antisocial or violent predispositions that qualified these youth as dreg man dem. It was their willingness and need to exchange violence on the market. More precisely, it was the capacities of their bodies to commit acts of violence that was fungible. That same capacity might as easily be called on for labor in the diamond pits, labor tapping rubber, labor felling trees, or labor standing in line at a disarmament center. For laborers in a violent economy, these were all qualitatively similar opportunities for work. The identity of those against whom that violence was arrayed mattered little, if at all. What mattered was being lucky, being clever, and being on the move.

NOTES

1. Historically, this has been true of a wide range of modes of work in the region, as in the case of Kru seafarers who worked the West African coast as free labor with the expansion of commercial shipping and the decline of the slave trade.

2. David Fithen (1999) describes in detail the various labor arrangements common in the diamond regions during much of the war and how the changing circumstances of the period altered existing practices.

3. Those who see post-Fordism as a discrete moment in the development of capitalism argue that it is a set of practices that developed to deal with what Marx called the perpetual crisis of overaccumulation.

4. By contrast, the armies of the United States and much of Europe were largely Fordist enterprises inextricably bound to national economies, at least through the end of the Cold War. This has been explored most notably in the work of Catherine Lutz (see esp. Lutz 2001). After the Cold War, and increasingly since 2001, the U.S. military has outsourced functions and relied more heavily on Special Forces–intensive counterinsurgency operations, a direction that appears increasingly post-Fordist (see Hoffman 2010).

5. This is an example I explain in more detail in Hoffman 2007.

1.5

WOMEN, ECONOMY, WAR
Carolyn Nordstrom

What takes place at the intersections where considerations of women, economy, and war meet? This is a question that I have followed in ethnographic fieldwork across three continents and over twenty-five years.[1] The answers I encounter seldom match prevailing "social wisdom"—Foucauldian epistemic knowledge that societies broadly take as true—on these topics. At the most basic level, for example, women's roles both in the economy and on the front-lines are far greater than many classic accounts recognize.

This disjuncture is in part due to an institutionalized failure to consider the full spectrum of political violence, and of economies, as wholes. Formal actors—that is to say, those populating legally recognized institutions (e.g., the military, government, industry, commerce)—are the focus of most reporting. Noncombatants, children, informal economic work, and extra-legal commerce appear far less in formal accounting, even though these represent the majority of people and the bulk of economic activity in many places (Nordstrom 1997, 2004).

I use the term "extra-legal" to refer to all that falls outside state-based definitions of "legal." This encompasses the informal, illicit, illegal, unrecorded, and undefined. The term "extra-legal" (and not "informal") is used exclusively in most of my publications because, as my research consistently demonstrates, no agreed definitions for any of these terms exist, and many of those arenas are blurred and overlap. But because this article explores women's working conditions that are frequently referred to as "informal" in the literature, I turn first to considerations of informality and then extend my examination to the more comprehensive concerns of extra-legality (Nordstrom 2007).

My interest is pragmatic: the informal economy today dwarfs the formal economy in a number of countries. . . . Women are overrepresented in the informal sectors worldwide. . . .

As evident as these trends are in peacetime, they are even more pronounced in times of political violence. For example, while I was conducting fieldwork during the final years of the war in Angola in the early 2000s, the United Nations offices there estimated that fully 90 percent of the national economy operated extra-legally. I found similar figures put forward in Mozambique during the last years of war. . . .

My fieldwork revealed that extra-legal economies worldwide are made up of everything from dangerous items such as arms and drugs, through luxury goods such as diamonds and designer clothing, to critical necessities such as energy, food, and medicine—and in ways that are foundational to the world's business, financial, and governing systems. Taken as a whole, the extra-legal constitutes a significant part of economies worldwide, at war and in peace (Naim 2006; Naylor 2005; Nordstrom 2007; van Schendel and Itty 2004).

Thus, exploring the intersections of women, economy, and political violence ethnographically often takes us out of the realm of formal institutions and public reporting and into the less reported and more invisible realms of the informal and extra-legal, going beyond what I introduce in this article as vanishing points: places where power and abuse thereof profit from general public invisibility. Here, women's role in solving aggressions and promoting development is substantial. And here, in these "shadows," opportunities for both economic development and oppressive abuses flourish. Given those realities, this article will, in considering the equations of women, war, and economy, focus largely on what predominates in actual practice—the informal and extra-legal.

Vanishing Points

Vanishing points, in terms of the concept that I introduce in this analysis, are the points where the normative (what should be) intersects with reality (what actually is). Ideally, research should illuminate both sides of this intersection: the ideals we hold as societies and the unfolding realities as people live them, regardless of how they may contradict our stated laws and values.

In point of fact, research may uphold a division that considers only the normative, as if it were reality. That which contradicts normative ideals is ignored and becomes invisible to formal analysis. Consider: formal country economic indices (generated by bodies such as the United Nations, World Bank, and International Monetary Fund) are based exclusively on legally regulated economies. Gross domestic product figures and formal policies are based on these indices (Kabeer 2008). Business and financial institutions publish only legally recognized expenditures and profits, despite the fact that, as a whole, industry's extra-legal activities can reach into the trillions annually, and money laundering is conservatively estimated to be 10 percent of global economic activity (Naim 2006).

What is most visible to policy makers, Naila Kabeer writes, are "paid activities carried out in formal establishments of a certain size, regulated and protected by the state, with policy preference given to 'internationally traded' activities that would save on foreign exchange." She concludes: "These biases gave rise to an 'iceberg' view of less monetized economies, since the bulk of the activities by which their populations met their basic needs and made plans for the future remained below the surface, hidden from the view of policy makers" (Kabeer 2008: 28).

Because women predominate in the "submerged" activities of the economy, they are relegated to the obscure side of arbitrary vanishing points created by the conventions of politics, research, and power (Carr and Chen 2004; Chant and Pedwell 2008).

To justify putting such blinders on "science," a general argument is made that the formal sector is, by definition, the paramount defining reality; anything outside this is by definition less significant. . . .

These practices are exacerbated by political instability and violence. Several contemporary trends concerning war are important to this analysis:

— Current wars are centered in less industrialized regions rich in the resources that fuel industrialized nations. Complex international economies, both legal and extra-legal, define war zones and their relationships with global markets.

— As violence disrupts governmental support systems, infrastructure, and trade routes, the general populace is thrown into increasing reliance on informal and extra-legal means to gain basic life necessities. . . .

No Man's Lands: From Informal to Extra-legal

In the latter years of the war in Angola, a division common to a number of war zones could be seen. The government forces tended to control the urban infrastructure, whereas the rebels held the more rural parts of the country. Both sides battled over areas rich in natural resources such as diamond mines and timber reserves. This split resulted in stark needs: government-controlled areas had more access to material goods, the rebel areas had greater access to food. Trade across political borderlines was both critical to survival, and an act of treason.

A dead zone—a depopulated strip five to ten kilometers wide that no one controlled—developed between the two sides. Trade between them took place across these no man's lands. Rogue troops and armed bandits preyed on the traders, who were frequently women. While some women did this voluntarily to support their families, many were forced with the threat that their children would be killed did they not (Nordstrom 2003).

In speaking with some of these women and the more powerful men controlling the lucrative trade, I found that the women who survived earned nothing more than the basic goods they could carry; the trade leaders reaped tremendous profits.

As Mary Douglas (2002) discusses in her classic work on purity and danger, the borders of in/formality and extra/legality[2] are imbued with power, fraught with myth, and guarded by violence. That which takes place beyond vanishing points can yield great profits, provoke abuse, and generate grinding poverty. Fortunes invisible to formal accounting are made here, and such fortunes can be brokered into economic prowess and political power. Such successes are often built on the work of disenfranchised people silenced by their invisibility. Examples of this are extra-legal gem mining (the proverbial blood diamonds) and timber logging, arms trafficking, and the exploitation of child labor.

Those able to control the borders where the extra-legal intersects the legal realm of the state enjoy considerable power. There is a qualitative difference between market women selling vegetables locally for a handful of coins and people who collect vegetables from growers and markets regionally to sell in multi-ton and multimillion-dollar shipments to cosmopolitan centers world-wide. These are profoundly gendered processes:

— While the majority of informal work is done by women, the most lucrative positions and products in the extra-legal world are held or controlled by men—for example, blood diamonds, illicit arms, technology, and drugs.

— The vanishing points themselves—the borders of the extra/legal and the in/visible (from transport and trade to financing and market management), and the violence that surrounds them—are likewise largely controlled by men;

— The people who create the definitions of what is, and is not, economic analysis and policy (the predominantly male political, business, and research elite) effectively create and maintain vanishing points and their profitability.

At the international level, a profound irony defines this trade: vast global trade networks, exchanging commodities produced in cosmopolitan centers for raw materials from less industrialized regions, rely in part on women initializing the trade across "no man's lands" in war zones and poverty, the ground zero of the global exchange circuits. These loci, however, are largely invisible in formal analysis: they are behind the vanishing point.

NOTE

1. I have spent roughly half of these two-and-a-half decades conducting ethnography in the field, working predominantly in southern Africa and South Asia, with shorter periods in contexts of political violence ranging from Southeast Asia and through the Balkans to the favelas of Brazil, and following the global networks of extra-legal commodity flows linking war zones through developing regions to cosmopolitan centers worldwide.

2. My use of the slash (in/formal, extra/legality) indicates that both meanings in the term are intended, e.g. informal and/or formal.

FIG. 2.0. Civilian contractors employed by a privatized military firm manually clear a mine field surrounding a Soviet-era monument located at Bagram Airfield in Afghanistan, September 2007. The workers were contracted by the Mine Action Center, part of NATO's International Security Assistance Force (ISAF). Military work increasingly relies on the labor of private contractors. Photograph by Sergeant James Wilt/U.S. Army.

SECTION II. MILITARY LABOR

Compiled by ANDREW BICKFORD

Introduction

"Military labor" is a surprisingly difficult term to define: we can define it narrowly, as simply labor in the military; we can broaden the definition and think of it as labor in and for the military; or we can define it even more broadly and think of it as labor—licit and illicit, voluntary and involuntary, forced or unforced—in and for the military. We can also think about it as a contradiction or misnomer: some scholars—such as Chris Tilly and Charles Tilly (1997: 26)—would probably not consider military service labor, as it did not "add a use value to goods or service." We might then think about it as "work," "employment," or a "job" in and for the military, as something that might not directly add value but is nonetheless seen as valuable and important by the military or by those seeking to make a living from the military in some form or the other. (Of course, for families with multigenerational military service, the military can be seen as a vocation.) We can also think about military labor as a living hell for those forced to labor or fight or perform services for the military against their will.

This section examines a variety of forms of voluntary and involuntary military labor and work in different states and settings: the use of Buddhist monks as soldiers in Thailand, forced laborers in Asia during World War II, child soldiers in Nepal, women traveling who find work as sex workers near U.S. military bases, the shift from a draft to a volunteer force in the United States, and the rise of privatized military firms across the globe.

In this section, Beth Bailey details the move toward an "all-volunteer force" in the United States military, and how the U.S. military drew on labor-market models to make military service enticing and appealing after the disaster of the Vietnam War.

Feminist scholars have noted that masculine labor forces often rely on the hidden labor of women, in the household and elsewhere, to function. Sealing Cheng's contribution examines military prostitution in South Korea, focusing on the global networks that bring women to South Korea to labor as sex workers and entertainers near U.S. bases. As Cynthia Enloe (1983) has argued elsewhere, female sex workers are often essential to the morale of masculinized militaries.

Children have long been forced to serve and fight in militaries, often co-erced or tricked into serving with promises of money or education. Militaries and paramilitaries depend on child soldiers not just for combat, but also for their (forced) labor as porters, cooks, and cleaners and to do other types of sup-port work. Brandon Kohrt and Robert Koenig discuss the use and experiences of child soldiers in Nepal's Maoist army.

"Ascetic soldiering" is a topic generally not considered when thinking about military labor and soldiering. In "Military Monks," Michael Jerryson examines the militarization of Buddhism in Thailand, and the intersections of military labor and religion in the training and deployment of Buddhist monks as sol-diers in clandestine units in the Thai military.

Civilians and prisoners of war have long been used as labor by militaries— by either their own or by that of a conquering force. In the introduction to his edited volume, excerpted in this section, Paul H. Kratoska examines the use of forced labor by both the Japanese military and the Allies during World War II. P. W. Singer concludes this section by examining how and why another group of civilians—"corporate warriors" or military contractors employed by private security firms—has increased in popularity since the end of the Cold War.

Taken collectively, the readings are intended to prompt discussion and thought about what the term "military labor" might mean in different contexts and times and how the term might be used as a productive and provocative analytical framework and engender new definitions and analytical conceptions of "military labor." While "labor" obviously intersects with many of the other parts of this reader, the following contributions focus on aspects of military labor that have gone largely unexamined.

READINGS

2.1 Excerpts from Beth Bailey, "Soldiering as Work: The All-Volunteer Force in the United States," in *Fighting for a Living: A Comparative Study of Military Labour, 1500–2000*, edited by Erik-Jan

Zürcher (Amsterdam: Amsterdam University Press, 2014),
581–612.

2.2 Excerpts from Sealing Cheng, "Sexing the Globe," in *On the Move
for Love: Migrant Entertainers and the U.S. Military in South
Korea* (Philadelphia: University of Pennsylvania Press, 2013),
15–20.

2.3 Excerpts from Michael Jerryson, "Military Monks," in *Buddhist
Warfare*, edited by Michael Jerryson and Mark Juergensmeyer
(Oxford: Oxford University Press, 2010), 182–85.

2.4 Brandon Kohrt and Robert Koenig, "Child Soldiers after War,"
Anthropology News 50, no. 5 (2009): 27.

2.5 Excerpts from Paul H. Kratoska, "Introduction," in *Asian Labor
in the Wartime Japanese Empire: Unknown Histories*, edited by
Paul H. Kratoska (New York: Routledge, 2005), xv–xviii.

2.6 Excerpts from P. W. Singer, "Corporate Warriors: The Rise of
the Privatized Military Industry," *International Security* 26, no. 3
(Winter 2001–2): 186–220.

2.1

SOLDIERING AS WORK
The All-Volunteer Force in the United States
Beth Bailey

On June 30, 1973, Dwight Elliot Stone, the last man to be conscripted into the
U.S. military, reported for basic training. The following day the United States
began its experiment with an all-volunteer force (Evans 1993: 40).

Most Americans understood this move as a major and unprecedented
transformation—even as a radical experiment—even though the long-
standing draft was, in fact, the aberration. Until Cold War pressures convinced
Americans that a large standing army was justified, the nation had relied on
a volunteer force, turning to conscription only in time of war. But memories
were short. Even though the draft had been in effect for only thirty-three years,
from 1940 through slightly more than three decades of war and tense peace,
conscription had come to seem normal, an expected part of young men's lives.

Short memories aside, however, those who saw the All-Volunteer Force
(AVF) as a radical experiment had a point. It was clear in 1973 that the nation would need to recruit 20,000–30,000 non-prior service (NPS) accessions

a month—vastly more than in the all-volunteer past. And they would have to do so from a population of youth that could generously be characterized as antimilitary, persuading them to join a troubled institution at the end of a difficult and unpopular war. The chair of the House Armed Services Committee was widely quoted as he quipped—repeatedly—that the only way the United States could get a volunteer force was to draft one (O'Sullivan and Meckler 1974: 228).

The American move from one military form to another was not messy and gradual. . . . Instead, it was clear and absolute from one day to the next, and both the end of conscription and the structure of the new system were argued over, legislated, planned, observed, analyzed, and evaluated. Thus, it is possible to discuss not only the key social, economic, demographic, and technological variables that produced the United States' modern volunteer force, but also the struggles to shape that force and to give meaning to the experience of military service in the post–Vietnam War United States. Significantly, many thought the AVF would simply replace the selective service system with an "economic draft" and that the new all-volunteer force would be filled with poor, alienated African American men (though some were objecting to such potential exploitation while others worried about angry black men with guns and weapons training). They believed it just could not be done. In the end, however, almost all involved in the debates over the AVF believed the volunteer force would serve as the core of the U.S. military and as the nation's peacetime force. In the event of a major conflict or long-lasting war, they assumed, the United States would once again turn to the draft.

THE MILITARY DID, in fact, face an enormous challenge, and the U.S. Army most of all. In the wake of a war gone badly wrong, an unpopular institution wracked by internal crisis had to recruit tens of thousands of Americans a month (by contrast, Army recruiting aimed for a total of eighty thousand NPS recruits in 2018) from a racially, culturally, and politically divided society in which young people were overwhelmingly opposed to the military and more comfortable with the urging to "question authority" than with an automatic "Yes, sir." . . .

Faced with such grim prospects, the Army began two linked efforts, each of which relied, at least partially, on models of civilian labor or the market. During the early 1970s, in an attempt to improve its image, the Army initiated a series of highly publicized reforms. Many were based on research into what young people would find acceptable work conditions and often relied on analogies to the civilian workplace. In the early 1970s potential volunteers were promised forty-hour workweeks and paid vacations. Announcing the end of reveille and bed checks, Army reformers made the point that civilian bosses did not check to see whether their employees were in bed at 10 P.M. More sophisticated arguments also used the language of work. When Pete Dawkins, a young and highly decorated major who, while at West Point, had won the Heisman Trophy for the most outstanding player in American college football, testified before Congress about the coming "modern volunteer army," he played down the reform of living conditions and the Army's newly competitive pay, emphasizing instead a different aspect of labor. To attract volunteers, he argued, the Army would need to offer recruits "the ability to grow in one's work, the ability to achieve recognition for achievement, the opportunity to really have work challenges." The army Dawkins envisioned would offer the satisfaction of meaningful labor.[1]

The military also began trying to compete more effectively in the labor market, offering benefits that, research suggested, would attract the sort of volunteers they wanted: bonuses for enlistment, money for college, job training, leadership skills, travel, adventure, and (initially, for women) good marriage prospects. Far-sighted reformers also began to focus on advertising (Bailey 2007). This was also, in a different sense, a turn to the market, though a market more broadly defined. Economists at that time had not yet begun to factor irrational forces into their calculations, and the economists whose arguments shaped the Gates Commission's conclusions had relied on fairly basic labor models of supply, demand, and competitive wages. [*Editors' note*: The President's Commission on an All-Volunteer Armed Force, known as the Gates Commission, submitted its final report to President Richard Nixon in 1970.] Offer young men a decent wage, the commission claimed, and a sufficient number would enlist. Individuals would make decisions based on rational understandings of their own economic self-interest.

These, however, were not days of measured rationality in American society. And the market, in 1970s America, was not simply a realm of rational economic choice. It was a site of consumer desire; it was a volatile space of inchoate needs, hopes, and fears. These military officers, paradoxically, understood the complexity of this "market" better than the Chicago School economists on the [Gates] Commission. . . . They adopted consumer capitalism's most powerful tools, turning to the most sophisticated marketing and advertising firms of the day in attempts to discover what young people wanted and sell it back to them in the shape of the military. Although the slogans varied ("Today's Army Wants to Join You" was the initial campaign), all attempted to convince young people that military service was not about obligation but opportunity.

That opportunity took different forms. Some of it was slightly misconceived reassurance: the initial advertisements made the unlikely claim that joining the army required no sacrifice of individuality—an important concept to '70s youth—not even the traditional "skin-head" haircut. At the same time, these ads offered a chance to "build your mind and body, further your education, become expert at a skill, have opportunities for advancement, travel, and 30 days vacation a year." One series of advertisements asked potential volunteers to "Take the Army's 16-month tour of Europe," a witty turn on the multiple meanings of tour that conflated the Army tour of duty with the grand tour of Europe that more prosperous youth enjoyed. But many ads made a more basic offer. "We've got over 300 good, steady jobs," read the headline on a *Reader's Digest* advertisement that prompted more than thirty thousand young men to send in postcards requesting more information. Another ad inquired, "What are you doing after school?"[2]

NOTES

1. Dawkins's comments in Special Subcommittee on Recruiting and Retention of Military Personnel, U.S. House Committee on Armed Services, *Recruiting and Retention of Military Personnel*, September 29, 1971, 59.

2. Advertisements created for the U.S. Army by N. W. Ayer are collected in the N. W. Ayer Advertising Records, Archives Center, National Museum of American History, Smithsonian Institution, Washington, DC.

2.2

SEXING THE GLOBE
Sealing Cheng

To understand the experiences of Filipina entertainers serving a U.S. clientele around U.S. military bases in South Korea, one necessarily has to grapple with the global forces that brought these disparate groups together. Equally, if not more, important: how are women's sexuality and labor both premises for their deployment and sites of agency to negotiate within globalized hierarchies of race, class, and gender? In very broad terms, *gijichon* is what Denise Brennan, following Arjun Appadurai's idea of "ethnoscapes," calls an individual "sexscape." [*Editors' note: Gijichon* is a term referring to red-light districts near military bases in South Korea.] Drawing on her study of sex tourism in a Dominican town, Brennan (2004: 16–17) suggests that "sexscapes link the practices of sex work to the forces of a globalized economy" and are characterized by travel from developed to developing countries, consumption of paid sex, and inequalities. Gijichon as a sexscape has been subjected to a distinct set of forces from sex tourism—most prominently Cold War geopolitics, post–Cold War economic liberalization, and intraregional labor migration in the 1990s. How do these processes of globalization shape individual experiences in gijichon? How may these experiences generate new insights into women's mobility, sexuality, and labor in the transnational field?

U.S. MILITARY CAMP towns in the Asia-Pacific region, in countries such as South Korea, Japan, Vietnam, and the Philippines, are a legacy of Cold War politics. Clubs for GIs in the Asia-Pacific region are the progeny of a global network of U.S. military bases established as part of U.S. policy to contain communism and preserve U.S. geopolitical interests.[1] Military stationed both onshore and offshore have access to the rest and relaxation (R&R) facilities around the bases. Prostitution has been a key component of these R&R sites.[2]

The Korean Peninsula is still technically a war zone, as there was only a truce but no peace treaty to conclude the Korean War (1950–53). U.S. military forces landed in southern Korea as an occupation force in 1945 at the end of World War II, ending Japanese colonial rule. The number of U.S. forces accelerated with the Korean War, and the Mutual Defense Treaty (effective 1954) formalized the stationing of U.S. troops in South Korea. This led, during the poverty and homelessness of the postwar years, to the rise of boomtowns around U.S. military bases, settlements that catered to the needs of U.S. military personnel for livelihood and included shopkeepers, club owners, and prostitutes.

The number of U.S. military personnel in Korea has been heavily tied to foreign-policy agendas in Washington, DC, and to concerns of a North Korean attack in Seoul. In 1971 the number of U.S. military personnel in South Korea decreased from 64,000 to 43,000 in conformity with the Nixon Doctrine, which aimed to reduce U.S. military involvement in Asia. In 2000, there were 37,000 U.S. military personnel at 120 military installations in Korea. This number had been reduced to 9,154 as of May 2006, as part of the restructuring of U.S. forces in the Pacific. The 2004 agreement between the U.S. and South Korean governments laid down plans to drastically reduce the Yongsan Garrison in central Seoul as part of the long-term goal to downsize U.S. troop presence in South Korea. When President Lee Myung-bak took office in 2008, he confirmed that U.S.-Korea relations would be placed at the center of his foreign policy. The U.S. and South Korean governments agreed to keep the number of American troops at 28,500. Thus, the continual presence of U.S. forces in Korea was assured, despite civilian groups' calls for their withdrawal (Sudworth 2008). Obviously, these governmental decisions regarding the presence, reduction, and redeployment of U.S. military forces in South Korea are central to the lives of those in gijichon and figure importantly in nationalist discourses in Korea.

In her study of gijichon women in the early 1990s, Katharine Moon makes an observation that forebodes the changing ethnoscape of gijichon. The Korean women Moon talked with in 1992 noted that the average GI could not afford to keep up with the high prices in the Korean economy and was no match for a Korean man in this respect, as the latter would "drop hundreds of dollars" in a bar. The U.S. dollars GIs had at their disposal had become "measly" and "ridiculous" at a time when the Korean Peninsula had become home to the tenth-largest economy in the world—an astounding economic advance from the war-torn country of the 1950s. For Korean women, the desirability of GIs as clients for a dependable income or a comfortable future began to decline with the rise of South Korean economic power.

Since the mid-1990s, foreign women, predominantly from the Philippines and the former Soviet Union, have entered the clubs to fill vacancies left by Korean women. Mr. Shin was a gijichon club owner who had been in Songtan, the gijichon right in front of Osan Air Base of the U.S. forces in Korea, for fifteen years when I interviewed him in 2000.[3] He was also chairman of the Songtan branch of the club owners' organization, the Korea Special Tourism Association (KSTA). He claimed to have come up with the idea of bringing Filipinas to work in the clubs to make up for the crippling shortage of Korean women. In 1990, he brought in some Filipinas on a trial basis, and the results were satisfactory to the KSTA, which then obtained permission from the Ministry of Culture and Tourism to bring in foreign women on E-6 (entertainer) visas in 1996. Diversification at a time of increased economic liberalism was, in Mr. Shin's view, favorable: "The American soldiers get fed up with women from only one country. We are thinking of getting women from other countries to come." During my fieldwork, women from mostly the Philippines but also Kazakhstan, Nepal, and Sri Lanka were working in both Dongducheon and Songtan. In 1999, club owners had to pay $1,300 for each entertainer recruited through the KSTA, followed by about $300 per month as salary for each woman in their employ. By August 1999, the KSTA alone had brought in 1,093 women, mainly from the Philippines and Russia, and had pocketed a total of $1.6 billion in agency fees." From my visits to most of the clubs in Dongducheon and Songtan, my estimate of the number of Filipino entertainers in Korean gijichon in 1999–2000 was six hundred.

Migrant entertainers enter into particular niches in the structure of the entertainment industry in gijichon, which has four broad levels. At the highest echelon are clubs and bars, usually with female entertainers who accompany customers for the price of a "ladies' drink" (some women may provide sexual services for an additional payment). Second in importance and price is street-level prostitution that usually relies on older women to solicit clients. The third level consists of "contract marriages," in which women play the role of wives for GIs during their stay in South Korea and receive monthly allowances in return. Independent streetwalkers, who are very few in number, make up the fourth level.

Foreign women work only in the clubs, which most GIs visit for drinks, music, dancing, shows, and female company. Club owners need young women to work in the clubs to attract GIs. Other jobs in gijichon are less profitable and are usually taken by older Korean women. Some of the Korean women who enter into "contract marriages" may also be working in the clubs as madams. Waitresses and cleaners are usually but not always Korean women who used to work in the clubs in their youthful days but could not make it as madams or club owners. Other older Korean women work as vendors, going from club to club selling GIs stuffed toys, flowers, and little souvenirs, which the GIs then give to the Filipinas.

Clubs attract GIs with their duty-free alcohol (around $2 for an imported beer), music, shows, and female entertainers. Since 1998, Filipinas have been present in most of the clubs. Only the larger clubs have shows, which are usually available on Fridays and Saturdays. The divide between clubs that served only blacks and those that served only whites, which created serious problems in the 1960s and 1970s, has been much eroded, although segregation still existed in Dongducheon in 2000. There is still a club that white GIs tend to avoid: the Black Rose, owned by an African American and his Korean wife. Some clubs specialize in Latino music and attract a more Hispanic following.

For those who are interested in female company, a "drink" for a woman costs $10 and usually entitles the customer to around twenty minutes of the woman's time—for conversation, dancing, or lap dancing. Rooms for VIPs are found in some clubs, and a customer may take a woman into the room (with her consent) for around half an hour if he buys her four drinks. A customer may pay a "bar fine" to take a woman out of the club. Depending on the time of the month (more expensive on paydays) and the length of time desired, bar fines range from $100 to $300. "Bar fine"—a term that has been used in the sex trade in the Philippines—was introduced into gijichon with the arrival of the Filipinas. "Short time" and "long time" were terms commonly used by the Koreans before that. The women usually get 20 percent of the money. Whatever happens in the VIP room or on a bar-fine outing is subject to negotiation between the woman and the customer.

In the 1990s, the profile of customers extended from U.S. military personnel to include foreigners on business trips or working in nearby factories, as well as Koreans. Korean men often visit these clubs because of the exoticism of foreign women. With greater spending power than GIs, and usually extravagant spending habits (drinking bottles of brandy rather than beer and giving tips more eagerly than GIs), these Korean men are often a more important source of revenue for gijichon clubs. This is particularly true in Songtan, where Koreans are basically free to enter all the clubs, while clubs in Dongducheon—particularly those with strip shows and sexual services available—follow more stringently the "foreigners-only" rule.

The labor shortage in gijichon that led to the introduction of migrant workers echoed the much larger-scale problem in the manufacturing sector, especially in what were commonly known as "3D" (dirty, dangerous, and difficult) jobs. Since 1991, an estimated 222,000 production jobs of all skill levels could not attract domestic workers. The problem was particularly serious for low-skilled jobs in plastics, electrical machinery, and commercial fishing. This need for cheap labor has thus been partly filled with the introduction of "industrial trainees"—not "workers"—from developing countries under restrictive terms. The globalization initiative (*segyehwa*) under President Kim Young-sam in 1993 came in on the heels of the burgeoning economic growth, market liberalization, and, finally, democratization that characterized the period of rapid industrial and financial development over the previous three decades. As Korean capital also found its way into many developing countries, foreign laborers entered South Korea as flexible workers.

The introduction of these foreign workers took place within the development of intraregional migration in Asia starting in the late 1980s. A shrinking labor force and robust economic growth in industrial economies such as South Korea and Japan have been drawing migrant workers from developing countries in the Asia region. The first significant influx of Filipino factory workers into South Korea took place after the signing of the Republic of the Philippines–Korea Economic and Technical Cooperation Agreement and the Korean Scientific and Technological Cooperation Agreement in 1986. Following the introduction of the "industrial trainee" system, the Agreement for the Promotion of Investment was signed in 1995, boosting overseas investment and exchanges of technology and labor. These measures by the Philippine and South Korean governments opened the official door for Filipinos' entry into Korea for work. In 2004, the Philippine government estimated that a total of 47,150 Filipino citizens were in South Korea, 9,015 of whom were irregular migrants (Philippine Overseas Employment Agency 2004).

Forged out of Cold War geopolitics, gijichon came to participate in global capital's search for flexible labor in the late 1990s. Not only do gijichon clubs participate in the transnational network of labor recruitment, but they also adopt new ways to manage these ethnic others and increasingly serve an ethnically diverse clientele. Even though gijichon is largely a marginal site in the larger Korean body politic, the globalization of its sexual economy provides important insights into South Korea's regional integration and global engagements.

NOTES

1. Shortly after the Korean War, the United States had about 450 bases in thirty-six countries and was linked by political and military pacts with some twenty countries outside Latin America (see Foot 1990: 5).

2. It is important to note that R&R facilities are not a universal corollary to U.S. military forces stationed abroad but are subject to negotiations between the United States and the host governments. There was no R&R during the Persian Gulf War, and soldiers were strictly prohibited from approaching local women by the military command.

3. Mr. Shin is a pseudonym.

2.3

MILITARY MONKS
Michael Jerryson

Military monks are fully ordained monks who simultaneously serve as armed soldiers, marines, or navy or air force personnel. This amalgam of Thai Buddhism and the military reflects the inherent violence. For many, the idea of a militarized monk conflicts sharply with a monk's most fundamental duties. A Buddhist monk's purpose is to avoid life's vulgarities, to aspire toward enlightenment. A soldier's life is virtually the opposite; that job requires confrontation with life's worst vulgarities.

In addition to these ideological complications, there is also an ecclesiastical interdiction that prohibits soldiers from becoming monks. However, as the anthropologist Hayashi Yukio (2003: 1) explains in his study of the Thai-Lao of northeastern Thailand, a people's religious practice is rooted in experience. Buddhism "does not consist merely of cultivated knowledge sealed in texts, or of its interpretation. Rather it consists of practices that live in the 'here and now.'" While the Buddhist textual tradition clearly disallows the existence of a military monk, lived Buddhist traditions demonstrate a different attitude. Throughout the development of Buddhism in such countries as China, Korea, and Japan, we find traditions that do not follow the idealized notions of Buddhism. Similar to Thai Buddhists, Chinese, Korean, and Japanese Buddhist monasticisms also have had military monks.

The Thai Theravada Buddhist tradition is unique among these monasticisms in allowing men to temporarily join the Sangha. It is common for Thai Buddhist men to ordain as monks for a short time at least once in their lives. Other Theravada, Mahayana, and Vajrayana traditions treat ordination as a permanent life decision. The anthropologist Charles Keyes notes that Thai men gain considerable esteem by their temporary ordinations, which generally occur during Buddhist Lent (*khaophansa* in Thai). By entering the Thai Sangha, all men, regardless of class, have access to education and a means of increasing their social status (Keyes 1987: 138–39). Moreover, in addition to these social benefits, it is also popularly believed that by becoming a monk, a son grants his mother merit to enter heaven.

According to the Vinaya, certain interdictions surround ordainment. Many such interdictions revolve around physical or social characteristics that would preclude ordination, such as if a person has a disease, is a criminal, or is disabled. Most of these guidelines resulted from the historical Buddha trying to cope with specific sociopolitical and economic dilemmas. For example, a prohibition evolved that specifically relates to the ordaining of soldiers:

> During the time of the Buddha there was a war on the border of the northern Indian kingdom of Magadha, one of the primary supporters of Buddhist monasticism. Several generals who did not want to join the battle entered the Buddhist Sangha. At the request of the king, the Buddha declared that henceforth soldiers were not allowed into the Sangha. (Vinaya I: 73–74)

Since this historical incident, the official doctrinal stance has been to prohibit active soldiers from entering the Sangha, though we have already noted that this interdiction is subject to regional and historical exceptions. Richard Gombrich, a well-respected scholar of Theravada Buddhism, has offered a slightly different context for this doctrinal prohibition: "A minister advised the king that anyone who thus deprived him of his soldiers deserved to be executed. As the king was on good terms with the Buddha, he advised him that other kings might not take such a thing lying down. Reading between the lines, we can deduce that he warned the Buddha that for their own good the Sangha had better not ordain soldiers" (Gombrich 1988: 116).

The Thai state has formally acknowledged and supported the ecclesiastical interdiction on ordaining soldiers. In 1905, to avoid the overlapping of duties to the state and Sangha, the Chulalongkorn administration created a legal provision called the Thai Military Service Act, exempting monks from military service. The act also eliminated the tensions concerning the possibility of monks enlisting in the army. Thus, in accordance with ecclesiastical restrictions, the Thai Military Service Act was designed to prevent the monk-to-soldier process. However, later in contemporary Thai society, it became clear that the tension was not the result of the monk-to-soldier process but the reverse: the soldier-to-monk process.

By means of its temporary ordinations, the Thai Buddhist tradition allows maneuverability around these obstacles to the existence of Buddhist soldiers. According to stipulations articulated by the Office of National Buddhism, soldiers are allotted one four-month paid leave of absence during their service in order to ordain at a local monastery (*wat*). Soldiers generally take this leave during the annual Buddhist Lent (which generally lasts from June until October). They return to duty after the rainy season retreat has ended. This leniency surrounding ordination is extended even further by another and more covert exercise regarding the status of military monks.

As early as 2002, a covert military unit (authorized by a confidential department) began directing Buddhist soldiers to ordain while remaining on active duty. Every year since, military monks have been assigned to specific posts. According to some of the military monks I interviewed, this secret military unit operates semi-independently. Its operations are unknown to most of the military in Bangkok, although there have been numerous reports implicating the Thai monarchy, especially Queen Sirikit. For example, there have been reports of groups of military monks becoming ordained in honor of the queen's birthday.

It is difficult to determine how many Thais in the military truly do not know about military monks as opposed to those who know but refuse to disclose what they know. As the state-appointed guardian of Thai monastic lifestyles and activities, the Office of National Buddhism does not acknowledge the presence of military monks. When asked about their presence, the director dismissed the issue, saying, "Why would soldiers have to dress like a monk? In dangerous monasteries, we have soldiers there to take care of them. And this point is a really serious point in Thai Buddhism. We can't let something like this exist. The monk can't fight and can't have weapons. People may think this is possible, but it's not."[1] The official position of the Office of National Buddhism mirrors that of the Thai Buddhist Vinaya. As the historian Craig Reynolds (2006: 237) notes, the Vinaya goes as far as to forbid monks from even observing an army in battle dress. Although the director of the Office of National Buddhism argues emphatically that military monks do not exist, they are a very real and active part of many monasteries in southern Thailand.

Accounts of military monks in southern Thailand are cloaked in rumors and secrecy.[2] In numerous interviews with abbots, journalists, and local Buddhists, there were allusions to military monks; they were short references but direct confirmations nonetheless. Such brief references to military monks were always followed by bouts of hesitation and reluctance. If not for the fact that I personally and directly interviewed military monks, I might have dismissed these informants' depictions as a communal fabrication.

To dismiss this atmosphere of secrecy as insignificant would be to dismiss the very real ideological efficacy of the military monk. Thai Buddhism is perceived as a peaceful, meditative, and supportive tradition, devoid of any violence. Monks, as embodied agents of this tradition, are considered diametrically opposed to violence and agents of war—that is, the military. Hence, there is a reluctance to talk about military monks. The anthropologist Michael Taussig postulates that truth comes in the form of a public secret. The importance of this public secret is *knowing what not to know* (Taussig 1999: 2). One clear indication of this tacit social understanding is the many interviews with abbots in the southernmost provinces who claim to know nothing about military monks. Contrary to their assertions, however, a high-ranking monk in the southernmost provinces confided that abbots throughout the region met in 2004 and discussed the issue of military monks receiving military stipends. Living in an environment that normalizes bombings and armed attacks, southern monks and some privileged members of the Buddhist laity are aware of military monks, but they also know that they should not openly speak of them. Such a discussion would combine elements that socially and religiously are considered opposites: Buddhism and violence.

NOTES

1. Personal communication with Nopparat Benjawatthananant, December 26, 2006.
2. There are no official reports on military monks. The only substantiation of their existence comes from interviews, personal observations, and local rumors in southern Thailand.

CHILD SOLDIERS AFTER WAR
Brandon Kohrt and Robert Koenig

"I was thirteen years old when I joined the Maoists," said Asha, a girl from a Dalit "untouchable" Hindu caste in southern Nepal, describing how she became associated with the Maoist People's Liberation Army (PLA). "I was born into a poor family." She pointed to a few pounds of cornmeal and then the one goat outside her thatched hut. "We just have this much, nothing more." Asha continued, "I was a very good student [but] after I took my exams for fifth grade my parents told me: 'We have no money so you have to leave school and take care of your brothers and sister.'" With few economic resources, Asha's mother decided to pay for her brothers' schooling rather than "waste money on a girl's education."

After Asha left school, Maoist women frequently visited her home and encouraged her to join the party. They told her that women and men were equal in the Maoist party and promised her an opportunity to continue her studies if she joined a women's division of the PLA. A few months later, Asha attended a Maoist cultural program and was impressed by the rhetoric: "Both sons and daughters should be treated equally, the Maoist leaders said. Husbands and wives should work together, too. . . . From that day, I didn't want to go back to my house."

Believing that the Maoists were her only option for a future beyond domestic servitude, Asha left home to join the armed struggle. During her time with the Maoists, she states, she was well treated, and the leaders encouraged her interest in art, enlisting her talents in painting propaganda signs. She encountered only one battle but saw a number of comrades killed.

Asha returned home for a brief visit after more than a year in the PLA, and her mother immediately married her to a man from a distant community to prevent her from returning to the Maoists. She was fourteen, and he was twenty-two. Asha describes her marriage as endless abuse and suffering. She was raped throughout the marriage by her husband and beaten by her in-laws. After two years of this abuse, Asha attempted suicide. Her father-in-law found her hanging from the ceiling. He cut her down, handed her the noose, and said, "Go to your mother's home and kill yourself." Asha now lives once again with her mother. She wept concluding her life story, "Maybe if I hadn't joined the Maoists, my parents wouldn't have forced me to marry, and I wouldn't have had such a life of suffering. At thirteen years old, what do you know? You just don't understand."

The exploitation of children by militaries and other groups around the globe is a gross human rights violation that bears lifelong consequences for children and communities. Despite increasing attention to the plight of child soldiers through powerful firsthand accounts, such as Ishmael Beah's *A Long Way Gone*, fictionalized depictions continue to dominate the public imagination, with important ramifications for the types of intervention and funding made available to support former child soldiers. In fictionalized accounts, life before becoming a child soldier is idyllic and the return home is seen as the panacea for all of the child's problems. However, as Asha's story illustrates, the return home can be far more painful than the experiences of war. An ethnographic approach to recording the experiences of child soldiers reveals these complexities.

Through anthropological research in conjunction with Transcultural Psychosocial Organization Nepal and ethnographic filmmaking, we have begun to understand the complex processes that make children vulnerable to recruitment and why the return home is so difficult. In Nepal, the recruitment of children into the Maoist army occurs against a backdrop of state-sponsored human rights violations, gender- and caste-based discrimination rooted in conservative interpretations of Hinduism, extreme poverty, and lack of education and other opportunities. Many see the Maoists as an escape from this, especially women. "After joining the movement women are taught to read and write," explained the Maoist party leader Chairman Prachanda, who later served as Prime Minister of Nepal. "When they fight . . . they understand the value of freedom."

We have found that approximately half of child soldiers in Nepal say that they voluntarily joined the Maoist army, often to escape harsh conditions at home. Thus, for some children their last choice would be returning to a community that they originally fled. Although Asha was in constant danger with the PLA, they offered her a sense of empowerment, a way out of domestic slavery, freedom from a rigid caste system, and an opportunity to learn from female leaders. For Asha, even gun battles were better than what she faced back home. Sadly, her story is not unique. Dalit boys also describe returning home to caste-based oppression after an environment of reported caste equality in the PLA.

Anthropological engagement with the lives of child soldiers is not simply an academic issue; it is crucial to help inform interventions. Anthropological research can address both sociopolitical issues that make children vulnerable to recruitment and postwar community responses to former child soldiers. A simple but important intervention in Nepal has been to support the enrollment of girls in school. If Asha's mother had supported her daughter's educational pursuits, this might have reduced the chances of her joining the Maoists. Although financial support is part of making this happen, changing attitudes toward girls' education is also crucial. Fortunately, there is a growing community of anthropologists engaged in research and intervention for child soldiers and other children affected by war, and intervention is focusing increasingly on reintegration as a crucial factor in well-being. Ultimately, a more complete anthropological view of the lives of children across the globe can help uncover the ways in which they are vulnerable to becoming soldiers and can go a long way to prevent other girls from suffering Asha's fate.

2.5

ASIAN LABOR IN THE WARTIME JAPANESE EMPIRE
Paul H. Kratoska

The mobilization of labor was a major feature of the Japanese empire in the 1930s and 1940s, and the number of people forced to work for the Japanese across Asia ran well into the millions. Japan needed soldiers, and it needed workers to produce military equipment and construct airfields and other military facilities and to grow food for the armed forces and the civilian population. As Japan expanded into China and then into Southeast Asia, the demand for labor increased, and people from these regions began to be pressed into service, some on a short-term basis but others for periods lasting months or even years. The prewar economy had collapsed, causing widespread unemployment, and workers initially responded positively to promises of generous wages and benefits. By 1944, labor reserves had been used up, and the Japanese turned to forced recruitment. Many workers were sent to distant locations, and a considerable number of them did not return. Theirs is a story of death and dislocation of Holocaust proportions, and remarkably it is a story that has received little attention from historians.

Conditions at the Japanese work sites were often extremely bad, with rudimentary housing, inadequate diets, little or no medical care, and strict labor regimens that showed scant concern for the loss of human life. Malaria and dengue fever were endemic at many project sites, and laborers brought in from other places often had little resistance to these diseases. Moreover, workers suffered from malnutrition, which left them weakened and lacking physical stamina. Bringing large numbers of unskilled workers to work sites with inadequate prior planning for sanitation resulted in outbreaks of dysentery, cholera, and other diseases. Laborers also developed debilitating tropical ulcers, leading in some cases to amputation of limbs or death. Finally, infractions of the rules or failure to work hard brought harsh corporal punishment, worsening the physical deterioration of the workers. Mortality rates of 30–40 percent appear to have been common, but there are few statistics, or even remotely reliable estimates, to indicate how many people died. It is certain from firsthand observations and anecdotal evidence that the numbers were very large.

Grief and despair find little place in most historical accounts and are absent from most of the source materials historians use, but the hundreds of thousands who died were sons, husbands, and fathers, or sometimes daughters, wives, and mothers, and had families awaiting their return. In some cases, their departures were recorded ceremoniously, with laborers affixing signatures or thumbprints to documents showing their home addresses and the names of their next of kin and acknowledging advances of cash against future wages. Deaths often went unrecorded. Coolies too sick to work were placed in death houses, where they spent their final hours in accumulated filth—mud and the vomit and excrement produced by those who had died before them—without food or medicine, and certainly without hope. Their corpses were thrown into unmarked graves, or burned, or abandoned in the forest, or tossed into rivers. Their families received no information and eventually had no choice but to presume the worst.

The suffering of European prisoners of war (POWs) forced to work for the Japanese, most famously on the Thai-Burma Railway, have been well chronicled, but the experiences of Asian laborers remain unstudied. There are many reasons for this omission. Most of the workers were illiterate, and those who had some education lacked the traditions of writing and publication that produced vivid accounts of European POW labor and of the Holocaust in Europe. Moreover, historians have little material with which to work because the Japanese destroyed the records of their wartime administration immediately after the conflict ended in August 1945. . . .

The use of Asian labor by Japan as part of its war effort in East Asia and Southeast Asia [was crucial], but labor is essential to any military effort, and the Allies also recruited Asian workers to support the military effort.[1] To meet its manpower requirements, Admiral Mountbatten's South East Asia Command made use of workers provided by the Indian Auxiliary Pioneer Corps (later called the Indian Pioneer Corps). Created early in the war, the corps was organized in companies, paralleling the military services. Companies belonging to the corps initially worked in the Middle East and India, where each battalion was assigned four labor companies consisting of 417 men each. In 1943, the corps was restructured under a group headquarters, which began assigning companies individually according to need. The Japanese thrust into Southeast Asia brought the creation of additional civil labor units in the form of state and provincial labor units, a Porter Corps, and Indian Tea Association labor forces.

Prior to January 1945, when Allied Land Forces, South East Asia (ALFSEA) headquarters consolidated these workforces, there was considerable overlap among these bodies. After the reorganization, Pioneer Corps group commanders became responsible for all labor employed within specified territorial zones. When Allied forces returned to Southeast Asia, labor companies were sent to Singapore and Malaya, Java, Siam, French Indochina, Hong Kong, and Borneo.

The workforce reached a very substantial size. In April 1945, ALFSEA operations included thirty-four Pioneer Group headquarters and 266 companies, and the Pioneer and Labor Directorate controlled 523,304 men. Following the Japanese surrender, local civilian labor replaced Pioneer Corps workers. By February 1946, the number of companies operating in Southeast Asia had been reduced by 50 percent, replaced by some 305,190 locally recruited civilians.

Pioneer labor companies carried out a wide range of activities, building roads, bridges, railways, and airfields; laying pipelines and signal wire; unloading ships; and manning storage depots. For example, nearly 54,000 workers took part in constructing airfields in Assam for supply missions to China, building the Ledo road, and laying pipelines in northern Burma.

Many of the laborers were Nepalese, and they performed impressive feats of endurance, marching as much as thirty miles a day to carry stores to the front lines and carrying back wounded soldiers. Pioneers often worked under fire, but they were neither armed nor expected to fight. Late in the war, in June 1945, the teams were "combatized," receiving rifles and training and a corresponding adjustment in pay. Following the Japanese surrender, Pioneers served as guards for working parties made up of Japanese "surrendered personnel," rode goods trains to protect shipments of supplies in Malaya, and guarded storage depots in Burma.

NOTE

1. Information in this section is from a paper entitled "Pioneer and Labour in South East Asia Command: A Survey of the Service," War Office (WO) 203/2192, in the British National Archives (Public Record Office), London.

CORPORATE WARRIORS
The Rise of the Privatized Military Industry
P. W. Singer

A failing government trying to prevent the imminent capture of its capital, a regional power planning for war, a ragtag militia looking to reverse its battlefield losses, a peacekeeping force seeking deployment support, a weak ally attempting to escape its patron's dictates, a multinational corporation hoping to end constant rebel attacks against its facilities, a drug cartel pursuing high-technology military capabilities, a humanitarian aid group requiring protection within conflict zones, and the world's sole remaining superpower searching for ways to limit its military costs and risks.[1] When thinking in conventional terms, security studies experts would be hard-pressed to find anything that these actors might have in common. They differ in size, relative power, location in the international system, level of wealth, number and type of adversaries, organizational makeup, ideology, legitimacy, objectives, and so on.

There is, however, one unifying link: when faced with such diverse security needs, these actors all sought external military support. Most important is where that support came from: not from a state or even an international organization but, rather, the global marketplace. It is here that a unique business form has arisen that I term the "privatized military firm" (PMF)—profit-driven organizations that trade in professional services intricately linked to warfare. They are corporate bodies that specialize in the provision of military skills, including tactical combat operations, strategic planning, intelligence gathering and analysis, operational support, troop training, and military technical assistance.[2] With the rise of the privatized military industry, actors in the global system can access capabilities that extend across the entire military spectrum—from a team of commandos to a wing of fighter jets—simply by becoming a business client....

The Global Reach of the Privatized Military Industry

Since the end of the Cold War, PMF activity has surged around the globe. Privatized military firms have operated in relative backwaters, key strategic zones, and rich and poor states alike. In Saudi Arabia, for example, the regime's military relies almost completely on a multiplicity of firms to provide a variety of services—from operating its air defense system to training and advising its land, sea, and air forces. Even Congo-Brazzaville, with less strategic importance and wealth, once depended on a foreign corporation to train and support its military—in this case, from the Israeli firm Levdan. Privatized military firms have also influenced the outcomes of numerous conflicts. They are credited, for example, with being or having been determinate actors in wars in Angola, Croatia, Ethiopia-Eritrea, and Sierra Leone.

The privatized military industry's reach extends even to the world's remaining superpower. Every major U.S. military operation in the post–Cold War era (whether in the Persian Gulf, Somalia, Haiti, Zaire, Bosnia, or Kosovo) has involved significant and growing levels of PMF support. The 1999 Kosovo operations illustrate this trend. Before the conflict, PMFs supplied the military observers who made up the U.S. contingent of the international verification mission assigned to the province. When the air war began, other PMFs not only supplied the logistics and much of the information warfare aspects of the North Atlantic Treaty Organization campaign against the Serbs, but they also constructed and operated the refugee camps outside Kosovo's borders (Copetas 1999). In the follow-on Kosovo Force peacekeeping operation, PMFs expanded their role to include, for example, provision of critical aerial surveillance for the force (Wall 2000). The U.S. military has also employed PMFs to perform a range of other services—from military instruction in more than two hundred Reserve Officer Training Corps programs to operation of the computer and communications systems at the North American Aerospace Defense Command's Cheyenne Mountain base, where the U.S. nuclear response is coordinated. . . .

Reasons Behind Military Privatization

The confluence of three momentous dynamics—the end of the Cold War and the vacuum this produced in the market of security, transformations in the nature of warfare, and the normative rise of privatization—created a new space and demand for the establishment of the privatized military industry. Importantly, few changes appear to loom in the near future to counter any of these forces. As such, the industry is distinctly representative of the changed global security environment at the start of the twenty-first century.

THE GAP IN THE MARKET OF SECURITY

Massive disruptions in the supply and demand of capable military forces after the end of the Cold War provided the immediate catalyst for the rise of the privatized military industry. With the end of superpower pressure from above, a raft of new security threats began to appear after 1989, many involving emerging ethnic or internal conflicts. Likewise, nonstate actors with the ability to challenge and potentially disrupt world society began to increase in number, power, and stature. Among these were local warlords, terrorist networks, international criminals, and drug cartels. These groups reinforce the climate of insecurity in which PMFs thrive, creating new demands for such businesses.[3]

Another factor is that the Cold War was a historic period of hypermilitarization. Its end thus sparked a chain of military downsizing around the globe. In the 1990s, the world's armies shrank by more than six million personnel. As a result, a huge number of individuals with skill sets uniquely suited to the needs of the PMF industry, and who were often not ready for the transition to civilian life, found themselves looking for work. Complete units were cashiered, and many of the most elite units (such as the South African 32nd Reconnaissance Battalion and the Soviet Alpha special forces unit) simply kept their structure and formed their own private companies. Line soldiers were not the only ones left jobless; it is estimated that 70 percent of the former KGB joined the industry's ranks (Lock 1998). Meanwhile, massive arms stocks opened up to the market: machine guns, tanks, and even fighter jets became available to anyone who could afford them. Thus, downsizing fed both supply and demand as new threats emerged and demobilization created fresh pools of PMF labor and capital.

At the same time, the ability of states to respond to many of today's threats has declined. Shorn of their superpower support, a number of states have suffered breakdowns in governance. This has been particularly true in developing areas, where many regimes possess sovereignty in name only and lack any real political authority or capability.[4] The result has been failing states and the emergence of new areas of instability. . . . The traditional response for dealing with areas of instability used to be outside intervention, typically by one of the great powers. The end of the Cold War, however, reordered these states' security priorities. The great powers are no longer automatically willing to intervene abroad to restore stability. . . .

Privatized military firms aim to fill this void. They are eager to present themselves as businesses with a natural niche in an often complicated post–Cold War world order. As one company executive explains, "The end of the Cold War has allowed conflicts long suppressed or manipulated by the superpowers to reemerge. At the same time, most armies have gotten smaller and live footage on CNN of United States soldiers being killed in Somalia has had staggering effects on the willingness of governments to commit to foreign conflicts. We fill the gap" (Lt.-Col. Timothy Spicer, quoted in Gilligan 1998).

Concurrent with the reordering of the security market are two other critical underlying trends. First, warfare itself has been undergoing revolutionary change at all levels. At high-intensity levels of conflict, the military operations of great powers have become more technological and thus more reliant on civilian specialists to run their increasingly sophisticated military systems. At low-intensity levels, the primary tools of warfare have not only diversified but, as stated earlier, have become more available to a broader array of actors. Increasingly, the motivations behind many conflicts in the developing world are either criminalized or driven by the profit motive in some way. Both directly and indirectly, these parallel changes have heightened demand for services provided by the privatized military industry. . . .

Fewer individuals are doing the actual fighting, while massive support systems are required to maintain the world's most modern forces. . . . The requirements of high-technology warfare have also dramatically increased the need for specialized expertise, which often must be drawn from the private sector, For example, recent U.S. military exercises reveal that its Army of the Future will be unable to operate without huge levels of technical and logistics support from private firms (Adams 1999). Other advanced powers are also setting out to privatize key military services. Great Britain, for instance, recently contracted out its aircraft support units, tank transport units, and aerial refueling fleet— all of which played vital roles in the 1999 Kosovo campaign (Sheppard 1999).

Another change in the postmodern battlefield requiring greater civilian involvement is the growing importance of information dominance (particularly when the military's ability to retain individuals with highly sought-after and well-paying information technology skills is well-nigh impossible). As one expert notes, "The U.S. [A]rmy has concluded that in the future it will require contract personnel, even in the close fight area, to keep its most modern systems functioning. This applies especially to information-related systems. Information-warfare, in fact, may well become dominated by mercenaries" (Adams 1999: 115). . . .

At the same time, the motivations behind warfare also seem to be in flux. This has been particularly felt at low-intensity levels of conflict, where weak state regimes are facing increasing challenges on a variety of fronts. The state form triumphed centuries ago because it was the only one that could harness the men, machinery, and money required to take full advantage of the tools of warfare (Tilly 1975). This monopoly of the nation-state, however, is over. As a result of changes in the nature of weapons technology, individuals and small groups can now easily purchase and wield relatively massive amounts of power. This plays out in numerous ways, the most disruptive of which may be the global spread of cheap infantry weapons, the primary tools of violence in low-intensity warfare. Their increased ease of use and devastating potential are reshaping local balances of power. Almost any group operating inside a weak state can now acquire at least limited military capabilities, thus lowering the bar for creating viable threats to the status quo (Klare 1999).

Importantly, this shift encourages the proliferation and criminalization of local warring groups. According to Stephen Metz (2000: 24), "With enough money anyone can equip a powerful military force. With a willingness to use crime, nearly anyone can generate enough money." As a result, conflicts in a number of places (Colombia, Congo, Liberia, Tajikistan, etc.) have lost any of the ideological motivation they once possessed and instead have degenerated into conflicts among petty groups fighting to grab local resources. Warfare itself thus becomes self-perpetuating as violence generates personal profit for those who wield it most effectively (which often means most brutally), while no one group can eliminate the others (Ignatieff 1997; Singer and Wildavsky 1993). Privatized military firms thrive in such profit-oriented conflicts, either working for these new conflict groups or reacting to the humanitarian disasters they create.

THE POWER OF PRIVATIZATION
AND THE PRIVATIZATION OF POWER

Finally, the past few decades have been characterized by a normative shift toward the marketization of the public sphere. As one analyst puts it, the market-based approach toward military services is "the ultimate representation of neoliberalism" (O'Brien 1998: 89).

The privatization movement has gone hand in hand with globalization: both are premised on the belief that the principles of comparative advantage and competition maximize efficiency and effectiveness. Fueled by the collapse of the centralized systems in the Soviet Union and Eastern Europe, and by successes in such places as Thatcherite Britain, privatization has been touted as a testament to the superiority of the marketplace over government. It reflects the current assumption that the private sector is both more efficient and more effective. Harvey Feigenbaum and Jeffrey Henig (1997: 338) sum up this sentiment: "If any economic policy could lay claim to popularity, at least among the world's elites, it would certainly be privatization." . . . Thus, turning to external, profit-motivated military service providers has become not only a viable option but the favored solution for both public institutions and private organizations.

1. I am referring here to the regime of Valentine Strasser in Sierra Leone, the Ethiopian military, the Croat army, the West African Economic Community Cease-Fire Monitoring Group (ECOMOG) peacekeeping force, Papua New Guinea, British Petroleum, the Rodríguez cartel, Worldvision, and the United States.

2. Many analysts have referred to some of these new firms as "private military companies" (PMCs). This term, however, is used to describe only firms that offer tactical military services while ignoring firms that offer other types of military services despite sharing the same causes.

3. Many groups are also suspected of having benefited from hiring some of the industry's more unsavory private firms. Examples include Angolan rebels and certain Mexican and Colombian drug cartels. The increased activity of PMFs also illustrates that many of these firms have no compunction about challenging state interests, even those of great powers, as long as the price is right (see Cullen 2000; Goodwin 1997; Linard 1998).

4. Examples range from Albania and Afghanistan to Somalia and Sierra Leone (see Jackson 1990).

FIG. 3.0. Militarism entwines with shifting ideas about manhood and femininity, embodied in the ideal masculine warrior. Yet a paradoxical dimension of male identity in the Western imagination is the glorification of sacrifice in war: the soldier is not only a trained killer but also a compassionate protector of small, vulnerable things. This photo depicts a U.S. Army medic caring for two puppies near Jalalabad, Afghanistan. Photograph courtesy U.S. Department of Defense.

SECTION III. GENDER AND MILITARISM

Compiled by KATHERINE T. MCCAFFREY

Introduction

This section considers the way ideas about femininity and masculinity are intertwined in militarism to justify killing, mobilize populations for war, and naturalize military priorities. Western rhetoric tends to contrast masculine bellicosity with feminine passivity and assign gender roles in warfare based on presumptions about biological difference or socialization. Ideologically, women's innate peacefulness has been marshaled as an argument against war. Indeed, the British feminist Virginia Woolf (1938: 13) famously claimed that "scarcely a human being in the course of history has fallen to a woman's rifle."

The selections excerpted here challenge such neat dualisms. Gender plays an important role in constituting military identities, but commonsense assumptions about women's passivity and men's aggression distort the reality of warfare. Kimberley Theidon's ethnographic research into the aftermath of armed conflict in Peru is a powerful example of the strength of an anthropological approach that draws on long-term field research to challenge such common sense. Theidon's ethnography reveals that Peruvian peace-building efforts were flawed by an essentialized view of "women's experience" that narrowly focused on sexual violence and presumptions of women's victimhood. Theidon demonstrates that women were not only victims but also perpetrators of violence; while they were subjected to brutal violence, they also defended their families in heroic ways. "When we speak of militarization," Theidon writes, "we need to think beyond the stationing of soldiers in the bases. Militarization also implies changes in what it means to be a man or a woman." Indeed, an important theme in two of the selections is the way masculinity and militarism are co-constructed. Militaries are hierarchical organizations whose core purpose is to create warriors who will kill and die for the state. To override social taboos against murder, militaries often mobilize notions of manhood to justify and inspire violence. Jean Bethke Elshtain's essay reveals that rather than aggression, the Western glorification of men's sacrifice in combat serves as a potent ideology driving support for war. Lesley Gill's ethnographic case study from Bolivia considers why young men from the most socially marginalized sectors of society are disproportionately motivated to risk death in warfare and suffer abuse at the hands of commanders who regard them as socially inferior. Gill examines how unequal class and ethnic relations inspire Bolivian indigenous men to join the national military as an act of masculine self-assertion, even though enlisting reinforces their own social subordination.

Women who eschew passivity and seek roles in combat clash with such a masculine warrior ethos. Cynthia Enloe (1988) pioneered a feminist critique of the armed forces, revealing how women's participation in the postwar North Atlantic Treaty Organization armies challenged entrenched male privilege. Women found themselves marginalized within the military, denied roles in combat, subject to sexual harassment and violence, and relegated to lower-status labor.

Today, the expansion of women's participation in professional armies and in combat has inspired new ethnographic research. In a case study from Argentina that ends this section, Máximo Badaró explores the complex and fluid nature of female identity in the armed forces. Badaró shows how Argentine female soldiers negotiate gender within a paternalistic framework, downplaying stereotypical femininity and asserting a desire to be treated "like one of the guys." As they embrace traditional military virtues such as obedience, bravery, loyalty, and honor, female soldiers also demand greater compatibility between family and professional life. Thus, female cadets not only challenge social conventions and expectations related to women's roles and capacity; they also reshape the internal politics of the Argentine military in ways that advance working conditions for women and men.

READINGS

3.1   Excerpts from Kimberly Theidon, "Gender in Transition: Common Sense, Women and War," *Journal of Human Rights* 6:4 (2007): 453–78.

3.2   Excerpts from Jean Bethke Elshtain, "The Compassionate Warrior: Wartime Sacrifice," in *Women and War*, edited by Jean Bethke Elshtain (Chicago: University of Chicago Press, 1995), 205–10.

3.1

___

GENDER IN TRANSITION
Common Sense, Women, and War
Kimberly Theidon

Within the context of the [Peruvian Truth and Reconciliation] Commission
(TRC), communal authorities set about developing their own "memory projects." . . . The truth commission conducted focus groups—in addition to taking individual testimonies—as part of their work on regional histories. . . . In
June 2002, the TRC team held two focus groups in the same community. . . .
The transcripts from these focus groups provide an opportunity to situate
truths within the dynamics of gender. . . .

The focus group was guided by some commonsense assumptions about
women and war. Convening a random group to talk "as women in total *confi-
anza*" resonates with well-intentioned feminist and therapeutic impulses. The
incitement to speech hinges on a belief that talking is intrinsically healing, and
thus participating in the focus group would provide the women "some relief."
This was at odds with the women's insistence on forgetting, and certainly at
odds with the woman who finally told the facilitators that she was "afraid to
talk." She called into question the gynofest premise of "talking as women."

In the context of civil conflict, one can only assume that the random assembly of a group of women is unproblematic if women are first defined as
peripheral to the conflict. By defining women as noncombatants—by assuming women are a homogeneous group of apolitical bystanders or victims—
one has the illusion of yielding a group with shared interests based on their
identity as women. This is a questionable assumption in many cases, and most
certainly in Peru, where an estimated 40 percent of Shining Path militants
were women.[1] . . .

My research team and I worked with this community and, thus, learned the
names of some of the women who participated in the focus group. One of the

women is the wife of a local Shining Path (ex-)militant, and we were assured she had been just as ruthless as he had. Thus, rather than [seeing the focus group as] a therapeutic environment, several of the women sitting in the group were very concerned about the consequences of anything they might say in front of someone they held responsible for lethal violence in their community. . . .

In both South Africa and Peru, the truth commissions held a series of public hearings, and women were invited to speak about violations of their human rights. Fiona Ross (2002) has demonstrated how the South African hearings essentialized suffering and gender, focusing on sexual violence and rape rather than the systemic injustice of apartheid or women's roles in resistance efforts. In Peru's Audiencias Públicas, several women talked about their experiences of rape, one introducing the audience to her six-year-old daughter, born as a result of the woman's gang rape in prison. For each viewer who squirmed in discomfort, there were others applauding the bravery of these women for coming forward and talking publicly about "their rapes."

These are troubling displays. By constructing these few women as courageous for speaking out, the implication is that only those women who choose a public forum to talk about rape are counted among the brave. Obscured are other forms of courage that women practiced on a daily basis during the internal armed conflict and, importantly, other messages are transmitted in the broadcasts of these public displays. The audience is told war stories replete with heroes and victims—a gendered dualism that is too familiar.

I want to foreground the protagonism of women confronted by sexual violence, motivated by a desire to question war stories that keep reproducing the heroism of men and the victimization of women. . . . As I have been told in every pueblo with which I have worked, women participated in the defense of their communities, their families, and themselves. War stories influence the public policies implemented in the postconflict period. These histories are a form of political action. Consequently, I want to explore multiple forms of heroism—not all of which are "male." . . .

In our research team, we talked at length about rape and how raped women are repeatedly violated: the first time during the rape itself and afterward because of the stigma that marks them in their communities. As Señora Prudencia lamented, "women like me" usually have not confided in anyone—before their eyes they have far too many examples of the price women have paid for talking, ending up the target of cruel gossip. Not one woman with whom we spoke had achieved justice with respect to the man or men who had raped her. Among the greatest injustices of war are the stigma of the raped and the impunity of the rapists.

Moreover, once again there is the parallel narrative structure and the insistence on context. Señora Prudencia was relating much more than her victimization. It was important to her that we know there were five soldiers pinning her down, armed with guns and a knife. She still fought, even though they punched her in the face and clearly outnumbered her. Over and over again she returned to her resolve: they would not touch her daughters unless they killed her first. She may have been raped, but she succeeded in protecting both of her young daughters. In her subsequent actions, she successfully out-strategized the soldiers, moving to her small house in the hills at night and ultimately deciding to get pregnant with her neighbor rather than the soldiers. When we listen to what she foregrounds in her story, we hear pride in how hard she fought defending herself and her daughters. This cannot be tidily compacted into the victim category without forcing her—and other women like her—to silence their courage. It may well be that courage that allowed her to preserve some sense of herself despite both the initial violation and the injustice of the events that followed. . . .

Forcing the women to *entregar sus cuerpos* (surrender or barter their bodies) was a widespread practice. In my conversations with ex-soldiers, they explained how they took advantage of their power to force young women to "barter sex" to save their loved ones. When the troops arrived in a pueblo, they would decide which of the young women were the prettiest. Their fathers and brothers would be rounded up and carried off to the base, denounced as *terrucos* [terrorists]. The women—a euphemism, given the age of some of the adolescents— would head up to the base in search of their fathers or brothers. There was a form of exchange: sex could save the lives of their loved ones.

This sacrifice had a price. Women who "have been with soldiers" are negatively viewed. Whether by rape or other forms of coercion, having been with a soldier carries its own stigma. In addition to stigma, several women assured us that husbands beat the wives they scorn as "soldier's leftovers." Elsewhere I have argued that there has been a "domestication of violence" following the war; while dead bodies in the streets may be a thing of the past, angry men and increased alcohol consumption are a nasty mix. One enduring impact of the militarization of daily life and the forging of militarized masculinities is an increase in domestic violence, a phenomenon noted in many post-conflict settings.

THUS I TURN now to the men, convinced that a gendered perspective on war should include an analysis of men and masculinity; "gender" is too frequently a code word for "women," leaving men as the unquestioned, unmarked category.

I want to discuss the rapists, convinced that gender-sensitive research should include studying the forms of masculinity forged during armed conflict as one component in reconstructing individual identities and collective existence in the aftermath of war.

In their research on sexual violence during the internal armed conflict in Peru, Carola Falconí and José Carlos Agüero (2003: 12) found, "In almost every case, those responsible for committing rape were members of the armed forces, especially the army, and to a lesser degree the police and Sinchis." [*Editors' note*: Sinchis are an elite special forces unit of the Peruvian National Police.] Similarly, in my research it became clear that although the Senderistas [followers of the Shining Path] and in some cases the *ronderos* (rural patrols) raped, the systematic use of sexual violence was a practice deployed by the *fuerzas de orden* (forces of order). In short, where there were soldiers there were rapes.

Also generalizable was gang rape. When women described their experiences with rape, it was never one soldier but several: "They raped the women until they could not stand up." The soldiers were mutilating women with their penises, and the women were bloodied. I want to think a bit more about these blood rituals.

When talking about gang rape, we should think about why the men raped this way. An instrumentalist explanation would indicate that the soldiers raped in groups to overpower a woman or so that one soldier could serve watch while the others raped. However, it would be a very limited reading that attributes this practice to the necessity for pure force or standing watch. When a soldier pressed his machine gun into a woman's chest, he did not need more force. When the soldiers came down from the bases at night to rape, "privacy" was not their primary concern. They operated with impunity.

Clearly there is a ritualistic aspect to gang rape.[2] Many people told me that after killing someone, the soldiers drank the blood of their victims or bathed their faces and chests with the blood. I want to think about the blood ties established among soldiers and the bloodied wombs that birthed a lethal fraternity. These blood ties united the soldiers, and the bodies of raped women served as the medium for forging those ties.

In their analysis of rape during the 1992–94 Bosnian war, Bulent Diken and Carsten Bagge Lausten (2005) offer a powerful assessment of the ways in which gang rape forges a "brotherhood of guilt" based in part on the abjection of the victim. For them, the men's guilt is the key emotion: guilt unifies the perpetrators, and rape is a rite of initiation. In addition, in tracing how women become "objects," they argue, shame resists verbalization while guilt incites it: "Whereas guilt can be verbalized and can perform as an element in the brotherhood of guilt, shame cannot, which is why it often results in trauma. War thus both creates and destroys communities (of the perpetrators and the victims respectively)" (Diken and Lausten 2005: 114).

I advocate shifting the focus from guilt to shame and shamelessness. Gang rape not only broke the moral codes that generally ordered social life. The practice also served to eradicate shame. Committing morally abhorrent acts in front of others not only forges bonds among the perpetrators; it also forges *sinvergüenzas* (shameless people) capable of tremendous brutality. To lose the sense of shame—a "regulatory emotion" because shame implies an Other in front of whom one feels ashamed—creates men with a recalibrated capacity for atrocity. Guilt unifies; shame individuates. Thus, acts that obliterate shame also obliterate a sense of self, lending themselves to processes aimed at subsuming the individual to create group cohesion and "selflessness" in the service of a collective. In addition, there is a temporal aspect to understanding these acts and the men who engage in them—and to understanding why the solidarity of guilt may well give way to a deep sense of shame over time. In my research, I am struck by the fact that "men don't talk"—at least, not in the first person—about their participation in rape.

But they certainly do talk during the act itself. Indeed, women emphasize what the soldiers said while raping them: "terruca de mierda" (terrorist of shit), "ahora aguanta terruca" (now take it, terrorist), "carajo, terruca de mierda" (damn it, terrorist of shit), and "India de mierda" (Indian of shit). The soldiers were marking the women with physical and verbal assaults. For example, there was a military base in Hualla, and the soldiers took the women from neighboring communities to the base to rape them, returning them with their hair cut off as a sign of what had happened. In other conversations in Cayara and Tiquihua, people told us the women returned to their communities "scarred" after having been raped on the bases. The women's bodies were made to bear witness to the power and barbarism of the so-called fuerzas de orden.[3]

However, one can imagine there were some men who did not want to participate in the raping. In my conversations with ex-soldiers and ex-sailors, they insisted that participation in the rapes was obligatory. It is possible that this fiction is a balm for their conscience; however, some men provided details about what happened to those soldiers and sailors who did not want to join in. Let me cite just one example from a conversation I had with someone who served in La Marina in Ayacucho during the early 1980s: "With the recruits, some of them were really young. They were just adolescents. They didn't want to participate (in the rapes). If someone refused, the rest of the men would take him aside and rape him. All of them would rape him, with the poor guy screaming. They said they were 'changing his voice'—with so much screaming, his voice would lower and he wouldn't be a woman anymore."

Raping was a means of establishing hierarchies of power, between armed groups and the population, but also within the armed forces themselves. It was common to force men in a community to watch as the soldiers raped their wives, daughters, and sisters. And it is striking that the soldiers raped according to rank, beginning with the officers and finishing up with the recruits. There were multiple audiences for this violent sexuality, and the performance was intended at least in part to impress other men with whom one jockeyed for status within the battalion.

When we speak of militarization, we need to think beyond the stationing of soldiers on the bases. Militarization also implies changes in what it means to be a man or a woman: the hypermasculinity of the warrior is based on erasing those characteristics considered "feminine" (Theidon 2003). This hypermasculinity is constructed by scorning the feminine, and one aspect of that scorn is feminizing other men by inflicting physical and symbolic violence.[4]

NOTES

1. See the TRC's Final Report (2003, vol. 8), on women in Sendero Luminoso.

2. For a discussion of war rape and male bonding, see Enloe 1988.

3. In its final report (Truth and Reconciliation Commission 2003), the TRC also notes the use of ethnic insults when raping and torturing both men and women. Fueling the violence was a sense that Quechua-speaking Others were semi-savage, which is also captured by the term *chuto*.

4. In her analysis of the gendered dynamics of armed conflict, Cockburn (2001: 16) argues that "male dominant systems involve a hierarchy among men, producing different and unequal masculinities, always defined in relation not only to one another but to women."

THE COMPASSIONATE WARRIOR
Wartime Sacrifice
Jean Bethke Elshtain

Our function was not to kill Germans, though that might happen, but to make things easier for men under our command.
—ROBERT GRAVES, *Good-Bye to All That*

Comrade, I did not want to kill you. . . . You were only an idea to me before, an abstraction that lived in my mind and called forth its appropriate response. . . . Forgive me, comrade.
—ERICH MARIA REMARQUE, *All Quiet on the Western Front*

I understand . . . why I jumped hospital that Sunday thirty-five years ago and, in violation of orders, returned to the front and almost certain death. It was an act of love. Those men on the line were my family, my home. They were closer to me than I can say, closer than any friends had been or ever would be. They had never let me down, and I couldn't do it to them.
—WILLIAM MANCHESTER, *Goodbye, Darkness: A Memoir of the Pacific War*

Man, as designated combatant, presents himself in his most prototypical guise in the West as neither a wholly reluctant warrior—there is much of that—nor as a bloodthirsty militant, though there is some of that. Rather, by his own account of wartime experience he constructs himself as one who places highest value not on *killing* but on *dying*—dying for others, to protect them, sacrificing himself so that others might live. This theme, resonating consistently and powerfully, cannot be ignored.

Although his sacrifice is seen by noncombatants, including women, as a sacrifice *for* the nation, for the collective, the soldier himself is far more likely to think and act in terms of his immediate cohort, that small number of men he is actually fighting, and possibly dying, with.

Loyalties of soldiers in wartime are to comrades and buddies, not to states and ideologies, or these are the exceptions. Ernst Junger (1975: 316), one of the least sentimental observers of World War I, valorizes the distillation of the Fatherland that emerged from the war as a "clearer and brighter essence," as men learned to "stand for a cause and if necessary to fall as befitted men." But Junger's voice seems rarer than the stark despair of Erich Maria Remarque's protagonist Paul Baumer, for example. Japanese soldiers in World War II played out the theme with their own variation: an oath of personal loyalty to the emperor. For those who volunteered to die as kamikaze, this oath was a matter of honor unto death, a sacrificial seal.

Richard Holmes (1985: 300) apprises us that, of eight medals won by U.S. Marines on Peleliu in 1944, "six were awarded to men who covered grenades with their bodies to save their comrades." Five black Marines earned the Medal of Honor in Vietnam. All five were killed shielding fellow Marines from exploding enemy grenades. One can put things even more strongly. S. L. A. Marshall (1947: 78), the great American military historian, concluded, as a result of his extensive study of American rifle companies in action in the Pacific and European theaters of World War II, that "fear of killing, rather than fear of being killed, was the most common cause of battle failure." Moreover, on average, only 15 percent of these men actually fired their weapons in battle, even when they were very hard pressed by enemy soldiers. Writes Marshall (1947: 77–78): "Seventy-five percent will not fire or will not persist in firing." Men behave defensively instead, trying to spare themselves and, more important, to protect their comrades. Inhabiting what John Keegan (1978) calls a wildly unstable environment, soldiers are bound up with their most immediate comrades and think of themselves as "equals within a very tiny group" of some six or seven men.[1]

J. Glenn Gray, from the soldier's point of view, examines the impulse to self-sacrifice characteristic of warriors who, from compassion, would rather die than kill. He calls the freedom of wartime a communal freedom as the "I" passes into a "we" and human longings for community with others find a field for realization. Communal ecstasy explains a willingness to sacrifice and gives dying for others a mystical quality not unlike the one abstractly depicted by Vera Brittain . . . at her safe remove from trench warfare. Because this fits no rationalist image of what human beings are all about and what makes them tick—sacrifice being implacably at odds with self-interest—rationalists must disdain the supramoral act of sacrifice or gloss it over: "Such sacrifice seems hard and heroic to those who have never felt communal ecstasy. In fact, it is not nearly so difficult as many less absolute acts in peacetime and civilian life. . . . It is hardly surprising that few men are capable of dying joyfully as martyrs whereas thousands are capable of self-sacrifice in wartime" (Gray 1959: 46–47).

Remarque's doomed protagonist reflects, "We are soldiers. It is a great brotherhood, which adds something of the good-fellowship of the folk-song, of the feeling of solidarity of convicts, and of the desperate loyalty to one another of men condemned to death, to a condition of life arising out of the midst of danger, out of the tension and forlornness of death" (Remarque 1975 [1929]: 236). Soldiers in wartime frequently make provisional peace, declaring their own truces on the front, showing one another pity and compassion. Siegfried Sassoon (1931: 39) noted a time when, on the Western front, the Germans could undoubtedly see the arduous effort their enemies were engaged in as they worked feverishly to repair the human and tactical damage done by a bomb explosion but "stopped firing: perhaps they felt sorry for us." For each instance of brutality, a deed of sacrificial courage or benign restraint can be proliferated—if one is telling the story *from the ground up*, as a narrative of men's experience rather than as an account of strategic doctrines or grand movements of armies and men seen from a bird's-eye view.

The lessons learned by Yoshida Mitsuru, a law student at Tokyo Imperial University in 1943 when he was called up into the Imperial Japanese Navy, and one of the few survivors of the sinking of the battleship *Yamato*, tells those who have not died in war (as he assumed he would), "Never underestimate how precious life is" (Mitsuru 1985: 45). Families of American marines killed in the barracks explosion in Lebanon on August 29, 1983, reading from letters they had sent home, reported hopes for peace. "He wanted peace," said Carol Losey, the mother of twenty-eight-year-old Second Lieutenant Donald Losey. "He [wanted to] help others." [Others read,] "I feel proud to be part of a peace-keeping force"; "I really want to go home. But deep down in my heart I want to be part of something that turned out good"; "I have a job to do. Protect the people."[2] What is remarkable about these expressions is their very unremarkableness. The soldier is one who serves and, if need be, sacrifices for others.

Visible on all battlefields, [along] with the powerful sacrificial possibilities and idealizations war fighting makes possible and crystallizes as a form of male identity, . . . is a category of concerned attachment that Gray calls "preservative love," an impersonal passion to preserve and to succor, to hold back the annihilation. This concern seems to Gray "maternal" in nature, protective in its unfolding. One finds side by side the paradox of organized mass killing and caring for small, vulnerable, particular things. Men grew flowers and vegetables outside their trenches on the Western Front. Adopting animals—stray puppies, even small mice—as pets is a common practice noted by war correspondents such as Ernie Pyle and described by men who have been in war, including Gray, Robert Graves, and Ernest Hemingway. "Waifs and orphans and lost pets have a peculiar claim on the affections of combat soldiers, who lavish upon them unusual care and tenderness," writes Gray (1959: 83). The spectacle of wounded or killed animals, especially horses dragged into the fighting, is scored as particularly abhorrent. "What struck me most"—Robert Graves (1929: 250) is the witness—"was the number of dead horses and mules lying about; human corpses I was accustomed to, but it seemed wrong for animals to be dragged into the war like this." One of the most horrifying of many horrifying passages in Remarque's *All Quiet on the Western Front* details the sharp, wounded cries and bellows of pain from injured horses stumbling erratically in no man's land—sounds that pierced the men with particular compassion, powerless as they were to go to the animals to dispatch them mercifully (Remarque 1975 [1929]: 61).

The warrior's compassion may be the spontaneous expression of young men in the midst of carnage or the more rule-governed response of the professional soldier who is scrupulous in adhering to wartime conventions. Evan Connell (1984: 118), for example, recalls messages exchanged between General George Armstrong Custer and a former West Point roommate, Thomas "Tex" Rosser, during the Civil War when they faced each other as opponents. Rosser's to Custer was addressed "Dear Fanny" (a nickname); Custer's to Ross, "Dear Friend." Attempting to destroy each other on the field of battle, they remained good friends capable of a caring and humorous relationship to each other. It is difficult for anyone who has not participated in war to understand this *impersonal* attitude of respect that does not destroy affection, even between foes— and it is difficult, as well, for some soldiers in war to understand. Often seen as the peculiar prerogative of the officer classes in modern European wars, the attitude I here describe is in fact more widespread. Sometimes it requires peace (or, better, the cessation of hostilities . . .) to flower fully.

In February 1985, two hundred ex-Marines and 132 of their Japanese counterparts returned to Iwo Jima—on the fortieth anniversary of the dreadful prolonged battle for possession of the island—in a ceremony of remembrance and forgiveness. As former enemies embraced, one American said, "I can expel some of the demons that have haunted me for forty years. Now my memories are tempered. Now I can die in peace" (quoted in Shapiro 1985). William Broyles, returning to Vietnam to confront some of his own ghosts, notes the "intimate combat" with the enemy, remarking, "I knew nothing about them." Finding the marker on a grave outside Hill 10, Broyles saw the name Ngo Ngoc Tuan, with the dates 1944–69: "It was the grave of a man born the year I was, and killed the year I arrived in Vietnam. . . . And I stood, a tourist from the land of his old enemy, and looked upon his grave and thought how it might have been my own. . . . We had tried to kill each other, but we were brothers now" (Broyles 1986: 273). Broyles discovered he had "more in common with old enemies than with anyone except the men who had fought at my side" (Broyles 1986: 235). This sort of recognition is one shared by all individuals who have gone through a powerful experience together, one that punctures routine expectations, that distills experience through a luminescent rush of heightened emotion. Survivors of shared catastrophes speak of similar recognitions, as do women who fought in partisan and resistance movements. But the clearest and most consistent expression of human companionship amid destruction and fellowship that can transcend enmities is in the practice and literature of war, in stories of the sacrificial soldier and the professional brotherhood.

NOTES

Epigraphs: Graves 1929: 290; Remarque 1975 [1929]: 147; Manchester 1979: 391.

1. Because this bonding of the small group has been essential to war fighting, Keegan concludes under modern conditions of techno-war, it will be less and less possible to develop the relations and identities necessary to carry out sustained war fighting among groups of men.

2. The soldiers' quotes are from "Families Talk of Victims' Hopes, Fears," *Boston Globe*, August 30, 1983, 11, and CNN, August 30, 1983.

3.3

CREATING CITIZENS, MAKING MEN
The Military and Masculinity in Bolivia
Lesley Gill

In Bolivia, young male military conscripts come from the most powerless sectors of society: Quechua, Aymara, and Guarani peasant communities and poor urban neighborhoods. Like recruits from impoverished ethnic groups and working classes elsewhere (Gibson 2000; Zeitlin et al. 1973), they are the foot soldiers who risk death in warfare to a greater degree than members of dominant social groups and frequently suffer emotional abuse at the hands of commanding officers. Their rural communities, mining camps, and urban neighborhoods have also long experienced repression in the military's fight against "internal enemies." Why, then, are these young men frequently eager to serve? And why do many experience social pressure from friends, family members, and their communities to enlist?

There is no simple answer to these questions; the reasons are both straightforward and complex. On the one hand, military service is a legal obligation for all able-bodied Bolivian men, and it is understood as a prerequisite for many forms of urban employment. Perhaps more important, young men may acquiesce to military service because Bolivia, unlike Peru and various Central American countries, has not been mired in bloody warfare for more than a generation. On the other hand, compulsory military service facilitates more ambivalent processes: even as the state attempts to create "citizens" out of "Indians" and "men" out of "boys," conscripts simultaneously lay claim to militarized conceptions of masculinity to advance their own agendas. They advance a positive sense of subaltern masculinity tied to beliefs about bravery, competence, and patriotic duty.[1] They do so to earn respect from women (mothers, wives, sisters, and girlfriends) and male peers, both as defenders of the nation and, more broadly, as strong, responsible male citizens who can make decisions and lead others.

Military service is one of the most important prerequisites for the development of successful subaltern manhood because it signifies rights to power and citizenship and supposedly instills the courage that a man needs to confront life's daily challenges. Through the experience of military service, men assert a dignified sense of masculinity that serves as a counterpoint to the degradation experienced from more dominant men and an economic system that assigns them to the least desirable occupations. Military service thus enables them to challenge their exclusion from full participation in Bolivian society and to contest more genteel notions of masculinity associated with upper-class men who avoid military service altogether.

Yet self-affirmation and the legitimate desire for respect are also inextricably tied to ongoing patterns of collusion with hegemonic uses and representations of subaltern men and bound to evolving relationships of inequality among subjugated peoples. Conscripts collude with hyperaggressive notions of masculinity that demean women, "weaker" men, and civilians in general and that conjoin maleness with citizenship. They further assert an imposed falsehood: soldiers like themselves defend the interests of all Bolivians from an array of internal and external threats. By so doing, they aggravate the estrangement between men and women and deepen their alienation from their class peers and the history of indigenous peoples in Bolivia. . . .

Sissies and "New Citizens": Suffering for Manhood

A complex array of pressures and motivations prompt young Bolivian men from La Paz and its surrounding hinterland to enlist in the armed forces every year. For some young men, the military offers the possibility of adventure and an opportunity to visit other parts of the country; for others, it is a way to obtain food and clothing in a time of need. According to the military itself, service provides recruits with opportunities to learn electrical, mechanical, and carpentry skills, yet only one of the men interviewed for this article mentioned the acquisition of useful skills for civilian life. Although the reasons have varied over time, two primary explanations for responding to the military's biannual calls for men stand out among former soldiers: (1) the importance of the *libreta militar* (military booklet), which documents the successful completion of military duty, for key transactions with the state and for obtaining work in urban factories and businesses; and (2) the desire to validate themselves as men in the eyes of families, peers, and communities. Establishing themselves as men requires the competence necessary to support themselves and a family amid considerable economic adversity and to participate in community positions of authority.

Obtaining the military booklet is not a concern for middle- and upper-class young men who wish to avoid military service. Once past age twenty-three, when an individual is no longer eligible for service, a man may pay a fee to obtain equivalent documentation. The cost, in recent years, has varied between $200 and $500, which is prohibitive for men from poor peasant and urban backgrounds, since they typically earn only a few dollars for an entire day's labor.[2]

For subaltern men, military service is the only practical means of acquiring the military booklet, which is quite literally a prerequisite for citizenship. Only with this document can a man register with the state and acquire a national identity card. The booklet is also indispensable for other key relationships with the state, such as obtaining a passport, a job in a government agency, or a degree from the state university. Similarly, military documentation is essential for obtaining employment in many of the businesses and factories of urban La Paz, where employers use it to guarantee themselves a disciplined, Spanish-speaking labor force.

The military booklet is thus part of the "civilizing process" through which young men are symbolically incorporated into the nation and the capitalist discipline of the labor process. Furthermore, with the collusion of their commanding officers, recruits may use the booklet as a way to change their Indian surnames to Spanish ones. But while it symbolically creates citizens, the booklet also facilitates the converse: the categorization of "aliens" within the boundaries of the state, a designation that is all too close to the lived experiences of poor men. . . .

For many young men, the importance of establishing their manhood is also a central reason for military service. They believe that service is indispensable to becoming responsible, disciplined men who are capable of making decisions, heading a family, and commanding others. As Felix Mamani, a rural immigrant who resides in El Alto, told me: "In the countryside, people think that you are a coward if you don't go to the barracks; that is, they think you're like a woman. The community pushes young men toward military service, and [we] have to go in order not to be faggots. It's a question of manliness." Peasant recruits who return to highland Aymara communities are referred to as *machaq ciudadano*, or, literally, "new citizen," and if domestic resources permit, their returns are celebrated with eating, drinking, and dancing. . . .

In the immigrant neighborhoods of La Paz, the connections between manhood and citizenship are equally evident, if somewhat more diffuse. Military service is not so directly linked to the assumption of community positions of authority, but young men still hope to earn the respect of families and peers by participating in a rite of passage that is understood as a prerequisite for full male adulthood and a duty of every good Bolivian man. They also hope to obtain the documentation necessary for permanent positions at a factory, business, or state agency and thus escape from the poverty and insecurity of the informal economy. . . .

Key to the transformation of these young men is the experience of suffering. Suffering is not only something that they anticipate before enlisting but also an experience that, when safely in the past, is constantly embellished and reinvented, as ex-soldiers represent themselves to others and assert claims within evolving social relationships. Given the myriad ways in which these young men and their families suffer every day of their lives with poor health, low wages, bad harvests, and racism, it is shocking to listen to them boast of their transformative experiences of hardship, which must be understood as part of a desperate and painful search for dignity and self-worth.

Rufino Amaya, for example, dreamed of and eventually received a posting on a distant frontier base in the tropical lowlands, where living conditions were particularly harsh. The isolation of the base meant that during weekend leaves he could not visit friends and family members, and he frequently did not have enough to eat because commanding officers were selling troop rations for personal profit. The food shortages prompted him to work as an agricultural laborer during leaves so that he could buy bread and other basic necessities, even though working for civilians was strictly forbidden by the military and considered a punishable offense. Yet, as Amaya told me, "The person who goes to the barracks, especially from the highlands, suffers a lot during the year, but those who do not serve never experience what corporal punishment is like and are more or less semi-men. [People in my community] criticize the ones who serve nearby. They say that they've just been to the kitchen."

Amaya went on to describe how highland men like himself were better suited for the rigorous tests of military manhood: "[In my group] we were 161 Paceños [residents of La Paz] and 80 Orientales [residents of the eastern lowlands]. The Orientales were very weak, and when things got rough, they started deserting. But the *colla* [highlander] man—as they call us—deserts very little, because he is able to endure any kind of hard work." Informants related similar accounts to me over and over. One individual even likened the Aymaras' propensity for military service and allegedly superior soldiering abilities to their history as a "warlike people."[3]

We can recognize a number of self-destructive beliefs in these assertions: suffering is a prerequisite for manhood; poor people can tolerate suffering more than others; and the Aymara have special abilities for warfare. To make these claims is to participate in the production of a dominant fiction. It is to create a virtue out of suffering, a condition imposed on the Aymara by both the military and, more generally, the form that class and ethnic domination takes in Bolivia. It is also to link extreme suffering in the military with an exalted form of manhood and thereby deny the very real daily suffering of women and other men who cannot or will not participate in the rituals of militarized masculinity. Finally, it is to misconstrue Aymara history, a history in which warfare was integral to the process of Incan and particularly European domination, but that has little to do with any essential Aymara characteristics. . . .

Contending with Militarism in Daily Life

Recruits never become true citizens after completing military service and returning to civilian life. This happens despite the civilizing mission of the armed forces, the concerted efforts to produce "real men," and the considerable extent to which young men claim and assert destructive, imposed beliefs about themselves in their search for respect. The realization of their continuing marginalization leaves many men feeling disillusioned and questioning the point of having dedicated a year of their lives to the armed forces. In most cases, they are no better prepared for a job than they were before they entered the military, and the few decent jobs that remain in La Paz, after years of economic crisis, restructuring, and state retrenchment, cannot possibly accommodate everyone. Young men typically return to their impoverished villages or seek a livelihood as gardeners, chauffeurs, part-time construction workers, and vendors in the urban informal economy and in low-paid positions in the state bureaucracy, such as policemen. Thus excluded from the economic rewards of the dominant society, they remain ineluctably "Indian" in its eyes, and some, not surprisingly, conclude that the entire experience was an enormous waste of time. . . .

The competence and citizenship equated with postmilitary manhood are also used by former conscripts to assert their dignity and claim respect from more powerful middle- and upper-class men, who view military service as a waste of time that can be more usefully spent studying; they also fear the prospect of serving with Indian and lower-class men in a context where military hierarchies theoretically take precedence over class and ethnic ones. Some even view the soldiers' claims to manhood as presumptuous. One individual, for example, criticized the peasant practice of requiring military service for male marriage partners because it was, he claimed, based on mistaken beliefs about how men acquire a sense of responsibility. Ex-soldiers are highly critical of these men, whom they view as unpatriotic sissies. One scoffed to me, "They're mamas' boys. They come from a different social class than we do, and their form of thinking and reasoning is so distinct that they forget about their patriotic duty. They are much more individualistic [than we are]; they forget about the nation so they can be totally independent. The upper class only thinks about its future and its social position and generally not about the country and what could happen one day."

This man and others like him were particularly critical when, in early 1995, a public scandal enveloped a high-ranking government official who had falsified his military booklet to avoid service. Sixty-year-old Rufino Tejar, for example, was absolutely disgusted. "These parliamentarians," he sneered, "say that they are the fathers of the country, but they are the first ones to avoid the barracks. These little gentlemen wouldn't know where to shoot. They always come from privileged families. They're mamas' boys. They can fix anything with money, but then they fill these government positions and demand that everyone else obey the law. They should be removed from their jobs and obliged to serve in the military at their age."

Tejar's remarks that these men claim to be "the fathers of the country" suggest something of the paternalism and the denigration that shape the reality of actual encounters among men of different classes. It is as waiters, gardeners, chauffeurs, shoeshines, handymen, and janitors that indigenous and poor urban men typically meet white men of the upper class. These structurally subordinate positions require them to display deference, subordination, and humility. Not only are they demeaning, but they also place men in relationships to more powerful men that are analogous to those of women in male-female relationships. Because they cannot command the labor power of others and possess none of the wealth necessary to embellish an elegant lifestyle and control, provide for, and protect women, lower-class men and men from subordinate ethnic groups experience greater difficulty backing up their claims of personal power and sexual potency than their class and ethnic superiors. Moreover, the class privileges of the latter enable them to develop a well-mannered, dignified, and controlled masculinity—one that is contrasted with the behavior of poor men, who, depending on the context, may be either labeled weak and ineffectual or condemned for impulsive and irrational outbursts of violence.

1. This article emerged from a research project conducted over an eight-month period between June 1994 and May 1995 on the relationship among nongovernmental organizations, the state, and popular organizations in La Paz. It draws on wide-ranging conversations with a large network of informants that I developed for that project and on focused interviews with thirty ex-soldiers from rural Aymara communities and poor neighborhoods in La Paz and El Alto. The men completed their military service between 1952 and 1994 and represented approximately equal numbers of urban- and rural-born individuals. Throughout this article, I use pseudonyms for the names of people I interviewed or spoke with during my field research in Bolivia.

2. There are other legal ways to acquire a military book without actually serving in the armed forces. Physical disabilities and family situations in which the son is the sole supporter of elderly parents exempt men from service. Students are also able to postpone service until the completion of their studies, at which time they must serve for one year at the rank of "honorary subofficer." They receive payment in accord with the rank and are employed as professionals. Engineers, for example, might teach, doctors provide medical services, and so forth. Student deferments are obviously not an option for poor men, who cannot afford the cost in time and money of a university education.

3. For similar assertions by Native Americans in the United States, see Holm 1992; Sider 1993: 203–7.

3.4

ONE OF THE GUYS
Military Women and the Argentine Army
Máximo Badaró

According to institutional rules and regulations, a soldier's gestures, uniform, shoes, personal hygiene, and hairstyle must all reflect both the emotional state of the individual and the moral position of the military institution as a whole. . . . Hair was the element most frequently named, specifically the "bun" that female soldiers are obliged to wear. . . . From the point of view of both male and female soldiers, this hairdo symbolizes the ambiguous, paradoxical place female soldiers occupy in the Argentine Army: reducing femininity to a bun helps integrate women into the armed forces while at the same time distinguishes them as women within the institution. . . .

In March 2010, while traveling with approximately fifteen cadets of different ages, half of whom were women, on the train connecting the Colegio Militar de la Nación (National Military College; CMN) with the city of Buenos Aires, I was surprised to see that, at a distance of around four stations from the academy, the female cadets, almost in unison, began letting their hair down; they not only changed their hairdo but in most cases also took off their ties and jackets, undid a few shirt buttons, and began putting on makeup. In only a few minutes, they had removed from their bodies all the symbols indicating they belonged to the army. By contrast, the male cadets did not alter their dress, and there was no way they could modify a haircut that denotes membership in the armed forces the world over.

The bun serves both as a symbol of women belonging to the military institution and as an instrument for manipulating and redefining the meanings associated with this membership. These women perform a doubly gendered mimetic action: when trying to be identified as "one of the guys" in the military, they imitate a stereotyped masculine behavior; when trying to highlight their womanliness in the face of military and nonmilitary interlocutors, they imitate a stereotyped feminine image based on the aesthetic aspects of their bodies and behavior. . . . Women's double mimesis in the army reflects a situational concept of military identity that contradicts the predominating holistic perspective—that belonging to the institution should encompass all aspects of a soldier's life. . . . Through their bodies, gestures, uniforms, and emotions, female cadets and officers unintentionally show that the masculinity-military link is indexical—that is, it is contextual, not categorical or "natural." These behaviors open a way to consider military activity more as a situational performance based on the deployment of professional training than as the exercise of supposedly natural corporal and emotional gendered attributes improved by military training.

The tendency of female soldiers to symbolically manipulate the signs indicating they belong to the army when in public has implications for the visibility of the Argentine armed forces in society at large. In public space, there are pathways, places, and presences inaccessible to direct observation; they exist only within the framework of a "sensibility regime" that grants them specific visibility. . . . In present-day Argentina, the sensibility regime orienting public perception of the armed forces oscillates between insult and praise for members. Soldiers in uniform rarely go unnoticed on the streets of Buenos Aires: seeing them either awakens images associated with the last military dictatorship or, less frequently, generates respect and admiration. Cadets and officers have told me they prefer not to wear their uniforms on the street to avoid conflict with civilians who have a "negative image" of the army. I have heard numerous accounts from soldiers of being denounced as "assassins" or "torturers" on the street. . . .

During my fieldwork I never heard a female soldier say she had received this kind of insult. In my view, there are at least two reasons for this. Any perplexity or surprise these female soldiers cause is due more to their gender identity than the recent past of the Argentine Army, and the image of the violent, authoritarian soldier predominating in many sectors of Argentine society is primarily a masculine one. In this sense, the sight of female soldiers in uniform frequenting public space, often accompanied by their male counterparts, represents for many people an image of a new military identity that is dissociated from the last military dictatorship. . . .

This image of the military woman acquires a different meaning inside the army. Many male soldiers still see their female counterparts, despite equal military training, as fragile, vulnerable, dependent beings who constantly require special treatment. This is the source of a comment frequently made by male soldiers: female soldiers are much more likely than male soldiers to report mistreatment, discrimination, and abuse of authority by superiors. What is interesting here is the implication that military women are associated with an increase in formal complaints and, above all, with the destabilization of discipline and authority—two mainstays of military life. According to this view, female soldiers constitute a threat to the stability of military life, and not only because they endanger the careers of those against whom complaints are lodged. By demanding the recognition and protection of their physical and moral integrity as individuals, they are also altering hierarchical relations within the army. Making a formal complaint can be viewed as an act of individuation that favors personal interest over and above collective values such as obedience and respect for hierarchical authority.

Yet most female soldiers reject this point of view, privileging compliance and respect for superiors over presenting formal demands and complaints. In 2011, I met Ana, a thirty-year-old officer who was particularly concerned about the notion that military women were more likely to report their superiors than men.[1] She had been working as an instructor at the CMN for two years. During her time as a cadet, she had had many problems with male cadets and some officers who discriminated against her. She dealt with the problem by discussing it personally with the men involved. But the discrimination continued, forcing her to leave the academy. When she recalled this part of her story during our talk in the CMN cafeteria, she shook her head and pursed her lips, looking both angry and sad. But she was also proud of the way she had handled the situation. She had made no formal complaint because she did not want to be considered "soft": reporting someone to the authorities went against her goal of being accepted as "one of the guys." Studies of military women in Japan (Frühstück

2007) and Israel (Sasson-Levy 2003) have identified similar attitudes, showing that female soldiers tend to "ignore" or "trivialize" situations of discrimination and harassment by men to avoid adopting a discourse of victimization that, in their view, would reinforce the image of vulnerability and weakness that many of their male counterparts already held of them. . . . It is worth noting in this case that Argentine military women's attitudes on gender relations had changed alongside transformations that took place in the criteria of authority and discipline of this institution. . . .

One of the primary changes that Ana identified in the CMN since her time as a cadet had to do with obeying orders. Current hierarchical relations are seen as more flexible, less distant, and more attentive to the recognition of individual needs. In the opinion of many present-day male soldiers, the most significant change in the army is that current military authorities pay attention to the individual interests, complaints, and rights of their subordinates. What is paradoxical about this institutional change is that it grants some degree of legitimacy to the argument that many male soldiers have used for years to stigmatize their female counterparts and criticize their presence in the army: the alleged propensity of women to make formal complaints and report physical or psychological mistreatment and abuse of authority. It would seem that the negative image that male soldiers have elaborated about female soldiers has contributed, to some extent, to the granting of greater visibility to individual interests, desires, and needs—formerly viewed as contrary to central values such as discipline, obedience, honor, and institutional loyalty—within the military institution.

According to Mariana, a twenty-seven-year-old army officer, male soldiers see these matters as endangering the "esprit de corps." In 2009, as we talked informally after a Council on Gender Policy meeting at the Ministry of Defense, she said, "Now women place great emphasis on work schedules that don't require late hours. Complaints of this kind are very frequent. The point is that men don't see this as a problem; for them being on call 24/7 is part of the job of being a soldier. Their idea is this: if you chose the military as a career, you've got to put up with it because they think their wife can take care of the children." Since their creation, the Council on Gender Policy and the Argentine Army's Gender Offices have become institutional spaces where long-standing tensions between individual rights and institutional values have acquired more visibility and relevance and where female soldiers have begun demanding, both officially and informally, greater compatibility between family life and individual rights, on the one hand, and institutional responsibilities, on the other hand.

While the tensions between individual rights and collective obligations reverberate in the army's Gender Offices, the number of official complaints filed at these offices is actually very low. The only accessible official statistics on these topics show that in 2009-10, the Gender Offices received fifteen formal complaints filed just by female soldiers. This statistic reports the results in these terms: 40 percent of the complaints were framed as "abuse of authority"; 20 percent as "discrimination"; 20 percent as related to problems in the "employment regime"; 6.6 percent as "sexual harassment"; and 6 percent as "domestic violence" (Ministerio de Defensa de la Argentina 2010: 52). While the first two categories refer primarily to disciplinary conflicts involving military personnel with different ranks, the third refers to conflicts regarding work requirements, especially time off during pregnancy and maternity leave. We can therefore say that 80 percent of all complaints involved two central values of military life: discipline (expressed as respect for hierarchical relations) and vocation (expressed as dedication to duty). By contrast, there were fewer complaints related to kinds of violent behavior that occur in both the military and society at large, such as sexual harassment and domestic violence, which can be explained by the fact that underreporting these issues in official statistics is a frequent behavior of most armed forces in the world and also of most of its victims, military and civilian.

Anthropological studies of norms and legal processes have shown that rights and laws serve as symbols and instruments for both oppression and social change (Lazarus-Black 2001; Merry 1995). As Mindie Lazarus-Black (2001: 389) points out, when subordinated actors struggle to "gain access to and recognition from dominant institutions that often contribute to their everyday oppression . . . [they] claim new rights and negotiate structural transformations that enable them to enact those rights." In the Argentine Army, female soldiers do not frame their claims in terms of individual rights; nor do they seek recognition for new legal systems. "Individual rights" run the risk of being perceived as "personal interests," a notion that clearly challenges the holistic cosmology prevalent in the army. Rather, when military women demand, officially or informally, greater compatibility between family and professional life, they appeal to symbols highly valued by the military institution such as family, motherhood, and being a responsible soldier, which carry normative prescriptions that, although not viewed as external to the military, open the way for the recognition of women's autonomy.

At first glance, the very existence of the Council on Gender Policy and the army's Gender Offices seem to indicate a certain "feminist militarism," a concept that Hugh Gusterson (1999a: 19) coined to refer to "feminist" women in the U.S. Army who agree to military norms but "struggle against discrimination and for a more complete incorporation into the military." However, in the

Argentine example, female soldiers did not identify themselves as "feminist" but, rather, as "women" or "professionals," which for them did not exclude their condition of mothers and wives. Initially created as places for institutionally discussing and dealing with gender issues in the military, the Council on Gender Policy and the army's Gender Offices have been rapidly transformed into spaces for making visible formerly unrecognized work problems. Placing gender issues on the agenda of defense policymaking and giving a role to female soldiers in this terrain has not only improved concrete aspects of a soldier's professional and family life; it has also introduced a long-resisted figure within the military institution: the soldier as worker. In fact, many of the changes brought about by gender policies have simply brought military normative systems into conformity with the rules and regulations governing the workplace in other areas of the public and private sectors (Ministerio de Defensa de la Argentina 2010). The attempt by female soldiers to be recognized also as mothers has raised the issue of the worker's rights in the military milieu and, by extension, the rights of the military individual as a citizen.

NOTE

1. All names of military personnel have been changed to safeguard their identities.

FIG 4.0. Indigenous Ixil Maya women celebrate after the former Guatemalan dictator Efraín Rios Montt is convicted of genocide against the Ixil people. In militarized societies, people often live in a constant state of fear, which erodes social trust more generally. The emotional and psychological scars of militarization can last for generations. Photograph by Elena Hermosa/Trocaire.

SECTION IV. THE EMOTIONAL LIFE OF MILITARISM

Compiled by CATHERINE LUTZ

Introduction

People in every social formation and historical epoch emerge with distinctive subjectivities, and the various forms that militarism has taken additionally shape those subjectivities in fundamental ways. A number of theorists and commentators have characterized the emotions, structures of feeling, and political aesthetics that are both responses to and foundations of contemporary militarism. Some are directly connected to military matters; others are their often unnoticed correlates in the civilian world, such as mass incarceration and its associated forms of torture that have become a tolerated and too invisible aspect of U.S. society, as Nancy Scheper-Hughes (2014) so vividly describes.

Fear has been a central affect of militarism, with anxieties about particular kinds of enemies and weapons growing and declining over time with a variety of government and military campaigns of threat inflation and deflation. Bioterrorism, for example, is a recent invention for which massive government investments have seemed to require a new and "unprepared" subject (Lakoff 2008). A new mode of collective health security emerges in which norms of prevention are replaced by those of preparedness in part through the migration of military thinking and techniques (particularly through scenario building and imaginative enactment) to the world of public health. With them come affects of urgency and fear of the future. The centrality of fear in the United States is particularly striking, given what historically is the relative absence of tangible external threats to life and liberty to that country over most of the past century. Militarism has made fear a way of life in a much more quotidian and bodily way elsewhere, however, as Linda Green shows for the U.S.-supported Guatemalan wars against native people in the 1980s.

The risk of nuclear war would appear to contradict the claim that fears have been unwarranted in the United States, but that risk has long been difficult for most citizens to assess independently, and it has been accompanied as often, or more so, by "numbing" as by fear, as Robert Jay Lifton notes in part of a 1999 interview that is excerpted in this part. He also attributes a sense of futureless-ness to Americans in the wake of Hiroshima/Nagasaki and the commitment to a vast nuclear arsenal. Joseph Masco's contribution to this part shows that the shaping of militarized affects has not been a simple psychological response to a technological invention and threat but the result of targeted propaganda campaigns that differentially describe the effects of the atomic bomb for various groups, including civilians, soldiers, and political elites. Nuclear scientists, however, have had immediate, intimate knowledge of the risks, but, as Masco (2004) has demonstrated in other work, they have been emotionally drawn into a historically morphing set of responses to different experimental regimes, with the bomb increasingly experienced as a pleasurable problem to solve rather than as a weapon of horrific consequence. The mediatized celebration of modern "humane" weaponry is another route to a desensitization to the realities militarism creates.

READINGS

4.1   Excerpts from Nancy Scheper-Hughes, "Militarization and the Madness of Everyday Life," *South Atlantic Quarterly* 113, no. 3 (2014): 640–55.

4.2   Excerpts from Linda Green, "Fear as a Way of Life," *Cultural Anthropology* 9, no. 2 (1994): 227–56.

4.3   Excerpts from Robert Jay Lifton, "Evil, the Self, and Survival" (interview with Harry Kreisler), November 2, 1999, Institute for International Studies, University of California, Berkeley.

4.4   Excerpts from Joseph Masco, "Target Audience: The Emotional Impact of U.S. Government Films on Nuclear Testing." *Bulletin of the Atomic Scientists* 64, no. 3 (2008): 23–31.

MILITARIZATION AND THE MADNESS OF EVERYDAY LIFE
Nancy Scheper-Hughes

Just as I was about to deliver a lecture on violence in war and peace in the auditorium of a large public university in the United States some years ago, the event was interrupted by police responding to a bomb threat. Although police dogs did not sniff out a bomb, the lecture was rescheduled and moved to the palatial home of the dean of undergraduate studies, who lived in a gated community that had grown, my genial host explained, like a solid wall of invading kudzu around his lovely faux–Frank Lloyd Wright home precariously encased in glass. The dean assured me that we would not be stopped or inspected by security guards posted at a kiosk at the gates of his community that evening. . . .

The security apparatus was an absurd performance, he said angrily. The real threat was not from the outsiders, the residents of the surrounding low-income neighborhoods, but rather from inside the gated complex itself. Scattered among the upper-middle-class professionals living there were a handful of unsavory newcomers who had climbed the economic, if not the social, ladder through involvement in the local drug trade. One was the dean's next-door neighbor with whose children my host's five- and eight-year-old son and daughter had struck up a casual after-school friendship. One afternoon, his son came home with the usual stories of "hide and seek" and "cops and robbers" but boasting about the use of real guns owned by the neighbor children's parents. Complaints were lodged; apologies were delivered; and the guns were moved to a locked cabinet, but the dean and his family remained trapped inside a pistol-packing, gun-loaded, gated community, a good enough metaphor of life in the United States today. . . .

It was not the first time I was involved in a lecture that was interrupted by violence; that would be in 1994 at the University of Cape Town (UCT), just before the election of Nelson Mandela, when a deadly period of political anarchy resulted in a series of deadly massacres in pubs, schools, workers' hostels, churches, and gasoline stations (Scheper-Hughes 1994). The UCT faculty knew how to duck and hide during academic lockdowns, which occurred frequently. . . .

These vignettes are meant to illustrate the militarization of everyday life in countries accustomed to war, either at home or abroad. Philippe Bourgois and I referred to a "continuum of violence" in which the tactics of war and war crimes gradually seep into domestic civilian life as the new norms, as in the proliferation of "armed" gated communities; the de rigueur house gun or house arsenal; and passive acquiescence to stop-and-frisk encounters (Scheper-Hughes and Bourgois 2004: 5, 19–22), whether at a corner 7–Eleven store, subway station, or domestic airport. The most egregious militarization of American life, particularly in California, has been the mass incarceration of black and Latino gang members and small-fry drug dealers who usually control no more than an evacuated city block in Philadelphia, South Central Los Angeles, or Detroit. Mass incarcerations have, for the most part, become routine and normalized in the American consciousness. . . .

The inverse relationship between war crimes and peacetime crimes is also apparent when private and domestic violences such as rape, homophobia, racism, misogyny, frat house initiation bullying, and child abuse (spankings, "time outs," and force-feeding) are deployed during wartime, consciously or unconsciously, to humiliate and torture war criminals, as in Abu Ghraib, where nudity, spankings, and homoerotic sexual abuse were used to crush prisoners of war, and in Guantánamo, where force-feedings evoked sadomasochistic fantasies of oral aggression and invasive perversions of paternal and maternal "care."

The gross abuses of our presumed enemy combatants in Abu Ghraib and Guantánamo Bay come back to haunt us as war crimes committed elsewhere affect behavior at home during peacetime. The grotesque expansion and deformation of U.S. prison culture—the excessive use of isolation, solitary confinement, and other dehumanizing practices—illustrate the militarization of American society over the past half century of wars abroad that spill over into wars at home. The mimetic recycling of war crimes and peacetime crimes was complete when the force-feeding of hunger strikers at Guantánamo Bay found its parallel in the force-feeding of hunger strikers at Pelican Bay in August 2013. . . .

The Normalization of the Abnormal: Mass Shootings and Self-Censorship

In an op-ed piece in the *New York Times*, Gabrielle Giffords (2014) speaks frankly about her uphill battle to regain her speech and the use of her right arm and leg after having been shot in the head. Giffords refers to the disappointing failure of Congress to approve a straightforward bill that would increase the use of reasonable background checks on gun owners while making sure that her readers know that she and her husband are not radicals but "moderates" and "proud gun owners" themselves. The redefinition of normal and moderate Americans is clear in this carefully worded and carefully self-censored piece, one that would not offend Kit Carson or Annie Oakley and that marginalizes and radicalizes those who believe that guns are dangerous and do not want their children playing in homes where guns may not be carefully stored.

The contradiction between the diminished rights resulting from stop-and-frisk laws, racial profiling, and the monitoring of telephone conversations and the robust rights of "proud gun owners" is quite astounding. The path forward, Giffords suggests, is a gradual, step-by-step process that would make it "illegal for all stalkers and all domestic abusers to buy guns and to extend mental health resources into schools and communities, so the dangerously mentally ill find it easier to receive treatment than to buy firearms" (Giffords 2014)....

In the months following the Sandy Hook Elementary School massacre, pundits suggested many reasonable strategies to help communities, parents, and professionals identify and respond to the assumed "early warning signs" capable of predicting a shooting disaster. Most of these strategies were implemented in 1999–2000 following the Columbine disaster that, like Sandy Hook, was another "tipping point."

A vigorous national dialogue followed an impassioned speech by President Bill Clinton in the Rose Garden following Columbine in 1999.... Clinton announced a National Campaign against Youth Violence.... The emphasis was on prevention, on desensitizing "at-risk youth" (inevitably meaning poor black and Latino urban youth) to the risks of subcultures of youth violence in gangs, hate crimes, drugs, and racist and misogynist rap music.

I participated in a Presidential Academic Advisory Board (1999–2001) led by the anthropologist John Devine that included some of the nation's leading scholars of urban America and youth violence.... We documented the links between isolated public mass shootings in schools and the broader social and political context of excessively high rates of youth homicides and suicides and of alienation and isolation of youth from their parents, schools, and communities. Drawing on the expertise of the advisory panel members, we explained the "code of the street" (Anderson 1999) and the "search for respect" (Bourgois 1995) that contributed to homicides and suicides among minority youth. Hypersensitivity and hyperreactivity to imagined insults were the offspring of a profound sense of shame and low self-esteem resulting from the extreme marginalization of unwanted and despised (even more than disrespected) populations. We described the culture of bullying in elementary schools that was not yet recognized as a trigger in some mass-shooting incidents. Finally, we touched on the lethal association of masculine honor with physical force and of power and might with deadly weapons, which led us to a critique of gun culture, but this conversation was derailed by those members of the board who labeled gun control a toxic subject, one that had to be carefully finessed.

We established connections between structural violence—the violence of poverty, exclusion, and extreme marginality—and everyday violence in the homes, streets, and schools of America. We described an epidemic of youth violence (Gillen 1997) that we linked to the punitive and carceral state and to the militarization of American society following the Vietnam War and the first Iraq War. We debated the problems of homelessness and of drug-addicted and traumatized veterans and their impact on children and adolescents. We introduced the concept of youth who were both dangerous and endangered, both victims and perpetrators of violence (Scheper-Hughes 2006). . . . The report's conclusions went against the grain, and, not surprisingly, it was contested and subjected to agonizing edits of passages dealing with the dangers of readily available weapons in American homes. . . . Today, one can barely find it online hidden in digitalized government archives. It was effectively, bureaucratically "disappeared."

After a brief respite, mass shootings in U.S. schools and other public venues resumed with a vengeance at an almost predictable rate. Americans failed to go deep enough inside our collective national unconscious. We continue to resist the fact that our nation is alone in the industrialized democratic world in tolerating subcultures of violence to form in our cities, towns, and suburbs. No other mature democratic nation allows its private citizens to assemble military arsenals in their homes, a practice that endangers the lives of all not only in our suffering postindustrial cities but also in our increasingly armed and dangerous suburbs, movie theaters, and picturesque New England towns. . . .

The public response to the shootings has focused on the mentally ill rather than on inadequate regulation of semiautomatic rifles and large-capacity ammunition magazines. At least Giffords's proposals highlight the problem of domestic violence and the correlation between private suicides and homicides and the family pistol in a sock drawer, the rifle under the bed, the gun in the closet. . . .

Americans in particular attribute magical powers to their guns. In many times and places people under siege have armed themselves with magical clothing or salves or incantations. From the Ghost Dance cult of the Plains Indians to Joseph Kony's child soldiers, people have maintained a mystical belief in their own invulnerability to silver bullets. The call by the National Rifle Association's chief, Wayne LaPierre, for armed guards to be stationed in all schools to prevent further gun massacres is a contemporary expression of the Ghost Dance, the belief in magical efficacy and invulnerability. The real danger is guns stockpiled in the house next door. . . .

The Two Specters

After the Columbine shoot-out, the national focus was on black youth, the "ghetto," and black rage and resentment. Black youth were readily turned into sacrificial scapegoats, the arbitrary objects of white middle-class fears and perceptions. The fact that the Columbine killers were, like most other school shooters, white and middle class had no bearing on the public discourse on youth violence, which was coded black. White children are not youth; they are adolescents or young people. Youth refers to minority children, the children of the other. Michael Greenberg and David Schneider (1994) . . . contest[ed] the then prevailing view that young black men are the cause of violence in U.S. cities. Their comparative study of urban violence in three relatively poor middle-size cities of New Jersey—Camden, Trenton, and Newark—reveals that violence is distributed among young and old; male and female; black, white, and Latino. They identify the real causes of urban violence as deindustrialization, unemployment, urban deserts, undesirable land uses, and the political and social abandonment of unwanted people: poor working-class whites as well as blacks. According to Greenberg and Schneider, violence and premature violent deaths (homicides, suicides, accidents) are caused by extreme marginalization, ghettoes, and segregation. . . .

The robust statistics [also] show that the mentally ill are less dangerous (except to themselves) than those who are not diagnosed with a serious mental condition, as defined in executive orders released by the president. Neither Adam Lanza nor his mother, who coached her unhappy son at a local shooting range and kept an arsenal of guns in her suburban home, would fall under the executive orders. The criminalization of mental illness for most of the late nineteenth to the mid-twentieth century, returning today in a new form and rationale, is a gross social injustice our nation should never seek to repeat. . . .

The Manufacture of Madness

If we nonetheless accept that certain forms of mental illness can be a contributing factor to acts of violence, from individual homicides to mass shootings— paranoid schizophrenia, for one, and post-traumatic stress disorder, for another—two institutions bear some responsibility in their florid eruptions: U.S. military involvement in unresolved warfare and multiple deployments of traumatized young men and women into uncertain and life-threatening situations; and high-security prisons with solitary confinement. When Thomas Szasz (1997) wrote about the "manufacture of madness," he was referring to the inquisitional approach of psychiatrists and their manufactured labels (that might as well have been diagnoses of witchcraft for the damage they did) and the failure to capture the existential experiences of human life and human suffering. When I refer, here, to the "manufacture of mental illness," I am referring to the actual production of madness in wartime deployments in dangerous and even useless wars and among prisoners in solitary confinement.

I have been inside many prisons, madhouses, and reform schools, orphanages that were international baby adoption supermarkets, and Dickensian poorhouses and homeless shelters over my forty-year career as a medical-psychiatric anthropologist. But the first time I saw humans locked up in animal cages was at the beginning of the new millennium. . . .

Like Argentina during and after the dirty war, California in 2000 and in the years since has been mired in another kind of dirty war—a war on drugs, gangs, and drug cartels—against the backdrop of a decade and a half of unresolved warfare in the Middle East. Our team's weekly visits to California's high- and maximum-security prisons—from the Pelican Bay, Tehachapi, and High Desert state prisons to the California Substance Abuse Treatment Facility in Corcoran, the Central California Women's Facility in Chowchilla, and the California Medical Facility Prison in Vacaville—were unforgettable. . . .

The shock of seeing solitary confinement prisoners being rolled out of the hole in individual cages on wheels, like a ferocious circus tiger, to defend themselves before a prison board of review or appeal remains fresh in my memory. I sat through a few of these kangaroo court hearings held in the inner sanctum of California state prisons and in full view of surrounding shelves of prison cells filled with angry men yelling and banging their cell doors to get the attention of the prison guards assembled around the table below. It could have been the eighteenth century. On one occasion I sat next to a clinical social worker already scribbling notes into the thick case record of a young male prisoner who was wheeled into the public space in his portable rolling cage, his legs in shackles as he tried to speak quickly and loudly to defend himself, begging to be released from months of solitary confinement, which, he said, quite understandably, was driving him mad. He had not meant, he said, to throw the contents of his chamber pot into the face of the prison guard who had come to check him out. It was "automatic," a "reflex," he said, nothing personal about it. He said that he had lost whatever self-control he once had. He was sure that he could behave reasonably if he were allowed back to a "normal cell," with other people nearby. "That would be very comforting," he said. But no one at the table was listening, least of all the psychiatric social worker who had already drawn his conclusions before the inmate was allowed to speak. He whispered to me from time to time saying that it was so loud in there, he couldn't hear a word of what the prisoner was saying anyway. The prisoner's petition was denied, and he was returned to stew in solitary confinement, to go mad, to lose his tentative hold on the world outside the cage. . . .

Today there are 33,000 diagnosed severely mentally ill people in California prisons, 12,000 of whom are in solitary confinement. The State of California continues to battle the Supreme Court and class-action lawsuits regarding overcrowding, access to medical and psychiatric care, and solitary confinement. No one knows exactly how many prisoners are in solitary confinement because the state does not acknowledge the term, which would be self-incriminating. . . . Meanwhile, every 120 days California correctional officers are required to "extract" people from their solitary cells in rolling cages to go through a hearing that will determine whether they can be reintegrated into the prison proper. Some prisoners are brought to the table in chains. Some are hallucinating; others are jiggling their feet and legs. Some are begging; some are crying. Others are trying to clear their heads while clearing their throats to speak. There is fear in their eyes.

Erving Goffman (1961) and Michel Foucault (1961) reminded us that prisons, like mental hospitals, are almost impossible to dismantle; they remain in place to recycle one stigmatized and despised population after another. Decarceration, as Andy Scull (1984) described it, existed as a policy for a few decades. But with the advent of a crack epidemic, crime and violence in the 'hood, the pileup of distressed returned war veterans, the eyesore of the mentally ill homeless, gentrification, and conservative politics, the State of California retrenched and began to build one of the world's largest and most densely populated prison complexes. . . .

Elsewhere, changes have begun. . . . Since the end of apartheid, the South African constitution has banned the death penalty, and more recently, in the 1998 Correctional Services Act, the state sought to incorporate the values embedded in the Bill of Rights to the prison population. The South African Constitutional Court has upheld the principle that a prisoner retains his personal rights, including the protection of human dignity; the equality of all people; and protection against cruel, inhuman, and degrading treatment or punishment. The state must provide prisoners with adequate accommodation, including adequate space for daily exercise, nutritious meals, access to books and other reading materials, and medical treatment. Nelson Mandela's last prison home at Victor Verster penitentiary in Paarl, Western Cape, is one showcase of prison reform. All new prisoners enter the gate greeted by a larger-than-life-size statue of Mandela striding out of the prison, his fist raised in victory and a broad smile on his face. The prison warden Manfred Jacobs said that prisoners are also released through the same gate "so that they can leave the prison with pride and hope."[1]

What, then, is the solution to the current impasse in the United States? Ultimately, we have to accept that our national commitments to interminable wars abroad and to dysfunctional wars on drugs and drug cartels along our borderlands with Mexico have consequences at home. The consequences of these wars spill over into our private lives—into our homes, schools, shopping malls, and other public institutions. We have to accept that our nation's growing isolation and arrogance toward the cultural norms that guide other mature democratic nations is hurting us. Above all, we have to resist the forces of censorship and self-censorship that have discouraged an open debate on militarization, incarceration, and public surveillance versus public security and a contemporary assessment of the right to bear arms in the context of late modern society.

NOTE

1. Personal communication with the author, August 2013.

4.2

FEAR AS A WAY OF LIFE
Linda Green

The tradition of the oppressed teaches us that 'the state of emergency' in which we live is not the exception but the rule.
—WALTER BENJAMIN, "On the Concept of History" (1940)

No passion so effectively robs the mind of all its powers of acting and reasoning as fear. To make anything terrible, obscurity seems to be necessary.
—EDMUND BURKE, A Philosophical Inquiry into the Sublime and Beautiful (1901)

People want the right to survive, to live without fear.
—DOÑA PETRONA, personal communication

Fear is response to danger, but in Guatemala, rather than being solely a subjective personal experience, it has also penetrated the social memory.[1] And rather than an acute reaction it is a chronic condition. The effects of fear are pervasive and insidious in Guatemala. Fear destabilizes social relations by driving a wedge of distrust within families, between neighbors, among friends. Fear divides communities through suspicion and apprehension not only of strangers but of one another.[2] Fear thrives on ambiguities. Denunciations, gossip, innuendos, and rumors of death lists create a climate of suspicion. No one can be sure who is who. The spectacle of torture and death and of massacres and disappearances in the recent past have become more deeply inscribed in individual bodies and the collective imagination through a constant sense of threat. In the altiplano, fear has become a way of life. Fear, the arbiter of power—invisible, indeterminate, and silent.

What is the nature of fear and terror that pervades Guatemalan society? How do people understand it and experience it? And what is at stake for people who live in a chronic state of fear? Might survival itself depend on a panoply of responses to a seemingly intractable situation?

In this article, I examine the invisible violence of fear and intimidation through the quotidian experiences of the people of Xe'caj. In doing so, I try to capture a sense of the insecurity that permeates individual women's lives wracked by worries of physical and emotional survival, of grotesque memories, of ongoing militarization, of chronic fear. The stories I relate are the individual experiences of the women with whom I worked, yet they are also social and collective accounts by virtue of their omnipresence (Lira and Castillo 1991; Martín-Baró 1988). Although the focus of my work with Mayan women was not explicitly on the topic of violence, an understanding of its usages, its manifestations, and its effects is essential to comprehending the context in which the women of Xe'caj are struggling to survive.

Fear became the metanarrative of my research and experiences among the people of Xe'caj. Fear is the reality in which people live, the hidden state of (individual and social) emergency that is factored into the choices women and men make. Although this "state of emergency" in which Guatemalans have been living for more than a decade may be the norm, it is an abnormal state of affairs indeed. Albert Camus (1955) wrote that, from an examination of the shifts between the normal and the emergency, between the tragic and the everyday emerges the paradoxes and contradictions that bring into sharp relief how the absurd (in this case, terror) works. . . .

The Nature of Fear

Writing this article has been problematic. And it has to do with the nature of the topic itself, the difficulty of fixing fear and terror in words.[3] I have chosen to include some of my own experiences of fear during my field research rather than stand apart as an outsider, an observer, for two reasons. First of all, it was and is impossible to stand apart. It soon became apparent that any understanding of the women's lives would include a journey into the state of fear in which terror reigned and that would shape the very nature of my interactions and relationships in Xe'caj. Second, it was from these shared experiences that we forged common grounds of understanding and respect.

Fear is elusive as a concept, yet you know it when it has you in its grips. Fear, like pain, is overwhelmingly present to the person experiencing it, but it may be barely perceptible to anyone else and almost defies objectification.[4] Subjectively, the mundane experience of chronic fear wears down one's sensibility to it. The routinization of fear undermines one's confidence in interpreting the world. My own experiences of fear and those of the women I know are much like what Michael Taussig (1992: 11) aptly describes as a state of "stringing out the nervous system one way toward hysteria, the other way numbing and apparent acceptance."

While thinking and writing about fear and terror, I was inclined to discuss what I was doing with colleagues knowledgeable about *la situación* in Central America. I would describe to them the eerie calm I felt most days, an unease that lies just below the surface of everyday life. Most of the time it was more a visceral than a visual experience, and I tried, with difficulty, to suppress it.

One day I was relating to a friend what it felt like to pretend not be disturbed by the intermittent threats that were commonplace throughout 1989 and 1990 in Xe'caj. Some weeks the market plaza would be surrounded by five or six tanks while painted-faced soldiers with M16s in hand perched above us, watching. My friend's response made me nervous all over again. He said that he had initially been upset by the ubiquitous military presence in Central America. He, too, he assured me, had assumed that the local people felt the same. But lately he had been rethinking his position since he had witnessed a number of young women flirting with soldiers, or small groups of local men leaning casually on tanks. Perhaps we North Americans, he continued, were misrepresenting what was going on, reading our own fears into the meaning it had for Central Americans. I went home wondering whether perhaps I was being "hysterical," stringing out the nervous (social) system. Had I been too caught up in terror's talk?[5] Gradually I came to realize that terror's power, its matter-of-factness, is exactly about doubting one's own perceptions of reality. The routinization of terror is what fuels its power. Such routinization allows people to live in a chronic state of fear with a facade of normalcy, while that terror, at the same time, permeates and shreds the social fabric. A sensitive and experienced Guatemalan economist noted that a major problem for social scientists working in Guatemala is that to survive they have to become inured to the violence, training themselves at first not to react, then later not to feel (see) it. They miss the context in which people live, including themselves. Self-censorship becomes second nature—Bentham's panopticon internalized.

How does one become socialized to terror? Does it imply conformity or acquiescence to the status quo, as my friend suggested? While it is true that, with repetitiveness and familiarity, people learn to accommodate themselves to terror and fear, low-intensity panic remains in the shadow of waking consciousness. One cannot live in a constant state of alertness, so the chaos one feels becomes infused throughout the body. It surfaces frequently in dreams and chronic illness. In the mornings, sometimes my neighbors and friends would speak of their fears during the night, of being unable to sleep, or of being awakened by footsteps or voices, of nightmares of recurring death and violence. . . .

The people in Xe'caj live under constant surveillance. The *destacamento* (military encampment) looms large, situated on a nearby hillside above town; from there everyone's movements come under close scrutiny. The town is laid out spatially in the colonial quadrangle pattern common throughout the altiplano. The town square, as well as all of the roads leading to the surrounding countryside, are visible from above. To an untrained eye, the encampment is not obvious from below. The camouflaged buildings fade into the hillside, but once one has looked down from there, it is impossible to forget that those who live below do so in a fishbowl. *Orejas* (spies; lit., "ears"), military commissioners, and civil patrollers provide the backbone of military scrutiny.[6] These local men are often former soldiers who willingly report to the army the "suspicious" activities of their neighbors.[7] . . .

One of the ways terror becomes diffused is through subtle messages. Much as Carol Cohn describes in her unsettling 1987 account of the use of language by nuclear scientists to sanitize their involvement in nuclear weaponry, in Guatemala language and symbols are used to normalize a continual army presence. From time to time army troops would arrive in *aldeas* (villages), obliging the villagers to assemble for a community meeting. The message was more or less the same each time I witnessed these gatherings. The comandante would begin by telling the people that the army is their friend, that the soldiers are here to protect them against subversion, against the communists hiding out in the mountains. At the same time, he would admonish them that if they did not cooperate, Guatemala could become like Nicaragua, El Salvador, or Cuba. Subtieniente [Second-Lieutenant] Rodriguez explained to me during one such meeting that the army is fulfilling its role of preserving peace and democracy in Guatemala through military control of the entire country. Ignacio Martín-Baró (1989) has characterized social perceptions reduced to rigid and simplistic schemes such as these as "official lies," in which social knowledge is cast in dichotomous terms—black or white, good or bad, friend or enemy—without the nuances and complexities of lived experience.

Guatemalan soldiers at times arrive in the villages accompanied by U.S. National Guard doctors or dentists who hold clinic hours for a few days. This is part of a larger strategy developed under the Kennedy doctrine of Alliance for Progress, in which civic actions are part of counterinsurgency strategies.[8] Yet the mixing of the two, "benevolent help" with military actions, does not negate the essential fact that "violence is intrinsic to [the military's] nature and logic" (Scheper-Hughes 1992: 224). Coercion through its subtle expressions of official lies and routinization of fear and terror are apt mechanisms that the military uses to control citizens, even in the absence of war. . . .

The presence of soldiers and ex-soldiers in communities is illustrative of lived contradictions in the altiplano and provides another example of how the routinization of terror functions. The foot soldiers of the army are almost exclusively young rural Mayas, many still boys of fourteen and fifteen, rounded up on army "sweeps" through rural towns. The "recruiters" arrive in two-ton trucks, grabbing all young men in sight, usually on festival or market days when large numbers of people have gathered together in the center of the pueblo. One morning at dawn, I witnessed four such loaded trucks driving out of one of the towns of Xe'caj, soldiers standing in each corner of the truck with rifles pointed outward, the soon-to-be foot soldiers packed in like cattle. Little is known about the training these young soldiers receive, but anecdotal data from some who are willing to talk suggest that the "training" is designed to break down a sense of personal dignity and respect for other human beings. As one young man described it to me, "Soldiers are trained to kill and nothing more" (sec also Forester 1992). Another said he learned [in the army] to hate everyone, including himself. The soldiers who pass through the villages on recognizance and take up sentry duty in the pueblos are Mayas, while the vast majority of officers are ladinos, from other regions of the country, who cannot speak the local language. As a second-lieutenant explained, army policy directs that the foot soldiers and the commanders of the local garrisons change every three months to prevent soldiers from getting to know the people. A small but significant number of men in Xe'caj have been in the army. Many young men return home to their natal villages after they are released from military duty. Yet their reintegration into the community is often difficult and problematic. As one villager noted, "They leave as Indians, but they don't come back Indian."

During their time of service in the army, some of the soldiers are forced to kill and maim. These young men often go on to become the local military commissioners, heads of the civil patrol, or paid informers for the army. Many are demoralized, frequently drinking and turning violent. Others marry and settle in their villages to resume their lives as best they can.

I met several women whose sons had been in the military when their husbands had been killed by the army. In one disturbing situation, I interviewed a widow who described the particularly gruesome death of her husband at the hands of the army, while behind her on the wall prominently displayed was a photograph of her son in his Kaibil [Special Operations Unit] uniform. When I asked about him, she acknowledged his occasional presence in the household and said nothing more. I was at first at a loss to explain the situation and her silence; later I came to understand it as part of the rational inconsistencies that are built into the logic of her fractured life. On a purely objective level, it is dangerous to talk about such things with strangers. Perhaps she felt her son's photograph might provide protection in the future. Although I ran into this situation several times, I never felt free to ask more about it. I would give the women the opportunity to say something, but I felt morally unable to pursue this topic. The women would talk freely, although at great pains, about the brutal past but maintained a stoic silence about the present. Perhaps the women's inability to talk about the fragments of their tragic experiences within the context of larger processes is in itself a survival strategy. How is it that a mother might be able to imagine that her son (the soldier) would perform the same brutish acts as those used against her and her family? To maintain a fragile integrity, must she block the association in much the same way women speak of the past atrocities as individual acts but remain silent about the ongoing process of repression in which they live? The division of families' loyalties becomes instrumental in perpetuating fear and terror. . . .

Silence and Secrecy

It was the dual lessons of silence and secrecy that were for me the most enlightening and disturbing. Silence about the present situation when talking with strangers is a survival strategy that Mayas have long utilized. Their overstated politeness toward ladino society and seeming obliviousness to the jeers and insults hurled at them—their servility in the face of overt racism—make it seem as though Mayas have accepted their subservient role in Guatemalan society. Mayas' apparent obsequiousness has served as a shield to provide distance; it has also been a powerful shaper of Mayan practice. When Elena disclosed to a journalist friend of mine from El Salvador her thoughts about guerrilla incursions today, her family castigated her roundly for speaking, warning her that what she said could be twisted and used against her and the family. This is reminiscent of what Alan Feldman, in writing about Northern Ireland, says about secrecy as "an assertion of identity and symbolic capital pushed to the margins. Subaltern groups construct their own margins as fragile insulators from the center" (Feldman 1991: 11).

When they are asked about the present situation, most people respond "pues, tranquila"—but it is a fragile calm. Later, as I got to know people, when something visible would break through the facade of order and the forced propaganda speeches, or in my own town when a soldier was killed and another seriously injured in an ambush, people would whisper fears of a return to *la violencia*. In fact, the unspoken but implied second part of "pues, tranquila" is "¿Ahorita, pero mañana saber?" (It's calm now, but who knows about tomorrow?). When I asked a local fellow, who was the head of a small (self-sufficient) development project that was organizing locally, whether he was bothered by the army, he said he was not. The army came by every couple of months and searched houses or looked at his records, but he considered this *tranquila*. Silence can operate as a survival strategy, yet silencing is a powerful mechanism of control enforced through fear. At times when I was talking with a group of women, our attention would be distracted momentarily by a military plane or helicopter flying close and low. Each of us would lift our heads, watching until it passed out of sight, yet withholding comment. Sometimes, if we were inside a house, we might all step out onto the patio to look skyward. Silence. Only once was the silence broken. On that day Doña Tomasa asked rhetorically, after the helicopters had passed overhead, why the government sent bombs to kill people. At Christmas Eve mass in 1989, twenty-five soldiers suddenly entered a church soon after the service began. They occupied three middle pews on the men's side, never taking their hands off their rifles, only to leave abruptly after the sermon. Silence. The silences in these cases do not erase individual memories of terror; instead, they create more fear and uncertainty by driving the wedge of paranoia between people. Terror's effects are not only psychological and individual but social and collective as well. Silence imposed through terror has become the idiom of social consensus in the altiplano, as Marcelo Suarez-Orozco (1990) has noted in the Argentine context.

The complicity of silence is yet another matter. During the worst of the violence in the early 1980s, when several priests were killed and hundreds, perhaps thousands, of lay catechists were murdered, the Catholic Church hierarchy, with the exception of several Guatemalan bishops, remained rigidly silent. Evangelical churches such as the Central American Mission, which lost large numbers of congregants, also remained silent. . . .

On Breaking the Silence

Despite the fear and terror engendered by relentless human rights violations and deeply entrenched impunity, hope exists. Since the appointment in 1983 of Archbishop Próspero Penados del Barrio, the Guatemalan Catholic Church has become increasingly outspoken in its advocacy for peace and social justice. The Guatemalan Bishops' Conference, for example, has issued a number of pastoral letters, beginning with the 1988 *Cry for Land*, that have become important sources of social criticism in the country. In 1990, the Archdiocese of Santiago de Guatemala opened a human rights office to provide legal assistance to victims of human rights abuses and to report violations to national and international institutions.

One of the collective responses to the silence imposed through terror began in 1984, when two dozen people, mostly women, formed the human rights organization called Grupo de Apoyo Mutuo (GAM). Its members are relatives of some of the estimated 42,000 people who "disappeared" in Guatemala over the past three decades. Modeling themselves on the Mothers of Plaza de Mayo in Argentina, a small group of courageous women and men decided to break the silence. They went to government offices to demand that the authorities investigate the crimes against their families. They also turned their bodies into "weapons" to speak out against the violence. As they marched in silence every Friday in front of the national palace with placards bearing the photos of those who had disappeared, they ruptured the official silence, bearing testimony with their own bodies about those who have vanished.

In 1990, Roberto Lemus, a judge in the District Court of Santa Cruz del Quiche, began accepting petitions from local people to exhume sites in the villages in which people claimed there were clandestine graves. Family members said they knew where their loved ones had been buried after being killed by security forces. While other judges in the area had previously allowed the exhumations, this was the first time that a scientific team had been assembled, in this case under the auspices of the eminent forensic anthropologist Clyde Snow. The intent of the exhumations was to gather evidence to corroborate verbal testimonies of survivors to arrest those responsible. Because of repeated death threats, Judge Lemus was forced into political exile in July 1991. Snow has assembled another team, sponsored by the American Association for the Advancement of Science, that continues the work in Guatemala at the behest of human rights groups. There are estimated to be hundreds, perhaps thousands, of such sites throughout the altiplano. The clandestine cemeteries and mass graves are the secrets *a voces*, or what Taussig (1999) has referred to in another context as the "public secrets"—what everyone knows about but does not dare to speak of publicly.

In Xe'caj, people would point out such sites to me. On several occasions when I was walking with them in the mountains, women took me to the places where they knew their husbands were buried and said, "Mira, él está allí" ("Look, he is over there"). Others claimed that there are at least three mass graves in Xe'caj itself. The act of unearthing the bones of family members allows individuals to acknowledge and reconcile the past openly, to acknowledge at last the culpability for the death of their loves and to lay them to rest. Such unearthing is, at the same time, a most powerful statement against impunity because it reveals the magnitude of the political repression that has taken place. These were not solely individual acts with individual consequences but public crimes that have deeply penetrated the social body and contest the legitimacy of the body politic.

NOTES

Epigraphs: Benjamin 1969: 257; Burke 1901: 130.

1. Paul Connerton (1989: 12) has defined social memory as "images of the past that commonly legitimate a present social order." In Guatemala, fear inculcated into the social memory has engendered a forced acquiescence on the part of many Mayas to the status quo. At the same time, a distinctly Mayan (counter-)social memory exists. Indigenous dances (especially the dance of the *conquista*), oral narratives, the relationship with the *antepasados* [ancestors] maintained through the planting of corn, the weaving of cloth, and religious ceremonies are all examples of Mayan social memory.

2. Fear of strangers is not a new phenomenon in Guatemala. Maude Oakes, in her study of Todos Santos, reported that in the late 1940s local people were reticent to talk with the few strangers who came to the community and that she, too, was treated with suspicion at the beginning of her fieldwork (Oakes 1951). With some, Oakes never developed a rapport of trust, a common experience for most fieldworkers. Since the last wave of violence, however, community loyalties have been divided, and a level of distrust previously unknown has permeated social life. A climate of suspiciousness prevails in many villages.

3. Michael Taussig's (1992) powerful treatise on the nervous system draws the analogy between the anatomical nervous system and the chaos and panic engendered by tenuous social systems. He notes that, across the fibers of this fragile network, terror passes at times almost unnoticed, and at others is fetishized as a thing unto itself.

4. See Elaine Scarry's discussion of the inexpressibility of physical pain. While she contends that it is only physical pain that can be characterized with no "referential content, it is not of or for anything" (1985: 5), I would argue differently. The power of terror of the sort that is endemic in Guatemala and in much of Latin America lies precisely in its subjectification and silence.

5. Taussig (1992: 17) notes that terror's talk is about "ordered disorder," a discourse that turns the "expected" relationship between the normal and the abnormal, the exception and the rule, on its head while it absorbs and conceals the violence and chaos of everyday life through a veneer of seeming stability.

6. Military commissioners are local men, many of whom have been in the army; in the villages, they serve as local recruiters and spies for the army (Adams 1970). The program was instituted nationwide in the 1960s and was one of the initial steps in the militarization of rural areas. The civil patrol system was created in 1982 and constituted a rural militia of more than one million men by 1985, more than half the highland male population older than fifteen. The PACs, as they are known, function to augment military strength and intelligence in areas of conflict and, more important, to provide vigilance and control over the local population. Although the Guatemalan Constitution states explicitly that the PACs are voluntary, failure to participate or opposition to their formation marks one as a subversive in conflictive zones in the altiplano (Americas Watch 1986; Stoll 1992).

7. The presence of civil patrols in communities has turned petty feuding into a conduit for vigilante justice, of which Benjamin Paul and William Demarest (1988) and Victor Montejo (1987) provide exemplary descriptions.

8. When the insurgents first appeared in the eastern part of Guatemala in the 1960s as a result of an unsuccessful military rebellion, a repressive state apparatus was already in place. Between 1966 and 1968, an estimated six thousand to eight thousand peasants were killed in a government campaign against five hundred insurgents. Subsequently, in an attempt to improve the relationship between the military and the rural population and to eliminate local support for the insurgency, a program of military/civil action was introduced into rural areas under the guidance of U.S. advisers.

4.3

EVIL, THE SELF, AND SURVIVAL
Robert Jay Lifton (interviewed by Harry Kreisler)

HARRY KREISLER: You [have mentioned] ... a concern with the "incapacity to feel or to confront certain kinds of experiences due to the blocking or absence of inner forms, or imagery, that can connect with experience." You go on to speak of the "more fundamental process of creation and recreation of images and forms within the mind." Why has that become such a central problem in our time, do you think?

ROBERT JAY LIFTON: I came upon the idea of what I call "psychic numbing," at first I called it "psychic closing off," in trying to understand what Hiroshima survivors were describing to me. They would say such things as, "the bomb fell"—or they would describe the experience they had: "I saw this array of dead and dying people around me. And I saw everything, but suddenly I simply ceased to feel anything." Some used the metaphor of a photographic plate that was overexposed. It was as though the mind was shut off. And I came to call that psychic numbing.

When I thought about that, I began to wonder not just about those who were exposed to the atomic bomb, [but] what about those who make not just atomic but nuclear weapons, hydrogen bombs? And I thought about the psychic numbing involved in strategic projections of using hydrogen bombs or nuclear weapons of any kind. And I also thought about ways in which all of us undergo what could be called the numbing of everyday life. That is, we are bombarded by all kinds of images and influences, and we have to fend some of them off if we're to take in any of them, or to carry through just our ordinary day's work, or really deepen whatever we have to do or say. And yet it isn't all negative. For instance, I realize that if you take the example of a surgeon who is performing a delicate operation, you don't want him or her to have the same emotions as a family member of that person being operated on. There has to be some level of detachment where you bring your technical skill to bear on it. And from that I formulated a model for professional work that I saw myself working at, and others, too, of a combination of advocacy and detachment. And the detachment could involve selective professional numbing of that kind, but one's advocacy was right out there as well, as was mine in studying as accurately and as rigorously as I could the effects of the atomic bombings, but at the same time coming to that study as a person very worried and critical about nuclear weapons.

KREISLER: In speaking of this problem of dealing with death and the new kinds of realities that we're creating in our world with things like nuclear weapons, what is available to terrorist groups in the way of biological warfare, you talk about how in previous times that we've had various ways of dealing with this problem of our own death, through children, through the notion of life after death, through our good works, our creative products, through identification with eternal nature. But you point to the notion that in our time what you call "experiential transcendence" seemed to be on the horizon more than it has been in the past.

LIFTON: What I was talking about was how all of us, not just religious people or people who think philosophically, but all of us need some sense of being part of something that precedes and extends beyond what we know in some parts of our mind, however we may deny it, to be our limited life span.

As human beings we are the animals or the creatures who know that we die, however we fend off that knowledge. And being part of something larger than ourselves is what I call the symbolization of immortality. And that can be done biologically through our children, or our works, our influences in the world, or through being bound up with eternal nature. And also through some sort of religious belief system. But all these are in some way called into question, both by the rapidity of historical change where we lose a clear sense of value structures or belief systems, and also through the existence of ultimate weapons or what I call "imagery of extinction" that accompanies ultimate weapons. Every adult in the world has some sense that he or she might be obliterated at any time by these weapons that we have created. And that at least it doesn't destroy our need for symbolic immortality or our ways of expressing it, but it does cast doubt to these ways. And I think that's why we tend to then embrace what I took to be a fifth form, which is the experience of transcendence or seeking high states, whether it's through meditation or drugs or something that takes us beyond ourselves or into something like what we call "ecstasy," which can be in quiet or very dramatic ways. And, of course, we have seen much of that, not just in the 1960s in this country and afterward, but I think continuously. And I think that nuclear weapons have something to do with it, importantly, and so do the speed and confusions of historical change. And then a third dimension that relates to both of these is the mass media revolution which feeds us with so much in the way of imagery as we were discussing before, that we become ever less certain of what structures we want to stay with or believe.

KREISLER: In the book on the Vietnam veterans [*Home from the War: Learning from Vietnam Veterans* (Lifton 1973)] you talk about confronting these realities, reordering the images within your own mind, and then seeking a renewal of both the self and the institutions around you.

LIFTON: Yes. I learned a lot from Vietnam veterans, especially as some of them turned against their own war. And I found that a lot of these young men, they were all men in the groups that I worked with and some other professionals, they had been used to the idea that when your country calls you to the colors, you go. They were patriotic. And they had a kind of macho feeling that war was a kind of testing ground for manhood. And also, the idea that in many cases they'd literally sat on their father's knee, he'd been a veteran of World War II and told them about the glorious victory, and they wanted their moment, with war glorified sometimes in that way. But when they experienced their first deads—sometimes that they had brought about in the Viet Cong or the enemy or else saw a buddy shot up next to them— . . . their comfort in all of this was shattered. And in many cases they simply could no longer justify their being there. And they felt everything there seemed strange and bizarre and, for many of them, wrong. There was something wrong or dirty about that war. And there were many atrocities that they witnessed or participated in. So an encounter with death could threaten one's entire belief system, and then one had to struggle with what one learned, what images came from that encounter, reorder them, put them back into some kind of structure that one could use, which is a whole restructuring process of the self. And then there could be a process of renewal. And that's what a number of the Vietnam veterans whom I and others worked with in so-called rap groups and individual exchanges were struggling to do.

4.4

TARGET AUDIENCE: THE EMOTIONAL IMPACT OF U.S. GOVERNMENT FILMS ON NUCLEAR TESTING
Joseph Masco

After World War II, the cinematic atomic bomb became the crucial way in which the government communicated the weapon's power to soldiers, civilians, and policy makers alike. It achieved two main purposes: first, it documented the effects of the exploding bomb; second, it shaped and controlled the meaning of the technology for each of these domestic audiences. This makes the visual record of the aboveground test era, which began in 1945 with the Trinity Test and ceased in 1963 with the landmark Limited Test Ban Treaty, a curious archive of scientific fact, speculation, and outright propaganda. It constitutes a detailed visual record of U.S. efforts to develop a state-of-the-art nuclear arsenal, along with a larger political effort to militarize American society through nuclear fear. This record is crucial to assess today, for in an age of terrorism, preemptive war, and renewed political mobilization of the term "weapon of mass destruction" at home and abroad, U.S. understanding of nuclear technologies has never been more important or more blurred.

Because atmospheric testing of nuclear weapons stopped in the early 1960s, it has been more than three generations since the explosive power of a U.S. nuclear weapon has been visible to the world and subject to detailed sensory assessment and understanding. Nuclear weapons science was conducted underground from 1963 until the current test moratorium began in 1992. Since then, programmatic efforts within the U.S. national laboratories have established a nuclear weapons complex capable of producing new nuclear weapons without conducting nuclear explosions at all—underground or otherwise.[1] As a result, while the weapons themselves have become more sophisticated and embedded within U.S. geo-strategic military policy, they have also become more invisible to the American public. Consequently, Americans are increasingly reliant on films, graphics, and computer programs to convey the bomb's destructive power (Eden 2004).[2]

The filmic record in particular is prolific. Each of the aboveground U.S. nuclear test series was extensively photographed, and the footage was edited into a variety of films aimed at specific audiences—from classified documentaries shown to policy makers to more general descriptions of test activities delivered to the public. The U.S. Air Force relied on a Hollywood studio, Lookout Mountain Laboratory, to produce classified technical films on weapons science, in addition to overviews of the major test series in the Marshall Islands and Nevada (Kuran 2006). Concurrently, the U.S. Defense Department made films to indoctrinate soldiers to fight on an atomic battlefield, and the Federal Civil Defense Administration produced films to prepare citizens for life in the Atomic Age.

Thanks to recent declassification efforts, we now have the ability to publicly assess the films used to craft the country's first official nuclear narratives. Three documentaries in particular (*Exercise Desert Rock*, *Operation Cue*, and *Special Weapons Orientation*) calculate the nuclear danger differently for specific sectors of U.S. society—soldiers, civilians, and policy makers. The two films directed at soldiers and civilians (*Exercise Desert Rock* and *Operation Cue*) help establish nuclear weapons as the new normative reality in the United States, grounded in the minute-to-minute possibility of nuclear war. This early effort to mobilize Americans as Cold Warriors was aimed directly at emotions rather than intellect, as soldiers and citizens viewing these films are presented with a highly politicized portrait of nuclear war. *Special Weapons Orientation*, aimed exclusively at policy makers, offers a different emotional appeal—possession of an absolute destructive power.

In each of these films, a new kind of governance grounded in nuclear fear, and mediated by secrecy, is taking shape. After Hiroshima and Nagasaki, the atomic bomb became a powerful psychological weapon in the United States—policy makers soon discovered that the political uses of nuclear fear worked as well domestically as they did abroad. Controlling the bomb's image—and thus the nuclear danger itself—became a multifaceted political tool.

Today, U.S. culture still relies on many of the images and political logics of self-discipline and nuclear fear first articulated in the government test films of the early 1950s, which we now read as propaganda or atomic kitsch. These films also dare today's public to interrogate a "war on terror"—not only for its technical

FIGS. 4.4.1–4.4.2. During Exercise Desert Rock, which the U.S. Defense Department ran at the Nevada Test Site from 1951 to 1957 and filmed for training, soldiers lined foxholes dug at a distance from ground zero. These arrangements allowed them to experience the shockwave that followed the blast. Photographs courtesy U.S. National Archives.

arguments about terrorism, dirty bombs, and weapons of mass destruction, but also for the political strategy of its emotional appeal.

PRIMARY AUDIENCE: Soldiers FILM: Exercise Desert Rock (1951)
PRODUCED BY: Defense Department RUNNING TIME: 27 minutes

From 1951 to 1957 at the Nevada Test Site, the Defense Department ran Exercise Desert Rock, a series of military training operations designed to prepare troops psychologically for fighting on an atomic battlefield. Each of the exercises consisted of a war game that involved the United States using tactical nuclear weapons against an imaginary invading army, followed by a march on ground zero by U.S. troops. First and foremost, the exercises were experiments designed to test the psychological responses of soldiers to atomic warfare. They also studied the effects of the exploding bomb on military equipment and warfighting strategy. The film *Exercise Desert Rock* presents an overview of the first Desert Rock experiment in 1951. It provides interviews with soldiers before and after the explosion and tracks their progress to ground zero. It was circulated within the military as a training film and became part of the indoctrination of U.S. military personnel for nuclear conflict.

Early in the film, the narrator informs viewers that the exercise intends to test the tactical field uses of nuclear weapons. But soon that message is refined, placing the focus on the psychological effects of nuclear fear on soldiers: "An understandable concern is usually expressed by troops about the dangers of entering an atom-blasted zone. In airbursts, like the one the men will see and the type which would normally be used against troop concentrations, no serious amount of radioactivity remains on the ground."

After promising that troops can be kept physically safe on a nuclear battlefield with careful planning, the problem ultimately becomes how to overcome and internally manage nuclear fear: "It is believed they will experience less fear during the blast because they have learned that radioactive elements from airbursts are carried into the stratosphere in a cloud, where they mix rapidly with the upper air currents. The bomb will be detonated only if all predetermined requirements are met, including weather conditions."

The test also exposed military equipment (tanks, artillery, bridges, planes, ammunition, communication systems) to the exploding bomb.... More than five thousand personnel participated in this nuclear warfighting exercise. Taught that "radiation is the least of one's worries" on an atomic battlefield, the soldiers watch the detonation from seven miles away. They turn away from the exploding bomb during the flash; seconds later, they experience a shockwave that covers them in dust. An interview with one soldier elicits the following discussion about the emotional costs of nuclear war:

INTERVIEWER: Can you tell us whether you think the orientation you had for this weapon prepared you for what you saw out here?

SOLDIER: Yes sir, it did.

INTERVIEWER: What about the fear that you felt? Did they prepare you against that?

SOLDIER: Yes sir, they did. They told us enough so that our fear was cut so much more than what it was before the orientation that we hardly had any fear at all.

INTERVIEWER: Do you have confidence that you would be able to go right in there now and carry out your tactical mission after the blast?

SOLDIER: Yes sir.

INTERVIEWER: How close, now that you've seen it, would you be willing to be?

SOLDIER: Well sir, I'll tell you that after I see them positions up there.

The staged nature of such interviews is apparent; the soldier knows exactly what he is supposed to say. But the startling confidence in his statements is undercut by nerves and a controlled hesitation about engaging the front line of a nuclear war.

The film then follows the troops as they march on ground zero and encounter a carefully prepared course of objects and animals exposed to the blast at different distances. Two miles from ground zero, little damage is visible, but after that, heat and blast have scorched military equipment and dummies. The sheep left in trenches are declared untouched by the bomb, but those situated aboveground have suffered burns that the troops carefully observe. The lesson: foxholes and good military planning can protect soldiers on the atomic battlefield, and nuclear fear is a greater danger than the bomb itself. The film ends with a radiation check of soldiers, a quick "decontamination" with brooms, and a voiceover that declares tactical field weapons can be used safely.

This scripting of danger and stage-managing of nuclear effects became increasingly sophisticated at the Nevada Test Site in the 1950s, eventually including parallel civil defense material aimed at civilians. Again, panic, not nuclear destruction, was positioned as the real danger in nuclear warfare. This argument was made with careful crafting of the images of nuclear warfare, censoring of nuclear effects such as fire and radiation, and focusing on atomic bombs rather than the much larger thermonuclear weapons already in the U.S. arsenal.

The inaugural head of the Federal Civil Defense Administration, Val Peterson, argued in August 1953 in *Collier's* magazine that emotional self-control was the primary goal of civil defense training, providing a detailed plan for how to become a "panic stopper." In his book *The Imaginary War: Civil Defense and American Cold War Culture* (1994), Guy Oakes documents how the ultimate goal of civil defense was to emotionally manage U.S. citizens through nuclear fear.

PRIMARY AUDIENCE: Civilians FILM: Operation Cue (1955) PRODUCED BY: Federal Civil Defense Administration RUNNING TIME: 16 minutes

Operation Cue was the largest civil defense exercise conducted at the Nevada Test Site. It involved the construction of a model U.S. city, complete with mannequins representing "Mr. and Mrs. America," which was then incinerated on live television for one hundred million viewers. The exercise promised to reveal what a postnuclear U.S. city would look like, and the Federal Civil Defense Administration went to extraordinary lengths to make the test city look real. Declaring "survival is your business," the Operation Cue exercise was part of a larger campaign to make Americans responsible for their own safety during a nuclear war. Contemporary-style homes were stocked with the latest furnishings donated by 150 industry associations. An elaborate food-testing program placed packaged and frozen food throughout the test site. The food that survived the explosion was later used as ingredients in dishes served during a post-blast feeding exercise.

Following the script developed in *Exercise Desert Rock*, the film takes viewers through test preparations, the detonation, and a post-test assessment of the ruins. But in *Operation Cue*, a female narrator introduces viewers to this "program to test the effects of an atomic blast on the things we use in everyday life." The mannequin families were posed in moments of domestic normalcy— eating at the kitchen table, napping in bed, or watching television. In other words, viewers were invited to think of themselves as mannequins caught in an unannounced nuclear attack and to watch *Operation Cue* for signs of what their postnuclear environment would be like.

Much as the soldiers did in *Exercise Desert Rock*, a group of civilian volunteers populated a forward trench to test their reactions to the nuclear blast. Testing the cognitive effects of a nuclear blast on civilians was part of Operation Cue's

FIGS. 4.4.3–4.4.4. For *Operation Cue* in 1955, the Federal Civil Defense Administration constructed a model U.S. city that it populated with mannequins. The city was destroyed with a nuclear weapon during a live television broadcast, scenes from which are pictured here. Photographs courtesy U.S. National Archives.

psychological experiment. The film ultimately promised viewers that nuclear war could be incorporated into typical emergencies and treated alongside natural disasters such as hurricanes, earthquakes, and floods. The overt message is that emotional self-discipline and preparation are the key to surviving a crisis— whether that crisis is a Soviet nuclear attack, fire, or bad weather.

In *Operation Cue*, there is no discussion about radioactive fallout or the extensive fires that the atomic bombings of Hiroshima and Nagasaki produced. Instead, the film provides a detailed portrait of a functioning postnuclear state. Rescue personnel pull damaged mannequins from the rubble, flying several to off-site hospitals; meanwhile, the mass feeding takes place alongside standing homes and power lines. Later, the mannequins scorched by Operation Cue went on a national tour of J. C. Penney department stores, which had provided the clothing used in the test, offering an explicit portrait of nuclear survival to the U.S. public.

A closer reading of *Operation Cue* reveals a more complicated message: the film is training citizens to accept nuclear war as a normative threat, employing nuclear fear to craft a militarized society organized around preparing for nuclear war every minute of every day. To accomplish this, the portrait of nuclear danger presented in *Operation Cue* is partial, a carefully edited version of nuclear science that the day's prevailing experts had already disproved via the test programs in Nevada and the South Pacific. In actuality, the fallout produced by nuclear tests such as Operation Cue traversed the continental United States, creating negative health effects for soldiers and civilians that continue to this day—a much starker reality than *Operation Cue* promises viewers (Miller 1986).

PRIMARY AUDIENCE: Policy makers FILM: Special Weapons Orientation: The Thermonuclear Weapon Part VI (1956) PRODUCED BY: U.S. Air Force RUNNING TIME: 29 minutes

A classified film made by the Lookout Mountain Laboratory, *Special Weapons Orientation*, provides a cumulative overview of the U.S. thermonuclear weapons program from 1950 to 1955. . . . Unlike *Exercise Desert Rock* and *Operation Cue*, this film takes as a central concern the effects of atmospheric fallout, indicating that there was an interest in the military uses of fallout and fire. Noting that "millions of tons of earth" are elevated into a cloud that rises above 70,000 feet in a high-yield explosion, the film reveals that fallout can traverse an enormous territorial range, delivering deadly levels of contamination for hours and days after detonation. The narrator explains that the widespread contamination produced by the first detonation of the 1954 Castle test series created an

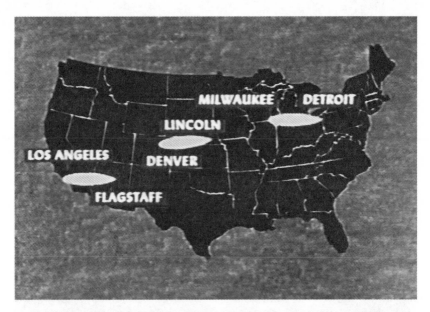

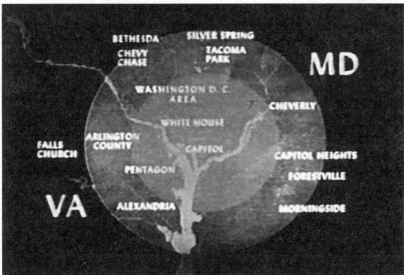

FIGS. 4.4.5–4.4.6. The films created for policy makers offered a more accurate accounting of the power of nuclear weapons than did the films intended for soldiers and civilians. Most notably, *Special Weapons Orientation* included information about fallout and fire. Photographs courtesy U.S. National Archives.

opportunity for biological research: "Wind factors caused contamination of distant populated atolls, providing a completely new source of study on these effects and showing graphically the tremendous area contamination from a high-yield surface burst. Two hundred and twenty-nine natives and twenty-nine American personnel received doses from 12 to 200 roentgens."

After images of Pacific Islanders with skin bleached by fallout are displayed, the narrator states that none of the exposure rates appears to be of "immediate combat significance," referencing official concern about how such exposures would affect soldiers (ours and theirs) on the atomic battlefield. Next, a graphic illustrating a zone of lethality in the Pacific covering some "7,000 statute square miles" for high-yield explosions is presented, changing the concept of nuclear war entirely. To drive the point home, a map of the United States is offered, with three comparable zones of fallout in California, Colorado, and Wisconsin. Here emotional management is subverted, and the hydrogen bomb's unprecedented destructive power is celebrated.

Special Weapons Orientation presents policy makers with a new range of weapons both capable of annihilating another country and offering little hope of a postnuclear society. The film concludes by assessing the effects of thermonuclear weapons on exposed troops and cities, using Washington, DC, as a reference point: "The real military importance of high-yield blast effects lies not in their type or quality but in their enormous range compared to kiloton weapons.... Two hundred and forty square miles, more than twenty Hiroshimas in a group, more than ten Manhattans, in which blast compounded with fire would bring almost total destruction. The big bonus from multimegaton weapons is the longer, positive phase, producing blast damage far beyond that of kiloton weapons."

In other words, the hydrogen bomb enables a new kind of total war—offering the capacity to annihilate whole civilizations—even as it installs new possibilities for domestic emotional management at home. *Special Weapons Orientation* ultimately documents the arrival of a new form of governance, as nuclear fear becomes the basis for both a new concept of global order and a new kind of American society—simultaneously militarized, normalized, and terrified.

NOTES

1. For further discussion, see Masco 2006.

2. Eden has shown that the extensive effects of fire after a nuclear detonation in an urban area were eliminated from nuclear war planning calculations in the United States during the Cold War, leaving policy makers today with models that can radically underestimate the power of urban nuclear warfare.

FIG 5.0. For centuries, the Japanese military aestheticized soldiers' deaths through the use of metaphor: falling cherry blossoms came to represent the self-sacrifice of military men. The rhetorical power of such symbolism continued well into the twentieth century. In this photograph from 1945, high school girls bid a kamikaze pilot farewell by waving cherry blossom branches as his plane departs.

SECTION V. RHETORICS OF MILITARISM

Compiled by ANDREW BICKFORD

Introduction

This section examines how rhetorics of militarism and militarization are used to naturalize war and violence, bring about support for and acquiescence to war and military action, and dehumanize the enemy. The work of turning soldiers into heroes and objects of veneration—and valorizing their deaths—are also key tasks and goals of militarized rhetoric.

The reading that opens this section traces how the regular, "normal" soldier becomes a symbol of unquestioned heroism and how fallen soldiers became the focus of cult-like worship in the modern state. Emiko Ohnuki-Tierney demonstrates how Japanese soldiers were closely identified with cherry blossoms as a way to aestheticize their deaths and prepare the country for war.

A different rhetorical strategy is described in the second selection, excerpts from an article by Stephen W. Silliman, who examines U.S. military officials' use of the "Indian Country" metaphor from the Vietnam War to the present day. His work provides insight into how past examples of U.S. imperialism and conquest are mapped onto the conflicts in Iraq and Afghanistan.

This is followed by a piece from Naoko Shibusawa, who carefully documents how the rhetorics of American exceptionalism, othering, and militarization coalesce to create arguments and justifications for Western imperialism and domination. Her work traces how postcolonial gender discourses construct "peoples" who are not yet ready for or capable of self-rule and governance. This "ideology of maturity," as she describes it, facilitates U.S. hegemony and the expansion of U.S. power around the globe.

In a similar vein, the last two contributions highlight the ways in which rhetorical arguments can cast the entire planet as a fundamentally dangerous place, necessitating a heavily militarized society. In "The Military Normal: Feeling at Home with Counterinsurgency in the United States," Catherine Lutz examines the public relations and propaganda work of the U.S. military and its attempts to engender support for the military and military action. Hugh Gusterson's analysis of what he calls "nuclear Orientalism"—the idea that the "nuclear other" cannot be trusted with nuclear weapons—plays on racialized stereotypes of Asia and the Middle East. By deploying such rhetoric, policy makers claim that "our" weapons are not a problem, while "their" weapons and attempts to develop nuclear weapons are a grave threat to global security.

Taken together, the selections illustrate how states can effectively deploy a wide range of rhetorical strategies to convince citizens of the need for a strong, well-funded military, of the "rightful" and "honored" place of the military and soldiers in society, and of the importance of the military in everyday life. Ultimately, such strategies often serve to normalize, glorify, and even perpetuate military violence, intervention, and domination.

READINGS

5.1   Excerpts from Emiko Ohnuki-Tierney, "The Militarization of Cherry Blossoms," in *Kamikaze, Cherry Blossoms, and Nationalisms: The Militarization of Aesthetics in Japanese History*, by Emiko Ohnuki-Tierney (Chicago: University of Chicago Press, 2002), 111–21.

5.2   Excerpts from Stephen W. Silliman, "The 'Old West' in the Middle East: U.S. Military Metaphors in Real and Imagined Indian Country," *American Anthropologist* 110, no. 2 (2008): 237–47.

5.3   Excerpts from Naoko Shibusawa, "Ideology, Culture and the Cold War," in *The Oxford Handbook of the Cold War*, edited by Richard Immerman and Petra Goedde (Oxford: Oxford University Press, 2013), 34–39.

5.4   Excerpts from Catherine Lutz, "The Military Normal: Feeling at Home with Counterinsurgency in the United States, in *The Counter-Counterinsurgency Manual*, edited by Network of Concerned Anthropologists (Chicago: Prickly Paradigm, 2009), 23–36.

5.5   Excerpts from Hugh Gusterson, "Nuclear Orientalism," from "Nuclear Weapons and the Other in the Western Imagination," *Cultural Anthropology* 14, no. 1 (1999): 111–43.

5.1

THE MILITARIZATION OF CHERRY BLOSSOMS
Emiko Ohnuki-Tierney

While the military identified itself with blooming cherry blossoms, it soon devised ways to aestheticize soldiers' deaths through the use of falling cherry blossoms as a metaphor, especially as threat of external wars became imminent. For example, it began using the term *sange*, or "to scatter like flowers" (like the petals of cherry blossoms). Not only was this term widespread in statements by the Japanese state, often issued through the media, but soldiers themselves began to refer to their own deaths as *sange*. The term derives from a Buddhist term referring to the practice of scattering flower petals in praise of Buddha as part of a complex ritual called *shika hōyō* (Amano 1995; Mochizuki 1958). The military transformed the term and used it to aestheticize the soldiers' deaths as "scattering like flower (cherry blossom) petals"—quite a departure from the original Buddhist usage.

To understand the military's larger scheme of aestheticization, a few examples not related to cherry blossoms will be reviewed later. One tactic was the creation of "war deities" (*gunshin*), the apotheosis of war heroes as deities. The term "war deities" originally referred to deities who guarded warriors. But the Meiji government refashioned the term to mean deified soldiers as a strategy to encourage soldiers to plunge to death as an honorable act and for the people not to object to their sacrifice. The government first resurrected past heroes who had fought on behalf of the emperors, making them models of loyal soldiers. An example was the resurrection of Yamato Takeru-no-Mikoto, a legendary figure who was said to have conquered the Kumaso in the west and the Emishi in the northeast so that the imperial ancestors could establish political control over rival regional lords.

Kusunoki Masashige (1294–1336) was the earliest and most important real figure in this development. He fought for Emperor Go-Daigo and successfully overturned the Kamakura shogunate.[1] Later, when Ashikaga Takauji, who once fought on the side of Emperor Go-Daigo, betrayed and attempted to enter Kyoto, where the emperor had established his government, Kusunoki Masashige valiantly fought against Ashikaga's force. He was first successful in defeating Ashikaga's force, but during the second advance by Ashikaga's force he was defeated in Minatogawa (Kobe), where he committed suicide as a result. Immediately after the "Restoration," in April 1868, before the era changed from Keio to Meiji, the Meiji emperor issued an ordinance to offer "deity title" (*shingō*) to Kusunoki Masashige and ordered the construction of the shrine at Minatogawa, which was completed in 1872 (Murakami 1970: 187–89). As a loyal hero who fought for the emperor, he became one of the most revered culture heroes among the Japanese, including Wada Minoru, one of the *tokkotai* [Special Forces] pilots.

The first "Ceremony for the Soldier Deities" (*gunshin-sai*) by the state took place at the Imperial Palace on March 20, 1868, followed by a second on April 9. On May 10, the government ordered a shrine built at Higashiyama in Kyoto to ensconce the soldiers who had fallen while fighting for the imperial side (Murakami 1970: 88–89).

Those who had died more recently were even more revered as "war deities" (Takahashi 1994b). Those who valiantly fought during the Russo-Japanese War (1904–1905) were the first to be deified, with Nogi Maresuke (1849–1912) as the most celebrated of all. He fought at Port Arthur, where many men, including his two sons, died. At the death of the Meiji emperor, as the corpse of the emperor was being taken across the Nijubashi, the bridge that spans the moat around the Imperial Palace, Nogi and his wife committed suicide—the practice called *junshi*, whereby someone close to a master will follow the master in death. In other words, he sacrificed both of his sons for the country *qua* emperor, and he and his wife followed the emperor in life and death. The state could not find a better model of *pro rege et patria mori*. Another war deity was Hirose Takeo (1868–1904), also a hero of the Russo-Japanese War. As a commanding officer of the battleship *Asahi* (Morning Sun; the naval flag), he was killed as he and his men attempted to blockade Port Arthur (Shimada 1995). Two other Russo-Japanese War heroes who were made into deities were Togo Heihachiro (1847–1934) and Tachibana Shuta (1868–1904). The government made these men into cultural heroes not simply by ensconcing them but also by praising them in countless stories in school textbooks and in popular and school songs.

The state also aestheticized the war effort through *gunkoku bidan* (heroic stories of the military nation) (Takahashi 1994a), in which war heroes and their activities were praised. There is a long folk tradition of storytelling (*kōodan*, which features war stories and warrior heroes of bygone days). But the new "heroic stories" were orchestrated by the state and disseminated from the top, especially through school textbooks and songs, rather than as a folk tradition. A famous example is the story "Nikudan San Yushi" (The Three Brave Heroes as Human Cannon). On February 22, 1932, three privates—Eshita Takeji, Kitagawa Jō, and Sakue Inosuke—carried a three-meter bamboo tube packed with explosives and dashed into a wire-fenced Chinese fortress in

Shanghai so the army could advance.[2] The army, always competing with the navy, seized the opportunity to make the most of this incident. In March 1932, the mothers of these three "deified soldiers" were summoned to Tokyo, where they were given an envelope containing money from Araki Sadao, the minister for the Imperial Army (Katō 1965). Throughout the country, the government erected statues of these soldiers carrying the land torpedo so that children and adults were regularly reminded to emulate them. Newspapers, radio, and other mass media told and retold the story of this heroic act. It was dramatized into a Kabuki play. Saijo Yaso, a famous composer, wrote a popular song about it titled "Yamato Damashii no Uta" (The Song of the Japanese Soul). It was also made into a school song for third- and fourth-graders (Matsui 1994: 136–37). The entire nation was caught up in a fervor over the heroic act. Donations of money for the families poured in. Until the end of World War II, the three brave heroes were celebrated and ingrained in the minds of the Japanese as the supreme model of patriotic self-sacrifice (Ohnuki-Tierney 1987: 121–22). Thirty-three years later, in 1965, Tanaka Takayoshi, then an army officer attached to the Japanese Embassy in Shanghai, announced on television that these soldiers' lives could have been saved had the commanding officer attached to the tube a fuse one meter long instead of one fifty centimeters long: their lives had in fact been deliberately sacrificed to enshrine them as models when the same military purpose could have been achieved without their deaths (Takahashi 1994a).

Similarly, the nine submarine pilots who plunged into the five vessels at Pearl Harbor were enshrined as war deities by the navy, while the tenth pilot, who was captured by the Americans, was erased from the navy record altogether (Takahashi 1994b). Katō Tateo, who led an army air attack over the Bay of Bengal on May 22, 1942, and supposedly gunned down 216 enemy planes, was another war deity, and a song in praise of his bravery became a hit (Takahashi 1994b).

A most blatant abuse of this notion of the war deity was when the government celebrated the so-called first war deity from Okinawa. Omasu Matsuichi, from Yonakuni-jima, Okinawa, had passed the difficult entrance examination and attended the Army Officers School. After serving in southern China, he led his division in the battle on Guadalcanal and perished at age twenty-five on January 1943, together with the rest of the men in the division. The army reported that the emperor was informed of his bravery. The prefectural funeral was performed at Naha, the capital of Okinawa, where ten thousand people gathered and six thousand schoolchildren marched. A play centering on his life was performed; a song about him was made; and his biography in 136 installments appeared in the local newspaper. In addition, his younger brother, Omasu Shigemori, had to appear at numerous events held in honor of Matsuichi. The fanfare was a cleverly orchestrated affair by the government, which knew that Okinawa was to be the battlefield in the near-future; it had to build up patriotism among the Okinawans, who had been marginalized as not quite belonging to Japan.[3]

Another term used to aestheticize deaths on the battlefield was *gyokusai* (a shattering crystal ball). The term originated in *The Chronicle of Beiqi*, a fifty-volume chronicle of the Beiqi dynasty (550–77), which was completed in 636 during the Tang dynasty in China. The term refers to the beautiful way in which a crystal ball shatters into hundreds of pieces. The Japanese military government adopted the term to encourage mass suicide when faced with a hopeless situation—an entire corps was supposed to shatter beautifully by mass suicide. The term began to appear as early as 1891 in a school song that declared that Japanese soldiers would fight until they died like a shattering crystal ball, no matter how many enemies there were. The most dramatic use of this term for the aestheticization of soldiers' sacrifice was on May 30, 1943, when the military headquarters reported the "shattering like a crystal ball" of the soldiers who died on Attu Island, the western-most island of the Aleutians. On May 12, 1943, eleven thousand Americans landed on Attu, which was held by 2,638 Japanese. When the Japanese military headquarters decided to abandon their men on the island, which was too heavily surrounded by American ships for them to be able to send in support, the battalion commander led the remaining 150 soldiers in a suicidal attack. Except for twenty-nine who were captured, all died or committed suicide. There were 550 American casualties (Takahashi 1994c). The state repeatedly aestheticized the gyokusai on Attu as the model for all Japanese when the tide of the war already shifting hopelessly against them. During World War II, the gyokusai was carried out twelve times altogether, with the involvement of civilians in the cases of Saipan and Okinawa (Hosaka 1985: 43–45). . . .

WITH THE REFASHIONING of the warriors' way, cherry blossoms were assigned the role of representing the souls of the Japanese—above all, of soldiers *qua* warriors, which "entitled" them to die without hesitation. The military construction of blooming cherry blossoms as apotheosized soldiers at the Yasukuni Shrine is most astonishing in that it represents a reverse of the ancient cosmological scheme. In ancient Japan, the Deity of the Mountains, the most powerful of all deities, came down to the rice paddies on the petals of cherry blossoms to offer his own soul, embodied in the rice grains, to humans, who would grow the grains of rice to full maturity and give the deity a return gift of multiplied seeds in the fall. The cosmological cycle of the "gift exchange of the self" was initiated by the deity's sacrifice for humans. In the Yasukuni scheme, it is the humans who fall/descend and sacrifice for the emperor, the "manifest deity." The soldiers' deaths are expressed through falling cherry blossom petals; these petals then ascend to become divine cherry blossoms, which in ancient times grew only in the mountains and thus represented the Deity of the Mountains.

The newly constructed idea of sacrifice in the modern military was the opposite both of Japan's own cosmological scheme and of Christianity, in which Christ is the Savior. The model for the Meiji emperor system, then, was the emperor system of ancient Japan, when the imperial guards were defined as the emperor's shields, rather than Christianity, where God is the shield protecting humans. In addition, the purpose of the Deity of the Mountains' sacrifice in ancient Japan was the reproduction of seeds—that is, production—since in ancient Japan production and reproduction were conterminous (Ohnuki-Tierney 1993: 55–57). In the modern military ideology, a most conspicuous analogy was that between cherry blossoms that fall before they bear fruit and young soldiers who die before bearing offspring. Both are stripped of reproductive capacity.[4]

It was the military state that transformed the image and meaning of cherry blossoms, such that falling blossoms represented sacrifice by the soldiers and blooming cherry blossoms were their souls. Yet, this 180 degree change in the meaning and appearance of cherry blossoms did not strike the Japanese as something odd or drastically different, since the Japanese shared a vast and rich field of meanings and images of cherry blossoms from which each could choose a meaning in a given context. The same was true of the phases of blooming: buds, slightly opening blossoms, full blooms, or falling petals—all are cherry blossoms with overlapping layers of meaning. The switch in emphasis was not consciously perceived, especially since the military simultaneously used blooming cherry blossoms as military insignia, celebrating the might of the soldiers, and as the metamorphosed souls of fallen soldiers at the Yasukuni Shrine. The symbolism of cherry blossoms was transformed from full blooms as a life force to falling petals as the sacrifice of soldiers, who then are reborn as blossoms at the Yasukuni Shrine. In other words, the same physicality—*blooming* cherry blossoms—came to represent both soldiers at their height of power and at their rebirth, predicated on death.

1. The part of the government effort was to establish the so-called Nan-chō, the southern imperial line, as the legitimate imperial line (Murakami 1970: 187–88).

2. *Asahi Shimbun*, evening edition, January 7, 1999.

3. The Japanese attribute this event to the so-called Manchurian Incident of 1931.

4. Michael Silverstein, personal communication, November 1999.

5.2

THE "OLD WEST" IN THE MIDDLE EAST

U.S. Military Metaphors in Real and Imagined Indian Country
Stephen W. Silliman

"Indian Country" is a complex metaphor. For Native Americans, it signifies home, territory, families and friends, sacred space, landscape, and community. One can hear of it from New England to the northwestern coast and from the Southwest to the Dakotas. It denotes particularly native spaces in the geographical and cultural landscape of the United States, ones that may comprise ancestral territories and reservations, refer to sacred spaces, be framed by wins and losses in federal acknowledgment battles, and crosscut rural and urban environments. "Indian Country" is not just one place; it is a metaphor for what it means (and where it means) to be Native American in the contemporary United States. The national newspaper *Indian Country Today* attests to the ways that Indian people welcome and use this venue to voice news and concerns about their current successes and struggles.

Counteracting this positive valence is the work that "Indian Country" does in another realm: as a metaphor used by U.S. military personnel to refer to hostile, unpacified territories in active war zones. From the Vietnam War to the occupation of Iraq by U.S. forces beginning in 2003, the notion of "Indian Country" offers a powerful heritage metaphor for the armed forces. The phrase summons the history of Native American and U.S. military encounters, particularly those of the nineteenth century, in ways that interpret the present in light of the past, that retell (or reinterpret) the past through present political filters, and that forecast the future while justifying the present. The metaphor draws on a narrative of U.S. colonialism, triumphalism, and Othering that operated in discourses about Native Americans in the past, that surround Native American struggles and communities today, and that appear to be recast in new (dis)guise in the Middle East in the early twenty-first century.

By exploring how the U.S. "Old West" is discursively and practically reca-
pitulated in the Middle East and how the national narrative of U.S. frontier
expansion receives embodied support by soldiers who live in and through these
heritage metaphors, I seek to explore why these metaphors work in imagined
"Indian Country" and how they do work in real Indian Country. I am interested here in metaphors that explicitly involve Native Americans and not in
the numerous parallel metaphors in U.S., British, French, and other national
media that refer to the occupation of Iraq and its overall management strategy
as reminiscent of the U.S. "Wild West," with gunslingers, sheriffs (a.k.a. "cowboy presidents"), John Wayne attitudes, and overall lawlessness. . . .

"Indian Country" Past and Present

Although I focus my argument here on the "Indian Country" metaphor in
twenty-first-century Iraq and Afghanistan, this context does not mark its
first usage in U.S. military parlance. A detailed history of the use of the term
"Indian Country" has not yet been traced (other than its likely origins during
the infamous nineteenth-century Indian Wars as the United States expanded
across the North American continent), but several observations can be made
about its role in twentieth-century military discourse.

The public first became aware of the "Indian Country" military metaphor
in the Vietnam War. . . . "Vietnam, the soldiers said, was 'Indian Country'
(General Maxwell Taylor himself referred to the Vietnamese opposition as 'Indians' in his Congressional testimony on the war), and the people who lived in
Indian country 'infested' it, according to official government language" (Stannard 1992: 251). Transcripts of the congressional war crime hearings following
the 1971 My Lai Massacre capture a revealing exchange between Captain Robert
B. Johnson and Congressman John Seiberling:

> JOHNSON: Where I was operating I didn't hear anyone personally use
> that term ["turkey shoots"]. We used the term "Indian Country."
>
> SEIBERLING: What did "Indian Country" refer to?
>
> JOHNSON: I guess it means different things to different people. It is like
> there are savages out there, there are gooks out there. In the same way we
> slaughtered the Indian's buffalo, we would slaughter the water buffalo in
> Vietnam. (Richter 2006) . . .

Despite the high numbers of Native Americans serving in the U.S. military
during the Vietnam War and the rising activism surrounding Native American

rights during that decade, the term did not disappear in the 1970s. The first Gulf War in 1991 revealed that such a term continued within military circles. Brigadier-General Richard Neal stated in a nationally televised broadcast that they had rescued a pilot "40 miles into Indian Country," a portion of Kuwait under Iraqi control (Dunbar-Ortiz 2004; Neal 1991). Not unexpectedly, Native American communities across the United States took notice and demanded an apology. As Paul DeMain (1991) reported, many Native American veterans recalled hearing this terminology during their service in Vietnam and resented the insults implied: accusations of non-patriotism and outright linkages with the enemy. However, instead of receiving an apology, they were told that although the term had been used commonly in the Vietnam War, it was not part of any official manual or training (DeMain 1991). However, what went unnoticed was the pervasiveness of this metaphor. Several prominent news sources contained quotations of U.S. soldiers in Kuwait who used the same terminology of "Indian Country" (see, e.g., Branigin and Claiborne 1991; Dowden and Fisk 1991; Galloway 1991). For example, consider this statement: "Beyond the berm, the immense sand wall running the length of the Kuwait border, lies what the grunts call Indian Country, a shell-pocked no man's land" (Nickerson 1991: 9).

The early twenty-first-century conflicts in Iraq and Afghanistan involving U.S. participation have not backed away from the "Indian Country" metaphor, and, in fact, may propagate it more than ever. The frequency with which this metaphor appears in military discourse indicates the comfort that its proliferators have with it as an efficacious, transparent, and acceptable "figure of speech." The availability of information on the Internet through media outlets, soldiers' accounts, and blog commentaries makes it clear that the terminology remains pervasive. . . .

As the *Atlantic Monthly*'s writer Robert Kaplan notes in a book that valorizes soldiers' experiences: "'Welcome to Injun Country' was the refrain I heard from troops from Colombia to the Philippines, including Afghanistan and Iraq" (Kaplan 2005: 4). . . . Some may use the metaphor haphazardly in everyday conversation, but others, like Kaplan, have reflected on it and embrace the imagery as evocative of U.S. soldiers' experiences past and present. In fact, Kaplan (2004, 2005: 4) claims that the use of the "red Indian metaphor" does not show soldiers' disrespect for Native Americans but, rather, honors them, much like the Indian names during radio calls that he also mentions. . . . Yet in Kaplan's writings, the metaphor becomes more than symbolic reinterpretation of past and present Native Americans and the U.S. military; it is racist in its extension of analogical reasoning:

The American Indian analogy went far in Mongolia, for the Plains Indians were descendants of the very peoples who had migrated from this
part of North-Central Asia across the Bering Strait and down into North
America. Gen[eral] Joseph Stilwell, the American commander in China
during World War II, remarked that the "sturdy, dirty, hard-bitten" Mongols all had "faces like Sitting Bull." The Mongolian long-song took you
back to the chants of the Sioux and Apaches. Helping matters were the
cowboy hats that Mongolians wore along with their traditional robes. As
[Lieutenant-Colonel Thomas Parker] Wilhelm never stopped saying [in
2003], "Mongolia is real Injun Country." (Kaplan 2005: 100)

Impacts in Real Indian Country

Conflating Indian Country real and imagined, past and present, sets the stage
for a dangerous symbolic inversion when the simile "Iraq is like Indian Country" transforms into "Indian Country is like Iraq" (or "Indians are like Iraqis").
The past is recast in the present, not only to confirm the assumptions about
the present but also to ensure that the past fits the expected mold. Referring
to the Iraq battlegrounds of the U.S. "global war on terror" as "Indian Country" means, quite simply, that Indians must have been (and still are?) terrorists. A Native American writer recently worried, "My immediate thoughts the
first time that I heard the reference to the war torn streets of Baghdad as 'Indian
Country'—was that after 515 years of conquest—in the minds of Imperial America the first Nations of the 'Americas' are still regarded as enemies, hostiles, obstacles to progress . . . as terrorists" (Starr 2007). Even if the rendering of terrorist
and infidel zones in the Middle East as "Indian Country" serves more as historical metaphor, and even if soldiers would not consider their Native American
neighbors or fellow soldiers today terrorists, one still cannot escape the problematic re-narration of those historical Indian Wars as conflicts with terrorists,
despite the obvious common thread of the United States as the invader. . . .

Not much reading between the lines in this discourse is necessary to realize that Native Americans who fought to keep their homelands against aggressive U.S. military encroachments now have become terrorists who caused
unexpected heavy casualties without provocation. How can an 1870s victory
in battle by Native Americans against a regiment of the U.S. Cavalry—led by
an aggressive General George Armstrong Custer, who was coming to force
them onto reservations and to help prepare the land for white settlement and
mineral extraction—be likened to the heavy civilian casualties suffered by U.S.
and world citizens in the surprise attack orchestrated by al-Qaeda on the Twin

Towers in New York City in 2001? It cannot. Suggesting otherwise involves (1) a misrepresentation of well-known U.S. history (one that is, in fact, commemorated by the U.S. National Park Service at the Little Bighorn battlefield with monuments to soldiers and monuments to Native American warriors and their bravery [see Elliott 2008]); (2) an attempt to instill fear by fabricating a threat of terrorism and savagery that, by extension, must have affected the United States since at least the 1870s and continues to require vigilance (see Ivie 2005); and (3) a complete disregard for the cultural and political casualties for Native Americans caused by such a flawed comparison.

More than history is at stake. The "Indian Country" metaphor also represents the language of colonization in the present. Summoning this kind of metaphor for a military effort in the Middle East conveys that the occupying troops are agents of colonization, imperialism, and the presumed highest orders of civilization. As a result, the military speaks of "Indian Country" as a place to dominate and control, not as the homelands of some of its current enlisted men and women who frequently serve their country in percentages higher than in the overall U.S. population. What must it be like as a Native American soldier to hear a phrase that means one's homeland being used to refer to a hostile and dangerous place that needs to be conquered and subdued? What are the implications of knowing that fellow soldiers are playing the proverbial cowboy? What dimensions are invoked when Native American visitors, such as the Native Star Dance Team from New Mexico headed by the retired Army Sergeant First Class Nick Brokeshoulder (Hopi-Shawnee), perform for soldiers in Iraq? How are these representatives of real Indian Country discursively and practically reconciled with references to imagined Indian Country in war zones? . . .

In the interim, one might propose that the effect, at a structural and discursive level, is recolonization in the heat of combat. These discursive moments involve social and psychological impacts during war, but these heritage performances do not remain in Iraq. If soldiers leave their imagined "Indian Country" in the Middle East as a place of violence, bloodshed, terrorism, savagery, and resistance, what is to encourage them to think differently of Indian Country in the United States, despite how Native American soldiers and civilians characterize it? It will insure that the war in Iraq becomes another arena for the complex perpetuation of U.S. colonialism on indigenous people within its own national boundaries. Recognizing this problem, Native American spokespeople demanded in 1991 that former President George Bush Sr. apologize for the U.S. military's use of such colonial metaphors and not expect Native American soldiers to fight in what the military deems "Indian Country" (DeMain 1991). Neither has happened. . . .

Conclusion

This analysis has served double duty as an academic exposé on the use of colonial heritage metaphors in U.S. conflicts in the Middle East and a critical examination of the complex ways that the past and present merge and undergo reinterpretation in deployment of such metaphors. It is important here to resist the claim that these are "mere semantics" or inconsequential references to vague histories with little import in people's lives since metaphors are fundamental to thought and not just incidental to communication of those thoughts (Lakoff and Johnson 1980). Uncritically attributing to them some entertainment value in combat, thanks to the proliferation of "cowboy and Indian" movies in the twentieth century, does not negate or depoliticize their impact either. Such an apologetic approach, in fact, accentuates the subtlety, pervasiveness, and longevity of those impacts. Linguistic practices and discourses have social, political, and cultural effects, particularly when they constitute the language of colonialism and of power.... The metaphor's ability to mobilize soldiers, Native Americans, anthropologists, and public commentators to very different positions reveals the power and the fragility of the narrative of both past and present to which it refers. Unlike the wars that the United States has fought outside of North America, the Indian Wars sit at the very foundations of colonial nationhood. Members of the U.S. Armed Forces use the "Indian Country" metaphor to negotiate a particular colonial and military legacy but one that is far from unequivocal and consensual....

Linguistically and practically, the discourse conveys an attempt to suppress and colonize those who are perceived as savage and uncivilized and to recapitulate the presumed successes of the U.S. military against Native Americans. To the editor of *Indian Country Today*, it "feeds the heart-wrenching realization that American public discourse is increasingly revisionist, distorted, inherently biased and so self-absorbed in its own supremacist thinking that it can only become the object of world condemnation" (Editor's Report 2004).

The problem is one of past and present. In the case discussed here, the past loses its difference and its independence to inform or critique the present; it becomes an inevitability and a figment of (re)imagination. History has been recast in present guise through a mere phrase that draws its meaning from shared ideology and powerful national narratives. The present suffers, as well, in the revived tropes of savagery and the continued neocolonial and racist treatments of Native Americans at home and abroad.

IDEOLOGY, CULTURE, AND THE COLD WAR
Naoko Shibusawa

Since the end of the Cold War, U.S. scholars have come to embrace a wider understanding of ideology. Ideology no longer signifies simply the flawed beliefs of communist enemies. Americans, too, have displayed ideological thinking in widely accepted narratives that pass for common sense. With this insight, scholars such as Michael Latham (2000) have been able to define "modernization" as an ideology, following Michael Hunt's (1987: xi) definition of ideology as an "interrelated set of convictions or assumptions that reduces the complexity of a particular slice of reality to easily comprehensible terms and suggests an appropriate way of dealing with that reality"?

Ideologies in this context are the varying and dynamic beliefs that enable the elite to exercise control with the consent of the ruled through what Antonio Gramsci called cultural hegemony. By "cultural hegemony," Gramsci meant the everyday narratives and ideas that make sociopolitical hierarchies and economic inequities appear natural and commonsensical. These naturalized narratives are not static, and they do not represent a conspiracy by ruling elites to hoodwink the poor and disempowered. Instead, they are deeply held beliefs shared by many within a society, regardless of socioeconomic status. They ultimately benefit the ruling elites, but the leaders themselves find the ideologies compelling because they cannot be "beyond" ideologies any more than they can be beyond their own cultures. Dominant ideologies, then, are a subset of culture or a discursive system. This culture or discursive system shifts as a small number of counterhegemonic narratives succeed in challenging the veracity and "common sense" of dominant ideologies.[1] . . .

Readiness for Self-Rule

Postcolonial critics have not ignored the liberating promises of modernity, among them self-determination and freedom from arbitrary and oppressive rule. In fact, their criticism comes from how most in the global South have been largely denied these promises. This denial of political freedom and economic justice has been possible with a series of rationalizations that have been sustained in one form or another since the Age of Enlightenment. Espousal of the "natural rights of man" did not hamper racial colonization because Westerners simply invented a range of rationalizations as to why some did not meet the qualifications of manhood. Or, to put it another way, they came up with reasons as to why some humans were not really adults capable of self-rule or ready to appreciate the social and political freedoms promised by modernity.

Along with race, two other criteria to rate readiness for self-rule were biologically based: gender and maturity. By virtue of their gender, of course, women did not fit into the category of "all men." But why gender was and continues to be a basis for exclusion and disempowerment is less apparent. To talk about gender does not mean a focus on women as subjects per se, but the perceived differences between the males and females beyond biological differences. This perception of difference has been common throughout many societies and eras—so common that the differences appear innate rather than as a consequence of socialization. Magnifying the supposed differences in temperament and thus ability between the genders signified relationships of power, as Joan Scott (1986) pointed out. Thus, power differences among nations have often been expressed through gendered references implying weakness, dependence, emotionality, and irrationality on one side and strength, rationality, discipline on the other.

Gender is a malleable ideology—indeed, this versatility is what gives any ideology its resilience and utility. Pundits and policy makers have frequently resorted to gendered metaphors to explain differentials in power and to argue for the subjugation of or guidance to another people. For example, the feminized rendering of occupied Germany by Americans after World War II was relatively brief compared with American notions of a feminized Japan or an effeminate India that predated the war and continued throughout the twentieth century (Goedde 2003; Rotter 2000; Shibusawa 2010). By virtue of being non-Western, the latter two nations were and are often Orientalized as being feminine in culture—and, by extension, as a people. Scholars who have expanded Edward Said's original thesis with a gendered analysis have demonstrated that gendered visions underlay notions about the exoticism (and eroticism) of the "Other."

Just as important, a gendered perspective frames what pundits and policy makers have thought not only of other peoples, but also of themselves. Thus, those who advocated war with Spain in 1898 derided William McKinley as an old woman when he hesitated about entering the conflict. while sixty years later, the Kennedy and Johnson administrations favored "toughness" with disastrous consequences in Vietnam (Dean 2001; Hoganson 1998). At the same time, the gendered self-image included a conviction that one's own society treated women better than other "less advanced" peoples. This notion can be seen in the Americas as early as [the Spanish explorer Álvar Núñez] Cabeza de Vaca's observation in the sixteenth century that the *indios* worked their women too hard but was often repeated during the Cold War and beyond regarding Asian men's treatment of Asian women. Since the end of the Cold War the trend is visible in American popular discourse about Muslim societies (Shannon 2010). This gendered rationale helped justify wars on Iraq and Afghanistan and has tragically brought more suffering, particularly to Afghani women.

Likewise, the ideology of maturity has helped to deny self-determination, usually to nonwhites. Analogies corresponding to the natural lifecycle have long been used as conceptual devices to justify political privilege and dominance. "Maturity" signified ability, wisdom, and self-control as well as entitlement to status and power. Colonial powers have used the rhetoric of maturity to justify their rule over nonwhite peoples. Images of the Filipinos, Cubans, Hawaiians, and Puerto Ricans as babies—often squalling—or as students in a classroom led by "Uncle Sam" were abundant in American media at the turn of the twentieth century. In the words of William Howard Taft, the first governor-general of the Philippines, "our little brown brothers" would require "fifty or one hundred years" of U.S. supervision "to develop anything resembling Anglo-Saxon political principles and skills" (quoted in Miller 1984: 134). This practice of depicting colonized or otherwise disempowered peoples as immature or even helpless "dependents" needing the firm hand of American guidance continued into the twentieth century and beyond.

Unlike race or gender, however, immaturity could be a transitional stage, not a permanent fate. After World War II, when the United States focused on exerting hegemonic power without formal colonial structures, it took more seriously its and other imperialist powers' previously false promises to bestow freedom when the natives grew up. American policy makers and media justified its occupation of Japan as necessary because the Japanese were "not yet ready to walk alone." Still, the Japanese were not expected to be under direct American "tutelage" forever, and indeed, after seven years of occupation, the Japanese regained their national sovereignty. Contrasting sharply with permanent colonial paternalism, this "liberal paternalism" was selectively applied during the postwar period—again, according to a perceived sliding scale of readiness for self-rule (Shibusawa 2010).

The ideologies of race, gender, and maturity were and are mutually reinforcing. Stereotypes or notions about women, nonwhites, and children not only overlapped but also provided rationales for the others. Women were considered weak, weepy, and emotional, like children. Children enjoyed frivolities and were fey like women. Nonwhites were deemed undisciplined, unschooled, and ignorant like children. Children were portrayed as "little savages" (and literally believed to be so, according to turn-of-the-century recapitulation theory

[Bederman 1996]). On the other side of the binary, then, were notions of white adult men being cool, levelheaded, responsible decision makers. This simplified worldview dovetailed with Americans' notions of their nation as exceptional. Ingrained belief about American exceptionalism, moreover, required vigilance in demonstrating American fitness to remain world leaders.

NOTE

1. For example, feminists and women's rights advocates pushed the discourse such that it is now "common sense" that women are capable of more responsibilities and skills than in the past.

5.4

THE MILITARY NORMAL
Feeling at Home with Counterinsurgency in the United States
Catherine Lutz

Here were two typical U.S. media moments in July 2008. On Fox News, Brit Hume opened his interview with two advocates of "victory" in Iraq—the pundits Charles Krauthammer and Fred Barnes—and by showing a video clip of George Bush explaining rising U.S. casualties in Afghanistan. "One reason why there have been more deaths [recently]," the president declared, "is because our troops are taking the fight to a tough enemy. They don't like our presence there because they don't like Americans denying safe haven."

This clip was followed by one of Admiral Mike Mullen, chairman of the Joint Chiefs of Staff, reminding Americans, "We all need to be patient. As we have seen in Iraq, counterinsurgency warfare takes time and a certain level of commitment. It takes flexibility."

Over on radio, National Public Radio's *Fresh Air* program featured an hour-long discussion with Lieutenant-Colonel John Nagl, a recently retired U.S. Army officer who led tank assaults in the first and second Gulf Wars; was one of the co-authors of the *U.S. Army/Marine Corps Counterinsurgency Field Manual*; and was now working with the ascendant, new Democratic-leaning think tank the Center for a New American Security. The gentle questions from the interviewer, Terry Gross, generally went like this one: "Ethics become very complicated because it's hard to tell who's a friend and who's the enemy. And that must make it hard to tell, too, when it's appropriate to fire and when it's not. Can you tell us about a difficult judgment call you had to make about whether or not to fire on individuals or on a crowd?"

Prevailing mainstream media discussions of counterinsurgency wars in Iraq and Afghanistan have this restricted kind of range, focusing on how the wars are being fought, or should be fought—with what tactics, for how long, and with what level of "success." The pundits, with the populace in tow, debate whether the military is stretched too thin, well-enough resourced (or not), or in need of tens of thousands more troops to do the job. They debate whether the Bush administration lied about the reasons for going into Iraq, but not about whether the nation should have been there or in Afghanistan under any circumstances. They debate timetables for bringing the troops home, not plans for accountability for illegalities of war and torture.

They do not ask whether the United States should have history's most lethal and offensively postured military, one with soldiers garrisoned in approximately one thousand bases around the world, waging wars covert and overt in numbers of countries, and with annual costs to citizens of $1.2 trillion and an arsenal of unparalleled sophistication in ways to destroy people and things. They treat it as a "no brainer" that the security of the United States grows when the military budget or the size of the army grows, and that it is sensible for the federal government to spend more on the military than on protecting the environment; educating children; building transport systems; developing energy sources, agriculture, and job skills in the populace; and getting people into housing—combined. In these discussions, it goes without saying that the military serves the nation and the world as a whole, "policing" it for the common good. These stories assume that above all we live in a world of threat and risk, of enemies and allies, and of national and state rather than global and human interests as operative values. They assume that all civilians addressed by those media outlets are American citizens who are happy to pay the Pentagon's bills and who want nothing but victory or honorable withdrawal from fights around the world. The dominant media narrative suggests the values associated with the military as an institution—obedience, loyalty, duty, honor, conformity—should be the primary values of the civilian world as well: it assumes that soldiering builds character more than nursing does.

While polls show the majority of Americans in 2008 wanted U.S. troops to return home from Iraq, the reasons pundits and populace most often gave for this did not question those basic assumptions: they argued the fight was elsewhere or that the military should be put in a more defensive rather than interventionist stance. Everyone is inside the consensus that makes an enormous military normal and acceptable: the most left-leaning think tanks tend to, at most, propose cutting military spending by 10 percent, pulling it back to levels it was at just a few years ago. Whether conservative or centrist, libertarian or liberal, the television, radio, and Internet sites from which the great majority of Americans get their news share these elements of a foundational narrative about the military, war, empire, and the world "out there," a world whose voices are rarely heard.

For expert comment on security, the media go to generals and civilian Pentagon employees who have made their careers preparing to make war far more than they go to diplomats, humanitarian officials, or civilians about to deal with the catastrophic consequences of war. Many of these experts, the *New York Times* reported in 2008, have been operating on specific Pentagon instructions as to message, with access to Defense Department power brokers and, in some cases, money as compensation. These Pentagon mouthpieces are but the tip of a very large iceberg of money invested in convincing the American public to support a government and economy on a permanent war footing, a point to which I return in a moment.

We can call all of this—the massive investments in war and in the public relations of war, and the assorted beliefs that sustain them all—"the military normal." . . .

Violence and the American Self-image

Despite the huge military budget, the frequent interventions overseas, and the morphing of foreign policy into military policy, Americans have been convinced that their nation is peace-loving (even when some relish the idea that no one trifles with the United States without swift retribution). In its long-standing war narrative, the United States fights reluctantly, rarely, and defensively, as Tom Engelhardt so eloquently noted in his *The End of Victory Culture* (2007). It is only when attacked that Americans rise to defend themselves. So it was a crucial and effective technique for the Bush administration to falsely link Iraq and the 9/11 attackers, to garner support for a war that was offensive in most senses of that term. Every invasion, in fact, has been portrayed this way—from the Dominican Republic in 1965 and Vietnam in the 1960s to Panama in 1989.

Remarkably, military and civilian leaders have even been successful in convincing people that the military rarely engages in killing. Military recruitment ads and official pronouncements from Pentagon, White House, and Congress suggest as much. As Elaine Scarry (1985) has pointed out, these discussions replace the broken bodies at war's center with war's supposed purpose, such as toppling a tyrant or freeing hostages. The preferential option for a view of the military as a defensive and innocent force for good in the world helps explain why U.S. soldiers participating in invasions and armed attacks are most commonly described as "putting themselves in harm's way." Even images of troops being killed are now censored, with the *New York Times* counting just six realistic images of dead U.S. soldiers over the entire war and across all media outlets. The work of moral hygiene that each day comes out of the mainstream media, and the Pentagon public relations and recruiting offices that feed them material, have made the war that most Americans know an almost nonphysical imposition of will on others.

The military normal is sustained in part through this sense of innocence, a sense bestowed and maintained in two ways. The first involves the fictionalization of American war history via the ascendance of the Hollywood definition of reality, many of whose war films have had official Pentagon support. Besides the large new harvest of Iraq and Afghanistan veterans who know what combat looks like, most students I teach about war have learned what they already know about it through the gloss of film and TV. They begin their questions and discussions with the military normal that those movies help reproduce, even if the message is sometimes the resigned notion that "war is hell."

The second involves the heavy censorship and cleaning up of actual wars' reality for public media consumption. The CBS network could receive a call from Dick Cheney in 2004 telling them not to publish the Abu Ghraib story, and it would sit on the information for several weeks, emerging with it only after a leak of the official Taguba report to the journalist Seymour Hersh made public knowledge inevitable. The embedding system for reporters [placing them within and under the control of military units] has successfully kept critical journalists from nonmilitary sources and outlets for their stories. It has also exerted great pressure on embedded journalists to report warmly on the men and women in uniform, an additional incentive being provided by the fact that these people help keep the reporter alive. This was all further strengthened by a concerted campaign to portray the U.S. military as having invented a new, humane, highly targeted form of warfare. It was one based in smart weaponry and new strategy that decapitates demagogues rather than assaults a nation, one that sends bombs through the eye of a needle to wreak vengeance only on "the bad guys." This vision of a new, even more civilized American Way of War predated the recent celebration of the rise of General David Petraeus's smarter, less kinetic brand of counterinsurgency warfare, but very much sets the context for the enthusiastic reception of Petraeus, the new *Counterinsurgency Field Manual*, and the idea of gathering academics to provide cultural knowledge to the military.

So the manual was launched in 2007, a year when, by conservative estimates, the U.S. military killed 713 Iraqi civilians and was involved in firefights where a thousand more were killed. The military normal is increasingly oriented around the idea of the exception—the civilian death as an exception, America as the exceptional nation, and the exception from rules called for by states of emergency, an emergency now decades long. It is guided by the spirit of a sign that Stan Goff, a Special Forces veteran, reports has hung in a Fort Bragg training area to encourage the sense of initiative desired in unconventional warriors: "Rule #1. There are no rules. Rule #2. Follow Rule #1." To be above the law is to be within the military normal.

This vision of the U.S. military is also sustained by having two versions of every document that guides military activity—one a document of civilization, and the other a document of barbarism. So the *Counterinsurgency Field Manual* published by the University of Chicago Press has a doppelgänger manual, the *Foreign Internal Defense Tactics Techniques and Procedures for Special Forces* (published in 1994 and 2004). The public relations version of past U.S. military action used by the Chicago version of the counterinsurgency manual sits in front of the well-recorded history of actually existing U.S. counterinsurgencies in places such as Vietnam and El Salvador, where the techniques of torture, assassination, and massive killing of civilians were in common and approved use.

The Counterinsurgency Campaign in the United States

It has often been said that modern warfare is centered in public relations more than weaponry, that the side that commands the story told about the fight—its rationale, justness, victims, and heroes—will win the war. Less often recognized is how much war and the military normal have depended on public relations campaigns at home, among the American public who must be convinced to continue to supply people to fight and money to buy weapons. From World War II's Office of War Information to the $20 million contract to monitor U.S. and Middle Eastern media coverage of news from Iraq to promote more positive coverage, reproducing support for war has required heavy lifting and significant investments.

The Pentagon has an annual budget of almost $3 billion for advertising and recruitment of new troops, a massive investment shaping domestic opinion. The U.S. General Accounting Office reported that, in the three years from 2003 to 2005, the Department of Defense spent $1.1 billion hiring advertising, public relations, and media firms to do the work of convincing the public that the war is important, going well, and requires new recruits and new dollars. The domestic propaganda is directed through the Pentagon's Soldiers News Service, Speakers Service, and other efforts to place news stories and advertising in U.S. media.

The military publishes hundreds of its own newspapers and magazines on bases around the world, from the *Bavarian News* at U.S. bases in Germany and the *Desert Voice Newspaper* in Kuwait to Fort Hood's *Sentinel* in Texas. It also has its own radio and television stations and a massive network of websites with news, as one site puts it, on the purpose and impact of Defense-wide programs, a number of which appear at first look to be civilian sites. The most effective part of the campaign focuses on soldiers' morale, recruitment, and public opinion simultaneously by encouraging civilians to respect and express gratitude to soldiers for what they do. This is affective labor that many find easy to do, especially when it is in exchange for not having to go to war or send one's children into the military.

This is itself a domestic counterinsurgency campaign, ongoing since World War II but especially intensified with the resistance that has emerged to the war and occupation of Iraq. The weapons of this campaign are the ideas articulated by powerful individuals in government and media, on the endless repeat that all marketers know is key to success. It centers on controlling what questions get asked—Is the surge working? Is the army large enough? Are Human Terrain Teams reducing casualties among civilians? Are our wounded veterans getting adequate care?—more than the answers. And the American public are more important long-term targets than "the Muslim world" or even the general population in Iraq and Afghanistan, because they theoretically control the purse strings and quite literally control whether they put their bodies or their sons' or daughters' bodies in uniform.

The military normal is constructed by a variety of factors, including the impact of years of advertising (becoming ubiquitous in the media only since the institution of the All-Volunteer Force in 1973) at a level that not only brings in the requisite number of recruits each year but convinces its other target audience, the American public in general, that the military is a reasonable and respectable institution, and that it makes our very way of life possible. In other words, without the military we would not have the right to free speech or the other democratic freedoms we enjoy. That these freedoms were in fact ensured by legions of civilians campaigning against a state and a military that had come down on the side of their opposite gets no attention, or that the military has frequently been used to deny those rights to others, as in Chile, Iran, or Guatemala. What also plays into the normalization and veneration of the military is the cumulative effect of the nation's twenty-five million veterans, many of whom are organized in powerful groups that act politically on military and foreign policy questions. . . .

NUCLEAR ORIENTALISM

Hugh Gusterson

According to the literature on risk in anthropology, shared fears often reveal as much about the identities and solidarities of the fearful as about the actual dangers that are feared (Douglas and Wildavsky 1982; Lindenbaum 1974). The immoderate reactions in the West to the nuclear tests conducted by India and Pakistan, and to Iraq's nuclear weapons program earlier, are examples of an entrenched discourse on nuclear proliferation that has played an important role in structuring the Third World, and our relation to it, in the Western imagination. This discourse, dividing the world into nations that can be trusted with nuclear weapons and those that cannot, dates back at least to the Non-Proliferation Treaty of 1970.

The Non-Proliferation Treaty embodied a bargain among the five countries that had nuclear weapons in 1970 and those countries that did not. According to the bargain, the five official nuclear states (the United States, the Soviet Union, the United Kingdom, France, and China), promised to assist other signatories to the treaty in acquiring nuclear energy technology as long as they did not use that technology to produce nuclear weapons, submitting to international inspections when necessary to prove their compliance. Further, in Article 6 of the treaty, the five nuclear powers agreed to "pursue negotiations in good faith on effective measures relating to cessation of the nuclear arms race at an early date and to nuclear disarmament" (Blacker and Duffy 1976: 395). One hundred eighty-seven countries have signed the treaty, but Israel, India, and Pakistan have refused, saying it enshrines a system of global "nuclear apartheid." Although the Non-Proliferation Treaty divided the countries of the world into nuclear and nonnuclear by means of a purely temporal metric—designating only those who had tested nuclear weapons by 1970 as nuclear powers—the treaty has become the legal anchor for a global nuclear regime that is increasingly legitimated in Western public discourse in racialized terms. In view of recent developments in global politics—the collapse of the Soviet threat and the recent war against Iraq, a nuclear-threshold nation in the Third World—the importance of this discourse in organizing Western geopolitical understandings is only growing. It has become an increasingly important way of legitimating U.S. military programs in the post–Cold War world since the early 1990s, when U.S. military leaders introduced the term "rogue states" into the American lexicon of fear, identifying a new source of danger just as the Soviet threat was declining (Klare 1995).

Thus, in Western discourse nuclear weapons are represented so that "theirs" are a problem whereas "ours" are not. During the Cold War, the Western discourse on the dangers of "nuclear proliferation" defined the term in such a way as to sever the two senses of the word "proliferation." This usage split off the "vertical" proliferation of the superpower arsenals (the development of new and improved weapons designs and the numerical expansion of the stockpiles) from the "horizontal" proliferation of nuclear weapons to other countries, presenting only the latter as the "proliferation problem." Following the end of the Cold War, the American and Russian arsenals are being cut to a few thousand weapons on each side. However, the United States and Russia have turned back appeals from various nonaligned nations, especially India, for the nuclear powers to open discussions on a global convention abolishing nuclear weapons. Article 6 of the Non-Proliferation Treaty notwithstanding, the Clinton administration declared that nuclear weapons would play a role in the defense of the United States for the indefinite future. Meanwhile, in a controversial move, the Clinton administration broke with the policy of previous administrations in basically formalizing a policy of using nuclear weapons against nonnuclear states to deter chemical and biological weapons (Panofsky 1998; Sloyan 1998).

The dominant discourse that stabilizes this system of nuclear apartheid in Western ideology is a specialized variant within a broader system of colonial and postcolonial discourse that takes as its essentialist premise a profound Otherness separating Third World from Western countries. This inscription of Third World (especially Asian and Middle Eastern) nations as ineradicably different from our own has, in a different context, been labeled "Orientalism" by Edward Said (1978). Said argues that Orientalist discourse constructs the world in terms of a series of binary oppositions that produce the Orient as the mirror image of the West: where "we" are rational and disciplined, "they" are impulsive and emotional; where "we" are modern and flexible, "they" are slaves to ancient passions and routines; where "we" are honest and compassionate, "they" are treacherous and uncultivated. While the blatantly racist Orientalism of the high colonial period has softened, more subtle Orientalist ideologies endure in contemporary politics. They can be found, as Akhil Gupta (1998) has argued, in discourses of economic development that represent Third World nations as child nations lagging behind Western nations in a uniform cycle of development or, as Lutz and Collins (1993) suggest, in the imagery of popular magazines, such as *National Geographic*. I want to suggest here that another variant of contemporary Orientalist ideology is also to be found in U.S. national security discourse.

Following Anthony Giddens (1979), I define ideology as a way of constructing political ideas, institutions, and behavior that (1) makes the political structures and institutions created by dominant social groups, classes, and nations appear to be naturally given and inescapable rather than socially constructed; (2) presents the interests of elites as if they were universally shared; (3) obscures the connections among different social and political antagonisms so as to inhibit massive, binary confrontations (i.e., revolutionary situations); and (4) legitimates domination. The Western discourse on nuclear proliferation is ideological in all four of these senses: (1) it makes the simultaneous ownership of nuclear weapons by the major powers and the absence of nuclear weapons in Third World countries seem natural and reasonable while problematizing attempts by such countries as India, Pakistan, and Iraq to acquire these weapons; (2) it presents the security needs of the established nuclear powers as if they were everybody's; (3) it effaces the continuity between Third World countries' nuclear deprivation and other systematic patterns of deprivation in the underdeveloped world in order to inhibit a massive north-south confrontation; and (4) it legitimates the nuclear monopoly of the recognized nuclear powers. . . .

I examine four popular arguments against horizontal nuclear proliferation. . . . All four are ideological and Orientalist. The arguments are that (1) Third World countries are too poor to afford nuclear weapons; (2) deterrence will be unstable in the Third World; (3) Third World regimes lack the technical maturity to be trusted with nuclear weapons; and (4) Third World regimes lack the political maturity to be trusted with nuclear weapons.

Each of these four arguments could as easily be turned backward and used to delegitimate Western nuclear weapons, as I show in the following commentary. Sometimes, in the specialized literature of defense experts, one finds frank discussion of near-accidents, weaknesses, and anomalies in deterrence as it has been practiced by the established nuclear powers, but these admissions tend to be quarantined in specialized discursive spaces where the general public has little access to them and where it is hard to connect them to the broader public discourse on nuclear proliferation. . . . Possible fears and ambivalences about Western nuclear weapons are purged and recast as intolerable aspects of the Other. This purging and recasting occurs in a discourse characterized by gaps and silences in its representation of our own nuclear weapons and exaggerations in its representation of the Other's. Our discourse on proliferation is a piece of ideological machinery that transforms anxiety-provoking ambiguities into secure dichotomies.

FIG 6.0. Militarization often alters landscapes in dramatic, lasting ways. In 2002, the
Israeli government initiated the construction of a concrete wall that is up to eight meters
high in some areas. The wall, euphemistically referred to as a "security fence" by some
Israeli officials, is a crucial part of an infrastructure of control created by the Israeli
Defense Forces to keep Palestinians sealed into the Occupied Territories. Photograph by
Justin McIntosh.

SECTION VI. MILITARIZATION, PLACE, AND TERRITORY

Compiled by ROBERTO J. GONZÁLEZ

Introduction

Militarization has had a profound impact on physical and cultural landscapes. Covert operations, military occupation, population control and resettlement, nuclear testing, secret interrogation, aerial bombardment, drone attacks, the creation of military bases, counterinsurgency, counterterrorism, and outright warfare—each of these activities has transformed regions in complex and sometimes destructive ways. Militarized geographies leave indelible imprints on place, space, and territory.

The articles in this section analyze how preparations for war—particularly through the construction of military bases and what might be termed zones of sacrifice—can change regions in unpredictable and enduring ways. Some dramatic examples come from areas in which military bases and weapons testing sites have been established. In the United States and beyond, bases bring with them a range of consequences. Surrounding towns become economically dependent on the base and its employees; toxic substances, explosives, and pollution degrade the natural environment and harm living things; and the status of women declines rapidly as sex work and sexism become normalized.

The section begins with a piece by Catherine Lutz, who provides a description of America's domestic "home fronts." She illustrates this by examining how Fayetteville, North Carolina, is deeply embedded within processes of militarization. The town is located near Fort Bragg, a massive army base that dominates the area's economy, politics, and culture. Lutz explores the historical connections between the region and the broader military-industrial complex of defense contractors and Pentagon officials.

The next piece, by Mark L. Gillem, focuses on the devastating impact of U.S. military bases in East Asia. Areas surrounding military bases are characterized by noise, preventable accidents, contamination, and red-light districts. Although Gillem's work is focused on South Korea, his observations can be extrapolated to Guam, Italy, Djibouti, Kuwait, and other places that host U.S. military bases.

Barbara Rose Johnston's contribution examines the environmental, geological, social, and physiological effects after the U.S. military tested weapons in the Marshall Islands more than half a century ago. Numerous regions of the world—the American Southwest, Kazakhstan, China's Xinjiang Province, and French Polynesia, to name but a few—have been profoundly affected by nuclear weapons testing. These lands, and the lives of those who call these places home, have been forever transformed by military activity.

Military and intelligence agencies have often manipulated space and place to control people. In some cases, the physical manipulation of space is paramount—for example, when military forces establish police checkpoints, erect concrete barriers or "security fences," install surveillance technologies to monitor border regions, or segregate viable neighborhoods along ethnic or sectarian lines. Such actions frequently provoke resistance from those being controlled.

Perhaps nowhere are these processes clearer than in Iraq and occupied Palestine. Julie Peteet focuses on the Middle East and the creation of a "new imperial cartography" in which military checkpoints, concrete barriers, and other structures have led to a fragmented landscape. Her article includes a discussion of the wall surrounding occupied Palestine.

The section concludes with Micheline Aharonian Marcom's interview with Jason De León, who is also interested in a wall—specifically, the wall being constructed between the United States and Mexico. He describes the structure not only as a militarized separation barrier, but also as a metaphor, a symbol that represents a deep cultural misunderstanding of broader global processes.

Control over space is a vital element in militaristic projects. Collectively, the contributions to this section clearly demonstrate the need to carefully analyze geographical and territorial structures of power.

READINGS

6.1   Excerpts from Catherine Lutz, "Making War at Home," in *Home-front: A Military City and the American Twentieth Century*, by Catherine Lutz (Boston: Beacon, 2001), 1–9.

6.2   Excerpts from Mark L. Gillem, "Spillover: The U.S. Military's Sociospatial Impact," in *America Town: Building the Outposts*

of Empire, by Mark L. Gillem (Minneapolis: University of
Minnesota Press, 2007), 34–70.

6.3   Excerpts from Barbara Rose Johnston, "Nuclear Landscapes: The
Marshall Islands and Its Radioactive Legacy," from "Nuclear Savages,"
by Barbara Rose Johnston, *CounterPunch* (online ed.), June 1, 2012.

6.4   Excerpts from Julie Peteet, "The War on Terror, Dismantling, and
the Construction of Place: An Ethnographic Perspective from
Palestine," in *Iraq at a Distance: What Anthropologists Can Tell Us
about the War*, edited by Antonius C. G. M. Robben (Philadelphia: University of Pennsylvania Press, 2009), 80–105.

6.5   Excerpts from Jason De León, "The Border Wall Is a Metaphor"
(interview with Micheline Aharonian Marcom), 2018, New
American Story Project, https://newamericanstoryproject.org.

6.1

MAKING WAR AT HOME
Catherine Lutz

I could see its seams as the huge warplane slowly lumbered overhead toward
its twilight landing at a military complex near Fayetteville, North Carolina.
It was mere feet above the flapping laundry and unlandscaped grounds of a
trailer park. A few miles farther away, people living in the houses of another,
greener area of Fayetteville straightened wall hangings set off-kilter by the
quiet boom of the post's artillery guns. Despite the chain-link fence separating
these neighborhoods from the installation, together they make up the single,
deeply entwined but often invisible world of America and its military.[1] There
are many places like this across the United States that the nation's massive state
of war readiness not only coexists with but has helped form. . . . As home to a
giant army post, Fort Bragg, Fayetteville may seem a very unusual place, but
it is America's twentieth-century history of militarization writ on a small but
human scale. . . .

Much of the history and contemporary reality of war and war preparation
has been invisible, though, to people both inside and outside the military—
because it has been shrouded behind simplified histories or propaganda,
cordoned off by secrecy laws, or been difficult to assess because so many of
the consequences of running our military institutions are not obviously war-
related. And so we have not evaluated the costs of being a country ever ready

for battle.[2] The international costs are even more invisible, as Americans have looked away from the face of empire and been taught to think of war with a distancing focus on its ostensible purpose—"freedom assured" or "aggressors deterred"—rather than the melted, exploded, raped, and lacerated bodies and destroyed social worlds at its center. And we have been taught to imagine the costs of war as exacted only on the battlefield and the bodies of soldiers, even as veterans' injuries and experience get scant attention, and even as civilians are now the vast proportion of war's clotted red harvest. . . .

There are many places like Fayetteville in America, from its nearly nine hundred other domestic military bases in such towns as Norfolk, Virginia; New London, Connecticut; and Killeen, Texas, to the thousands of places from Seattle, Washington, to Binghamton, New York, where weapons and equipment are made. In an important sense, though, we all inhabit an army camp, mobilized to lend support to the permanent state of war readiness that has been with us since World War II. . . .

Fayetteville: Almost Anytown, Almost Spectacular

A city of 100,000 souls near the interstate that runs between Boston and Miami, Fayetteville is a place both familiar and strange. Most cities share its mix of boosters and detractors; of gracious, friendly people and misanthropes; of activists and watchers. Most have a version of its tale of postwar growth and suburbanization, mushrooming malls and declining downtowns. And like almost every other American urban area, it is really two cities, one of pedicured lawns and plush square footage, and the other, small weather-beaten cottages and policed public housing. And this city is like the rest of America in its relationship to militarization: its people pay military taxes and send sons and now daughters to war, and it includes nationalists and interventionists, Quakers and libertarians.

Fayetteville is both a city of cosmopolitan substance and humane striving and the dumping ground for the problems of the American century of war and empire, the corner of the American house where the wounds of war have pierced most deeply and are most visible. With the post as its neighbor since World War I, the city has come to have among North Carolina's smallest tax bases, voter registration rates, and number of sidewalk miles, and its county appears near the top or the bottom, whichever is worse, in many lists of North Carolina's one hundred counties' features, including those for poverty, child abuse and other crime, women's unemployment, and auto accidents per capita. It has a striking number of pawnshops and strip joints and of prostitutes and prostitute murders. And while many of its veterans are successful small-business people or civic activists, some live with horrific physical and psychological injuries, and they make up a quarter of the city's substantial number of homeless people.

America's international military interventionism is everywhere visible in the city, whose Okinawan, Korean, and Vietnamese residents stage an annual International Folk Festival but remain outsiders to City Hall. Those twentieth-century military missions are also written on its citizens' memories and their imagination of Fayetteville's future. The refugees and veterans who now make up a large segment of Fayetteville's population have seen Guatemalan terror and the secret war in Laos and authoritarian regimes in Asia, and their politics have been shaped there. And while areas near the post are among the nation's least racially segregated, the city remains a place of stark racial tension and inequality. More generally, there is a widespread sense that someone else (on-post or in the Pentagon) controls Fayetteville's people's fate. The city's wealth is in real estate and retail sales, with a virtual riot of shopping malls and "big box" outlets on eight-lane highways near the post where civilians and soldiers buy fashions and movie tickets with their literally billions of salary dollars. Many chain stores find that their Fayetteville outlets produce more dollars per square foot than any others around the country, but the people who work there make lower wages than in any city in the state.

The drive into Fort Bragg and Fayetteville, if you come in from the west or the north, is through rural countryside dotted with the golf courses of wealthy Southern Pines on one side and with the multiple prisons and chicken-processing plants of nearby Hoke County on the other. Entering Fort Bragg's open gateways, you feel the transition to a more environmentally pristine roadside, often dotted with enlisted men and women on litter patrol. Environmental management practices are evident in the burned-off underbrush and pine trees tagged with signs warning of nesting sites of the endangered red-cockaded woodpecker. You can drive for miles across the bottom edge of the post's 160,000 acres, passing sandy tracks into the piney woods where soldiers gather under camouflage tents for war exercises, parachute into the Sicily Drop Zone, or target practice into various "impact areas." Near the eastern side of the installation, you drive past the ammunition dump and a sprawling area of administration buildings, huge barracks, and family housing in neighborhoods with battlefield names such as Normandy Heights, Anzio Acres, and Corregidor Courts. There live about half of the installations 43,000 soldiers; the rest live in town. Soldiers and their families head in and out of the Post Exchange (PX) to shop, the white-steepled church to worship, and their cars to commute to work on- and off-post. You pass a daycare center with dozens of matched Fisher-Price toddler cars parked near its playground, recreation centers, golf courses, and, after a wooded buffer, you suddenly feel your arrival in Fayetteville itself, as miles of strip malls and strip joints appear. Its highway face begins with business flotsam and jetsam: a used car lot flapping with red, white, and blue bunting; a two-story pawnshop painted completely in camouflage; a sign with silhouetted thin-ankle strippers.

But two very different routes can take you, a few miles later, to downtown Fayetteville. One winds past the malls through miles of wealthy neighborhoods, from Van Story Hills to Haymount, with comfortable housing of most every era since the 1920s, reflecting the absence of any sustained recession in military salaries. Here are the people who sell car insurance to soldiers, market houses at a steady clip sustained by station reassignments, and own the fast-food franchises that feed young soldiers' appetites. These neighborhoods house most of the medical professionals whose incomes rival any of their peers around the country, given the special market conditions of lush military medical funding and thin medical personnel supply.

Just a few miles to the east and directly below the residential area of the post, Murchison Road takes you through a very different landscape—an urban wasteland of razed and weedy lots and deteriorated housing untouched by the billions of dollars that have come into Fort Bragg over the years. In this area live many of Fayetteville's African Americans, the racial integration that characterizes some, more military-populated neighborhoods, absent. Sources of community strength are certainly evident—churches and a mosque, NAACP headquarters, and the new Sickle Cell Association building. And just before arriving downtown by this route, one comes to Fayetteville State University, a historically black college with an illustrious past and a promising future. It helped form a surrounding community at College Heights through waves of refugees who came from the 1920s on to find public education for their children and freedom from rural racial oppression.

These two routes converge and clash symbolically at the central rotary that twists around the Market House. This building means starkly different things depending on the road taken there: it is a former slave market and a current developer boondoggle for most coming down Murchison Road, but it is a nostalgic sign of a more glorious past for many coming down from Haymount Hill. The Market House's uses over the past two centuries do tell stories about the city's tragedies and transitions. It was a market for produce and estates—including slaves—before the Civil War; a meat shop swarming with flies until health regulations were instituted in the early twentieth century; an information center for America's first conscripted soldiers in World War I; a first-aid station for the hundreds of soldiers injured on town liberty each month in the World War II era;

and, in the 1990s, a booster organization's headquarters and icon in a struggle for tourist dollars and rejuvenated land values, as well as in skirmishes over what version of city history will prevail. For this past can be deployed as a prologue, defining the city's present dilemmas and future directions in specific ways.

The physical view of the city for any newcomer is almost always preceded by an imaginary one, and it is less pretty. The city has a bad reputation, to say the least. Many people think of Fayetteville, as I have been told again and again, as a place to get a dozen beers and a sexual disease. People have long called its main downtown thoroughfare "notorious Hay Street," and the epithets "Fat-alburg" and "Fayettenam" have been among the most popular. One can trace the transmission routes of that diseased reputation through every one of the now millions of soldiers and family members who have seen the worst the city has to offer or who have simply seen its unregulated highway detritus. But it is also viewed through the class- and race-inflected fantasies of people around the state who have never seen the city or met a resident. For it suffers the fate of all victims of poverty and racism, which is to be seen as the complete master and architect of their own sad fate. Working-class enlisted soldiers suffer the class prejudice as well, sometimes erroneously assumed to be a main source of the city's crime, at worst, and of its "lack of class," at best. The city's notoriety and neglect also result when people conflate the city with the wounds of war themselves or turn away from them in revulsion or fear. . . .

I BEGAN VISITING Fayetteville to learn how America's military has affected daily life in this country, knowing I would learn much from people who have lived with an army for part or all of their lives. While there are many military facilities within a several-hour drive of my day job as an anthropologist at the University of North Carolina, Chapel Hill, Fayetteville drew me because its experience with the installation covers most of this century. The city had a significant population and economy and a distinct identity both before and after the post arrived, allowing me to see the problems of the military in society in that scale and relationship to each other. . . .

In my first visits to Fayetteville, I went to see what I and others construed as a "military city." While some in town may think of it that way as well, most people with longer residence prefer to think of themselves as living in a town next to a military installation. In that distinction they hope to preserve their autonomy and, perhaps, the respect they might be accorded by others for whom they otherwise become latter-day "camp followers." This is despite the fact that, from the beginning, the camp followed them.

I also came to Fayetteville thinking that I would primarily study "civilians" living alongside "soldiers." I came to see, though, that this distinction between things civil and things military—while a distinction that in some ways is getting sharper over time and abrading political culture—has been for decades an illusion, artificially maintained. The blurred boundaries of the civilian and military worlds, and of war and peace, might have become visible to me because I grew up, like millions of other Americans, with a father who was a war veteran and then a military reservist. For all of my childhood, he was both and simultaneously in the military and in a civilian job. And like all of us, I grew up with that form of peacetime that is in fact war—war "over there" in Korea, Vietnam, Central America, the Persian Gulf, or war threatened or held at bay by the wisp of deterrence theory, or war denied or spectacularized by daily Hollywood and television fare.

I remember vividly when I first became aware of the problem of how human communities can sustain or question organized violence. It was in the early 1960s and my middle childhood when, walking past my living room TV, I was stopped dead by ghostly images of ash and jumbled bones in Nazi ovens and skeletal human forms in the liberated concentration camps, And later, too, from the comfort of my home and through the mediations of those with the power to name the significant and choose the images, I saw the ravages of the Vietnam War on bodies and relationships. Two methods presented themselves to me for understanding how cultures and political economies came to shape people's view of war and the choices they had to make: anthropology, which demands listening and suggests how good people could disagree about important matters, how evil could be justified, how power shapes the currency of ideas and the well-being of individuals and groups; and history, which shows how things have not always been as we see them now, how we might have shifted from a nation suspicious of standing armies to one whose military patrols the globe in all of its corners twenty-four hours each day.

NOTES

1. The military facilities near Fayetteville include the Army's Fort Bragg and Pope Air Force Base.

2. Many claims have been made for the benefits: freedom from foreign tyranny, aggression between other states deterred, military technologies that spin off to civilian use, and youth disciplined through soldier training. With few exceptions, these are unproved or disproved propositions.

SPILLOVER
The U.S. Military's Sociospatial Impact
Mark L. Gillem

I was just starting to doze off after a day of meetings at Kunsan Air Base in southwestern South Korea. A gentle breeze from the Yellow Sea, which was less than a half-mile from my fourth-floor hotel room, kept the small, sparsely decorated space cool. Then, without warning, a piercing alarm broke through the calm evening. After the noise subsided, a loud voice from outside my window took over and announced in a slow, drawn-out monotone, "ALARM YELLOW; ENEMY AIRCRAFT EN ROUTE; PROTECT VITAL RESOURCES."

My heart skipped several beats, and I jumped out of bed, wondering what was going on. The day's news reports were uneventful. North Korea's leader, Kim Jong-il, had done nothing out of the ordinary. His army was reportedly surviving on the barest of rations, and those few North Koreans unlucky enough not to be in the military were near starvation. Surely they did not have the energy to mount a surprise attack on South Korea. Then the voice from above echoed again through the previously peaceful village: "EXERCISE, EXERCISE, EXERCISE." With relief, I approached the window and noticed a loudspeaker mounted on a telephone pole just inside the base perimeter, which was less than 1,200 feet from my window.

After my pulse slowed and the adrenaline rush subsided, I tried to get some sleep. But the voice kept all of us informed as to the progress of the "war," whether we were on or off the base, whether we were military or civilian, whether we cared or not. Unfortunately, at least from my selfish perspective, the voice's reach did not stop at the base perimeter, which surely kept the locals awake as much as it kept me awake.

As I walked around the base the next morning, barbed wire and sandbag revetments were going up around nearly all the buildings. Soldiers lumbered around the best they could in the ninety-degree heat, even though chemical gear covered them from head to toe—thick chemical-resistant pants and coats, steel helmets, black rubber gloves and boot covers, gas masks, and vinyl hoods. They were in MOPP 4, which is military-speak for the highest level of "Mission Oriented Protective Posture," during which they must wear all the gear.

For the next seventy-two hours, the base was much more like a prison. The soldiers had hunkered down in exercise mode, practicing for what could only be a worst-case scenario. After all, for North Korean warplanes to make it to Kunsan, they would have to first get by Seoul's impressive defenses. Nevertheless, sentries at every door checked ID cards. American security police with grenade launchers and automatic weapons augmented the lightly armed South Korean guards at the main gate. Air Force personnel placed blackout boards on windows around the base. Throughout the exercise, the base's fighter jets kept a very busy schedule. Day and night, the eerie glow from their engines illuminated the sky, and their din saturated the landscape.

This visual and audible spillover is not confined to exercise days. Neighbors living in the flight pattern of America's outposts must deal with the noise, the contamination, and the accidents that occur regularly because of military operations. Moreover, horrific crimes and the sociospatial impacts of prostitution routinely make headlines in the newspapers of the host nation. While the articles in these papers frequently show the bases in a regional context, the planning maps produced by the U.S. military rarely show anything beyond the fence line. For the Americans, the white space around their outposts is just that: it is nothing, and it is nowhere.

During multiple visits to bases in South Korea, Japan, and Italy, the only documents I found that showed the outposts in their regional context were aerial photos taken as a perfunctory part of the General Plan process. A checklist required an aerial photo. Check, one aerial photo is complete. Check, thinking about the context is complete. While they made for attractive posters on the walls of planning offices and were interesting graphics for the covers of planning documents, planners rarely referenced these photos, and they therefore served little useful purpose. The widely used documents were facility maps and infrastructure plans that stopped at the border. The production of these maps reflects a deeply ingrained base-planning mind-set. Like the maps, the thinking about empire's impacts stops at the fence lines. However, the piercing sounds of an F-16 or the plumes from underground oil leaks do not stop when they reach the edge of the map. Before the United States made these maps, the land under each base was not an island of empire, floating in a sea of white space. Rather, the land belonged to a nation, a people, a family, and oftentimes to an individual farmer struggling to survive.

Legalizing Colonization: The Okinawan Example

The confiscation and consumption of land is clearly a form of spillover, but military leaders using the rhetoric of national security too quickly dismiss the cost. Military commanders justify their land needs with little consideration given to the sordid history of expropriation that preceded their tours of duty. Following the examples of earlier empires, the United States has adroitly practiced displacement and demolition. As a nation that governs itself by the rule of law, the United States justifies many of these actions through one-sided legal frameworks signed more than fifty years ago in the name of freedom and democracy. A relevant example of this approach is the case of Okinawa, Japan. In Okinawa, as in so many other locations around the globe, the "price of freedom" for local residents in the way of American power has been their own land. . . .

The controversy over U.S. land use in Okinawa is nothing new. It dates back to World War II, when the Americans engaged in a ferocious battle with Japanese forces dug in on the island. Left dead were 12,000 Americans, 75,000 Japanese soldiers, and more than 150,000 Okinawans caught in the crossfire. American forces killed many of the local residents; Japanese forces killed some; and a few killed themselves. The tropical island became a deathbed, nearly stripped of its people, its landscape, and its heritage. To be sure, the Okinawans first suffered under the Imperial Japanese Army. Land confiscations, rapes, and evictions turned much of the local population against the Imperial Army. After the Americans won the Battle of Okinawa, they moved onto the island in force and began converting it into a staging ground for a possible assault on the Japanese mainland. Many Okinawans remember a welcome period of relief beginning with the American arrival. The American soldiers studied Okinawan culture and dedicated five thousand personnel to the work of meeting the needs of the civilian population. . . .

The welcome aspects of the American arrival did not last long, however. Although President Harry Truman's decision to subject Hiroshima and Nagasaki to nuclear attack obviated the need for a staging location, the United States continued to build up its outposts on the island despite growing local resistance. Within one year, the United States took more than 40,000 acres as an act of war, including 20 percent of all arable land on the island, and by 1955, justified by the Cold War, the United States had displaced 250,000 people, or nearly half of the island's entire population. The Americans even shipped 3,218 Okinawans to Bolivia in a largely failed bid at transcontinental displacement (U.S. Congress, House Armed Services Committee 1955).[1] Across history, the hands of empire predictably travel past the same markers: displacements and demolitions are the norm. . . .

While some Okinawans did profit from the construction efforts and employment opportunities at the bases, many more had to find their own incomes and were unable to buy into the "benefits" of capitalism. Naha's shopping centers and the island's roads essentially belonged to the wealthy or the occupying force.

The near-total destruction of all pre-1945 buildings facilitated the remaking of the island into a spatial setting more similar to Cold War suburbs in the United States than prewar villages in Okinawa. Making room for shopping centers and wide boulevards on an island with a population density of 1,270 persons per square mile (twenty-three times greater than that of the United States in 1955) forced even more Okinawans into the few crowded urban centers on the island. In a decade, the island went from being a largely self-sufficient agricultural economy to one heavily dependent on handouts from Tokyo and the United States. There were not enough jobs or arable land in the hands of Okinawans. Despite the economic impact of the U.S. military, Okinawa remains the poorest prefecture in Japan, with an unemployment rate nearly twice the national average (Ota 1996). . . .

Living under Imperial Wings

The fighter planes and fuel trucks that supported this imperial expansion ushered in new forms of spillover. These impacts fall into four broad categories: clamor, calamity, contamination, and crime. Each category reveals that sociocultural practices have spatial consequences.

CLAMOR

Perhaps the most studied spillover concerns the noise generated from military operations. This applies primarily to outposts with significant flying missions: naval and Marine Corps air stations, army posts with flying operations, and air force bases. While public address systems and partygoers are noisy, jets and helicopters can be deafening. The noise, though, is not just a nuisance. It is a significant public health issue. In 1995, a study by Asahikawa Medical College in Okinawa found that 480,000 residents of Okinawa (38 percent) lived in areas with noise levels that exceeded Japanese environmental noise standards. In the four-year study, researchers analyzed more than 350,000 medical records, sent questionnaires to 1,580 schoolchildren and their parents, and surveyed 4,245 residents living on the island and concluded:

— Lower than average birth weights around the bases were due to aircraft noise.
— Children living around these bases had greater emotional and health problems than their peers on other parts of the island.
— Adults experienced higher stress levels that disturbed their work and sleep patterns. . . .

While clamor can make life unbearable and even lead to health problems, more deadly examples of spillover have been the calamities surrounding the operation of American warplanes and fighting vehicles overseas. Airplanes and tanks crash. "I'm astonished," said Shigeyoshi Suzuki, mayor of Misawa, after one airplane crash that narrowly missed Japanese homes in 2001. "It would have been a disaster if this happened over a residential area" (quoted in Specht 2001). . . .

Planes crashing into schools, parts falling from the sky, and pilots ejecting into the ocean are not welcome news headlines for residents living around America's outposts. While there has not been an accident as catastrophic as the one in 1959 that killed eleven children, with dense development abutting almost every base, the chances of a similar accident are high. . . .

CONTAMINATION

While aircraft accidents make the headlines, largely unseen environmental contamination seeps into the soil of the nations that house U.S. forces. Fuel spills, chemical leaks, and illegal dumping continue to plague military bases. A few examples may suffice. In Japan, engineers at Misawa Air Base have attempted to clean up a plume of aviation fuel twenty-five feet deep that seeped into the ground and beyond the base's boundary following an explosion of a 420,000 gallon fuel tank in 1955. They have spent $1.5 million to clean up the spill since engineers discovered the plume in 1996. In January 2003 in South Korea, two thousand gallons of diesel fuel leaked out of a fuel tank at Osan Air Base, and seven hundred gallons of jet fuel leaked out of a containment system following a spill at Kunsan Air Base. In Seoul, oil leaks around Yongsan garrison and at a religious retreat center near Mt. Namsan have saturated the ground, contaminating spring water in the process (Lee 2002). . . .

Another type of spillover that can lead to contamination is the disposal of trash. Okinawa, for example, is running out of landfill space and may have no room left for trash in the near future. At Kadena Air Base, it costs $2 million per year to dispose of 21,416 tons of trash. "We live on an island of limited land mass with a large number of people," said Richard Kuehn from Kadena. "We cannot indefinitely amass trash without running out of room, and we're rapidly running out of room." Americans apparently have a difficult time managing the eighteen different categories of recycling used by the Japanese, so many of them just dump their trash illegally on the base. Base personnel then must relocate this garbage to a local landfill. Moreover, the American culture of consumption follows these families to their overseas assignments. Americans bring their big-screen televisions and their barrels of trash. In 2001, Americans generated about 2.5 times the daily household garbage per capita as their Japanese neighbors living on Okinawa. An American produces 1,500 pounds of trash a year. An Okinawan produces 590 pounds per year. But Americans in Okinawa are no different from their colleagues back home, who, it turns out, spend more on garbage bags than ninety of the world's 192 countries spend for everything. Imperial excess extends into the wastebasket (Bongioanni 2003; Gittler 2004).

CRIME

While formaldehyde flowing into the Han River draws out the protestors, and landfills reaching capacity are a worry for some, other heinous examples of spillover result from crimes committed by U.S. soldiers on foreign soil. Following World War II, the American occupation of Germany, Italy, Japan, and Korea opened up these countries to the needs of capitalism while also exposing their residents to the occupation mentality and spatial demands of American soldiers.... U.S. soldiers have been responsible for deadly traffic accidents, beatings, robberies, rapes, and murders. These acts can quickly become major international incidents involving presidents and prime ministers. While rapes have caused the most outrage, U.S. soldiers commit many other types of crimes. In addition to their human cost, these crimes have a direct financial cost. Between 1992 and 2003, for instance, the South Korean and U.S. governments paid $27.3 million in compensation for damage caused by American soldiers. In South Korea, between 1999 and 2001, Americans committed 1,246 criminal acts, from misdemeanors to felonies (Kim 2003).[2] ...

Spillover's Surprise: The Land-Use Connection

The spillover seeping out of America's outposts is profound. Some in the military call this "the price of freedom." But for the Okinawans shipped to Bolivia or the farmers left with nothing, freedom came with a steep price tag. For four thousand Okinawan children fathered and then abandoned by U.S. soldiers, the price is a childhood in orphanages and foster homes (Sims 2000).

For the families living under the noisy flight paths and the falling parts, for the children who endure the constant "sound of freedom," and for the women coerced into satisfying the desires of the young men "defending" freedom, the homes and schools and the basements and bars that frame their existence are far from free.

Admittedly, the United States is making some changes. It has changed its policies regarding prostitution and embarked on an educational campaign to make its soldiers aware of the sociocultural and personal impacts of exchanging money for sex. It has modified flight schedules and improved the reliability of its aircraft. It has even reduced the number of soldiers who can drive off its bases to minimize traffic accidents. However, apart from offering to give back largely rural land and vulnerable bases near the South Korean demilitarized zone, the United States has done little to curb its appetite for valuable land. On the contrary, it has maintained planning policies and implemented new regulations that only drive up the demand for land around many of its outposts....

"The real crime of the American bases," according to Sheila Johnson (2001), who has studied the situation in Okinawa, "consists of far more than the rapes and other ugly incidents committed by a few servicemen. The real crime is that these bases occupy one-fifth of the island, often polluting it with dangerous chemicals and preventing sensible urban planning." Living under empire's wings means living with an occupying force justified through legal documents signed not among equals but among unequals, where the power disparity was and is profound. It means living with the din of fighter jets roaming the sky. It means living with the crime and contamination that comes with imperial arrogance. It means living with aircraft and their parts falling from the sky. Moreover, for South Koreans and residents of 142 other countries, it means living with a foreign power on their land. Sadly, the U.S. military largely refuses to acknowledge the impact of the spatial spillover resulting from its actions.

NOTES

1. For a discussion of the Bolivian connection, see Amemiya 2002.

2. For a discussion of crimes committed by members of the U.S. military, see Johnson 2001.

6.3

NUCLEAR LANDSCAPES
The Marshall Islands and Its Radioactive Legacy
Barbara Rose Johnston

Following World War II, the Marshall Islands became part of the Trusteeship of the Pacific, and in 1946, after the detonation of two atomic bombs in the

Bikini lagoon, the United States was given the authority to administer the islands as a Strategic Trusteeship. The terms of this agreement included the U.S. obligation to "protect the inhabitants against the loss of their lands and resources" and "protect the health of the inhabitants of the Trust Territory" (United Nations Security Council 1947).

Between 1946 and 1958, the United States tested sixty-six nuclear weapons on or near Bikini and Enewetak atolls, atomizing entire islands and, according to records declassified in 1994, blanketing the entire Marshallese nation with measurable levels of radioactive fallout from twenty of these tests. To consider the gravity of this history, the total explosive yield of nuclear militarism in the Marshall Islands was ninety-three times that of all U.S. atmospheric tests in Nevada, and more than seven thousand Hiroshima bombs. Hydrogen bomb tests were especially destructive, generating intense fallout containing an array of isotopes, including radioactive iodine, which concentrates in the thyroid and can cause both cancer and other medical conditions.

All told, by U.S. estimates, some 6.3 *billion* curies of radioactive Iodine-131 were released into the atmosphere as a result of the nuclear testing in the Marshall Islands—forty-two times greater than the 150 million curies released as a result of the testing in Nevada, 150 times greater than the 40 million curies released as a result of the Chernobyl nuclear disaster. And, while comparison to the ongoing Fukushima meltdown is difficult as emissions continue, estimates to date have ranged from 2.4 million to 24 million curies. Simply put, radioactive contamination in the Marshall Islands was, and is, immense. Radioactive fallout from the 1954 Bravo Test not only blanketed a populated nation but also severely harmed the twenty-three Japanese crew members of the *Daigo Fukuryu Maru* (No. 5 Lucky Dragon) who were in Marshallese waters harvesting a school of tuna when fallout blanketed their vessel. The United States provided antibiotics to treating doctors at the Atomic Bomb Casualty Commission in Japan. One of the crew members, Kuboyama Aikichi, died a few weeks later. In the Marshall Islands, residents of Rongelap and Rongerik atolls who were evacuated in earlier weapons test but not informed or moved before this largest of all detonations, experienced near-fatal exposures.

News of the disastrous exposure of Japanese fishermen and Marshallese island residents fueled international outrage, prompting demands in the United Nations for a nuclear weapons test ban. It also prompted a series of pacifying news releases from the United States about the rapid return to health of exposed civilians.

What was not reported to an interested world public was the news that the heavily exposed people of Rongelap, once evacuated, were immediately enrolled as human subjects in a top-secret study, Project 4.1, which documented the array of health outcomes from their acute exposures but did not treat the pain or discomfort of radiation burns or use antibiotics to offset potential infection.

Nor did the United States make public the full array of findings from its extensive documentation of the character and extent of radioactive fallout during the 1954 and other nuclear weapons tests, which demonstrated the deposition, movement, and accumulation of radioisotopes in the marine and terrestrial environment of Rongelap and other northern atolls.

In 1957, the people of Rongelap were returned to their homelands with great fanfare, moving into newly built homes on islands still dangerously contaminated from prior nuclear weapons tests and clearly vulnerable to the fallout from the thirty-three bombs detonated in 1958. This repatriation of the Rongelap community was both planned and celebrated by scientists and officials at the U.S. Department of Defense and the Atomic Energy Commission, who saw a significant opportunity to place a human population in a controlled setting to document how radiation moves through the food chain and human body. Annually, and then, as the years progressed and degenerative health symptoms increased, biannually, the U.S. medical teams visited by ship to examine—with X-ray; photos; and blood, urine, and tissue samples—the relative health of the community . . . , illustrating both the abusive disregard and human consequences of experiments that violate U.S. law, the Nuremburg Code, and Article 7 of the International Covenant on Civil and Political Rights, which states that "no one shall be subject without his free consent to medical or scientific experimentation." . . .

The long-term study of the human health effects of exposure to fallout and remaining nuclear waste in the Marshallese environment extended over four decades, with a total of seventy-two research excursions to the Marshall Islands involving Marshallese citizens from Rongelap, Utrik, Likiep, Enewetak, and Majuro atolls. Some 539 men, women, and children were subject to studies documenting and monitoring the varied late effects of radiation. In addition to purposeful exposure to the toxic and radioactive waste from nuclear weapons, some Marshallese received radioisotope injections, underwent experimental surgery, and were subjected to other procedures in experiments that addressed scientific questions that, at times, had little or no relevance to medical treatment needs and in some instances involved procedures that were detrimental to their health. The U.S. Department of Energy acknowledged in 1994 the administration of Chromium-51 and tritiated water, and in at least three instances Chromium-51 was injected in three young women of childbearing age. A 2004 review of declassified research proposals, exam reports, and published articles in support of a Marshall Islands Nuclear Claims Tribunal proceeding found that a broader array of radioisotopes were used—radioactive iodine, iron, zinc, carbon 14—for a wide array of experiments that included research demonstrating the linkages among radiation exposure, metabolic disorders, and the onset of type 2 diabetes.

Arguably, while these experiences were abusive, a broader public health interest was being served, as the results of such science could potentially influence government policy and actions to protect humanity from the adverse health outcomes of nuclear fallout. And indeed, significant scientific knowledge was accumulated. However, the bulk of these findings demonstrated varied degenerative health effects resulting from chronic exposure to low-level radiation in the environment, findings that threatened political (nuclear proliferation) and economic (nuclear energy) agendas. Such findings were buried in the classified files.

For example, the presence and bioaccumulation of radioiron (Fe-55) in fallout from the 1958 detonations of nuclear bombs was documented in terrestrial and marine environments, including lagoon sediments, coral reefs, and reef fish, with alarming levels in goatfish liver, but this knowledge was not shared with the larger scientific world until 1972; nor was it shared with the Marshallese until the declassification process supporting an Advisory Commission on Human Radiation investigation forced bilateral disclosure to the Marshall Islands government in the 1990s. The movement of cesium through the soils and bioaccumulation in coconut crabs, trees, and fruit—primary sources of food and liquid in the Marshallese diet—was also documented, with restrictions on the consumption of coconut crab periodically issued without explanation. The movement through the food chain, bioaccumulation, and biological behavior of radioiodine in the human body was documented, and when thyroid nodules, cancers, and disease resulted, these conditions were studied and treated through various experimental means, though the relationship of nuclear weapons testing, fallout, contamination of the environment, and human subsistence in that environment was not explained until decades had passed.

In short, a wide array of other degenerative health outcomes were documented, including changes in red blood cell production and subsequent anemia; metabolic and related disorders; immune system vulnerabilities; musculoskeletal degeneration; cataracts; cancers and leukemia; miscarriages, congenital defects, and infertility....

However, when Marshallese residents suggested to U.S. scientists that these and other unusual health problems were linked to the environmental contamination from nuclear fallout, their concerns were repeatedly and, because of the classified nature of the science, easily dismissed then. And because time and

U.S. power over the narrative of radiation's health effects is so immense and entrenched, they continue to be dismissed now.

The experiences of the Marshallese are particularly relevant to a world still coming to terms with the ulcerating disaster that is Fukushima, a point that is not lost to the members of United Nations Human Rights Council, which has been engaged in an effort over the past number of years to explore the varied means by which humans are unable to enjoy their right to a healthy environment, including the human rights abuses associated with movement and dumping of toxic and dangerous products and wastes.

Călin Georgescu of Romania, then United Nations Special Rapporteur for toxics and human rights, had a mandate that included, among other directives, a country-specific mission to investigate these concerns in the Marshall Islands, especially the human rights consequences of environmental contamination from nuclear weapons testing and other U.S. military activities. In March 2012, Georgescu visited the Republic of the Marshall Islands (RMI), interviewing displaced members of the Bikini, Enewetak, and Rongelap atolls and other Marshallese citizens whose health and other rights have been severely impacted by living in a contaminated environment.

In April 2012, he traveled to Washington, DC, where he interviewed U.S. government officials, met with independent experts such as myself, and discussed his investigation with the Marshall Islands' ambassador and the RMI's United Nations representative . . .

Why should a world community care about Cold War nuclear militarism in the Marshall Islands and its varied ulcerating consequences, especially given the many urgent and all-to-current crises we now face?

The United States knowingly and willfully exposed a vulnerable population to toxic radioactive waste as a means to document the movement and degenerative health outcomes of radiation as it moves through the food chain and human body. This human-subject experiment extended over decades, with profound consequences for individual subjects and the Marshallese nation as a whole. The Marshallese have become a nation whose experience as nuclear nomads, medical subjects, citizen advocates, and innovators is shared by many citizens, communities, and indigenous peoples around the world. Their experiences, consequential damage, and struggles to restore cultural ways of life, quality of life, intergenerational health, and long-term sustainability are especially salient to a nation and a world concerned with the lingering, persistent, and invasive dangers of a nuclear world.

With both the United States and the RMI participating in the United Nations Special Rapporteur's investigation, there is an obligation for both governments to receive and respond to the report's recommendations in a timely fashion and, in subsequent reviews, to demonstrate truly meaningful remediation and reparation for their nuclear legacies in the Marshall Islands. . . . Given the historical role of the United Nations in designating the Marshall Islands as a strategic trust, there is a moral and legal obligation for the United Nations community to assist in the remediation, restoration and reparation due to the environment, health, and dignity of the Marshallese nation. International attention to this history and experience is long overdue, and sadly and sorely relevant to a post-Fukushima world.

6.4

THE WAR ON TERROR, DISMANTLING, AND THE CONSTRUCTION OF PLACE
An Ethnographic Perspective from Palestine
Julie Peteet

For Palestinians in the West Bank and displaced Iraqis, the vision of the "new Middle East" encompasses a significant remapping and corresponding reterritorializing of people with serious consequences for demography, mobility, access to resources, and human rights. . . . In both Palestine and Iraq, a strategy of control exercised through extreme violence, separation, and confinement crafts spaces where a particular form of power is wielded and a vision of the ethnic, sectarian, and national composition of space is enacted. . . . On a regional level, a new colonial cartography is taking shape in the Middle East (Khalidi 2004). . . .

Centered in once largely secular Iraq, the war on terror unleashed sectarian (Sunni and Shia) and ethnic (Arab, Kurdish, and Turkmen) violence and dismantled the geography and notion of a unified, secular Iraq. . . . A temporal dimension can be discerned here, as well, that resonates with Palestine: the U.S. administration imagined Iraqis as memoryless; the past and collective memory were to recede into the background. The looting of the National Museum of Iraq certainly fits this mode of thinking. Israelis have long attempted to deny Palestinians a past in the space of Palestine; Iraqis and Palestinians are to have a future, just not one of their own making. . . .

Zionism, which posits ethnic and religious affiliation as the basis of political belonging and the allocation of rights, conceives of the region as an ethnic and sectarian mosaic. Concomitantly, Israel has consistently rejected the notion of a secular, democratic state of its citizens. In Iraq, U.S. actions also point to such a conceptualization, with each ostensibly bounded group increasingly occupying its own geospatial enclave and with political power and representation apportioned by sect. It has taken incredible levels of violence to force Iraqis into sectarian and ethnic enclaves. . . . The impulse to territorialize—to separate, segregate, and miniaturize—is apparent in both Israel-Palestine and Iraq. . . .

Ethnography of Closure: "Permission to Breathe"

What is now known as "closure" began in 1991 when Israeli checkpoints suddenly mushroomed around Jerusalem to control Palestinian access to the city. "Closure" refers to Israeli restrictions on the movement of Palestinian goods, labor, and people into Jerusalem, within and between the Gaza Strip and the West Bank, and between them and Israel. Illegal Israeli settlements and closure, with its wall, bypass roads, permit and visa system, and checkpoints—around five hundred checkpoints dot the landscape of the West Bank—form an interlocking set of architectural and bureaucratic controls over Palestinian mobility. These spatial features, architectural forms, and bureaucratic rules facilitate the continuing acquisition of Palestinian land and natural resources, impose economic crisis, and incorporate significant tracts of the West Bank into Israel. . . .

Our sense of distance is socially produced and often violently so, especially in Palestine. With closure, once short distances have become monumental exercises in mobility, fraught with anxiety and danger. . . . Spatial tactics that limit Palestinian mobility encapsulate and thus clarify and make visible and tactile the social hierarchy.

Current Israeli spatial practices in the West Bank are components of a continuing policy to dilute an Arab presence in historic Palestine. Palestinian refugee camps are spaces where those excised from the new Jewish state in 1948 were relegated and managed as a population. . . . Closure to effect demographic transformation has been Israeli policy; its goal is to *remove the land* from them and reduce their numbers—to make Palestinian places into empty space that, through Jewish settlement and the extension of sovereignty, can then be reconfigured as exclusively Jewish places. . . . Draconian controls over the economy and mobility, as well as pervasive settler and military violence, proceed apace and are intended to encourage emigration, also known as slow-motion ethnic cleansing. . . . Ultimately, the goal seems to be to generate migrants rather than refugees who have a legal status and a presence in the international arena.

Closure: Chaos and Transforming the Landscape

In a number of public talks, the Israeli journalist Amira Hass has referred to settlements, checkpoints, road barriers, and the wall as "the violence of cement." Landscape is the meaning imputed to the environment and its inscription with meaning, referring to the way people narrate space. Israeli settlements, checkpoints, military installations, blocks of cement obstructing roads, barbed wire, trenches, and bypass roads, starkly etched into the rural topography, scar the landscape of Palestine. The wall's rough cement slabs speak to the raw power to immiserate. Jewish settlements, illegal according to international law, now house 430,000 Jewish settlers. . . .

Closure's most immediate effect has been to obstruct Palestinian mobility. In trying to grasp daily life ethnographically, I came up with the phrase "calibrated chaos." An acquaintance working with a nongovernmental organization said, "The soldiers have told us chaos is their policy." Control through the imposition of calibrated chaos, the conscious policy of changing rules and regulations at will, with no warning or explanation, is accomplished through a rich variety of techniques to inhibit mobility and induce anxiety: checkpoints, the wall, metal gates, earth mounds, trenches, and concrete slabs that block access to villages as well as the permit system. Intermittent and prolonged curfews punctuate these measures. Unpredictability is now the norm; it shatters trust in the routines of daily life. . . .

If the wall divides a town and the hospital is on other side, Palestinians may have to drive for hours, through multiple checkpoints, to reach a hospital that is just a few miles away. Ambulances are routinely obstructed at checkpoints. Soldiers step into them and check the wounded, often causing delays; sometimes they compel patients to walk or be carried through the checkpoint to take another ambulance on the other side. Closure has produced mass impoverishment because of the lack of work and lack of access to markets in Israel. Seventy-five percent of Palestinians live below the poverty line, a figure that has tripled since 2000. . . . Palestinians are suffering a collective and individual loss of control over the most basic elements of daily life. . . .

Mobility, Checkpoints, and Permission to Move

Palestinian mobility is a scarce commodity, almost completely under Israeli control, a tangible thing that Israelis have and Palestinians are denied. Spatial difference is arbitrarily imposed on contiguous spaces and is activated by barriers that control mobility. . . . Checkpoints are spaces where the body is forced to undergo a disciplinary regime of coercive and subordinating power. Israeli power is displayed and strutted in this highly performative encounter between two vastly unequal sides. The participants know the script well; there is little ambiguity in this encounter. Enacting the script reaffirms and reproduces Palestinian subordination and Israeli rule. The sectarian and ethnic basis to mobility is part and parcel of a regional remapping and the differential allocation of access to space and mobility. It is similar to that which now exists in Iraq, where mobility is determined by sectarian identity, which can be a ticket to mobility or a death sentence.

Checkpoints range from small posts manned by two or three soldiers to large sites such as Kalandia (just outside Jerusalem), which resembles an international border through which thousands of people are processed every day. Only those with Jerusalem identity cards or a permit to enter the city are allowed to enter the Jerusalem side. Long lines at checkpoints are standard; metal turnstiles force the body into an assembly line procedure of mobility.... The rules of opening and closing checkpoints are quite arbitrary; one can wait hours or minutes, regardless of how many cars are there or how many soldiers. The soldiers take everyone's papers and often disappear, usually without a word, and return them, sometimes quickly and sometimes hours later.... People are forced to wait in cars in the heat or cold; this can be quite difficult for the elderly and those with small children.... Palestinians watch bitterly as Israeli cars whiz through checkpoints with a friendly wave of the hand and a smile while Palestinian cars wait for permission to pass....

In expansionist settler-colonial projects, the familiar landscape rapidly becomes the strange and unknown. Dramatic changes, such as new settlements, checkpoints and flying checkpoints, and new signage in a foreign language are disorienting to those who know the terrain through a lifetime of intimate use. Palestinians now have a new lexicon of topographic names and spatial locators, which continue to expand as new spatial tactics are devised: flying checkpoints; terminals; underground passages; gates; areas A, B, and C; and bypass roads. This new geography of the homeland and its lexicon are embodied as well. The Palestinian collective is being fragmented by multiple kinds of identity cards and permits endowing each individual holder with varying degrees of mobility and differential access to space, and thus different privileges. The Palestinian body is perceived as transgressive and thus subject to extensive regulation; it is punished for the smallest infraction and sometimes for no infraction at all. Beatings, arrests, confiscations of the identity card, forced waiting, and shootings face the Palestinian body that transgresses Israeli rules of access to space....

Access to the road system in the West Bank is organized according to ethnic and national affiliations. Only cars with Israeli plates can drive on the well-paved bypass roads; these crosscut the West Bank and connect settlements to Israel. They allow settlers direct access to Israel without having to drive through Palestinian areas. Cars have color-coded license plates so their drivers can be easily identified. Bypass roads and the wall now prevent line of sight. In other words, Israeli settlers do not have to see the indigenous population. Their line of vision includes colorful pastoral scenes painted on the Israeli side of the wall; the Palestinian side has eye-riveting graffiti graphically expressing protest, anger, and solidarity. . . .

The permit system permeates the minutest details of everyday life. . . . For example, Selma has a Palestinian West Bank identity but is married to a Palestinian with a Jerusalem identity. Palestinians who do not possess an Israeli-issued Jerusalem identity card are not allowed in the city without a permit, even if they are married to a Jerusalem identity card holder. . . . The policy of closure, identity cards, and permits determines Palestinian mobility, enhances chaos, and generates uncertainty and anxiety. [Selma said:]

> If I had known it would be like this I wouldn't have married him! I have a baby girl. We are living in Beit Hanina, very close to Jerusalem and Ramallah. . . . I have to pass checkpoints to go home. My daughter is registered with her father. She cannot travel with me because she is registered with him. If I try to give her a Palestinian identity and passport, she will lose the Jerusalem identity.
>
> When I gave birth, my husband managed to bring my mother. . . . I remember once she was supposed to come to the hospital, but no taxi would take her. They asked her, "Do you have a Jerusalem identity?" She told them, "No I have a West Bank identity." And they said, "Sorry, we can't." So no taxi would take her; they don't want to be imprisoned for driving someone without a Jerusalem identity card. So I spent the day alone. . . . The future—it is so dark. . . .

The Wall

An age-old technique of controlling population movements, defending territory, and quelling resistance, walls are hardly a historical novelty. Indeed, the Great Wall of China and Hadrian's Wall in England, built to prevent "barbarian" incursions, are United Nations Educational, Scientific, and Cultural Organization World Heritage sites. The wall is also thought to indicate the drawing of a unilateral border. It could incorporate into Israel as much as 53 percent of the West Bank or as little as 10 percent.

The stark slabs of upright concrete form a cement wall that snakes through populated areas, punctuated by watchtowers and firing posts every three hundred meters or so. In some areas it is composed of razor-wire fence. Accompanying the wall is a one hundred- to three hundred-foot-wide buffer zone that often includes trenches, electric fencing, remote sensors, a parallel road for military patrols, and cameras. At nearly twenty-five feet high (eight meters—about three times the height of the Berlin Wall) and an estimated four hundred miles (seven hundred kilometers) in length, it is significantly longer than the twelve kilometer Berlin Wall.

Palestinians argue that if security were the issue, [the wall] could have been built on the Green Line [the pre-1967 border]. Yet tellingly, it is deep in Palestinian territory. In some places it extends up to fourteen miles into Palestinian territory and indeed cuts the West Bank into three parts, making the territorial contiguity of a Palestinian state dubious. The wall erases the 1967 border and isolates Jerusalem. . . . To construct the wall and its buffer zone has meant large-scale house demolition; thousands of acres of agricultural land have been confiscated, and thousands of trees have been uprooted. Some small towns and villages are completely surrounded by the wall, with only one point of entry and exit controlled by the Israelis. . . .

The New Cartography in the Middle East

Spatial fracturing and divisions that separate and transform landscape and place are crucial to maintaining and reproducing a hierarchy of access to natural resources, sovereignty, and human rights. Palestinian/Israeli difference is cast as one between spaces of law, civilization, and democracy and spaces of terror, lawlessness, and militant Islam. As such, the latter can be attacked without recourse to the conventions governing international conflict. Afghanistan, Palestine, Lebanon, and Iraq are all currently such spaces. . . .

Colonial and occupying regimes classify and partition space discursively and on the ground in such a way that eventually their meaning will become part of the taken-for-granted, routine aspects of daily life. The politics of space, enclosure, and displacement deprive those excluded from familiar places. Memories of past spatial formations may gradually fade as new memories are created in their place. At a time of a now tempered, although in some instances still celebratory, attitude toward transnational space and mobility, Israel has put Palestinians behind a wall to achieve demographic exclusion and national homogeneity, and Iraq has been effectively dismembered, and a significant proportion of its population has been displaced.

The colonial cartography being inscribed in the West Bank and Iraq is dramatically recrafting ethnic and sectarian spaces, the space of human rights, and national landscapes. In Palestine, the new spatial ordering allocates space, mobility, and rights according to ethnic-religious-national belonging. In this form of modern colonialism, spaces are hierarchized along a scale of premodern to modern coinciding with ethnicity and allocating rights and privileges accordingly. . . .

In pursuit of this policy, fragmentation of the region, the breakup of states along ethnic-sectarian lines, conforming to an Orientalist imagery of the region as a mosaic of "peoples and cultures," is materializing through invasions and prolonged occupations. The human cost has been continuing humanitarian crises and massive numbers of displaced. The most immediate lesson is that in pursuit of these policies the Arab world will not be allowed to control either its resources or its destiny. On the flip side, the level of sustained resistance by both Iraqis and Palestinians, in the face of the world's most technologically sophisticated military forces, shows little sign of abating.

6.5

THE BORDER WALL IS A METAPHOR
Jason De León (interviewed by Micheline Aharonian Marcom)

The border wall is a metaphor for all sorts of anxieties. . . . People still think that it's the solution to all of our problems, foreign and domestic. The problem is that the farther away you go from the U.S.-Mexico border, the less understanding people have about the border and how it's secured, so the idea of what the border looks like is fundamentally flawed for most of the general American public. But obviously, every election cycle we see right-leaning politicians really playing up on border security, on the role that a potential gigantic wall could play in defending the country from terrorism, from undocumented migrants.

The Walls Today

The walls that exist currently are around ports of entry. They're fairly difficult to scale over because they're so tall, although people do it. But once you hop over that wall, there are hundreds of agents on the ground, there are motion detectors, there are infrared cameras. It's really difficult to cross into the United States at a port of entry.

But if you walk five miles west of a town like Nogales, Mexico, you get to the desert, and the only thing between the United States and Mexico is a two-strand, three-strand, barbed wire fence. There are no agents waiting there because they know that if you really want to get into this country, you will first have to walk thirty-five miles through one of the most remote and inhospitable natural environments in the Western Hemisphere.

The Natural Environment as a Weapon

Prior to the 1990s, the U.S.-Mexico border was a much more fluid space. People were moving back and forth with relative ease. You didn't need a passport to go into Mexico, and for the most part, it was pretty easy to get across the U.S.-Mexico border into border towns. People didn't have to walk for six days through the Arizona desert; they didn't have to walk twenty miles east or west of a port of entry to find a place where they could get through. It was a pretty easy time to move back and forth.

Our take on border security has evolved over the past two to three decades. Policies were put into place to exploit the natural environment as a weapon against undocumented migration. The idea was: we can't stop people with a wall, but we can redirect them. Some strategist at Border Patrol eventually said, "If we force people to try to cross the border in those areas where it's hundreds of square miles of wilderness, where they can drown crossing the American Canal in San Diego, or die in the desert of dehydration or heatstroke—those things that are natural deterrents to migration—they can be used effectively against migrants."

Everybody knows that it's a lot cheaper to use the desert as a deterrent than it is to try to construct a wall there.

Post-9/11

Following 9/11, we had a surge in people signing up for the Border Patrol. I know a lot of agents who are good-hearted, sensitive people who joined the Border Patrol to fight terrorism. We sold it to them. The government sold these recruits by saying, "You join the Border Patrol and your number-one job will be to protect the homeland from terrorists." The sleight of hand that has happened is that we now conflate terrorism with undocumented migration across the southern border. And there has been no evidence that terrorists are coming across the U.S.-Mexico border. We do know that terrorists come through official ports of entry: they come with fake identification cards, they come with Green Cards, they overstay visas. But we have done this incredible sleight of hand to confuse these things.

We spend billions of dollars on border security. We've militarized the border, put more agents on the ground, but we haven't necessarily slowed down border crossers. But it made a lot of government contractors incredibly wealthy. A lot of it has been shown to not be very effective.

We Are All Involved

I think we, the American public, want these very simple answers. We want to narrow things down to: "Tell me who the bad person is." Or "How do we keep folks out?" Nobody wants to hear about the messiness of stuff, right?

So we say, "We're worried about Mexico as a failed state, the narco-state." But we're not worried about who's supplying them with guns. We're not really worried about who's snorting the cocaine and the other things they're producing that are leading to these violent things that are happening in that country—the accountability stuff.

I think that's a very difficult thing for the American public to wrap its head around: that we are all involved in this process. The things that we do in the United States impact the things, obviously, that happen in Central America, that happen in Mexico, and in many ways, we created this problem. . . .

Interconnectedness

I had a journalist once, a British journalist, ask me about immigration reform. She said, "What are some policy solutions?"

I said I think the best place to start for any kind of immigration reform is to work on political and economic stability in these countries where people are fleeing. Doesn't matter what we do at the border, doesn't matter how many people we give amnesty to, or Green Cards to, people are still going to be coming if things are horrible in their home countries. We need to be responsible and figure out what we can do to help out these situations.

And this person said to me, "Well, don't you think that that's those countries' problems? Shouldn't Mexico fix itself?" And that is the problem. We have to think about these countries as being partners, true partners. Not just partners we can get cheap labor from, or outsource jobs to, but partners. It shouldn't be combative, because I think we look for them to be friendly to us when we need stuff, but then we're incredibly combative when we don't like things that are going on here. It's very frustrating that we're just not globally aware, as a country, about all of these things.

I'm trying to get people to think more globally and understand that, number one, it's inescapable: we are a globalized world now, and these isolationist policies aren't going do us any good. We're moving forward with globalization, and it can go one of two ways. We can either work for it to be productive and positive, or we can maintain the status quo, which is going to end so poorly for so many people, both here in this country and elsewhere. But it's disheartening. And I think if I had to say anything about the kind of current stuff, at least with the Central Americans, is that people need to start conceptualizing the migrant experience as one that is not wholly economic—at least, not in terms of the driving motivation to leave home. This problem is not going anywhere anytime soon.

I'VE HAD SOME very difficult things happen during the process of this work. I had a very good friend, a kid that I worked with last year, who was murdered right after I left Mexico. And I had two choices. It was either stay in a kind of depression that I had fallen into following that event or pick myself up and figure [it] out. . . . I told him I was going to write his story, and now I've got to do that. He trusted me enough to share a lot of his life with me, so it's a mutual kind of relationship. . . . If I can raise awareness about these global inequalities and not just tell an immigration story, but tell a human story, that's what I want to do.

FIG 7.0. In many regions of the world, the provision of humanitarian aid is increasingly handed over to local, foreign, and multinational military forces. Here, soldiers from the Philippine Army help the British crew of a Royal Air Force transport plane deliver aid to victims of Typhoon Haiyan in 2013. Intertwining humanitarian aid and military intervention enables new forms of military occupation and the militarization of social life. Photograph by Russell Watkins/U.K. Department for International Development.

SECTION VII. MILITARIZED HUMANITARIANISM

Compiled by CATHERINE BESTEMAN

Introduction

This section charts the turn toward military intervention for purportedly humanitarian purposes since the 1990s by the United Nations and relief agencies for managing complex emergencies such as famines, civil and regional wars, and natural disasters. The section begins with Mariella Pandolfi's call for critical analyses of the power dynamics and discourses that emerge from and structure zones of humanitarian-military intervention as "states of exception," in which foreign military and humanitarian actors attempt to implement local transformation according to utopic universalizing models. Michael Barnett provides an overview of the decision-making processes that resulted in humanitarian military interventions in Somalia and Kosovo, analyzing the implications for humanitarian nongovernmental organizations (NGOs) working in those areas as the form of military intervention shifted from protecting relief workers to supervising relief operations. Barnett echoes the charges by other researchers, such as Alex de Waal, who resigned from Human Rights Watch in 1992 to protest that organization's support for U.S. military intervention to protect food relief efforts in Somalia, that military interventions in humanitarian disasters have worsened rather than alleviated conflict.

The remaining essays examine the local and global power dynamics that structure and legitimize militarized humanitarian interventions. Anne Orford poses the difficult question of when and why it is considered acceptable to kill in the name of humanitarianism. Orford queries the moral calculus that justifies civilian death and absolves killers in contexts of "international" interventions. Mahmood Mamdani suggests that the powerful countries, including the United

States and its European allies, call themselves "the international community" and use the language and tools of humanitarianism to police and intervene in weaker countries, while, as Orford notes, escaping accountability for their own humanitarian crimes. Mamdani questions the moral calculus that assigns different understandings to the 2003–2004 violence in Sudan and the 2003 U.S. invasion of Iraq, resulting in an indictment at the International Criminal Court for one president but not the other. Finally, Chowra Makaremi examines the new United Nations discourse of "human security," which when allied with the United Nations–endorsed concept of the "responsibility to protect" (R2P) extends the role of international intervention to promote security through militarized humanitarian interventions by the powerful North in places in the global South labeled as chaotic or anarchic.

Together, these essays chart the transformation in humanitarian ideology and practice from the Cold War years, when relief agencies promoted the goal of political neutrality, through the 1990s, when some relief agencies began calling for military intervention in complex emergencies, to the 2000s when the concept of R2P emerged and humanitarianism became a justification for military intervention to effect regime change. The essays scrutinize the implications of military intervention for relief operations in conflict zones, arguing that such intervention often exacerbates conflict and hinders local conflict resolution. Amid this New Humanitarian Order, these authors warn that more powerful governments will hijack the moral authority of humanitarianism to use military force to pursue their own interests in weaker regions and will face no accountability for the violence unleashed in the name of saving lives.

READINGS

edited by Didier Fassin and Mariella Pandolfi (New York: Zone, 2010), 335–56.

7.4 Excerpts from Mahmood Mamdani, "Responsibility to Protect or Right to Punish?" *Journal of Intervention and Statebuilding* 4, no. 1 (2010): 53–67.

7.5 Excerpts from Chowra Makaremi, "Utopias of Power: From Human Security to the Responsibility to Protect," in *Contemporary States of Emergency: The Politics of Military and Humanitarian Interventions*, edited by Didier Fassin and Mariella Pandolfi (New York: Zone, 2010), 107–27.

7.1

LABORATORY OF INTERVENTION

The Humanitarian Governance of the Postcommunist Balkan Territories
Mariella Pandolfi

In order to understand the role that anthropologists stand to play in laying bare the dynamics of humanitarian intervention, it is necessary to reflect on how we can conceive of humanitarian intervention in the context of new global and local landscapes. Intervention most often occurs in areas undergoing rapid transformation. Intervention is a necessarily mobile phenomenon and can be conceived of as the complex deployment of a network of military forces, non-governmental organizations (NGOs), and international institutions, including, among others, United Nations agencies, the International Monetary Fund, the World Bank, and the Organization for Security and Cooperation in Europe. It is difficult to define humanitarian intervention according to specific "goals" or technical means because these are constantly changing in light of shifting local and global circumstances.

For example, the United Nations first approached the subject of humanitarian intervention through the notion of "complex emergencies." This concept was used to denote a phenomenon characterized by a host of causes (including conflict, war, and famine) and requiring a diverse array of responses (such as military, peacekeeping, and relief efforts). This militarized approach to humanitarian intervention would later replace the humanist approach, exemplified by the category "the right of interference." This category emerged out of the European, and particularly French, humanist tradition and became a dominant force in the humanitarian realm in the 1980s. Against the backdrop of a new world order, the international community relied on this new notion to lay claim to its right to interfere in any area for the purpose of upholding human rights. Most recently, the terminology of humanitarian efforts has shifted again, inventing a new discourse: "the responsibility to protect." This term was instituted in 2005 and was specifically aimed at protecting populations from genocide, ethnic cleansing, and other crimes against humanity. If a government is deemed unwilling to protect or incapable of protecting its own citizens, this doctrine asserts that the international community has the duty to ensure the protection of that state's citizens. This final categorization of humanitarian intervention represents the merging of prior militaristic and humanist perspectives, for it unites the benevolent responsibility to intervene in times of suffering with an unquestionable right to employ force in the protection of global citizens.

Indeed, intervention has been the preferred foreign-policy tool of the post–Cold War order, and over the years it has taken on many guises: "humanitarian" when it seeks to redress the suffering of civilian populations; "military" when it seeks to restore international security and order; and "political" when it seeks to reconstruct states and societies. As a flexible tool that can he applied both to postcommunist societies in "transition" and to societies in the aftermath of war, intervention has become a common foreign-policy solution to the varied crises of our times. Intervention is the standard response of an outside force to the local problems of societies undergoing multiple, simultaneous transitions. It is composed of a set of complex social relations that exist within a particular framework of power and a landscape marked by a distinct temporality and a politics of "emergency." The procedures of intervention are justified in the name of coping with "economic" and "democratic" emergencies. The "emergency" period is an administrative definition that permits the loosening of rules for the allocation and distribution of resources, irrespective of the situation on the ground. Yet these procedures often provoke shifts in power where local populations lose control over the agenda of political reform and the processes that create new social hierarchies (Lafontaine 2002).

Whether speaking of the dissolution of Yugoslavia or regime change in Afghanistan and Iraq, intervention entails the invocation of a particular "state of exception" (Agamben [1995] 1998, [1995] 2000, [2003] 2005), a suspension of previously valid norms and rules arising not only from the collapse of existing social and political structures but from the fact of intervention itself. Intervention presupposes the very exceptions it creates. Speaking in terms of power, is it possible to conceive of this reduction in terms of what Michael Hardt and

Antonio Negri (2000) define as "empire"? Examining this issue from the point of view of populations, it might be useful to reflect on Giorgio Agamben's radical biopolitics of "bare life."

As Mark Duffield (2004: 13) underlines, "The insistence that humanitarianism is 'neutral' and separate from politics, means that humanitarians can only grasp human life as bare life. By excluding the political, humanitarianism reproduces the isolation of bare life and hence the basis of sovereignty itself." While Agamben ([1995] 1998, [1995] 2000) worked in a very different context, his theoretically evocative approach to biopolitics offers important insight into the dynamics of power at work in the new realm of humanitarian intervention (Pandolfi 2000).

This deeply political and inherently mobile field poses many challenges for anthropological fieldwork. It is challenging for anthropologists to work in a field that is so widely covered by the media. Yet anthropological expertise has much to offer to this situation, for anthropologists are particularly adept at calling into question the logics associated with emergencies and "humanitarian catastrophes." Humanitarian intervention clings to international institutions and to certain segments of local elites, weakening the society that it proposes to reconstruct. It works on fragile territories whose tenuous position renders them porous to the imposition of Western political logic. Anthropological studies demonstrate that humanitarian intervention conceals the link between its actions and the priorities of Western states by relying on a rhetoric of generosity and the claim that its actions are independent of political forces. The links between military and humanitarian intervention have long been obscured, necessitating a critical examination of the strategies driving humanitarian intervention and the risks inherent in invoking the right to interfere. . . .

Since the mid-1990s we have witnessed the exponential and uncritical growth of what I call a "gray zone" among humanitarian intervention, military humanitarianism (Pandolfi 2006), and the humanitarian war. The gray zone is a fluid space that is alternatively political, civil, and military in nature. This varied space confronts us with an ambiguity that undermines humanitarian intervention (Prendergast 1997). The mixing of military and humanitarian aid results in a hybrid dislocation of political space (Pandolfi and Abélès 2002) that is "locally constructed" around a mobile international community, composed of both civil and military experts. This gray space acts as a third social actor within a universalizing, apolitical utopia, intended to promote and maintain peace and bring aid to the victims of emergencies. This procedure is enacted in a top-down manner that places itself squarely within a space that is neither local nor national. This new space is sustained by a standard universal discourse that progressively eliminates all historical and cultural contextualization. This new zone progressively marginalizes the kind of contextualized accounts produced by anthropologists and promotes prefabricated schemes produced by international human rights lawyers and political scientists. These schemes outline standardized responses to violations of human rights, the exportation of democratic institutions, and the construction of new civil society. Within this new gray zone, humanitarian actors tend to focus narrowly on their work at the local level. . . .

Positing humanitarian and military intervention as the object of fieldwork raises two important issues for anthropologists: marginality and the politics of collaboration. . . . Given their limited access to the field, anthropologists have not been able to study the impacts that the international military and civilian presence have had on local society.

Anthropological fieldwork in humanitarian and military zones raises thorny issues that can be summarized under the term "politics of collaboration." Anthropologists may take on a collaborative role in such settings, becoming directly involved in the humanitarian industry as volunteer workers or "experts," or as officers or project directors. If an anthropologist becomes professionalized within the industry it is difficult for him or her to maintain a critical perspective. Anthropologists working in these situations are often pulled in opposing directions. Faced with the very real problems of human suffering it is difficult for anthropologists to refrain from intervening. Yet intervention complicates an anthropologist's ability to maintain a critical and distanced stance.

The temptation, therefore, is to treat the humanitarian industry in a way that is perhaps not dissimilar from how our disciplinary ancestors treated their isolated villages: as remnants of a pure precapitalist solidarity. Yet wars and postwar zones are no place for fabricated utopias, and critical anthropological work on humanitarian intervention must testify to the more difficult truths that remain once the media spotlight has dimmed. There is an urgent need for anthropology to critically address this issue that so radically departs from the discipline's classic, focused engagement with a single locality and its local social group, language, and culture. The humanitarian industry is a primary effect of globalization (Stiglitz 2002) and as such invites the attention of contemporary anthropology (Abélès 2006; Agier 2002; Appadurai 1996; Fassin and Vasquez 2005).

ARMED FOR HUMANITY
Michael Barnett

Violence is part of humanitarianism's history. The violence we usually associate with humanitarianism is the violence that causes humanitarian action. But there also is the violence deployed in the name of humanitarianism. As famously observed by Hannah Arendt, the first signs that humanitarianism could legitimate bloodshed occurred with the French Revolution, when proclamations of humanity, fraternity, and liberty inspired beheadings, riotous behavior, and mass killings. Some of the greatest crimes of the past few centuries have been carried out in the name of alleviating suffering and improving human welfare. Violence also has been justified for protecting those whose lives are at immediate risk from malevolent forces, a notion closely associated with humanitarian intervention. Not everyone who claims to be a humanitarian shares the same views regarding the use of force for protecting lives. Some see humanitarian intervention as a necessary possibility. Others ridicule the idea of humanitarian war as an oxymoron or insist that if war must be waged in the defense of human rights, it should be called anything but humanitarian. These debates regarding the relationship between humanitarian action and the use of force are as old as humanitarianism itself, but in the last decade of the last century they became a point of controversy among humanitarian organizations. . . .

Although various events over the 1990s reflected the meandering and momentary reactions of aid agencies to the use of force during emergencies, Somalia, Bosnia, Rwanda, and Kosovo were the most consequential. Over the course of the decade, a silent pattern developed: whereas at the beginning of the decade aid agencies tried to recruit states for their cause, by the beginning of the next decade they had discovered that states had already coopted humanitarianism for their interests.

Somalia and Armed Protection

Beginning in the late 1980s a power struggle erupted in Somalia. At the outset, the contest was between the Ethiopian-funded Somali National Movement (SNM) and the Somali government of Siad Barre, but it took a violent turn in 1988 when the SNM launched a guerrilla war against Siad. An increasingly unpopular Siad began to retaliate severely and indiscriminately, and soon thereafter it seemed as if every clan had its own militia and was vying for political power. The greatest military threat, however, came from General Mohamed Farrah Aidid, and he defeated Siad in 1991, resulting not in his coronation but, rather, in an increase in clan-on-clan violence. Their war destroyed most urban centers, political institutions, and the economy and left upward of twenty thousand civilian casualties, a million displaced people, and the specter of mass starvation.[1]

Nongovernmental organizations wandered into a situation unlike anything previously encountered. There was no central government, not even in name only. There were dozens of militias, each answering only to themselves. Nor were they fighting for the familiar ideological goals of the Cold War. Instead, they seemed to be motivated by a strange mixture of long-standing grudges, new power plays for political power, turf protection, and revenge. Aid organizations confronted a bewildering maze of violence and politics as they attempted to negotiate access to the hundreds of thousands of Somalis who were on the verge of starvation. In order to have the privilege of delivering assistance, the militias extorted food aid from the relief agencies. If they did not comply, then either they would not be allowed to pass or they would be attacked (de Waal 1998: 168–79).

Aid agencies had several alternatives, none of them good. They could decide to withdraw, but with fatal consequences for those in the camps. Or they could hire "protection" from the local clans. James Orbinski [of the NGO Médecins sans Frontières (MSF)] captures the moment well: "The needs were overwhelming. Some of the old humanitarian rules of neutrality and independence seemed to be falling apart, and it wasn't clear what the new rules would be. For the first time ever, the Red Cross, MSF, and other aid agencies were paying armed guards from various clans to protect aid workers and food supplies (Orbinski 2008: 81). But still the militias were able to make out like the bandits that they were, confiscating, according to various estimates, anywhere from 20 percent to 80 percent of the food, depending on the time and place (Foley 2010: 54–55). The only way to secure aid from the poachers was to be protected by a local clan. Once a group did that, though, its neutrality became suspect. Nevertheless, aid workers could operate in relative safety, captured by the following exchange. One worker asked another whether they were at risk of being shot. No, the other replied, "Because if we get shot, then the NGOs leave, and there's nobody left to pay protection money or salaries. They want us afraid and alive. So you should be afraid and happy, because it means you can work. It's a little fucked up, isn't it?" ([quoted in] Orbinski 2008: 81). In any event, the aid agencies quickly realized that they were contributing to the famine because the militias had every intention of keeping it alive in order to keep the aid flowing.

Given the unprecedented nature of the challenge—or, at any rate, the belief that Somalia had no precedents—aid agencies had no ready-made answers for how to provide relief without also fueling the war.

One possible escape from this nightmare was an international force. Various NGOs, alongside a growing number of United Nations officials and human rights activists, began campaigning for a humanitarian intervention. After a gun battle ensued when a Cooperative for Assistance and Relief Everywhere (CARE) convoy refused to give a payout to the militias, killing five relief workers, CARE's president, Philip Johnston, began to call for armed protection, appealing to the United States, the United Nations, and anyone else who would listen; in his judgment, this was the only way to save starving Somalis. Unlike years before when no one would have bothered to listen, in this early post–Cold War moment the United Nations was beginning to consider various forms of armed intervention in the defense of human life.

In 1991, the United Nations established Operation Provide Comfort to provide aid to the Kurds who were fleeing Saddam Hussein, and the following year it began playing a role in Bosnia. For a mixture of reasons, including a desire to demonstrate that the United Nations also cared about emergencies in Africa, the UN Security Council decided to provide armed protection for the relief convoys, which proved to be the first step on a slippery slope toward an all-out war between United Nations forces and Mohamed Farrah Aidid. Not only did most aid agencies go along with a new arrangement that they helped to create, which some later sarcastically dubbed "Operation Shoot to Feed," but many American NGOs, operating under their umbrella organization, Interaction, began pushing Washington and New York to up the ante. But not everyone was thrilled by this; the European NGOs in particular were generally unified that this was a bad idea (Rutherford 2008: 96). Médecins sans Frontières had reluctantly agreed to seek the protection of local militias, but the situation became intolerable when the United Nations began doing "peace enforcement." As Rony Brauman reflected, it became impossible to contemplate humanitarian neutrality when licensed defenders were firing into crowds and delivering aid directly to the very people who were the executioners of the population: "For the first time in Somalia, they killed under the banner of humanitarianism" (Vallaeys 2004: 509–10). Médecins sans Frontières closed the mission and walked away, leaving other agencies to deal with the dilemmas. Asked whether he has any regrets, Johnston said, "Hell no. Hell no."[2] While armed force might now be possible, aid agencies relied on their instincts, often fueled more by passions than by well-honed ideas. . . .

Kosovo and Humanitarian War

Kosovo was an autonomous province of the Yugoslav Republic until 1990, when Yugoslav President Slobodan Milošević formally abolished its autonomy. The situation in Kosovo remained fairly stable during the Yugoslavian Wars, but once they ended, it deteriorated. In response to continuing repression by the Federal Republic of Yugoslavia, a previously unknown organization, the Kosovo Liberation Army (KLA), carried out a series of attacks in April 1996. . . . In March 1998, the Security Council adopted Resolution 1160, which called on the KLA and Belgrade to negotiate a political settlement, imposed an arms embargo on both parties, and warned of the "consideration of additional measures" in the absence of progress toward a peaceful solution. . . . In June, UN Secretary-General Kofi Annan informed the North Atlantic Treaty Organization (NATO) of the possible need for the Security Council to authorize military action. In September, the Security Council adopted Resolution 1199 declaring that Kosovo was a "threat to peace and security in the region." . . .

Citing "humanitarian intervention" as the legal justification for any possible use of force, on October 9, 1998, NATO Secretary-General Javier Solana warned of future military action if Belgrade did not comply with international demands.[3] . . . Following through on its threat, NATO launched air strikes on March 24, its first active military encounter in its fifty-year history. Many world leaders, from Czech President Václav Havel to U.S. President Bill Clinton, offered the decision to bomb Kosovo as evidence of cosmopolitanism and a growing sense of international community. . . .

The NATO bombing campaign, however, seemed to trigger the very humanitarian emergency it was designed to prevent. Milošević responded by unleashing a torrent of ethnic cleansing, causing hundreds of thousands of Kosovar Albanians to flee. Within two weeks, a half-million Kosovars had crossed into Albania and gathered at the Macedonian border, producing the largest refugee flight in Europe since World War II. This spectacle—mass displacement caused by a humanitarian war—was quickly becoming a major public relations disaster for an organization that had initially seen this operation as a public relations savior. . . . But NATO was not the only organization overwhelmed by the flood of refugees. So, too, were the United Nations High Commissioner for Refugees (UNHCR), the lead humanitarian agency, and most relief agencies. In any event, it was NATO that was accused of creating the situation, and it was NATO that was expected to do something about it. Given all of this, NATO decided that relief was too important to be left to the relief agencies (Orbinski 2008; Suhrke et al. 2000). It began holding immediate discussions with the UNHCR.

On April 3, 1999, one day before NATO's fiftieth anniversary, UN High Commissioner Sadako Ogata requested NATO's assistance. This was an unprecedented and highly controversial decision because never before had the UNHCR approached a combatant for direct assistance. Many at the UNHCR objected on the grounds that whatever temporary benefit the UNHCR might receive from NATO's assistance would be outweighed by the cost to its independence and ability to work in the field. Ogata overruled these objections on the grounds that the UNHCR needed NATO to help overcome Macedonia's unwillingness to permit entry of refugees (the government feared destabilizing the ethnic balance) and logistical problems in Albania (Morris 1999; Ogata 2005); NATO stepped in and acted as a "surge protector" (Minear et al. 2000). . . .

The North Atlantic Treaty Organization became a "full-service" relief agency, helping to build camps, distribute relief, ensure security, coordinate the actions of relief agencies—and set the agenda (Rieff 2002: 204). Its decision to overstay its welcome and extend its activities into unauthorized areas had relatively little to do with the needs of the refugees and everything to do with NATO's need to maintain support for the air campaign (Porter 2000: 5). By continuing to play a coordinating role, NATO was able to cast its actions as humanitarian and thus continue to legitimate the war. . . .

Although most agencies resented the hit to their autonomy, the surprise was that there was little outrage or outright rebellion. After all, the same agencies that had strenuously guarded their humanitarian space—their independence, impartiality, and neutrality—in places such as the Congo and Sudan were now working alongside, getting assistance from, and being directed by a combatant—and doing so with relative ease (Vaux 2001: 66–67). Médecins sans Frontières was one of the few organizations that refused to participate on the grounds that doing so violated basic principles of humanitarian action and placed refugees at risk (Roggo 2000). In general, while some NGOs attempted to distinguish themselves from governments, one observer concluded that "most were happy to go along with these arrangements" (Porter 2000: 5).

Why? Certainly, some relief organizations believed that they had little choice. The financial independence of MSF might allow it to walk away, but those agencies that relied on Western funders could not be so high-minded. To criticize NATO's heavy-handed presence in the humanitarian operation overtly or to refuse to work in camps run by their own governments would have cut against their short- and long-term interests . . . (Porter 2000: 5).

Yet their willingness to ally themselves with NATO also owed to their perception that they were on the same side. Many openly supported NATO action because they had watched the lack of a response to Bosnia and now were desperately worried they were about to see indifference redux" (Orbinski 2008: 326). . . . As the violence continued with no political settlement in sight, more agencies made increasingly urgent appeals for a more forceful response (Minear et al. 2000). Accordingly, once the diplomatic talks collapsed and the bombing began, they saw themselves as allied with NATO as part of a humanitarian operation designed to protect civilians. Oxfam appeared so enthralled with the idea of a NATO intervention that one journalist called the British Army "a bit like Oxfam's military wing" (Norton-Taylor, cited in Foley 2010: 36) In general, human rights organizations and relief agencies that had integrated a rights discourse into their operations turned out to be humanitarian warriors.

NOTES

1. For a good overview of the historical setting and a detailed account of the intervention, see Rutherford 2008.

2. Interview with the author.

3. See "Letter from Secretary-General Solana to Permanent Representatives of North Atlantic Council," October 9, 1998, cited in Simma 1999: 7.

7.3

THE PASSIONS OF PROTECTION
Sovereign Authority and Humanitarian War
Anne Orford

The centrality of the U.S. military to much humanitarian strategizing has not been seriously challenged. While much of the human rights movement has been properly appalled by the abuses carried out by U.S. military and security forces in the "war on terror," advocates of humanitarian intervention still do not question whether increased intervention by the U.S. military under its current rules of engagement offers the best strategy for the protection of individuals in Darfur or elsewhere. Indeed, in many critical appraisals of the conduct of the war on terror, politicians and their advisers are indicted, while the U.S. military and the existing laws of war are redeemed. . . .

At the same time, the push for greater military intervention in the name of protecting suffering peoples in Africa, Asia, and the Middle East has received an enormous boost through the adoption of the notion of the responsibility to protect in international relations. The language of the responsibility to protect has gradually colonized the legal and political debate internationally since its development by the International Commission on Intervention and State Sovereignty (ICISS) in 2001. The ICISS was an initiative sponsored by the Canadian government that was designed to respond to the perceived tension between state sovereignty and humanitarian intervention in the aftermath of the NATO action in Kosovo. When the concept of a responsibility to protect was introduced into the mainstream institutional debate by the ICISS report, it was presented as a new way of talking about humanitarian intervention, as well as a new way of talking about sovereignty. Both were organized around protection. This new way of talking about sovereignty was to argue that "its essence should now be seen not as control but as responsibility" (Evans 2006). If a state is unwilling or unable to meet this responsibility to protect its population, it then falls on the international community to do so. The new way of talking about humanitarian intervention involved recharacterizing the debate "not as an argument about any right at all but rather about a responsibility—one to protect people at grave risk." The people at grave risk were those "millions of human beings" who, in the words of the ICISS report, "remain at the mercy of civil wars, insurgencies, state repression and state collapse" (International Commission on Intervention and State Sovereignty 2001: 11). . . .

In this essay I am interested in making sense of the relation between these two features of contemporary international humanitarianism: the claim that the modern military state, and in particular the United States, has abandoned cruelty as an official instrument of warfare, and the claim that it is through increased international policing and military intervention that the state can be perfected and protection of those at risk achieved. . . .

The Calculation of Suffering

Both international humanitarian law and the broader legal prohibition against torture during war or peace can be understood as part of a modern project to eliminate what international law describes as "cruel, inhuman, or degrading treatment or punishment" (Asad 2003: 100–103). Humanitarian intervention can be understood as an extension of that project—as an attempt not just to prohibit, but to eliminate certain forms of suffering in this world. Central to this task is the distinction between torture and cruel, inhuman, or degrading treatment, on the one hand, and justifiable suffering, on the other. . . . International law, like modern statecraft, envisages that certain kinds of suffering are authorized. Some forms of suffering are understood as necessary or inevitable—in particular, the suffering that is authorized in terms of the reason of state or proportional to military necessity. International law thus prohibits suffering that is excessive, suffering that is beyond what is calculated as necessary to protect state security or to enable human flourishing. It is on the basis of this logic that the use of military force against peoples and territories in Africa, Asia, and the Middle East can be understood as humanitarian or that aerial bombardment can be understood as humane.

We can see this logic in action if we look at the ways in which international humanitarian law deals with the killing and wounding of civilians. The norms of international humanitarian law prohibit the targeting of civilians in armed conflict, requiring attackers to direct their actions against broadly defined "military objectives," rather than "civilian objects" (Rogers 2004). Civilians can be killed "incidentally," but the risk of endangering civilians as "collateral damage" must not be disproportionate to the military advantage to be gained by the attack (Fenrick 2001). The utilitarian language of this balancing test reveals that the lives of civilians can be sacrificed if the value of their existence is weighed against the importance of "military objectives" and found wanting. Similarly, while it is illegal to target purely civilian infrastructure, "dual-use" infrastructure can be targeted. "Dual use" relates to infrastructure that serves both a civilian and a military function. For instance, roads, electricity distribution systems, and communications networks might all have this dual function, depending on the extent to which they form part of the "command and control" aspect of a state's military activities. . . . The "harm to the civilian population" caused by attacks on dual-use targets must therefore be weighed against the military objectives that such attacks are calculated to achieve (Human Rights Watch 2003). . . .

The extent to which civilian deaths are seen as legitimate in conflict situations is dependent also on the determination of the facts of each case. In a subtle way, this also involves taking the perspective of the state in many situations of modern warfare. In international law, as in domestic law, the application of law depends on the determination of "facts." In the case of international humanitarian law and its capacity to protect civilians, these "facts" include decisions about whether the targeting of a particular object to further a military objective may pose a risk to civilians and whether particular infrastructure is "dual use." . . .

The questions prior to "Who applies the law?" must always be "Who determines the facts?" and "Who determines which facts are relevant?" Facts cannot simply be found. In domestic legal systems, the removal of ambiguity through the writing of facts and the determination of their relevance is part of the practice of judgment. In the world of international humanitarian law . . . , a great deal of deference is paid to the intelligence, and therefore the sovereign authority, of powerful states. Thus, while some protection is offered to civilians by international humanitarian law, this protection is offered within a framework in which strategic calculations about military necessity and state survival are privileged and in which facts are often determined by the intelligence of the attacking state. Having adopted this perspective, it becomes difficult to argue with the targeting expert who asserts that striking a particular target is proportional and necessary. The deaths of civilians, the ruination of cities, the destruction of livelihoods, and the pollution of the environment can ultimately be justified if these means are deemed proportional to the ends of military necessity....

Protection, Shock, and Awe

So far, this essay has explored the implications of the representation of military statecraft as a rational process involving the weighing and balancing of individual life and state survival. I would like now to argue that the history of the modern state suggests grounds for questioning even this claim that reasoned calculation governs the practice of statecraft. And while the rational explanation for state violence would seem to make human beings disposable, the irrational or perhaps passionate explanation for state authority renders us even more vulnerable.

The state is often represented as the ultimate achievement or expression of rationality. Modern state theorists certainly promoted the idea that obedience to the state is a rational choice on the part of its subjects.... Something similar is being staged with the turn to protection as the basis of international authority today. The responsibility to protect concept is presented as a rational solution to the problem of creating political order in situations where such order is nonexistent or under threat. It is premised on the notion that authority, to be legitimate, must be effective.... If a state proves unable to protect its citizens, the responsibility to do so shifts to the international community. The advocates of the responsibility to protect seek to make an argument for the lawfulness of both state and international authority without reference to self-determination, popular sovereignty, or other romantic or nationalist bases for determining who should have the power to govern in a particular territory. Rather, the legitimacy of authority is determinable by reference to the *fact* of protection.

This grounding of authority on the capacity to preserve life and protect populations rejects the more familiar claims to authority grounded on right, whether that right is understood in historical, universal, or democratic terms. By focusing on de facto authority, the responsibility to protect concept implicitly asserts not only that an international community exists, but that its authority to govern is, at least in situations of civil war and repression, superior to that of the state. . . . What matters for those advocating the responsibility to protect is the effectiveness of the techniques available to achieve protection and the maintenance of a functioning security machine. War or police action may be necessary—and thus individual lives may have to be sacrificed—in order to protect a population at risk. The population here functions as a "transcenden- tal form of life" in the name of which mere "biological life" can reasonably be sacrificed (Campbell 2008: xii, xv). . . .

Life and Critique

What, then, should a critical engagement with military statecraft entail? Do we moderns need to seek a more perfect calibration, a more precise balancing of the costs and benefits involved in warfare? International humanitarian law is in part a call to do just that—to calculate, to evaluate risk, and to measure the suffering that is justified to defend the state. Should we try to respond to this call by entering more fully into the world of "impossible calculations," of "secret debts," of "the charges on the suffering of others" (Derrida 1987: 56)? Should we take part in the ongoing task of differentiating lives to be saved, lives to be risked, and lives to be sacrificed? Should we consider it "moral progress that such a calculation is even possible"—that individual lives count enough that counting deaths seems necessary (Fassin 2007: 513)? . . .

Or should we instead refuse the call to make the suffering inflicted by mod- ern wars, including humanitarian wars, comprehensible? . . .

It is better to refuse the invitation made by state militaries and international law—to refuse, in other words, to become part of a system that weighs things that are presented as substitutable one for the other—these human lives, those wounded bodies, that sovereign state. Perhaps, after all, we should welcome the inability of humanitarian law ever successfully to bury the dead.

7.4

RESPONSIBILITY TO PROTECT OR RIGHT TO PUNISH?
Mahmood Mamdani

When World War II broke out, the international order could be divided into contradictory parts: on the one hand, a system of sovereign states in the West- ern Hemisphere, and on the other, a colonial system in most of Africa, Asia, and the Middle East. Postwar decolonization embraced state sovereignty as a universal principle of relations among states. The end of the Cold War has made for another basic shift, heralding an international humanitarian order that promises to hold state sovereignty accountable to an international human rights standard. Many believe that are we are in the throes of a systemic transition in international relations.

This new humanitarian order claims responsibility for the protection of "vulnerable populations." That responsibility is said to belong to "the international community," to be exercised in practice by the United Nations and, in particular, by the Security Council, whose permanent members are the great powers (Lloyd 2006; Pawson 2007). The new order is sanctioned by a new language that departs markedly from the older language of democracy and citizenship. It describes as "human" the populations to be protected and as "humanitarian" the crisis they suffer from, the intervention that promises to rescue them, and the agencies that seek to carry out intervention. Whereas the language of sovereignty is profoundly political, that of humanitarian intervention is profoundly apolitical, and sometimes even antipolitical. Looked at closely and critically, what we are witnessing is not a global, but a partial, transition. The transition from the old system of sovereignty to a new humanitarian order is confined to those states defined as "failed" or "rogue" states. The result is a bifurcated system whereby state sovereignty obtains in large parts of the world but is suspended in more and more countries in Africa and the Middle East.

The Westphalian coin is still the effective currency in the international system. It is worth looking at both sides of this coin: sovereignty and citizenship. If one side reads "sovereignty," the password to enter the passageway of international relations, the other side upholds the promise of "citizenship" as the essential attribute of membership in the sovereign national political (state) community. Sovereignty and citizenship are not opposites but go together: the state, after all, embodies the key right of citizens, the right of self-determination.

The international humanitarian order, in contrast, is not a system that acknowledges citizenship. Instead, it turns citizens into wards. The language of humanitarian intervention has cut its ties with the language of citizens' rights. To the extent that the global humanitarian order claims to stand for rights, these are residual rights of the human and not the full range of rights of the citizen. If the rights of the citizen are pointedly political, the rights of the human pertain to sheer survival; they are summed up in one word, "protection." The new language refers to its subjects not as bearers of rights—and thus active agents in their own emancipation—but as passive beneficiaries of an external "responsibility to protect." Rather than rights-bearing citizens, beneficiaries of the humanitarian order are akin to recipients of a charity. Humanitarianism does not claim to reinforce agency, only to sustain bare life. If anything, its tendency is to promote dependence. Humanitarianism heralds a system of trusteeship.[1] . . .

The era of international humanitarian order is not entirely new. It draws on the entire history of modern Western colonialism. At the very outset of Western colonial expansion in the eighteenth and nineteenth centuries, leading Western powers—the United Kingdom, France, Russia—claimed to protect "vulnerable groups." When it came to countries controlled by rival powers, such as the Ottoman Empire, Western powers claimed to protect populations they considered "vulnerable," mainly religious minorities such as specific Christian denominations and Jews. The most extreme political outcome of this strategy can be glimpsed in the confessional constitution bequeathed by France on independent Lebanon.

When it came to lands not yet colonized by any power, such as South Asia and large parts of Africa, the practice was to highlight local atrocities and pledge to protect victims against rulers. It was not for lack of reason that the language of modern Western colonialism juxtaposed the promise of civilization against the reality of barbaric practices. . . .

From this history was born the international regime of trusteeship exercised under the League of Nations. The league's trust territories were mainly in Africa and the Middle East. They were created at the end of World War I, when colonies of defeated imperial powers (the Ottoman Empire, Germany) were handed over to the victorious powers, who pledged to administer them as guardians would administer wards, under the watchful paternal eye of the League of Nations. One of these trust territories was Rwanda, administered as a trust of Belgium until the 1959 Hutu Revolution (Mamdani 2001). It was under the benevolent eye of the League of Nations that Belgium hardened "Hutu" and "Tutsi" into racialized identities, using the force of law to institutionalize an official system of discrimination between them. Thereby, Belgian colonialism laid the institutional groundwork of the genocide that followed half a century later. The Western powers that constituted the League of Nations could not hold Belgium accountable for the way in which it exercised an international trust for one simple reason: to do so would have been to hold a mirror to their own colonial record, for Belgian rule in Rwanda was but a harder version of the same indirect rule practiced—to one degree or another—by all Western powers in Africa. This system did not simply deny sovereignty to its colonies; it redesigned the administrative and political life of colonies by bringing each under a regime of group identity and rights. Though one could argue that Belgian practice in Rwanda made for an extreme version, it certainly was not exceptional. Given the record of the League of Nations, it is worth asking how the new international regime of trusteeship would differ from the old one. What are the likely implications of the absence of citizenship rights at the core of this system? Why would a regime of trusteeship not degenerate yet again into one of lack of accountability and responsibility?

On the face of it, these two systems—one defined by sovereignty and citizenship, and the other by trusteeship and wardship—would seem to be contradictory rather than complementary. In practice, however, they are two parts of a single but bifurcated international system. One may ask how this dual bifurcated order is reproduced without the contradiction being flagrantly obvious, without it appearing like a contemporary version of the old colonial system of trusteeship. A part of the explanation lies in how power has managed to instrumentalize the language of violence and war to subvert its meaning to advantage. . . .

In the era of nationalism and nation-states, power, as well as its adversaries, tends to be identified with entire national communities, whether defined racially, ethnically, or religiously. Yet the regime identified with the international humanitarian order makes a sharp distinction between genocide and other kinds of mass violence. International legal norms tend to be tolerant of counterinsurgency as integral to the exercise of national sovereignty and war as a standard feature of international politics—but not of genocide. The point of the distinction is to reserve universal condemnation for only one form of mass violence—genocide—as the ultimate crime and thus call for "humanitarian" intervention only where "genocide" has been unleashed, but at the same time to treat both counterinsurgency and war between states as normal developments, one in the internal functioning of nation-states, and the other in the international relations between them. Even if not made explicitly, the point is clear: counterinsurgency and interstate violence is, after all, what states do. It is genocide that is violence gone amok, amoral, evil. The former is normal violence; only the latter is bad violence.

But what is genocide, and what are counterinsurgency and war? Who does the naming? To consider this question is to focus on the question of power. The year 2003 saw the unfolding of two counterinsurgencies. One was in Iraq, and it grew out of war and invasion. The other was in Darfur (Sudan), and it grew as a response to an internal insurgency. If you were an Iraqi or a Darfuri, there was little to choose between the brutality of the violence unleashed in either instance. Yet much energy has been invested in how to define the brutality in each instance: whether as counterinsurgency or as genocide. We have the astonishing spectacle whereby the state that has authored the violence in Iraq, the United States, has branded an adversary state, Sudan, one that has authored the violence in Darfur, as the perpetrator of genocide. . . .

The debate over how to name the mass violence in Sudan is instructive. For anyone familiar with the documentation that came out of the debate between the United States (on the one hand) and the United Nations and the African Union (on the other) on how to name the violence in Darfur, it is clear that the real disagreement was not over the scale of the violence and the destruction it had wrought, but over what to call it. . . . Labeling performs a vital function. It isolates and demonizes the perpetrators of one kind of mass violence and, at the same time, confers impunity on perpetrators of other forms of mass violence.

My point here is not to enter the debate around the definition of genocide but to show that the depoliticizing language of humanitarian intervention serves a wider function; "humanitarian intervention" is not an antidote to international power relations but its latest product. If we are to respond effectively to a humanitarian intervention, we need to understand its politics. The discourse on rights emerged historically as a language of resistance to power. Its political ambition was to turn victims into agents. Today, the tendency is for the language of rights to become the language of power. The result is to subvert its very purpose, to put it at the service of a wholly different agenda, one that seeks to turn victims into so many proxies. It justifies interventions by the big powers as an antidote to malpractices of newly independent small powers.

The International Criminal Court

The emphasis on big powers as the enforcers of rights internationally is increasingly being twinned with an emphasis on big powers as enforcers of justice internationally. . . .

Its attempted accommodation with the powers that be has changed the international face of the International Criminal Court (ICC). Its name notwithstanding, the ICC is rapidly turning into a Western court to try African crimes against humanity. Even then, its approach is selective: it targets governments that are adversaries of the United States and ignores U.S. allies, effectively conferring impunity on them.[2] . . .

My point is not that those tried by the ICC or the International Tribunals have not committed crimes, including mass murder, [but that] the law is being applied selectively. Only some perpetrators are being targeted and not others. The decision as to whom to target, and whom not to, is inevitably a political decision. When the law is applied selectively, the result is not a rule of law but a subordination of law to the dictates of power so flagrant that the outcome is more reminiscent of feudal privilege than of a bourgeois rule of law. . . .

The case of the ICC raises a more general question: that of the relationship between legal and political questions. One may begin by asking: what is a legal issue, and what is a political issue? In a democracy, the domain of the legal is defined through the political process. Even where there is a human rights regime, both the fact and the content of rights (e.g., the Bill of Rights in the United States) is defined in the country's constitution—that is, in its foundational political act. At the same time, its actual operation in any given period is subject to the will of the country's political organs, which have the political power to qualify it in light of the changing context (e.g., with the Homeland Security Act in the U.S. war on terror).

What happens if one detaches the legal from the political regime? Two problems arise, both related to the question of political accountability. The only formal gathering of the global community today is the United Nations, where the General Assembly has a full representation of states, but the Security Council is a congress of big powers that emerged from the ashes of World War II. To the extent that the ICC has any accountability, it is to the Security Council, not the General Assembly. It is this relationship that has made it possible for the only superpower of the post–Cold War era to turn the workings of the ICC to advantage. . . .

Those who face human rights as the language of an externally driven "humanitarian intervention" are required to contend with a legal regime where the very notion of human rights law is defined outside of a political process— whether democratic or not—that includes them as meaningful participants. Particularly for those in Africa, more than anywhere else, the ICC heralds a regime of legal and political dependence, much as Bretton Woods institutions pioneered an international regime of economic dependence in the 1980s and 1990s. The real danger of detaching the legal from the political regime and handing it over to human rights devotees—shall we say, human rights fundamentalists, meaning those who believe that the pursuit of human rights should not be qualified by any external considerations?—is that it will turn the pursuit of justice into revenge seeking, thereby obstructing the search for reconciliation and a durable peace.

NOTES

1. The UN Security Council's response to mass violence in Darfur has been to pass Resolutions 1590 and 1591. Together, these resolutions have the effect of placing Sudan

under foreign trusteeship. Resolution 1593 charged the ICC with responsibility to try the perpetrators of human rights violations in Darfur.

2. If the ICC is turning into a Western court to try African perpetrators of mass crimes, genocide, too, is becoming a non-Western crime. The official genealogy of genocide excludes the crimes perpetrated against Native Americans and against Africans in the course of modern transatlantic slavery and the colonial era that followed it, as well as those perpetrated by the United States in the course of the Indochinese and Iraqi wars and counterinsurgencies.

7.5

UTOPIAS OF POWER
From Human Security to the Responsibility to Protect
Chowra Makaremi

In what follows, I examine the genesis of this concept of human security and its development within institutions as attempts to redefine security have shifted from the idea of "human development" originally concerned with "basic needs" to norms and techniques of humanitarian actions, military doctrines, and, finally, the legalization of interventions in the name of a "responsibility to protect." While acclaimed as a demilitarized approach to security, the concept of human security has been remilitarized in humanitarian interventions, promoting notions of emergency and safety as moral grounds for political action. This legacy introduces the idea of human security as a practice of government in response to the narrative of global chaos.

Securitizing the Patterns of Daily Life

Since the 1990s, questions of environment, identity, crime, and welfare have been reframed in terms of "security" (Booth 1991: 527–45; Buzan 1991). A turning point in this process was the introduction of a new word in the 1994 Human Development Report, redefining security as "humane" and broadening the use of the concept from exclusive military threats to economic, social, and environmental threats. . . . This concept of human security has resulted in imperatives of protection, care, and emergency. In practice, over the past decade, the project of "developing humans" has supported the normalization of humanitarian interventions and opened the floor to a new doctrine of interventionism in the UN Security Council. The Plenary Meeting of the United Nations General Assembly on September 15, 2005, declared: "We recognize that all individuals, in particular vulnerable people, are entitled to freedom from fear and freedom from want, with an equal opportunity to enjoy all their rights and fully develop their human potential. To this end, we commit ourselves to discussing and defining the notion of human security in the General Assembly." . . . Introduced into the preamble of the 1948 UN Declaration of Human Rights, freedom from fear and freedom from want have become the aim of the new paradigm of human security, which is used to manage violence through intervention in the post–Cold War era. . . .

Of the two, it appears that a concern for achieving freedom from fear is prevailing as the notion of human security evolves. Following the rupture of several states in civil conflicts and the defeat of UN-led humanitarian interventions in Somalia, after difficulties in Bosnia, and failure and shame in Rwanda, the context of the late 1990s marked the narrowing of human security from holistic and development programs to a concern for safety and protection from violence. While UN police operations stumbled (the interventionist being treated as another party to decentralized conflicts), principles of human security were reinvested in an effort to conceptualize a discursive and operational apparatus of civil-military intervention. In the UN arena, the idea prevailed that a reform should "allow the Security Council to authorize action in situations within countries, but only if the security of people is so severely violated as to require an international response on humanitarian grounds" (Carlsson 1995: 181). At the same time, state powers such as Japan, Norway, Canada, and, more recently, the European Union became interested in human security as a possible program of foreign policy. It may seem contradictory that states would support a people-centered redefinition of security. The notion, however, turned out to be a useful and flexible tool to manage new conditions of sovereignty in the global context. . . .

The Human Security Network

Since 2000, the concept of human security had framed a "foreign policy ethics" for Western democracies that are evaluating "how to restore the usefulness of their armed forces in a world redefined by the United States over the skies [*sic*] of Kosovo and Afghanistan" (Axworthy 2004: 349). Particularly Canada, as well as the European Union, have embodied the institutional concept in coordinated humanitarian and military operations in areas defined by emergencies. More than a mere ethical slogan for interventionist foreign policies, the paradigm has been based on two principal ideas: first, a globalized vision of security in which the safety of the populations of others and their resources is the guarantee of one's own national security, and [second], the management of global disorder as a goal of national self-interest. The idea of justifying one's concern for the security of others in this way acquired a new dimension after September 11, 2001, and the reconfiguration of security discourses. "The whole point of a human security approach is that Europeans cannot be secure while others in the world live in severe insecurity. National borders are no longer the dividing line between security and insecurity: insecurity gets exported," Marlies Glasius and Mary Kaldor (2009: 7) declare.... "The call for humanitarian action brought together concern for the care of victims and a traditional security approach to conflicts around the idea of a win-win situation: the securitization of the victims' basic needs is also the guarantee of the security of Western states."

Humanitarian intervention, as a political process, thus becomes a pact of security anchored in the bodies of aid beneficiaries.... This apparatus translates all dimensions of life in terms of security and, at the same time, fuses together issues of development, the military, and humanitarian assistance in one and a same process, phrased in terms of human security.

The process of redefining our ideas of war and peace in this way and of bringing about new configurations of life in the name of human security has developed as an answer to how Western democracies should address the threat of global disorder that is bursting existing frameworks such as traditional ideological oppositions, existing assumptions about the conduct of wars, established international agreements on the conduct of hostilities, and so on. In the past decade, Mary Kaldor has become one of the most acclaimed theorists of "new wars" understood in this way (Kaldor and Johnson 2007). She has argued, in particular, that since the end of the Cold War there has been a reconfiguration of warfare—and more broadly, a reconfiguration of the relationship between violence and the political....

The disorder occurring in several parts of the world is said to be marked by an economy of war based on pillage and by an "extreme" form of globalization: transnational, informal, illegal networks, remittances, and the diversion of humanitarian aid.... The new wars are said to be marked by two forms of violence: the genocidal violence of states and a free, generalized violence derived—at best—from older forms of identity politics. This quite unintelligible violence is marked by anomie, as well as by a withdrawal from the political—Kaldor's core argument. Another important result of such disorder is a change in warfare, which becomes unrestrained, technologically archaic, and barbaric.

In the end, like many analysts of "global chaos," Kaldor advocates a "civilizing process" of cosmopolitan law enforcement (i.e., an international law for individuals) and, finally, the use of force that resembles that employed by the police. This way of thinking posits the idea of human security as a practice of governments in response to the specter of global chaos. It follows that such a response is not about instituting order but about "managing global chaos," as the title of a book by Chester C. Crocker, Fen O. Hampson, and Pamela R. Aall (1996) forthrightly puts it. Within these perspectives, the shift from political order to the management of disorder becomes a shift in the technology of government, a shift advocated as a way to cope with "new wars" and to gain control over "moving power systems." Evolving modes of intervention under the banner of human security have come to depend on the notion of policing violence.

Policing Violence as a Technique of Government

In the past several years, Canadian peace operations—that is, operations undertaken under a UN peacekeeping mandate or within a (usually NATO-led) "coalition of the willing"—have deployed police officers in addition to traditional military forces, a policy for which Canada claims "leadership." The use of police as peacekeepers in war-torn areas illuminates how the securitization process is imagined under the paradigm of human security. It defines intervention as a combination of several strategies: the coercive exercise of force ("executive policing"), the humanitarian securitization of lives ("assisting aid and humanitarian assistance"), the normalization of social relationships by a "neutral" third party ("monitoring and investigation of human rights violations"), and the normative implementation of political organization ("institutional capacity building," lending "support to electoral process," "security sector reform"). . . . Intervention in the name of human security thus merges military and civilian agents, with the focus of the intervention being the government of populations. In this sense, it confirms what already is taking place in the management of zones of disorder: the co-engagement of international and state-based public forces and elements of the private sector—whether they are NGOs, experts working on short-term contracts, private military companies, or private security companies—through mechanisms of funding, subcontracting, and lobbying (Duffield 2001). . . . The rise of this private-public and civilian-military complex marks the emergence of new modes of warfare—Kaldor's new wars—that fit the rationale of global governance. The human-security doctrine solidifies and gives a frame to ad hoc practices of population management inherited from the evolution of capitalist economics and public policies in the West.

FIG 8.0. For many years, governments around the world have used media of all kinds to garner public support for war, censor inconvenient information, and improve the image of the military as a whole. Those seeking to support militaristic approaches use newspapers, films, museum exhibits, the Internet, and much more in the battle to win hearts and minds. Here, NBC reporters interview a member of the Illinois National Guard engaged in training exercises at Fort Bragg, North Carolina. Photograph courtesy U.S. Army Public Affairs Midwest.

SECTION VIII. MILITARISM AND THE MEDIA

Compiled by HUGH GUSTERSON

Introduction

This section surveys both press coverage of war and the representation of war and militarism in movies, literature, museum exhibitions, and popular culture. The U.S. government, particularly the Department of Defense, has sought to shape representations of the military in the press and in popular culture. They have, in Noam Chomsky's famous phrase, set out to "manufacture consent." David Barstow, David L. Robb, Mark Pedelty, John Whittier Treat, and Peter Van Buren shed light on the processes involved here.

In an interview with Amy Goodman, David Barstow reveals that the "independent" military analysts who are quoted in the media often have financial ties to the military-industrial complex and rely on privileged access from the Pentagon for the knowledge that enables their commentary in the media. These analysts are, in fact, embedded in the military-industrial complex while representing themselves as commenting on its affairs from outside.

The next piece in this section features an interview with David L. Robb, who relates how Pentagon officials have succeeded in shaping Hollywood representations of war and of the U.S. military, even to the point of demanding script changes, in exchange for providing film studios with the military equipment, access to bases, and expert advice they need. Meanwhile, Mark Pedelty shows how U.S. officials in El Salvador manipulated access as a way to control journalists.

John Whittier Treat writes about the Smithsonian Air and Space Museum's failed attempt to mount a major exhibition in 1995 on the bombing of Hiroshima, in which methods of outright intimidation were used to silence critique. He offers a thought-provoking account of an episode in what some have called call "historical cleansing." Pundits, politicians, and veterans came together to intimidate the museum's officials to make sure that the American people would remain ignorant of the lively debate among professional historians about whether the bombing of Hiroshima constituted an atrocity or a mercifully swift end to a ferociously violent war.

Popular consent to militarism and support for particular wars are also shaped through popular culture: films, television shows, music, museum exhibitions, and even fashion trends. As Peter Van Buren demonstrates in his contribution to this section, Hollywood war films have followed a formulaic pattern that glorifies American soldiers and erases the moral complexities of armed conflict. He documents how these techniques have been used for well over half a century and notes that they have been compelling enough to convince young men and women to sacrifice their lives on the battlefield.

READINGS

8.1   Excerpts from Amy Goodman, "Pentagon Pundits: Interview with David Barstow," *Democracy Now!*, May 8, 2009.

8.2   Excerpts from Jeff Fleischer, "Operation Hollywood" (interview with David L. Robb), *Mother Jones*, September 2004, https://www .motherjones.com/politics/2004/09/operation-hollywood/.

8.3   Excerpts from Mark Pedelty, "Discipline and Publish," in *War Stories: The Culture of Foreign Correspondents*, by Mark Pedelty (New York: Routledge, 1995), 85–98.

8.4   Excerpts from John Whittier Treat, "The *Enola Gay* on Display," *Positions* 5, no. 3 (1997): 863–78.

8.5   Excerpts from Peter Van Buren, "War Porn: Hollywood and War, from World War II to *American Sniper*," *Truthout.com*, February 19, 2015.

8.1

_____

PENTAGON PUNDITS

David Barstow (interviewed by Amy Goodman)

AMY GOODMAN: [The *New York Times* reporter David] Barstow uncovered Pentagon documents that repeatedly refer to the military analysts as "message force multipliers" or "surrogates" who could be counted on to deliver administration themes and messages to millions of Americans in the form of their own opinions. The so-called analysts were given hundreds of classified Pentagon briefings, provided with Pentagon-approved talking points, and given free trips to Iraq and other sites paid for by the Pentagon.

David Barstow [recently] wrote . . . , "Records and interviews show how the Bush administration has used its control over access and information in an effort to transform the analysts into a kind of media Trojan horse—an instrument intended to shape terrorism coverage from inside the major TV and radio networks."

The officials appeared on all the main cable news channels—Fox News, CNN and MSNBC—as well as the three nightly network news broadcasts.

The Pentagon program started during the build-up to the Iraq War. . . . The Pentagon continued to use retired generals to counter criticism on various issues, ranging from Guantánamo to the surge in Iraq. In some cases, analysts would appear on cable news programs live from the Pentagon just minutes after receiving a special briefing. . . .

DAVID BARSTOW: [T]he program had its roots in the 2002 buildup to the war in Iraq. The main architects were folks inside the Pentagon, notably Torie Clarke, who was the main spokesperson for the Pentagon at the time and a former public relations executive who had some pretty sophisticated ideas about how it is that you influence the American public in a spin-saturated world, where people are increasingly cynical both of journalists and of official spokespeople of the government. The idea that she pitched to Don Rumsfeld, then the Secretary of Defense, was that the way to really influence the American public was to try and find people who were viewed as independent of both government and the media, people who were considered authoritative and expert, people who would have an ability to cut through the spin.

The group that they began zeroing in on were all the military analysts who were being hired in droves after 9/11 by the major TV networks. In the view of Torie Clarke and her staff, these guys were the ultimate key influencers. They were seen as retired decorated war heroes. They were, many of them, retired generals, some three- and four-star generals. They came from an institution that traditionally is extremely trusted by the American public. They were seen by the public not really as of the media, but not of the government, either.

Torie Clarke and her aides, with the strong support from the White House and from her bosses, set out to target this group and to make them one of the main vehicles for reaching the American public and building support for the war on terror. So that's how it began, with this idea that they could take this thing called the military analyst, which is a creature that's been around for a long time—going back to the first Gulf War, we remember some of the retired generals first coming on-air—and they could take this and the fact of 9/11 and the fact of how prevalent they were on air, sometimes appearing segment after segment after segment, getting more air time than many correspondents were getting, holding forth, not just on the issues of where the airplanes were flying and where the tanks were moving, but weighing more heavily on even the strategic issues of what should we do next and how should the war on terror unfold, what should be the next targets. . . .

Effectively what they were doing was writing the op-ed on air for the networks and for the cables. And they noticed the way the relationships between the anchors and their sort of in-house generals, there was a sort of bond between anchor and general . . . . You didn't see the kind of challenging questioning that would go on if you had sent, for example, a representative of the Pentagon to the TV station. It was a much more— almost fawning kind of relationship between anchor and general. So they saw in this group a way of taking the media filter, which politicians are always so fond of complaining about, and turning the media filter into more of a media megaphone. . . .

GOODMAN: According to Media Matters, the army of analysts that you identified made 4,500 appearances and quotations on ABC, CBS, NBC, MSNBC, CNBC, CNN, Fox News and NPR. . . . Give us the story, one of the case studies. . . . Tell us the story of Barry McCaffrey. . . .

BARSTOW: General Barry McCaffrey is really one of the most impressive military leaders. He was the youngest four-star U.S. Army general, I believe, in history. He was the man who became famous during the first Gulf War for leading the left hook into Iraq. He also then became the drug czar under President Bill Clinton.

And in September 2001, an odd thing happened. Actually, the week before 9/11, he was asked to join the . . . defense advisory board of a major private equity firm in New York called Veritas Capital, which at that moment, just at that moment, was making plans to invest heavily in defense contractors. [Then] 9/11 happened. Weeks later, General McCaffrey was hired by NBC to be one of its military analysts. . . . He has been on, time and time again, talking about the war in Iraq, the war in Afghanistan, but at the same time, most notably through his ties to Veritas Capital, he has been deeply involved in the business affairs of some of the major defense contractors who are operating in both of those war zones.

And what's more, none of those ties have been disclosed to NBC's viewers when they're bringing him on to talk about the wars in Iraq and Afghanistan. One of the threads that we followed was, how did his appearances on television, and what did he say on television, to what extent did his positions on TV overlap with the undisclosed business interests of these major defense contractors?

In addition, General McCaffrey . . . has his own consulting firm. And what that consulting firm does is it helps defense contractors gain access and win contracts. So, at the same time, while he might be going over to Iraq, for example, in his capacity as a military analyst for NBC and getting access to all of the top generals in Iraq, he's also representing companies who are trying very hard to get into that market. . . .

GOODMAN: You interviewed the president of NBC News, Steve Capus?

BARSTOW: I did, yes. What I've learned since the story ran is that although they, for the most part, defended their use of General McCaffrey after the story on General McCaffrey ran, they have begun relooking at their internal ethics policies, their standards and practices. And what I've noticed in the past couple of months, I did see an appearance where General McCaffrey was on TV, and David Gregory in fact did tell viewers, "OK, he sits on the board of DynCorp." And so there was at least a move toward a little bit more disclosure.

But . . . there are a lot of retired military officers who have great expertise out there who in fact don't work for defense contractors who are over in Iraq and Afghanistan, and there is this question: if a network wants to make use of that expertise and bring that to the table in their coverage, why not find somebody who doesn't have these outside entanglements to do that? . . . I mean, one thing that we did discover through the reporting of this is that the military analysts, many of them, aren't just having an on-air role, but they're having an off-air role, as well. They're in some cases participating in the editorial meetings where coverage of the war is being discussed. They're weighing in on story ideas. In some cases, they were suggesting story ideas that were suggested to them from the Pentagon. . . .

It's probably a little bit of a surprise for viewers, who became so accustomed to seeing these generals as part of the news coverage, to now be told, "Well, wait a minute, they're actually not considered journalists in any way, shape, or form. I mean, they're consultants, and so therefore they're not beholden to any of our other ethical standards that would, for example, make it impossible for Tom Brokaw to go over and cover Iraq but at the same time be representing a defense contractor seeking business in Iraq." If that were to happen, we all know that would be a huge scandal in journalism. But when it comes to these guys, those rules didn't apply. . . .

It's important to note that some of the [analysts], during moments of the war, developed deep misgivings about what they were being told in these briefings. They began to suspect that they weren't really getting the straight truth, that they were getting a sort of a rose-colored view of what was really happening in Iraq and Afghanistan. And yet when those guys began to go off the reservation and began giving voice to those doubts on the air, what we saw happen was that some of them found their access rather abruptly cut off.

There was this effort on the part of the Pentagon to use access as the carrot and the stick. And access is a really important thing to focus in on here, because if you're in the world of defense contracting in Washington, access to people and to information is really the coin of the realm. It is so important to have that kind of granular, up-close, frequent contact with the very top people at the Pentagon to understand what are their needs, what are they thinking about next. And in some cases, you would see these guys go back out into the marketplace and advertise the special access they were getting as military analysts to people who they were trying to bring in as clients or as consulting arrangements or as board—to win a seat on a board of a company. . . .

What we don't know, and it's important to note, that not only were these relationships not disclosed to the viewers of either CNN or NBC, but CNN at least claimed that they weren't even aware that General [James "Spider"] Marks, their main military analyst, in fact had this role with this company, was deeply involved in fighting for this contract. And then, indeed, when they found out in mid-2007 or later on in 2007 that he, in fact, did play this role with this company, CNN pretty quickly severed its ties with General Marks, and he no longer appears on the air as military analyst for them. . . .

One thing that I wanted to look at closely [was] . . . what was the information being told to this group? Was . . . it truthful? Was it accurate? Or was it spin? Was it whitewash? And the problem [was] . . . when you looked at the transcripts of the conference calls between the military analysts and the Pentagon officials, while certainly there was plenty of truthful information that was given to them, time and time again they were also given information that deeply contradicted what we now know to be the truth, the truth that was known inside the Pentagon and the White House, about the true state of affairs in Iraq and Afghanistan.

So . . . , for example, let's take the effort to train up Iraqi security forces. These guys were constantly being told one story about how wonderful the effort was going, even though the White House and the Pentagon knew all along that the training effort was a mess in lots of different ways. You could also see it—even, I remember talking to a couple of these guys who were brought in just before the war began, and they were brought in for a presentation about WMD [weapons of mass destruction]. What do we know about WMD in Iraq? And even the guys who were there in these secret briefings about the WMD in Iraq, as they listened to the story they were being told by the Pentagon officials, had a clear instinct at the time that they were being given information that either wasn't very strong or wasn't accurate or didn't hold up.

So in other words . . . , if what the White House was doing was giving really a thorough briefing of what the White House and Pentagon knew about the situation in Iraq and Afghanistan, the war on terror at large, you know, that would be one thing. But that, in fact, is not what was happening in many of these sessions. And when you looked at the transcripts of these sessions, the other thing that jumped out at me was that there was never the normal kind of relationship you would see in terms of the tension between people who are journalists, who are independent-minded, and a government official. There was never that sort of questioning, that probing, to see whether or not the information was really correct, whether they're being told the whole story, whether they're being told the story straight. Instead, what you often came away with was this feeling that you were watching kind of like a sales meeting, where the military analysts were sort of syncing up with the Pentagon and almost brainstorming together about, you know, what would be a better way to explain this, what would be a better way to communicate the themes and messages in order to keep the support for the war strong here at home. . . .

When things like Abu Ghraib happened, when questions were being raised about the adequacy of the armor being given to American troops, invariably they would pull these guys in, bring them in to neutralize the critical coverage, sometimes the critical coverage that was coming from the network's own war correspondents.

8.2

OPERATION HOLLYWOOD
David L. Robb (interviewed by Jeff Fleischer)

To keep the Pentagon happy, some Hollywood producers have been known to turn villains into heroes, remove central characters, change politically sensitive settings, or add military rescues to movies that require none. . . .

"The only thing Hollywood likes more than a good movie is a good deal," David Robb explains, and that's why the producers of films such as *Top Gun*, *Stripes*, and *The Great Santini* have altered their scripts to accommodate Pentagon requests. In exchange, they get inexpensive access to the military locations, vehicles, troops, and gear they need to make their movies.

During his years as a journalist for *Daily Variety* and the *Hollywood Reporter*, Robb heard about a quid pro quo agreement between the Pentagon and Hollywood studios and decided to investigate. He combed through thousands of Pentagon documents and interviewed dozens of screenwriters, producers, and military officials. The result is his new book, *Operation Hollywood*. . . .

JEFF FLEISCHER: What steps does a producer take to get assistance from the military? How does the process work?

DAVID ROBB: The first thing you have to do is send in a request for assistance, telling them what you want pretty specifically—ships, tanks, planes, bases, forts, submarines, troops—and when you want this material available. Then you have to send five copies of the script to the Pentagon, and they give it to the affected service branches—Army, Air Force, Navy, Marine Corps, Coast Guard. Then you wait and see if they like your script or not. If they like it, they'll help you; if they don't, they won't. Almost always, they'll make you make changes to the military depictions. And you have to make the changes that they ask for or negotiate some kind of compromise, or you don't get the stuff.

So then you finally get the approval, after you change your script to mollify the military, put some stuff in about how great it is to be in the military. Then when you go to shoot the film, you have to have what I call a "military minder"—but what they call a "technical adviser"—someone from the military on the set to make sure you shoot the film the way you agreed to. Normally in the filmmaking process, script changes are made all the time; if something isn't working, they look at the rushes and say, "Let's change this." Well, if you want to change something that has to do with the military depictions, you've got to negotiate with them again. And they can say, "No, you can't change it, this is the deal you agreed to." . . .

After the film is completed, you have to prescreen the film for the Pentagon brass. So before it's shown to the public, you have to show your movie to the generals and admirals, which I think any American should find objectionable. . . .

FLEISCHER: At that stage, with the film finished, what can the military do if they have a problem?

ROBB: This happened on the Clint Eastwood movie *Heartbreak Ridge*. He finished the film, showed it to them, and they went through the roof. There was a scene in the script where he shoots an injured and defenseless Cuban soldier. They said, "You have to take that out. It's a war crime. We don't want that." They hate having war crimes in movies. So with *Heartbreak Ridge*, Eastwood shot the film, and the scene ended up in the movie anyway. They said, "We told you to take that out." He said he thought it was only a suggestion. . . . So they withdrew their approval. The film was still released, of course. . . . And they can stop it from being shown in military theaters overseas or on bases in the United States, which can really hurt the box office of a film. They've done this to numerous films. Also, at that time Clint Eastwood was the chairman of Toys for Tots, the Marine Corps Christmas gift program for poor children. He wanted to screen the movie at a premiere to benefit Toys for Tots, and they said, "We're not going to let you do that." They can be very spiteful; they can hurt the box office of a film, and they don't forget, either. . . . They can't stop the film. But if you want cooperation again, . . . you're not going to get it. . . .

FLEISCHER: What criteria do the Pentagon use in deciding whether to help a film?

ROBB: The most important criterion is that the film has to "aid in the retention and recruitment of personnel." . . . They also say it has to reasonably depict military operations. And if it's based on history, they say it has to be historically accurate, which is really a code. They're much less interested in reality and accuracy than they are in positive images. They often try to change historical facts that are negative. Like with the movie *Thirteen Days*, which was very accurate but very negative toward the military during the Cuban Missile Crisis, showing that they would have taken us down the path toward World War III. During the negotiations with the producers, Peter Almond and Kevin Costner, the military tried to get them to tone down the bellicose nature of General Maxwell Taylor and General Curtis LeMay. . . . To their credit, Kevin Costner and Peter Almond stood up to the military, refused to buckle under, and made their film without military assistance.

FLEISCHER: Why don't more producers take that approach?

ROBB: A lot of the studio heads tell their producers, "We're not going to make this film unless we get military assistance, because it would be too expensive. So you'd better make sure the script conforms to what they want." Also, what you don't see in these documents is the self-censorship that goes with knowing you need their assistance and that they're going to be your first audience. Writers write stuff to get that military assistance. So there's no documents saying, "In *Black Hawk Down*, let's leave out the whole part about the soldiers being dragged through the streets of Mogadishu." Jerry Bruckheimer knows that if they have that in there, the military's just going to tell them to take it out or won't help them. . . . When you know the government is looking over your shoulder while you're typing, that's a very bad situation.

FLEISCHER: Aside from showing war crimes, what are some of the other things the military balks at?

ROBB: They never—at least that I've seen—help movies with aliens. Usually in those movies, the military is shown to be ineffective in combating the aliens. . . . They wouldn't help *Independence Day*. The military could not get over the fact that one of the key plot points was that the United States was secretly working on a spaceship captured at Area 51, so the film ended up not getting assistance. . . .

They don't like drinking or drugs in the military. . . . Like in *Stripes*, they made them take out all drug references. . . . They don't want to see any pot smoking, even in Vietnam. The former Navy Secretary James Webb, after he left that post, he became a book writer. He'd been a Marine in Vietnam, and one of his books was semiautobiographical, with many of the things he saw and knew for a fact happened in Vietnam: fragging of officers, smoking pot, burning Vietnamese villages. He had a screenplay and wanted to turn it into a movie. They said, "No, you have to change all this stuff," and he wouldn't do it. So that's a film that never got made. Many films have never been made because they couldn't get assistance.

FLEISCHER: In the book, you give examples of how the Pentagon won't allow military characters to be depicted as bad guys.

ROBB: Right. For example, there was an HBO movie, *The Tuskegee Airmen*, where the military made them replace the villain. This was a movie about the first black airmen during World War II, where the bad guy was a general at the base where these guys were training, and the good guy was a white congressman. Well, the army said they didn't like that, so they ended up changing it. . . . Now when people saw that film, they had no idea that the good guy and the bad guy had been reversed just so the military could meet its recruiting goals.

FLEISCHER: You also talk about the military targeting children by encouraging pro-military storylines in shows such as *The Mickey Mouse Club* and *Lassie*.

ROBB: In those cases, they recognized that children are the future recruits. . . . One of the best examples [was] *The Right Stuff*, about the early days of the space program. The original script was filled with vulgarity and cussing, and the military sent the producers a letter. It reads, "The obscene language used seems to guarantee an 'R' rating. If distributed as an 'R,' it cuts down on the teenage audience, which is a prime one to the military services when our recruiting bills are considered." Of course, an "R" rating means children under seventeen have to be accompanied by a parent, so a lot of sixteen- and seventeen-year-olds couldn't see this picture. And the Air Force wanted young people to see it so they'd get a good, positive image of the military and join up. So they changed it. . . .

Major Georgi, who had been the military minder on many movies, said that one of the targets of this program is Congress—that Congress goes to movies, and when they see positive images of the military, that makes it easier for them to vote for that $500 billion military appropriation. They also target voters, the people who are really footing the bill. Really, if you talk to soldiers and sailors and Marines, many of them will tell you they joined the military because of some movie that they saw. The former head of the Marine Corps film office, Matt Morgan, told me he joined the military after seeing *Top Gun*. After *Top Gun* came out, there was a huge spike in recruitment for the Navy flying program. They know that it works. People are going off to war and getting killed in part because of some movie they saw that was adjusted by the military. . . .

The Writers' Guild, whose stated mission is to protect the creative and economic rights of its members, has never made a single protest that its members' scripts are being manipulated and changed by the military. Congress has done nothing. Hollywood likes the way it is, and the military likes the way it is. . . . The only people who have a real interest in this are the American people. They're being saturated with military propaganda in their mainstream movies and TV shows, and they don't even know. But I think there's a very good argument that can be made that over the past fifty years, this chronic sanitization of the military and what war is has affected the American character; that we're now a more warlike people than we were fifty years ago. . . . When the world's most powerful medium colludes with the world's most powerful military to put propaganda in mainstream films and television shows, that has to have an effect on the American psyche.

8.3

DISCIPLINE AND PUBLISH
Mark Pedelty

The U.S. State Department imposes strict guidelines of attribution that reporters must follow faithfully or lose access to embassy staff. These rules were explained to me in detail by a U.S. Information Service attaché. The first rule is that all interviews must be conducted under the rubric of "deep background." Under these conditions, quotes cannot be attributed directly to the source. In news reports, such information is preceded by phrases such as, "It is generally understood that . . ." or "It is widely believed . . ." Following the terms of deep background, the specific words of the State Department are posited as the general opinion of local society.

After conducting an interview, journalists may negotiate on a quote-by-quote basis to move information into the category of "background." Under the rules of background attribution, the source may be cited as a "Western diplomat." Under this guise, actual quotations may be reproduced. Therefore, journalists always hope to be accorded the privilege of "background" status.

Background attribution assumes less generality. A "Western diplomat" is an actual person rather than an amorphous social collective, as implied by the phrase, "It is widely believed." . . . The great majority of statements attributed to "Western diplomats" in the U.S. press come directly from the State Department. Beyond deep background and background, there is "on the record." Few journalists are granted this right to direct attribution, and once again, only on a quote-by-quote basis. . . .

In our initial interviews I asked journalists what readers should know in order to better understand the news coverage of El Salvador. Several cited the State Department rules of attribution. Bob answered:

> People should know about the incredible involvement of the U.S. Embassy and how, when they read a mainstream story and it says "Western diplomat," that three out of four times, or probably higher, that is going to be a U.S. official who has deliberately spoken on the record on background so he doesn't have to take responsibility for his views. Yet he allows you to use his views under the rubric "Western diplomat," which gives the impression that the source is a noninvolved person—just a detached, objective diplomat who is speaking—when in fact it is someone who is a major player.

Stringers were not alone in complaining about embassy influence. After volunteering that "a diplomat close to the [Salvadoran] government" quoted in one of her articles was in fact Ambassador "Bill" Walker, Katherine admitted she does "not like using the embassy people that much." Unfortunately, she finds them "impossible to avoid in El Salvador because they are key players" who are "running a war." . . .

Despite their discomfort with the practice, reporters work extremely hard to obtain "inside" embassy quotes, no matter how prefabricated and banal they may be (Sigal 1986: 22). The main reason journalists tolerate the embassy's restrictive rules of attribution, opacity, and obstructionism is the editors' preference, if not requirement, that official U.S. government positions be included in most news reports. . . . As a result of this editorial pressure, reporters with the Salvadoran Foreign Press Corps Association will print the words of State Department officials even when they know the information is inaccurate. . . .

If editors feel that they "must" print such falsehoods, then reporters are obligated to do the same. Reporters are "tempted not to quote them," explained Paul, "but the editors won't run it." The rules of objectivity, as currently conceived, further constrict the reporters' ability to qualify or contextualize the State Department frame. On several occasions, the State Department charged Farabundo Martí National Liberation Front (FMLN) guerrillas with carrying out or inventing atrocities that were, in reality, the work of the military or its closely affiliated death squads. . . .

They were unable to present that historical qualification, however, when reporting the recycled embassy assertions, since that would be seen as "editorializing." This duplicitous process of editorial, state, and narrative disciplines creates a "string," in the words of a U.S. journalist working in Honduras, that "runs from the administration and State Department through almost all news coverage."

Those willing to offend the embassy have come under sharp attack from what Bob calls "the sleazy tactics" of the State Department. The ambassador and his staff have made repeated calls to the top editors of newspapers for which Bob has submitted reports and have even spoken with his publisher. Bob explains the effects of this flak, saying, "It weakens your credibility, especially if you are a stringer. The publication listens to this supposedly authoritative and professional State Department functionary calling up and saying, 'Your reporter has made a whole bunch of mistakes, and his reporting is tendentious and biased.'"

This is one reason reporters feel compelled to represent elite sources in a favorable light. Another is their need to maintain privileged access. . . . Only those who were already disenfranchised from the embassy and relatively free from editorial pressure could afford to violate this system of corporate, state, and narrative structures.

"Editors Suck"

Reporters conduct their work within extremely hierarchical bureaucracies (Gans 1979: 83–87). Most of them are at the bottom of their respective organizations, beneath ascending levels of editors, managers, and owners. The field reporter must constantly defer to her immediate and ever present boss, the editor. The professional promise of freedom—the cherished sense (and pretense) of autonomy—is contradicted in practice by realities of constraint and control.

Such is the recipe for frustration. These frustrations are most often projected on the editor, the most obvious and immediate symbol of institutional discipline. Youthful reporters, those who have not completely acquiesced to the disciplines of mainstream press work, are particularly vigilant in fighting to maintain a space, however small, within which they may retain a sense of professional autonomy. It is the job of editors to collapse that space, to facilitate the assimilation of institutional ideology into the individual journalist's regimen. As a result, all reporters share a degree of antipathy toward editors. . . .

Editors not only edit reporters but also decide proper placement for articles, anywhere from "Column One" to the back pages, where the story may be dwarfed by a Macy's ad. Editors often reject a reporter's work altogether. Likewise, editors influence the journalists' daily reporting agendas and geographic distribution as they cast their institutional "news net" across the world (Tuchman 1978: 15–38). In addition to all of these functions, editors keep in constant contact with their correspondents, suggesting stories and discussing news concepts. They are not only "gatekeepers" (White 1950) but overseers as well. Editors not only filter out unwanted materials from the news hole but actively involve themselves in the reporting process. . . .

Editors also perform the difficult task of writing headlines. Headlines are an extremely influential framing device that summarize, contextualize, and even replace news reports as hurried readers breeze through the morning paper. Reporters are often angered by headlines. For example, an editor entitled one of Shawn's articles, "HOPES RISE IN EL SALVADOR," even though the article clearly argued against an optimistic view of the negotiations. Furthermore, the article was edited in a manner that favored the optimism of the headline, contradicting the text Shawn originally submitted.

Further frustration is added by the fact that most editors know very little about Latin America and think of Latin American culture almost solely in terms of violence. "Editors want bang bang," complained Michael, "If there is no bang bang, they figure 'Why pay attention to it?' They are very Eurocentric. They don't appreciate Latin America for what it is." Similarly, Pati complained, "Editors . . . need to know that not everyone is carrying an AK-47 and wearing a red bandanna, and that just because a journalist is interviewing campesinos and guerrillas doesn't make them a communist." . . .

As a reporter for *Time* explained in *Deciding What's News*, "Every writer has a working knowledge of what his editor wants. Unless he's incorrigibly stubborn or independently wealthy, he tries to give it to him" (Gans 1979: 102). Although editors are themselves subservient to a number of institutional superiors, they represent nearly absolute power from the perspective of the field journalist. It is little wonder reporters do not like to talk about them. The editors' existence serves as a reminder that they work near the bottom of hierarchical organizations and that the power of authorship does not flow from their pen but from the structure as a whole.

The Ray Bonner Effect

Journalists who continue to breach the parameters of permissible discourse despite routine editorial attempts at correction often receive punishment in the form of unwanted assignments, rejected reports, demotion, or even loss of a job. One of the best-known cases of journalistic censure involved Raymond Bonner of the *New York Times*. On January 27, 1982, Alma Guillermoprieto and Bonner published front page stories describing the aftermath of the now infamous El Mozote massacre. At least seven hundred peasants were murdered at El Mozote, many of them children. Several of the corpses displayed signs of torture. The massacre was committed by the Atlacatl battalion, the officers of which were trained in the United States (Danner 1993).

Bonner's report of the El Mozote massacre was published one day before the Reagan administration was legally obliged to assess the human rights situation in El Salvador before Congress, making it a great embarrassment for U.S. foreign-policy makers. The State Department claimed the massacres never took place. According to the administration's testimony before Congress, embassy officials in El Salvador had visited the site and found no evidence of an attack or massacre. A decade later, those officials admitted they had lied to Congress. No U.S. officials had ventured anywhere near the site of El Mozote (Hertsgaard 1988: 190).

Predictably, Guillermoprieto and Bonner came under attack from the U.S. government and conservative institutions such as Accuracy in Media and Freedom House (Hertsgaard 1988: 190; Hoyt 1993: 22). Perhaps most disturbing, however, was the flak generated by other media institutions. The *Wall Street Journal* started the wave of criticism, claiming the reporters were duped by a "propaganda exercise" of the FMLN. The *Washington Post* editorial board rejected Guillermoprieto's evidence, writing an editorial endorsement of the Reagan administration's claim that things were improving in El Salvador. . . .

The editors of the *New York Times* responded to the flak by pressuring Bonner to moderate his reporting. When Bonner failed to do so, he was removed from the bureau. A little later he was demoted to the New York metropolitan desk. Finally, Bonner resigned on July 3, 1984. Another *New York Times* reporter explained, "The board came down hard on [executive editor] Abe Rosenthal, who was a conservative guy anyway, and he fired Ray." Perhaps during a moment of less intense government interest in El Salvador Bonner would have gotten away with reporting the truth, but not in the midst of a foreign-policy crisis. As another reported explained, "Bonner was crucified for telling the truth." . . .

According to many reporters working in the early 1980s, Bonner's removal by the *New York Times* had a "chilling effect" on news coverage (Hertsgaard 1988: 196–97; Parenti 1986: 57). What little space had been opened for critical news reporting quickly slammed shut, leaving a brisk chill of caution as its legacy. Shari claimed that a conservative shift in the writing of several reporters, including a man she now calls an "archenemy," was precipitated by Bonner's firing. She and others call this "the Ray Bonner effect." The Ray Bonner effect is manifested in an extreme, yet rational, fear of editorial retribution. . . .

As a U.S. Marine-turned-lawyer-turned-stringer-turned correspondent, Bonner was very unusual. The *New York Times* took a risk in hiring the untested stringer and paid dearly. What it got was a reporter with strong ideas and values he was unwilling to compromise for the sake of career or country. Most media hires are much more willing to compromise their values, have relatively few conscious political values, or are in general political agreement with their institutions from the start. In other words, Bonner's experience could not have chilled the other staff correspondents because most of them were already cold. . . .

8.4

THE *ENOLA GAY* ON DISPLAY
John Whittier Treat

The lines were long in Washington the summer of 1995. The National Museum of American History, the National Archives, the National Air and Space Museum, and the U.S. Holocaust Memorial Museum all attracted visitors curious about a war that few of us are old enough to remember. Yet each of these museums chose that commemorative summer to make "memory" their common theme.

Washington would not have seen such numbers of museumgoers without the months of media attention focused on the Smithsonian Institution's controversial exhibit—eventually reduced to a mere "display"—of the *Enola Gay*. Americans are not usually students of August 1945: a recent poll reveals that 60 percent of us do not know which president dropped the bomb on Japan, and a third of us do not know that the first A-bomb was used on Hiroshima.

But what happened to make us now so keen on history was the alleged assault on it by scholars and Smithsonian bureaucrats intent on revising our understanding of events half a century ago. These events, which stand, if not securely, in the American imagination as one of our finest hours, seemed in danger in the summer of 1995 of being turned into a rout of our claims to moral as well as military certitude. . . .

Reacting to a lack of historical consciousness that some attribute to a deadening postmodernity, it has been argued that today we celebrate our "sites of memory" because we have no "environments of memory." Those sites can be anything we invest with a confidence missing in our more ephemeral understandings. After President Bill Clinton and the U.S. Postal Service canceled a planned mushroom-cloud stamp, an ex-Marine in Ohio privately printed 1,800 copies for himself and friends, explaining, "It's history." And after a year in which experts in and out of the universities failed to provide us with any acceptable definitive account of the end of World War II, no one is in a position to tell that veteran he is wrong. . . .

Perhaps it was an awareness of how treacherous memory can be that led the Smithsonian's Secretary I. Michael Heyman and his institution to cleanse the *Enola Gay* exhibit of all memories save those of the plane's small crew. But even the voices of the pilot Paul W. Tibbets and his four surviving comrades, shown on a brief videotape continuously displayed near the exit of the small exhibition, did not quite have the ring of genuine recollections. Half a century of telling their tales of August 1945 has rendered their "memory" a scripted performance, as polished as the fuselage of the plane itself and honed to fit a consensus that came into being after the events in question. "Hiroshima," Tibbets tells us, "was definitely a military objective." All traces of ambiguity, of guilt, or even of doubt were excised from their testimony as neatly as the Smithsonian stripped the original exhibition of all its purposeful suggestions of stubborn ethical conundrums. . . .

THE *ENOLA GAY* display . . . was confined to a single gallery in a first-floor corner of the museum. To reach that gallery, visitors had to pass immense monuments that celebrate American technological achievement in both war and peace: sleek fighter planes, space capsules that have been to the moon and back, towering rockets that presumably kept the nuclear peace in the years between Hiroshima and the present. . . .

The political solution to putting the *Enola Gay* on public display was to strip it bare of all analysis, consequence, and context. The plane and its crew, according to Secretary Heyman, would "speak for themselves." But Heyman felt it necessary to preface the visitors' entrance to the gallery with a placard explaining, if not why the bomb was used, then how the display came about. The placard stated that originally there had been planned "a much larger exhibit" that would have concentrated "attention on the devastation." But what we have now, it went on to explain, is something "much simpler," "essentially a display."

In referring, albeit obliquely, to the controversy, Heyman did the minimum he had to do. After all, more than $1.5 million of taxpayers' money had been spent planning the full, subsequently censored, exhibition. Still, both the display and its audiences were there to appreciate not the complicated politics of American history but the "simpler" fascination with a very famous airplane, which, after all, is why the National Air and Space Museum exists. There is across the mall a National Museum of American History, where any exhibition on the meaning of Hiroshima for us today might have been more logically staged. But in the Air and Space Museum, among the antique machines of both our early civilian aviation and our arms race with the Russians, the *Enola Gay* was another example of inspiringly successful American engineering, not American brutality.

The original plan called for the first two rooms of the exhibition to review the war in the Pacific after the defeat of Germany and culminate in *The Decision to Drop the Bomb*. But not in the scaled-down version: those same rooms explained first the history of how the B-29 Super Fortress was designed and built and then how this particular plane was painstakingly restored in what was the most ambitious such project in the Smithsonian's history. The details of this restoration occupied nearly half the total space of the gallery. The American heroism that this museum everywhere celebrates was especially found here, in the 55,000 man hours of labor that brought this plane "back to life." Only just before the exhibit of the fuselage itself were visitors finally confronted with the human history of this aircraft: a large blown-up photograph of the *Enola Gay*'s crew in 1945 features a group of smiling young men who were surely aware and at the same time not aware of what the mission they were about to embark on would accomplish and come to mean.

The *Enola Gay* came upon visitors suddenly. Fifty-three feet of fuselage, awkwardly amputated of its wings, slowed tourists who until now had been fairly racing through the gallery. Cut-away views into the interior of the plane, the original casing for the Little Boy bomb, the single photograph of the mushroom cloud (devoid of any human reference), the plaques explaining how the markings of the plane had been altered to trick the Japanese into thinking the *Enola Gay* was a harmless reconnaissance plane—all these things interested museumgoers and slowed their progress through the rest of the otherwise tedious display. The brief video made about and from the recollections of the *Enola Gay* crew was the only place where memory was explicit, and it was the often defensive memory of a handful of men whose lives have been defined and overwhelmed by this single mission. According to the original exhibition plan, this alcove was where taped interviews with Hiroshima survivors would have played.

It took less time to see this display than it did any other at the National Air and Space Museum. That may be because the *Enola Gay* alone had been purposefully stripped of the explanations, elaborations, and contextualizations that attended the other exhibitions. . . . The Smithsonian's display of the *Enola Gay* failed to suppress the kind of information, imagining, and even identification that it encouraged upstairs. Heyman made the *Enola Gay* display as meaningfully spare—which is not to say empty—as Japanese aesthetics would have insisted on. Removing the burned and melted artifacts that the city of Hiroshima had wanted to lend, and the photographs of actual burn victims that so "disturbed" . . . the veterans' groups, may have "sanitized" the exhibit, but in making it less pornographic they also made it more sublime. The cool, technical, and even scientific mood of the display stood in contrast to what some museumgoers must have imagined was the real-life consequence of this impressive technology and planning. . . .

The National Air and Space Museum's perfectly polished *Enola Gay* . . . , left stranded outside the history in which it looms large, could not help but generate metonymy, metaphors, and analogies. The few signs that did surround the display reassured visitors that the bomb casing "contains no nuclear material and presents no radiation hazard"; as to whether the *Enola Gay* itself is radioactive, the signs stated, "This exhibit poses no health hazards to museum visitors." Such guarantees would not have been needed unless the museum knew that this was precisely what worried the public: could they, too, be made victims of this weaponry, this airplane? Or was the museum worried that visitors were, despite everything, liable to imagine themselves . . . at ground zero?

The original *Enola Gay* exhibition would have concluded with a room called *The Legacy of Hiroshima and Nagasaki*. In this room, the Cold War and the arms race would have been presented as the legacy this plane willed us. But that—and, indeed, the nuclear regime we live under—were banished from what the public was finally permitted to see. Still, in a city full of museums and monuments that command us to remember the past, here in one small corner was the "simple" display that might have made some of us "remember the future"—that is, it might have made some of us use our imagination of the

Hiroshima victims to picture what might lie in store for everyone today, when we are all still universally menaced by even more powerful nuclear weapons. To "remember" the future may seem a contradiction, but it is always the past that governs the terms of our anterior historical speculation. . . .

One lesson of the *Enola Gay* display is that supposing memory is multiple also means that its truth is not singular, or legislated in advance. But another, more unsettling lesson would have to be: remembering the past does not guarantee understanding it. . . . The fact is that there is no reified memory. There is only remembering—remembering by human beings, with all of their biases and frailties. To treat memory as anything else is to make rhetoric out of it. To make memory serve, we need what might look like its opposite: metaphor. Cynthia Ozick once said that we cannot imagine—remember—how others live without the "reciprocal agent" of metaphor, the metaphor that is both memory and history. Ozick knows exactly what is wrong with the *Enola Gay* on display. Its businesslike order took metaphor away from us, and we could only try hard to bring it back and turn what was meant to be a monument into a memorial. Fifty years after Hiroshima and Nagasaki, we had to learn what happened there by imagining, by using the memory that Ozick's metaphor gave us. And to do that, you never had to go to Washington anyway.

8.5

WAR PORN
Hollywood and War, from World War II to *American Sniper*
Peter Van Buren

In the age of the all-volunteer military and an endless stream of war zone losses and ties, it can be hard to keep Homeland enthusiasm up for perpetual war. After all, you don't get a 9/11 every year to refresh those images of the barbarians at the airport departure gates. In the meantime, Americans are clearly finding it difficult to remain emotionally roiled up about our confusing wars in Syria and Iraq; the sputtering one in Afghanistan; and various raids, drone attacks, and minor conflicts elsewhere.

Fortunately, we have just the ticket, one that has been punched again and again for close to a century: Hollywood war movies (to which the Pentagon is always eager to lend a helping hand). *American Sniper*, which started out with the celebratory tagline "the most lethal sniper in U.S. history" and now has the tagline "the most successful war movie of all time," is just the latest in a long line of films that have kept Americans on their war game. Think of them as war porn, meant to leave us perpetually hyped up. Now, grab some popcorn and settle back to enjoy the show.

There's Only One War Movie

Wandering around YouTube recently, I stumbled across ... a video clearly meant to stir American emotions and prepare us for a long struggle against a determined, brutal, and barbaric enemy whose way of life is a challenge to the most basic American values. Here's some of what I learned: our enemy is engaged in a crusade against the West; wants to establish a world government and make all of us bow down before it; fights fanatically, beheads prisoners, and is willing to sacrifice the lives of its followers in inhuman suicide attacks. Though its weapons are modern, its thinking and beliefs are two thousand years out of date and inscrutable to us.

Of course, you knew there was a trick coming, right? This little U.S. government-produced film wasn't about the militants of the Islamic State. Made by the U.S. Navy in 1943, its subject was "Our Enemy the Japanese." Substitute "radical Islam" for "emperor worship," though, and it still makes a certain propagandistic sense. ... The age of the Internet, with its short attention spans and heightened expectations of cheap thrills, calls for a higher class of war porn, but as with that 1943 film, it remains remarkable how familiar what's being produced remains.

Like propaganda films and sexual pornography, Hollywood movies about America at war have changed remarkably little over the years. Here's the basic formula, from John Wayne in the World War II–era *Sands of Iwo Jima* to today's *American Sniper*:

— American soldiers are good; the enemy, bad. ... Our country's goal is to liberate; the enemy's, to conquer. ... It's beyond question that the ends justify just about any means we might use, from the nuclear obliteration of two cities of almost no military significance to the grimmest sort of torture. In this way, the war film long ago became a moral free-fire zone for its American characters.
— American soldiers believe in God and Country, in "something bigger than themselves," in something "worth dying for," but without ever becoming blindly attached to it. The enemy, by contrast, is blindly devoted to a religion, political faith, or dictator. ... As one critic put it back in 2007 with just a tad of hyperbole, "In every movie Hollywood

makes, every time an Arab utters the word 'Allah' . . . something blows up."

— War films spend no significant time on why those savages might be so intent on going after us. The purpose of American killing, however, is nearly always clearly defined. It's to "save American lives." . . . In Kathryn Bigelow's *The Hurt Locker*, for example, the main character defuses roadside bombs to make Iraq safer for other American soldiers. In the recent World War II–themed *Fury*, Brad Pitt similarly mows down ranks of Germans to save his comrades. Even torture is justified, as in *Zero Dark Thirty*, in the cause of saving our lives from their nightmarish schemes. . . . When an American kills in war, he's the one who suffers the most, not that mutilated kid or his grieving mother—I got nightmares, man! I still see their faces!

— Our soldiers are human beings with emotionally engaging backstories, sweet gals waiting at home, and promising lives ahead of them that might be cut tragically short by an enemy from the gates of hell. The bad guys lack such backstories. They are anonymous fanatics with neither a past worth mentioning nor a future worth imagining. . . .

— Our soldiers, anguished souls that they are, have no responsibility for what they do once they've been thrown into our wars. . . . In the film *First Blood*, for example, John Rambo is a Vietnam veteran who returns home a broken man. He finds his war buddy dead from Agent Orange–induced cancer and is persecuted by the very Americans whose freedom he believed he had fought for. Because he was screwed over in the 'Nam, the film gives him a free pass for his homicidal acts, including a two-hour murderous rampage through a Washington State town. . . .

— Americans always win, even when they lose. . . . A loss is still a win in *Black Hawk Down*, set amid the disaster of Somalia, which ends with scenes of tired warriors who did the right thing. *Argo*—consider it honorary war porn—reduces the debacle of years of U.S. meddling in Iran to a high-fiving hostage rescue. . . . In *American Sniper*, the disastrous occupation of Iraq is shoved offstage so that more Iraqis can die in Kyle's sniper scope. . . .

In sum: gritty, brave, selfless men; stoic women waiting at home; noble wounded warriors; just causes; and the necessity of saving American lives. Against such a lineup, the savage enemy is a crew of sitting ducks who deserve to die. Everything else is just music, narration, and special effects. . . .

A Fantasy That Can Change Reality

But it's just a movie, right? . . . Don't underestimate the degree to which such films can help create broad perceptions of what war's all about and what kind of people fight it. Those lurid on-screen images, updated and reused so repetitively for so many decades, do help create a self-reinforcing, common understanding of what happens "over there," particularly since what we are shown mirrors what most of us want to believe anyway. . . .

War films have the ability to bring home emotionally a glorious fantasy of America at war, no matter how grim or gritty any of these films may look. War porn can make a young man willing to die before he's twenty. Take my word for it: as a diplomat in Iraq, I met young people in uniform suffering from the effects of all this. . . .

Learning from the Exceptions

There are indeed exceptions to war porn, but don't fool yourself: size matters. How many people have seen *American Sniper, The Hurt Locker,* or *Zero Dark Thirty?* By comparison, how many saw the antiwar Iraq War film *Battle for Haditha,* a lightly fictionalized, deeply unsettling drama about an American massacre of innocent men, women, and children in retaliation for a roadside bomb blast? . . .

War is not a two-hour-and-twelve-minute hard-on. War is what happens when the rules break down and, as fear displaces reason, nothing too terrible is a surprise. The real secret of war for those who experience it isn't the visceral knowledge that people can be filthy and horrible, but that you, too, can be filthy and horrible. You don't see much of that on the big screen. . . .

If the core propaganda messages the U.S. government promoted during World War II are nearly identical to those pushed out today about the Islamic State, and if Hollywood's war films, themselves a particularly high-class form of propaganda, have promoted the same false images of Americans in conflict from 1941 to the present day, what does that tell us? Is it that our varied enemies across nearly three-quarters of a century of conflict are always unbelievably alike, or is it that when America needs a villain, it always goes to the same script?

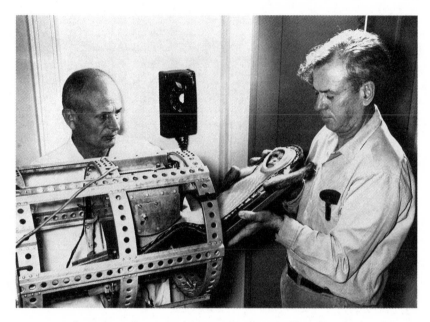

FIG 9.0. Militarization often means that scientists are coopted by military and intelligence agencies seeking to reap the benefits of basic research. For example, the physical, biological, and social sciences were commandeered by the US military during and after the Cold War. Scientists from the National Aeronautics and Space Administration (NASA) engaged in "dual-use" research that could be used by the U.S. military. In this photograph from 1958, NASA scientists prepare Sam, a rhesus monkey, for space flight. Photograph courtesy NASA.

SECTION IX. MILITARIZING KNOWLEDGE

Compiled by **DAVID H. PRICE**

Introduction

American universities have long-standing links to military and intelligence agencies, and academics often have uncomfortable reactions to these relationships. During the mid-twentieth century, American universities hosted research centers and training grounds for a broad range of military intelligence-related tasks as the needs of World War II pushed the hard sciences, soft sciences, and humanities to produce knowledge needed for the global war.

While the contributions of physicists, chemists, and biologists to World War II are widely recognized, social scientists also made significant contributions. Psychologists such as Rensis Likert developed techniques to measure public opinions related to war activities. Sociologists such as Samuel Stouffer produced classified reports on soldiers' attitudes for the Research Branch of the War Department. Hundreds of anthropologists performed war-related tasks that ranged from teaching "strategic languages," writing intelligence assessments, and managing War Relocation Authority camps to conducting dangerous secret missions for the Office of Strategic Services (OSS). Many of the OSS's top analysts came from Ivy League literature departments, with heavy recruiting for the Central Intelligence Agency (CIA) after the war.

Public reactions to military and intelligence agencies or their funds coming onto American campuses has shifted through time. During World War II, the militarization of campuses occurred rapidly with little critical opposition, as the dire needs of a nation at war overran whatever concerns about academic freedom and independence lingered. After the war, the GI Bill of Rights transformed

American college and university campuses as a wave of first-generation students came in droves to campuses.

After World War II, funds from government sources and private foundations established research programs in the physical sciences with military applications and funded foreign language and area study programs. These programs supported the Cold War's need for specific forms of geocultural knowledge. Bruce Cumings's essay explores links connecting the formation of interdisciplinary intelligence operations at the OSS and other agencies and the postwar proliferation of interdisciplinary programs at elite universities' Area Study centers and other programs, while Ellen Herman's contribution shows how the Cold War helped shape individual disciplines.

During the 1960s and '70s, shifts in campus political orientations and broad opposition to American military and intelligence actions in Vietnam and elsewhere in Southeast Asia led to movements to remove classified research projects, CIA recruitment, and military- and intelligence-linked projects from university campuses. Johan Galtung's essay on the now infamous Project Camelot records the passions and arguments of broadly shared academic opposition to collusion with military and intelligence work. The Beals Report (Beals 1967) marked a significant shift in academics' relationships with military and intelligence agencies. These campus attitudes and policies limiting military and intelligence work on campuses remained largely in place until after the September 11, 2001, attacks as a new national wave of fear brought an acceptance of new reductions of civil liberties and weakened resistance to intrusions of military and intelligence agencies into all spheres of civilian life, including universities and other knowledge producers (Price 2011).

The interview with Henry A. Giroux demonstrates how the rise of military-linked campus ties has evolved in tandem with increased militarization and decreased open public funding for universities. As civilian students take on tens of thousands of dollars in debt, new military education programs create a new class of citizen-students emerging from school with debts now payable by employment at military and intelligence organizations.

READINGS

9.1   Excerpts from Bruce Cumings, "Boundary Displacement: The State, the Foundations, and International and Area Studies during and after the Cold War," in *Parallax Visions: Making Sense of American–East Asian Relations*, by Bruce Cumings (Durham, NC: Duke University Press, 1999), 173–204.

9.1

BOUNDARY DISPLACEMENT

The State, the Foundations, and International and Area Studies during and after the Cold War

Bruce Cumings

After World War II ended, the new area programs and associations (such as the Association for Asian Studies) instantly confronted the existing boundaries of the social science and humanities disciplines; this often made for interesting intellectual confrontation, as well. William Nelson Fenton was present at the creation of area studies, and in 1947 he wrote that area programs faced fierce resistance from the "imperialism of departments" since they challenged the fragmentation of the human sciences by disciplinary departments, each endowed with a particular methodology and a specific intellectual subject matter (Fenton 1947: 26).

The anthropologist Cora DuBois thought that the collaborative work of the oss during the war was the prelude to a new era of reformist thinking on an interdisciplinary basis: "The walls separating the social sciences are crumbling with increasing rapidity. . . . People are beginning to think, as well as feel, about the kind of world in which they wish to live" (Du Bois 1949: 10–11). Postwar area studies, much maligned as the precinct for atheoretical navel-gazing and Orientalia, was beginning to challenge the parochialism of the disciplines in the name of a unified knowledge.

Still, these were not the power lines that counted. The state was less interested in the feudal domains of academe than in filling the vacuum of knowledge about a vast hegemonic and counterhegemonic global space; it was the capillary

lines of state power that shaped area programs. This was effected in the first instance by the relocation of the OSS's Soviet division to Columbia University as
the basis for its Russian Institute, which opened in September 1946, and in the
second instance by a Carnegie Corporation grant of $740,000 to Harvard to
establish its own Russian Research Center in 1947. Soon the Ford Foundation
put in much more money, a total of $270 million to thirty-four universities, for
area and language studies from 1953 to 1966.

This munificent funding created important area programs throughout the
country and provided numerous fellowships that allowed scholars to spend
years in the field acquiring difficult languages and other forms of area knowledge. McGeorge Bundy, however, was much closer to the truth in linking the
underpinnings of area studies to the intelligence agencies—the OSS and, subsequently, the CIA. William Donovan may have directed the wartime OSS
and then returned to Wall Street, but he was also in many ways the founder
of the CIA. In his papers, combed through by the CIA and then deposited at
the Army War College, there is a brief account of the original development of
"foreign area studies," in which Donovan, George F. Kennan, and John Paton
Davies played the major roles. Davies had a plan to transform area studies and
bring enormous amounts of government and foundation funding into U.S.
universities through what was originally to be an institute of Slavic studies but
that subsequently became a model for the organization of studies of the communist world of threatened Third World areas.

Donovan, who was then with the Wall Street firm Donovan, Leisure, was
at the center of this effort, working with Davies in 1948 and helping him to
get foundation funding. The organizers specified that the government was not
to be involved publicly in developing area studies to allay suspicions that such
programs were little more than "an intelligence agency." Their work should be
"impartial and objective," clear of conflicts of interest, and so on. (Indeed, the
files on this project are full of concern with academic independence and proper
procedure.) However, in a letter to Donovan, Clinton Barnard of the Rockefeller
Foundation—which with the Carnegie Corporation funded this effort at the
beginning—wrote, "The most compelling aspect of this proposal is the intelligence function which the Institute could perform for government" (Barnard
1948).

Sigmund Diamond (1992) greatly expanded our understanding of the establishment of area studies centers during the early years of the Cold War in his
book *Compromised Campus.* Diamond paid particular attention to the Russian
Research Center at Harvard, which, following Columbia's Russian Institute
and Davies's Slavic studies institute, became a model for other area programs

on Eastern Europe and China. It was also a model of cooperation with the CIA and the Federal Bureau of Investigation (FBI).

Although Diamond's government documents on Harvard in this period have been greatly expurgated—and Harvard's own papers remain closed to scholars under a fifty-year rule—he was able to document that the Harvard Russian Research Center was based on the wartime OSS model (like Columbia's); that the center was deeply involved with the CIA, the FBI, and other intelligence and military agencies; that several foundations (Carnegie, Rockefeller, Ford) worked with the state and the center to fund projects and, in some cases, to launder CIA funding; that the same scholars who undertook this activity often were themselves subjects of FBI investigations; that some of these scholars, in turn, were responsible for denouncing other scholars to the FBI; and, finally, that these academics were major figures in the postwar development of Russian area studies in the nation as a whole. By 1949, Harvard and the center had established a mutually satisfactory relationship with the local FBI office—indeed, results of the Russian Research Center's work were "made available to the Bureau officially through contact with President James B. Conant of Harvard University, who has on occasion indicated his respect for the Bureau's work and his understanding for its many and varied interests in connection with internal security matters" (quoted in Diamond 1992: 47). At roughly the same time, Conant also negotiated basic arrangements between Harvard and the CIA.

I frequently chide myself for running afoul of what I might call the fallacy of insufficient cynicism. I had not, for example, thought that J. Edgar Hoover enjoyed being wined and dined by major figures in organized crime, or that the Mafia had blackmailed him (either because of his closet homosexuality or his gambling debts) into refusing for years to investigate organized crime, even into denying that there was such a thing. Nor had I imagined the lengths to which the FBI would go to investigate even the most trifling aspects of life in academe in the early Cold War period. It is only a bit of an exaggeration to say that for those scholars studying potential enemy countries, either they consulted with the government or they risked being investigated by the FBI; working for the CIA thus legitimized academics and fended off Hoover (something particularly important for the many scholars born in foreign countries, or the many onetime communist émigrés now engaged in anticommunist research).

Diamond's papers contain large files of the Freedom of Information Act material on nationwide FBI investigations of academics in the early 1950s. Although most of the files are still thoroughly blacked out by "declassification" censors (in truth, there has been hardly any declassification on this issue), there is enough to indicate that any hearsay, any wild charge, any left-of-center organization joined, any name entered on a petition for whatever cause unacceptable to the FBI (such as peace or racial integration), any subscription to a magazine the FBI didn't like (e.g., *The Nation* or the *New Republic*) was enough to get an entry in the file. The FBI routinely checked the credit records of academics, tailed them around, monitored their lectures, questioned their colleagues and students, and sought out reliable campus informants. (William F. Buckley Jr. distinguished himself at Yale by becoming an important source for the FBI, as did Henry Kissinger to a lesser degree at Harvard.)

One FBI memorandum on Harvard goes on for forty-two pages with a detailed account of its courses on the U.S.S.R., complete with syllabi, teachers, and the content of the courses. Another has extensive reports on lectures at Harvard sponsored by the John Reed Club (which the future Japan scholar Robert Bellah chaired, and which had as its members the future China scholars Albert Feuerwerker and Franz Schurmann). Academics working on East Asia, of course, were particularly vulnerable to FBI harassment; those working on the U.S.S.R. were, as well, but more Asianists seemed to have come to the FBI's attention. The reasons for this were deeply involved with the history of those fields—the fact that the U.S.S.R. never inspired much sympathy among academics in the postwar period, but China, pre- and post-1949, did. The Korean War, for example, had an immediate impact on Harvard's policies toward the John Reed Club. Two months after the war began, Harvard banned the club from using Harvard facilities, unless it went through a lot of formalistic procedures (membership lists, sources of funds, and so forth) not required of other groups. In the same period, Harvard security people blocked the China hand Israel Epstein from speaking at a club gathering. An FBI informant in the Reed Club reported that the war in Korea was the cause of this new policy and that some club members did not want to register with Harvard for fear that their names would be turned over to the government.

9.2

THE CAREER OF COLD WAR PSYCHOLOGY
Ellen Herman

Between 1945 and the mid-1960s, the U.S. military was, by far, the country's major institutional sponsor of psychological research, a living illustration of what socially minded experts could accomplish, especially with a "not too gentle rain of gold" (Darley 1952: 720). Some of the reasons for the meteoric rise of military psychology were not very subtle. The military had more money than any other public institution during these years, and during the Korean War, the Department of Defense spent more on social and behavioral science than all other federal agencies combined (National Science Foundation 51, 1952). Projects that would have represented heavy investments for civilian bureaucracies could, on occasion, simply be ways of satisfying the military's curiosity or appeasing psychology's overheated advocates. Although impressive, the staggering sums that were spent on military psychological services between 1945 and 1970 are not, in themselves, convincing evidence that the military establishment had been thoroughly enlightened by psychology or converted to the experts' worldview. The military spent staggering sums on many things during these years, and psychology was—in relative terms, at least—dirt cheap.

Many of the academic professionals who had worked in the World War II military were relieved to return home to their universities in 1945, much like the ordinary soldiers they had studied. Samuel Stouffer, who had managed the Research Branch of the U.S. Army's Information and Education Division, returned briefly to the University of Chicago, then moved on to Harvard, where he became director of the new Laboratory of Social Relations. Rensis Likert, head of the Department of Agriculture's Division of Program Surveys and director of the Strategic Bombing Survey's Morale Division, went to Ann Arbor, where he headed the Institute for Social Research at the University of Michigan. Leonard Doob returned to his post at the Yale Institute of Human Relations. Even from such scattered locations in civilian academic life, however, World War II–era experts kept close tabs on the progress of military psychology (typically by serving as Defense Department advisers) and carefully nurtured the professional networks they had constructed during the world war, to their lasting benefit. According to Nathan Maccoby, a psychologist who worked in the Army Research Branch under the direction of Samuel Stouffer, "The Research Branch not only established one of the best old-boy (or old-girl) networks ever, but an alumnus of the Branch had an open door to most relevant jobs and career lines. We were a lucky bunch" (quoted in Simpson 1993: 12–13).

Those who chose to stay on in the military, or young professionals who spent their entire careers in the new defense-oriented research organizations that proliferated in the postwar era, were fond of pointing out that nothing much distinguished psychology on campus from psychology administered, directly or indirectly, by the Pentagon; virtually all psychological research had military applications (Geldard 1953). Further, work that was officially nonmilitary took on a military flavor, if only because association with national defense during the Cold War ensured the government's generous and sustained patronage. The National Institute of Mental Health (NIMH) and the National Science Foundation (NSF), both important civilian sources of funding for psychological and behavioral research in the postwar years, came into existence on the heels of World War II (Parsons 1986). The NIMH was established in 1946 as one component of the National Mental Health Act. General Louis Hershey, head of the Selective Service and one of the most vocal lobbyists for this legislation, made liberal use of the military's mental health data and warned that the psychiatric casualties of World War II were but the tip of the iceberg. The NSF was created four years later, after five years of congressional debate over twenty-one separate bills. By 1950, the Cold War climate was firmly in place, and the Korean War had just begun. The NSF and the NIMH were sensitive to military requirements and institutionally bound to the Defense Department in a number of ways, in spite of their allegedly nonmilitary purposes (Meyers n.d.: 20). The director of the NSF, for example, served on the President's Defense Science Board and was responsible for initiating and supporting military research at the request of the Secretary of Defense. Employment patterns were also quite fluid, and experts moved back and forth between military and civilian institutions. Theodore Vallance, for example, a psychologist and the director of the military research organization, the Special Operations Research Office (Camelot's sponsoring organization in the early 1960s), became chief of the NIMH Planning Branch just a few years later. Job location changed frequently; the nature of the work did not.

During the 1950s, all the types of work that psychological experts had done in the World War II military were further institutionalized (in the Defense Department and on campus) with the support of military funding: psychological warfare, intelligence classification, training, clinical treatment, and "human factors" (previously called "man-machine") engineering. Even the mysteries of morale and other fields of human relations research were vigorously pursued on the theory that, however speculative in the short run, their potential military payoff was large enough to justify the investment.

In the wake of World War II, practical applications counted above all, and the patriotic rush to make psychology (and other behaviorally oriented disciplines) serviceable generated expectations that at least certain kinds of expertise would be dependable enough, and hence indispensable enough, to be called "policy sciences" (Lerner and Lasswell 1951). Lingering skeptics typically confronted the passion—and sometimes the arrogance—of true believers, such as the sociologist Talcott Parsons (1986: 107), who wrote:

Do we have or can we develop a knowledge of human social relations that can serve as the basis of rational "engineering" control? . . . The evidence we have reviewed indicates that the answer is unequivocally affirmative. Social science is a going concern; the problem is not one of creating it, but rather of using and developing it. Those who still argue whether the scientific study of social life is possible are far behind the times. It is here, and that fact ends the argument.

Such confidence drowned out whatever tentative speculation existed that the explosion of job opportunities in the military, and elsewhere in government, was turning experts into obedient servants of the state.[1] The panic set off by Sputnik in 1957 about the state of U.S. scientific and technological know-how did nothing, of course, to inspire a more critical mood; it only increased the gush of defense dollars.

By the early 1960s, the Defense Department was spending almost all of its social science research budget on psychology, around $15 million annually, more than the entire budget for military research and development before World War II (Riecken 1962: 300). By the end of the 1960s, the figure had almost tripled, but even the huge sums spent by the Defense Department had been swamped years earlier by Great Society programs wishing to direct psychological expertise toward domestic policy problems. Whatever the intentions of military planners for their in-house and contract research during the Cold War, psychologists were hopeful, during the years following World War II, that "the military [might] serve for psychology the role that the industrial revolution served for the physical sciences" (Melton 1952: 136).

After 1945, and until the formal establishment of the NSF in 1950, the federal agency most responsible for funding psychological research was the Office of Naval Research (ONR). Established in August 1946 as the first federal agency dedicated to supporting scientific research, it took up pretty much where World War II left off. The ONR inherited many wartime research contracts that employed psychologists in areas of personnel and training (test design and measurement), group dynamics (conformity, motivation, and leadership studies), human factors engineering (equipment design), and physiological psychology (sensation and perception). With a total budget for psychological research of around $2 million each year, the ONR represented a military commitment to psychological research and expertise that far outstripped that of other public agencies. A decade after its establishment, the American Psychological Association celebrated this work at an elaborate Washington banquet "in recognition of the exceptional contributions of the Office of Naval Research to the development of American psychology and other sciences basic to the national welfare" (Darley 1957).

In 1950, the Korean War confirmed the wisdom and reliability of the military-psychology combination. Widely publicized "brainwashing" of U.S. prisoners of war by Chinese communists gave special impetus to studies of sensory deprivation and techniques of ideological conversion, although there was a concerted effort to keep this kind of politically sensitive military research quiet.[2] Ultimately, research related to the mechanisms of mass communications and persuasion found their most eager customer in the evolving U.S. intelligence community.[3] The CIA, in particular, launched an ambitious mind-control program during this period.[4] With a professional self-image that leaned heavily on psychological factors, the agency's embrace of behavioral technologies—including personality measurement and assessment—was not at all surprising. Consider the following description of an agent's primary mission by the CIA's inspector general in 1963: "The CIA case officer is first and foremost, perhaps, a practitioner of the art of assessing and exploiting human personality and motivations for ulterior purposes . . . by bringing the methods and disciplines of psychology to bear. . . . The prime objectives are control, exploitation, or neutralization. These objectives are innately anti-ethical rather than therapeutic in their intent" (quoted in Marks and Greenfield 1987: 25).

While the CIA's determination to train agents in the intricacies of psychological manipulation and its research into mind control were covert, not a matter of public record until decades later, the military's response to the Korean War was to reaffirm, often quite publicly, the fundamental lesson learned during World War II: war should be treated as a psychological struggle and laboratory. The Personnel Research Branch of the U.S. Army, along with several new contract research outfits (including the army's Operations Research Office of Johns Hopkins University and the U.S. Air Force's Human Resources Research Institute) sent psychologists to Korea to pursue the question of what exactly made a good soldier. These investigations proceeded under the watchful eyes of advisers, including Samuel Stouffer, who had pioneered this sort of attitude assessment effort in World War II. The army also launched Project CLEAR, an effort to check up on the slow progress of military racial integration after President Harry Truman issued an executive order in July 1948 to desegregate the armed forces. These studies, too, were reminiscent of the work of the Army Research Branch during World War II. Finally, the U.S. Psychological Strategy Board, which coordinated all psychological warfare campaigns in Korea, consulted with behavioral experts including Hadley Cantril, Daniel Lerner, Harold Lasswell, Rensis Likert, Gabriel Almond, Clyde Kluckhohn, and Alexander Leighton.[5] The result was that the World War II experience was grafted onto the Cold War conflict. The commitment to psychology as a weapon continued unabated.

NOTES

1. For one such prophetic warning, see Shils 1949.
2. Psychologists, such as McGill University's Donald Hebb, whose work on sensory deprivation for the Canadian Defense Research Board emerged directly out of war-inspired concerns with "brainwashing," were not permitted to say as much in their published studies (see Gilgen 1982: 122).
3. For a general discussion of this development, see Simpson 1993.
4. The most important CIA experiments of these kinds occurred from approximately 1945 to 1965 and included 149 projects, 80 institutions, 183 researchers (many of them academics), and $25 million. They were known as MK/ULTRA and MK/DELTA, and details of their existence were not exposed until the late 1970s. Much of the research involved laboratories at home, but the CIA also sent teams composed of a psychiatrist, a hypnotist, and an interrogator to communist countries to try out their scientific techniques (see Marks 1979).
5. See Proposed Consultant Panels, Records of the Psychological Strategy Board (cited in Simpson 1993: 13a–13b).

9.3

SCIENTIFIC COLONIALISM
Johan Galtung

Project CAMELOT is a study whose objective is to determine the feasibility of developing a general social systems model which would make it possible to predict and influence politically significant aspects of social change in the developing nations of the world.

> The project is conceived as a three- to four-year effort to be founded at around one and one-half million dollars annually. It is supported by the Army and the Department of Defense, and will be conducted with the co-operation of other agencies of the government.
>
> The U.S. Army has an important mission in the positive and constructive aspects of nation building as well as a responsibility to assist friendly governments in dealing with active insurgency problems.

These quotations are taken from an official document (dated December 4, 1964) from the Special Operations Research Office of the American University in Washington, DC, to introduce Project Camelot. . . .

The project was well prepared in the United States by a committee of social scientists, and the final research design was to take place in the summer of

1965. However, when this information was made available to Latin American social scientists, they refused indignantly to cooperate. The matter was brought first to national attention in Chile, then to international attention. The result was that on July 8 the project was canceled by the Office of the Secretary of Defense, and on August 5, an order was issued by the U.S. president that "no government sponsorship of foreign area research should be undertaken which, in the judgment of the Secretary of State, would adversely affect the United States' foreign relations."

The affair was much discussed by professional social science associations (particularly the anthropologists' association). But that does not mean that the essential lessons have necessarily been drawn from the matter or that it is entirely clear what these lessons might be. Many U.S. social scientists seem to understand little of the complexities of emotions and arguments in an affair of this kind. . . .

WHAT, THEN, WAS essential in this project? Certainly, its political nature, on which I comment first. But the question is: precisely what makes a project of this kind more political than academic? . . .

I would prefer to take as my criterion simply *the design of the project itself.* What kind of perspective on the political system studied is implicit in the design? Is this perspective one that expresses one political view rather than another so that it is already built into the design that findings can be used in favor of one political course of action rather than another? If, in addition, the sponsorship is political and even military, and the project is launched in a secretive manner, then the political nature of a project is unmistakable.

In defining the problems of the world in terms extremely close to exactly what people of the left, all over the world, feel to be the U.S. perception of world problems, Camelot was political. That the project also had considerable potential scientific value and that parts of it were brilliantly designed does not detract from this.

The social sciences are now rapidly developing in the Soviet Union and Eastern Europe. Imagine the Soviet Defense Ministry launching a sociological/anthropological project to inquire into the nature of unrest in Hungary, Poland, and East Germany, say, in early 1953 or early 1956.

From most Latin American points of view, outside some very special circles, participation in Project Camelot was a clearly political action, raising all of the problems of the role of social scientists relative to their governments. As the chairman of the special investigation by the Chilean House of Representatives into Project Camelot, Andres Aylwin, said:

In this project one pretends to make an analysis of the problems of man, of hunger, of unemployment.... However, these vital problems are not studied because of the significance they have in themselves but only insofar as they can be causes of rebellion or revolution. Said in other words, in Project Camelot one does not analyze unemployment to find its causes and study its solutions, it is not a question of studying human needs to try to satisfy them. Social problems are only important insofar as they can lead to tensions. In short, this project has not been conceived to try to solve the problems of hunger in Latin America, only to avoid revolution (quoted in Chilean House of Representatives, Special Investigation Committee 1965).

The many U.S. social scientists of world renown who participated in this project might protest this description of it. They would point to other aspects: the emphasis on nonmilitary rather than military approaches to these problems, the possibility of supporting the "softs" rather than the "toughs" in the Pentagon by giving them social science software that could serve as a substitute for their traditional military hardware....

If Project Camelot had been launched as intended, it would have led to the end of Latin American social science for, say, ten or twenty years. The suspicions the radical left has always entertained in Latin America as to the true nature of non-Marxist sociology would have been confirmed: a design to perpetuate the capitalist system internally and the imperialist system externally. Even with the development that actually took place, the project seriously affected intellectual—and, to some extent, political—confidence between North America and South America.

ANOTHER, EQUALLY SERIOUS aspect of Project Camelot is its "scientific colonialism." This, indeed, is an emotionally loaded term. But it is better than a neutral one such as "asymmetric patterns of research." ...

Scientific colonialism is that process whereby the center of gravity for the acquisition of knowledge about the nation is located outside the nation itself. There are many ways in which this can happen. One is to claim the right of unlimited access to data from other countries. Another is to export data about the country to one's own home country to have it processed there and turned out as "manufactured goods," as books and articles....

And then, most important, there is the biased distribution or accumulation of personally acquired knowledge about the "colony." At present, this is expressed in terms of the high number of doctoral theses, journals, and institutes that specialize in area studies (Latin American studies, African studies, studies of the "capitalist world") found in the scientifically most developed nations of the world (among other reasons because this mirrors the structure of their foreign ministries). Scholars from the scientifically powerful nations often know more about other nations than these nations know about themselves . . . the studies tend to be extremely adequate and relevant, and often quoted by nationals of these nations as the best ones available.

But is this not to be commended? Is it not a great favor to these nations that others contribute to their self-image? In one sense it is, and in another it is not. Knowledge is known as a good thing, but in human affairs it is not immaterial how that knowledge was acquired. . . .

Scientific colonialism as such is different from mixing politics and science. But it is also obvious that the two can easily be combined, with Project Camelot as the most glaring example. Social science knowledge about a small nation in the hands of a big power is a potentially dangerous weapon. It contributes to the asymmetric patterns already existing in the world because it contributes to manipulation in the interests of big powers.

A major aspect of scientific colonialism is the idea of unlimited right of access to data of any kind, just as the colonial power felt it had the right to lay its hand on any product of commercial value in the territory. How would the United States react to a commission of Soviet social scientists investigating the assassination of President John F. Kennedy? Or investigating the roots of the Cuba invasion? Or investigating the interests behind the Santo Domingo intervention?

In a sense this is a question of simple human decency. But it is also one of fundamental human rights. . . .

MUCH MORE CHALLENGING and much more important than the analysis of what happened is the effort to find workable solutions to the problems raised by the Camelot affair. Essentially, there are only these two problems: *the problem of combination of scientific and political goals*, and *the problem of scientific colonialism*. Whether governments should ever sponsor scientific research is not a problem—they maintain state universities in most countries, and it is difficult to argue that there is anything intrinsically wrong in government-sponsored research without denouncing the greater portion of research that has ever been carried out. Whether military agencies should ever sponsor research is not an issue either: they do so for military purposes, which one may like or dislike, or they may do so for nonmilitary purposes, which should then be evaluated on scientific merits.

Nor is the issue one of dishonesty: most people today will probably subscribe to (if not live up to) an ethical code whereby lies are permitted only under conditions of extreme *force majeure*—in matters of life and death—and would not include the operation of a research project under this heading. Moreover, since scientists presumably are engaged in the pursuit of truth, lies seem antithetical as means to this end. But many of the social science techniques for launching a project come dangerously close to infringing such a code.

The following extract from a letter from the faculty of the Catholic University, Santiago, Chile, to the president of the International Sociological Association gives some explanation of such attempts to deceive:

> In fact, Dr. Hugo Nuttini, professor in the Department of Anthropology at the University of Pittsburgh, who came to Chile to establish contact with Chilean sociologists to make them interested in participating in Project Camelot, affirmed both in writing and orally that the project was financed by the National Science Foundation when in reality it was financed by the Army of the United States and the Department of Defense of that country. Moreover, in the copy of the Project Design that he gave to Chilean sociologists all references to the Army had been meticulously erased. Finally, efforts were made to make us believe that it pursued purely scientific interests when in reality it was intended to serve as a basis for the counterinsurgency policies of the United States. [*Editors' Note*: This quotation was presumably obtained by the author, who played a leading role in exposing the proposed Project Camelot.]

The tensions that may arise from the problem of mixing politics and science may be eased if some principles can be applied, and the first of these is that of *frankness where purpose and sponsorship are concerned*. No bona fide social scientist should ever withhold both the purpose and sponsorship of his project. Second, social science projects should be *unclassified*, with the obvious limitations due to rules of anonymity, general considerateness, and so on. But as mentioned earlier, much too much emphasis has been put on this condition, probably because it is easily understood and relatively unproblematic both to implement and to circumvent.

Third, the tools of social science are more equally distributed. This political weapon must not become the monopoly of one group or one nation. This is not only a question of free access to theory and methods and effective technical assistance, but also one of devising social science methods that are so good and so cheap that they can be used by anybody with a sufficient level of training. At present, the costs of large-scale projects of the Camelot type are prohibitive for all but the bigger nations of the world. Realistically, all these technical-assistance efforts should be seen not only as measures to diffuse social science, but also as measures of self-defense for the nations in the periphery of the world.

Fourth, much research of a politically touchy nature should be handled not by the parties to the conflict but by third parties or by international institutes. Finally, one should above all be willing to see and to admit the political aspect of such research and not be lured and distracted by too much talk about the freedom to do research. We all believe in the value of science, but not at all costs; to do so would be to put knowledge higher than, say, freedom, autonomy, dignity, life, and death.

The key to the problem of *scientific colonialism* is asymmetry. The epitomized asymmetric project is carried out by the social anthropologist: when the design is his own, he himself carries out the data collection, although he may hire natives to do some of the prospecting for data for him and to function as interviewers, interviewees, or informants. The data are then carried home, and the processing, analysis, theory formation, and final write-up are all his. He leaves his country with the design, collects his data abroad, and comes with his suitcase filled with data extracted, to be processed at home. More often than not, he does not even inform his subjects as to his findings prior to the publication or afterward.

To this it will be objected that he does not have much of a choice: he is studying primitive peoples who have been discovered by social science but who have not themselves discovered social science, so they cannot possibly participate on an equal level, let alone carry out their own projects in the country of the social anthropologist. But this objection becomes increasingly invalid as the social sciences are developing around the world. . . .

In the Camelot case, [equal participation might] mean a design that would have been expanded to include, for instance, a study of the conditions of military intervention by the United States, a study of the ramifications of the famous "military-industrial" complex alluded to by President Dwight Eisenhower, a study of general attitudes to developing countries, a study of the potentials for violent and nonviolent change in U.S. society, and so on, all to be carried out by mixed U.S.-Latin American teams. With appropriate sponsorship, Camelot might have become an extremely useful project for other purposes, as well:

- It would give scholars from the developing countries a chance to gain more insight into the nature of the social and political systems they are emulating;
- It would enrich social science in the developing nations by forcing them to use other methodologies and theories. . . .
- It would give them a chance to get out of a certain self-centered frame of reference into a more global vision. . . .
- It would contribute to insights about the most powerful nations of the world, since they would no doubt be studied from other angles by scholars from developing countries (as examples, think of what Alexis de Tocqueville's and Gunnar Myrdal's studies have meant to the self-image held by Americans). . . .
- It would contribute to better social science by making it more universal and by exploiting more systematically the difference in research perspectives.
- It would contribute to more equality in the international system by institutionalizing equality in nations' access to knowledge about one another. . . .

The potential gains would be many. . . . It is also to be hoped that the fate of Project Camelot will serve as a warning to those who still feel such projects may be legitimately launched in the name of social science as well as to those who may become the targets of such projects, that they are not blind to their political overtones and are able to react toward them accordingly.

9.4

RESEARCH IN FOREIGN AREAS
Ralph L. Beals

As an aftermath of the Camelot affair, a Presidential Order directed the U.S. Department of State to review all government-supported research outside the United States. The Department of State proceeded to establish a Foreign Affairs Research Council for this purpose. The department—quite wisely, in the opinion of our committee—exempts grants and fellowships awarded by the National Science Foundation and the National Institutes of Health from the review procedure, although they must be reported for the information of the research council. . . . Reports of the volunteer area chairmen contain rich and instructive information concerning the difficulties and obstacles met by anthropologists in the field. Many of these problems are essentially unique or of limited occurrence since they relate to the peoples studied and their particular sensitivities, or to transitory local situations and personalities, or to the preparation and personality of the field investigators. . . .

There are areas in the world, we believe, where Americans are liked and welcomed and where anthropologists meet only the normal problems of adaptation to local situations. There, excluding personality clashes or manifest incompetence or ineptness by the fieldworker, official cooperation is freely given, and most Americans are respected and readily accepted by the people they plan to study. At the opposite extreme are countries (of which the U.S.S.R. and mainland China are the principal examples) in which American anthropologists can do virtually no field research, or where it can be done only under very restricted and often indirect circumstances. Between these extremes, most countries fall along a spectrum ranging from indifference and lack of official cooperation to the prohibition of entry or proscription of studying selected topics. It seems that there now is a trend toward more restriction and greater criticism of anthropologists and their research.

There are many causes for this growing suspicion, antagonism, and restriction on research. Some are particularly relevant to the research of U.S. anthropologists in foreign areas; others are international in their scope and implications and apply generally to anthropologists doing research outside their homelands. Some problems are particularly acute in the so-called developing countries, especially where there is limited understanding of social science and its purposes and possible utility, or where anthropology formerly was associated with the goals and administration of colonial governments. . . .

Research problems in foreign areas have multiplied with the substantial increase in the number of U.S. anthropologists doing research or being trained in other countries. Another complication has come with an increasing number of other social scientists recently undertaking foreign research. It is clear from the reports of the volunteer area chairmen that too many anthropologists engage in research abroad without adequate preparation and background for the area. This is far more true, however, of social scientists in other disciplines, many of whom have little or no preparation or experience, or who have worked only in European areas. It may also be said that the same criticisms can be made of anthropologists and social scientists from other countries. Finally, it appears that the foreign research projects that most frequently arouse criticism have been large and highly visible projects, often involving survey research techniques, frequently studying topics of national sensitivity, and designed or administered by people with little specific training for foreign area research.

Whenever U.S. anthropologists undertake research in foreign countries, they necessarily do so as guests, subject to whatever restrictions or restraints their hosts wish to impose.... Where civil disorder exists, anthropologists can expect restrictions on access to designated regions and groups. Anthropologists who engage in local politics or social movements, who promote ideologies, or who criticize local administrators or governments may expect to encounter hostilities and restrictions on their activities. In short, reports indicate that a noticeable number of anthropologists encountering problems in research abroad have created their own difficulties....

A major problem for anthropology and anthropologists in many parts of the world is the suspicion or belief that they are engaged in nonanthropological activities, or that the information they are collecting will be used for nonscientific and harmful ends. There is some basis for these suspicions and beliefs.... But what is more important than the question of the validity of these reports is the fact that the belief or suspicion that they may be true has already been harmful to legitimate anthropological research.

1. It is reported that agents of the intelligence branches of the U.S. government, particularly the CIA, have posed as anthropologists or asserted that they were doing anthropological research when in fact they were neither qualified as anthropologists nor competent to do basic anthropological studies. Journalists and others from the United States and elsewhere have also posed as anthropologists, and even though not involved in secret intelligence work for agencies of their governments, they have, through their behavior, created difficulties for legitimate anthropologists and their research.

2. It is reported that some of those qualified by training to call themselves anthropologists, and representing themselves as engaged in anthropological research, have actually been affiliated with U.S. intelligence agencies, especially the CIA. This has come about through direct employment by these agencies, or through accepting grants from certain foundations with questionable sources of income, or through employment by certain private research organizations. In some cases, such people have falsely represented themselves as still being associated with universities, although their prior academic affiliations no longer existed. It should be noted that situations of the same kind exist among anthropologists from

countries other than the United States. However, one deplorable aspect of the present situation is the frequency of loose, completely unsubstantiated, and often scarcely credible allegations of spying or intelligence activities made by a few anthropologists against their colleagues.

3. It is said that some anthropologists, particularly younger ones, who have encountered difficulties in securing funds for legitimate research have been approached by obscure foundations or have been offered supplementary support from such sources, only to discover later that they were expected to provide intelligence information, usually to the CIA. Some anthropologists are reported to have sought such support and to have accepted commissions willingly. . . . Such foundations or alleged foundations cannot be listed by name but may be identified among those that do not publish balance sheets indicating the sources of their funds.

A few anthropologists report that they were approached by U.S. Embassy officials in the countries where they worked or that they were interviewed by representatives of intelligence agencies after they had returned. In some cases, the information requested appears to represent legitimate interests, as when an anthropologist returned from an area that no member of the U.S. Embassy had visited and the information requested was of a general and public nature.

The reactions of anthropologists to such situations have varied greatly. A few would give no information to any government agency or representative. However, some have volunteered information when they encountered situations that they felt might be harmful to relations between the host nation and the United States. . . . It should be observed, however, that even in such situations the overwhelming majority of anthropologists have said they would give no information that might prove harmful either to the host nation or to its citizens, whether the data were given in oral, written, or published form.

A few cases have been reported to the committee in which anthropologists who have worked for intelligence agencies have not been granted visas for travel and research abroad once their former activities became known. Some universities also have declined to offer positions to anthropologists who have been employed by one or another intelligence agency. . . .

4. It is reported that the disclosure of contractual arrangements between universities and the CIA, even though these did not involve research in foreign areas, has in a number of cases cast doubt on university sponsorship of research abroad, especially in South America and Central America.

The belief has been voiced that some museums and other institutions that were conducting large research projects in foreign countries often unwittingly permitted intelligence agents to be included on the staffs of such projects.

The success with which academic institutions can function as sponsors of anthropological research is affected by their contracts and activities in nonanthropological, as well as in anthropological, matters. Although some individual anthropologists have been guilty of behavior that threatens to impair access to foreign areas by their colleagues, the greatest dangers have actually come from contracts, actions, and projects of the U.S. government and of some academic and private research organizations, even though these did not primarily involve anthropological activities. . . .

5. It also is reliably reported that in several countries of South America and Central America, Africa, and Asia, financing from certain U.S. government sources is suspect, and in some cases completely unacceptable. These sources include such mission-oriented agencies as the Department of Defense, CIA, U.S. Information Agency, and Department of State. Support by the Agency for International Development, the Peace Corps, and similar agencies is less suspect. . . .

The seriousness of the problems involved in the foregoing varies in different countries and areas of the world and may rapidly change, depending on international relations and attitudes toward the United States. One anthropologist reports that in the course of two years of fieldwork he was accused variously of being a Castroite, a Chinese communist, a Russian communist, a CIA agent, an FBI agent, a spy for the host nation's taxing agencies, and a Protestant missionary. Only the last caused him serious difficulties, and such an identification given anthropologists generally seems to be the most important field problem in much of South and America Central America. . . .

No easy or complete solutions to these problems can be proposed, of course. Most anthropologists have expressed disapproval of any activities, or the appearance of such activities, that are likely to arouse suspicion or resentment and hence restrict future anthropological research abroad. It also appears from their reports that suspicion has been allayed when anthropologists who are engaged in legitimate research openly explain their professional affiliations, sponsorship, source of funds, and the nature and purposes of their research—even when such explanations have to be expressed in simple terms to fit the knowledge and experience of the people concerned.

RETHINKING THE PROMISE OF CRITICAL EDUCATION
Henry A. Giroux (interviewed by Chronis Polychroniou)

I don't think there is any question that the neoliberal reconstruction of higher education has reached alarming heights in many countries, but we would be remiss not to recognize that there are other dangerous forces attempting to shape the university in ways that undermine its promise as a Democratic public sphere. For instance, while there has been an increasing concern among academics and progressives over the growing corporatization of the university, the transformation of academia into a militarized knowledge factory has been largely ignored as a subject of major concern and critical debate. Such silence has nothing to do with a lack of visibility regarding the shift toward militarization taking place in higher education.

Attempts to inject a military and security presence into American universities certainly have not been covert. Not only is the militarization of higher education made obvious by the presence of more than 150 military-educational institutions in the United States designed to train a youthful corps of tomorrow's officers in the strategies, values, skills, and knowledge of the warfare state; it is also evident, as the American Association of Universities points out, in the existence of hundreds of colleges and universities that conduct Pentagon-funded research, provide classes to military personnel, and design programs specifically for future employment with various departments and agencies associated with the warfare state. After decades of underfunding, especially within the humanities, faculty are lured to the Department of Defense, the Pentagon, and various intelligence agencies either to procure government jobs or to apply for grants to support individual research in the service of the national security state, which in turn provides backing for the U.S. government's commitment to global military supremacy. Military-oriented research programs and knowledge are now being funded to produce new and innovative ways to fight wars, develop sophisticated surveillance technologies, and produce new military weapons. Based on the assumption that weapons of destruction, surveillance, and death insure freedom and security, such research not only displaces compelling environmental, health, and life-sustaining projects in the interests of military priorities, but it is also antithetical to fostering a culture of public disclosure, transparency, questioning, dialogue, and exchange, all of which are central to the university as a democratic public sphere.

Similarly, the sixteen intelligence agencies in the United States are using higher education to train potential spies or other national security operatives, often under the cloak of secrecy. In such cases, the fundamental principles of public accountability, academic freedom, and open debate are either compromised or severely endangered. Moreover, an increasing number of colleges and universities are trying to attract Pentagon money by jumping into the market for online and distance-learning programs, often altering their curricula and delivery services to attract part of the lucrative education market for military personnel. The rush to cash in on such changes has been dramatic, particularly for private online educational institutions. What I think is problematic is both the nature of these programs and the wider culture of privatization and militarization legitimated by them. With respect to the former, the incursion of the military presence in higher education furthers and deepens the ongoing privatization of education and knowledge itself. Most of the players in this market are for-profit institutions that are problematic not only for the quality of education they offer, but also for their aggressive support of education less as a public good than as a private initiative and salable commodity. And as this sector of higher education grows, it will become not only more privatized, but also more instrumentalized, reducing the university to a credentializing factory designed to serve the needs of the military and coming closer to falling into the trap of confusing training with a broad-based education. Catering to the educational needs of the military makes it all the more difficult to offer educational programs that would challenge militarized notions of identity, knowledge, values, ideas, social relations, and visions.

At a time when civil liberties are under attack, intelligence agencies are illegally engaged in data mining; the separation of powers is increasingly undermined by an imperial presidency; and the CIA abducts people who then "disappear" into the torture chambers of authoritarian regimes, it is all the more imperative that higher education educate students to consider the consequences of the creeping militarization of American society. In addition, military institutions radiate power in their communities and often resemble updated versions of the old company towns of nineteenth-century America—inhospitable to dissent, cultural differences, people who take risks, and any discourse that might question authority. What all of this suggests is that the sheer power of the military apparatus, further augmented by its corporate and political alliances and fueled by an enormous budget, provides military-oriented institutions with a powerful arm-twisting ability capable of shaping research agendas, imposing military values, normalizing militarized knowledge as a fact of daily life, supporting military solutions to a range of diverse problems, and bending higher education and individual researchers to its will, an ominous and largely ignored disaster that is in the making in the United States.

Another threat that the university now faces comes from a newly reinvigorated war that is currently being waged by Christian nationalists, reactionary neoconservatives, and right-wing political ideologues against all of those independent institutions that foster social responsibility, critical thought, and critical citizenship. And there is more at work in this current attack than the rampant anti-intellectualism and paranoid style of American politics outlined in Richard Hofstadter's (1966) *Anti-Intellectualism in American Life*, written more than forty years ago. There is also the collective power of radical right-wing organizations, which, in spite of a democratically controlled Congress, continue to have a powerful influence on all levels of government and feel compelled to dismantle the open, questioning cultures of the academy. While the attack on dissent is being waged on numerous fronts, higher education in the United States seems to be the primary target of several right-wing forces that are waging an aggressive and focused campaign against the principles of academic freedom, and seem more than willing to sacrifice critical pedagogical practice in the name of patriotic correctness. Ironically, it is through the vocabulary of individual rights, academic freedom, balance, and tolerance that these forces are attempting to undermine the ideal of the university as a bastion of independent thought and uncorrupted inquiry; to slander—even vilify—an allegedly liberal and left-oriented professorate; to cut already meager federal funding for higher education; to eliminate tenure; and to place control of what is taught and said in classrooms under legislative oversight.

Underlying recent attacks on the university is an attempt not merely to counter dissenting points of view, but to destroy them, and in doing so to annihilate all of those remaining public spaces, spheres, and institutions that nourish and sustain a culture of questioning so vital to a democratic civil society. Within the conservative rhetoric, dissent is often equated with treason, and the university is portrayed as the weak link in the war on terror by powerful educational agencies. Professors who advocate a culture of questioning and critical engagement run the risk of having their names posted on websites such as DiscovertheNetworks.org and CampusWatch.org and being labeled un-American, while various right-wing individuals and politicians increasingly attempt to pass legislation that renders critical analysis a professional and personal liability and to reinforce a rabid anti-intellectualism under the call, with no irony intended, for balance and intellectual diversity. Genuine politics begins to disappear as people methodically lose those freedoms and rights that enable them to speak and act in public spaces, to exercise their individual right to dissent, and to advocate a shared sense of collective responsibility.

While higher education is only one site under attack, it is one of the most crucial institutional and political spaces where democratic subjects can be shaped, Democratic relations can be experienced, and anti-democratic forms of power can be identified and critically engaged. It is also one of the few spaces left where young people can think critically about the knowledge they gain, learn values that refuse to reduce the obligations of citizenship to either consumerism or the dictates of the national security state, and develop the language and skills necessary to defend those institutions and social relations that are vital to a substantive democracy. As the philosopher Hannah Arendt insisted, a meaningful conception of politics appears only when concrete spaces exist for people to come together to talk, think critically and act on their capacities for empathy, judgment, and social responsibility. What all this points to is a dire need for educators and others to recognize and take measures against the current attack on higher education that is now threatening to erase the ideas and the practices that enable the academy to fulfill its role as a crucial democratic public sphere, offering a space both to resist the dark times in which we now live and to embrace the possibility of a future forged in the civic struggles requisite for a viable democracy.

FIG 10.0. Militarization's effects can alter human bodies in many ways. Soldiers' bodies may be subjected to rigorous discipline or abuse and exposed to chemical, radiological, or pharmaceutical substances that can have lethal effects. In the era of modern warfare, however, civilians' bodies are far more susceptible to being damaged or destroyed, as in the case of the victims of the Isaaq genocide in northern Somalia, which occurred in the late 1980s. Photograph by Alison Baskerville.

SECTION X. MILITARIZATION AND THE BODY

Compiled by ROBERTO J. GONZÁLEZ

Introduction

War and militarization affect the natural world and social relationships in complex ways, but they also have intimate effects on human bodies. Since ancient times, bodies have been inscribed, altered, damaged, and destroyed by military action. Questions of long-term human survival have been of great interest to anthropologists, and studying militarism's effects on health and well-being is a productive way to approach these concerns.

The following selections review different ways in which militarism has affected human bodies. The section begins with an excerpt from Hugh Gusterson's "Nuclear War, the Gulf War, and the Disappearing Body" and analyzes the ways in which governments and military institutions essentially erase the destructive effects of modern warfare on human bodies. By examining official accounts of nuclear bombardment and the Persian Gulf War of the early 1990s, Gusterson convincingly argues that masking the violent nature of military action makes it difficult to see its human costs.

The next selection focuses on war's embodiments. It is taken from Elaine Scarry's *The Body in Pain*. Her analysis of war as a series of acts explicitly designed to injure human bodies is supplemented by a consideration of how injury often disappears from view in written accounts of war. Scarry's work can be applied to the use of torture in the early years of the so-called war on terror. Horrific accounts of bodily and psychological injury suffered by men held at the U.S. detention facility at Guantánamo Bay (see, e.g., Rasul et al. 2004) illustrate one of the most extreme embodiments of militarism: torture, abuse, and degradation of captive bodies.

The next selection, by Kenneth Ford and Clark Glymour, focuses on the creation of "the enhanced warfighter"—a new kind of technologically formed subject resulting from the genetic and computational alteration of the body, close physiological monitoring, and the increasing use of pharmaceutical drugs. Their article analyzes soldiers' bodily relationships with technologies that keep them alive yet, ironically, may also be exposing them to harm. On the one hand, disciplinary processes and technological tools are designed to create bodies that are more capable of overcoming near-term injury or death. On the other hand, these same innovations may increase the long-term risks of servicemen and servicewomen who use them.

The section ends with a contribution by James Quesada, who illustrates how psychological injuries can linger for decades, long after military actions have ceased. By ethnographically analyzing the experiences of a Nicaraguan boy and his family, Quesada demonstrates that war's legacy can be embodied through the lived experience of chronic social suffering.

READINGS

10.1 Excerpts from Hugh Gusterson, "Nuclear War, the Gulf War, and the Disappearing Body," *Journal of Urban and Cultural Studies* 2, no. 1 (1991): 45–55.

10.2 Excerpts from Elaine Scarry, "The Structure of War: The Juxtaposition of Injured Bodies and Unanchored Issues," in *The Body in Pain: The Making and Unmaking of the World*, by Elaine Scarry (Oxford: Oxford University Press, 1985), 60–122.

10.3 Excerpts from Kenneth Ford and Clark Glymour, "The Enhanced Warfighter," *Bulletin of the Atomic Scientists* 70, no. 1 (2014): 43–53.

10.4 Excerpts from James Quesada, "Suffering Child: An Embodiment of War and Its Aftermath in Post-Sandinista Nicaragua," *Medical Anthropology Quarterly* 12, no. 1 (1998): 51–73.

10.1

NUCLEAR WAR, THE GULF WAR, AND THE DISAPPEARING BODY
Hugh Gusterson

The human body is a place where objectivity and subjectivity meet. As Elaine Scarry (1985) and Michel Foucault (1979, 1980) observe, the human body can be treated as an object to be tortured, wounded, dismembered, and destroyed—in other words, engraved by the powerful with the marks of their power. The very limit of this power is the ability to make human bodies completely disappear. However, the human body is also a place where pain, desire, and personhood are experienced as subjectively real. In matters of contemporary war, the human body can be both a blank page awaiting the violent inscriptions of power and, when its subjectivity escapes subjection, a source of embarrassment and resistance to that power.

Contemporary American war-fighting strategies involve not only the destruction of human bodies on a massive scale, but also an ambiguous marginalization of the body's presence. War has not always been this way. In the simple wars of small-scale, so-called primitive societies, the human body was the focal resource, target, and visual center of fighting. Descriptions of fighting among the Iroquois Indians (Wallace 1970), the Yanomami Indians (Chagnon [1968] 1977), the Dani of New Guinea (Heider 1979), and the Ilongots of the Philippines (Rosaldo 1989), for example, emphasize that the point of fighting was to jubilantly kill, wound, or torture the bodies of enemy men and, in some cases, to rape or capture the bodies of enemy women. Both victory and heroism were judged in terms of damage done to bodies.

In recent history, technological advances have multiplied the volume of damage done to human bodies in war, but, ironically, the importance of bodies as targets has become increasingly marginal to warriors, who now score success mainly in terms of territory captured, enemy weapons destroyed, or industrial infrastructure disabled (Clausewitz 1976; Gray and Payne 1980). In our contemporary postmodern era of nuclear and smart weapons, the unprecedented ability of commanders to destroy entire bodies of bodies is matched by a partial preemptive disappearance of the body from representations of war.

This becomes clear if we investigate the representation of the body in nuclear discourse, a subject I have looked at as an anthropologist writing an ethnography about a nuclear weapons laboratory in California. The history of the nuclear age can be written partly as the story of the objectification and disappearance of the subjective human body. Nuclear discourse estranges the masters of the discourse from their own bodies, while the victims of nuclear weapons disappear either literally or figuratively as they encounter the objectifying practices of Western scientific militarism.

Nuclear War

Michel Foucault (1979) and Talal Asad (1983) have argued, in regard to ritual torture and execution in premodern Europe, that mutilated bodies are points of exchange between power and knowledge. They suggest that the inscription of pain on the body produces social and political effects of truth, either by producing confessions or by transforming bodies into texts inscribed with the marks of power. According to Foucault, however, Western societies in the past two centuries, partly out of sensitivity to popular opinion at a time of increasing democratization, have become much more circumspect about displaying such marked bodies in public.

Applying this argument to war rather than to domestic social discipline, we can say that nuclear weapons afford an unprecedented power to produce effects of truth and domination by marking docile human bodies. Yet the mutilated bodies of atomic bomb victims, as well as the fearful bodies of those who have yet to be annihilated, have an inflammatory potential that also makes them dangerous. . . .

Nuclear weapons first proved their power by destroying the bodies of about 200,000 people in Hiroshima and Nagasaki and leaving marks on the surface and in the interior of countless thousands more living but wounded bodies. These marks on the destroyed or damaged bodies of the Japanese came to constitute a kind of collective text for American scientists to decode as they sought scientific truths about nuclear weapons that would, in turn, be used to establish political regimes of truth in the form of ideologies of deterrence, targeting doctrines, and so on. Thus, American scientists have spent years keeping careful track of Japanese casualties, trying to document the exact numbers killed and wounded by the initial flash, blast effects, the fireball, instantaneous radiation effects, and subsequent cancers. Their findings have been used to calculate the strength of the nuclear explosions in Japan and to help plan hypothetical nuclear attacks against other countries (Luke 1989). . . .

Although they are an essential medium for recording the bomb's power, there is a sense in which these bodies disappear in the process of being read. Photographs of atomic bomb survivors feature close-ups of burns, mangled limbs, and exposed nerves that are often taken from the back or focus so closely on ravaged tissue that the race, age, and sex of the victim cannot be known. In these photographs, human bodies are metamorphosed into body parts and pieces of human matter—pieces of bodies that have been fragmented not only by the weapon but also in the act of documentation, by the photographers whose cameras sever limbs from bodies as sharply and quickly as the bomb itself did. There is a politics of representation here that, in its attention to detail, objectifies damaged bodies, makes them disappear, and impedes sympathetic identification with the people who live in them.

This point is best illustrated by contrasting two texts that describe the effects of nuclear weapons on the human body, but in different voices and with different results. The first, from John Hersey's *Hiroshima*, was read into the congressional record by Senator Mark Hatfield . . . :

> He found about 20 men and women on the sand pit. He drove the boat onto the bank and urged them to get aboard. They did not move and he realized they were too weak to lift themselves. He reached down and took a woman by the hands, but her skin slipped off in huge, glovelike pieces.
>
> Then he got into the water and, though a small man, lifted several of the men and women, who were naked, into his boat. Their backs and breasts were clammy, and he remembered uneasily what the great burns he had seen during the day had been like: yellow at first, then red and swollen, with the skin sloughed off, and finally, in the evening, suppurated and smelly.
>
> With the tide risen, his bamboo pole was now too short and he had to paddle most of the way across it. On the other side, at a higher spit, he lifted the slimy living bodies out and carried them up the slope away from the tide. He had to keep consciously repeating to himself: "These are human beings. These are human beings."[1] . . .

Contrast the following passage from *The Effects of Nuclear Weapons*, a Pentagon publication widely read by nuclear weapons scientists and defense planners: . . .

> Because of the relatively small size of the body, the diffraction process is quickly over, the body being rapidly engulfed and subjected to severe compression. . . . The sudden compression of the body and the inward motion of the thoracic and abdominal walls cause rapid pressure oscillations to occur in the air-containing organs. These effects, together with the transmission of the shock wave through the body, produce damage mainly at the junctions of air-containing organs and at areas between tissues of different density, such as where cartilage and bone join soft tissue. (Glasstone and Dolan 1977: 548)

This account, abstracted from the experiences of Hiroshima and Nagasaki victims, has a generic quality. The use of objectifying language to describe body components undermines our sense of the body's subjectivity, of our own embodiment, and of our relationship to other bodies. . . .

The damaged bodies of human beings have now disappeared and been re-constituted as a body of knowledge.

Bodies can become sites of resistance to such discourses and practices when their subjectivity escapes discipline. One physicist who had refused to work on nuclear weapons explained her decision to me in these terms: "There's this thing in my stomach. My head understands the reason to work on the weapons, for deterrence and so on, but when I think about doing this work I feel this thing in my stomach." This visceral rebellion of the body can be spontaneous and powerful. In the documentary film *The Day after Trinity*, the physicist I. I. Rabi recalls his reaction to seeing the first nuclear test: "It took a few minutes until I realized what had happened. I had gooseflesh when I thought of the consequences for the world." . . .

Meanwhile, the scientists' discourse on weapons is flecked with traces of a repressed and transposed identification with bodies. In the metaphorical world inhabited by the scientist, there is a sense in which the machines become surro-gate bodies. . . . Thus, nuclear weapons are spoken of as "arms," and the American nuclear triad is said to stand on three "legs" (air-, sea-, and land-based missiles). Nuclear missiles have heads—"warheads"—and certain kinds of attacks on enemy hardware are described as "decapitation attacks." . . .

The Gulf War

The representation of the Gulf War to the American public, by both the media and the U.S. government, brings many of these themes into sharper focus. This representation was remarkable for the way in which it treated bodies as objects for mechanical enhancement and weapons as surrogates for the bodies of war-riors, and, above all, for the extraordinary visual and thematic absence of dead, maimed, mutilated, strafed, charred, decapitated, pierced human bodies in a heavily televised war that surely claimed at least 100,000 casualties.

American supremacy in the Gulf War was often portrayed in terms of the United States' ability, through technology, to transcend the limitations of the human body or to reengineer the human body. While the Iraqis' ability to fight was constrained by their bodies' need to sleep and their inability to see in the dark, American pilots were using amphetamines to suppress their body rhythms so they could bomb around the clock, and American pilots and ground forces were using night-vision goggles and thermal sights to enable them to see targets in the dark that would not usually be visible to the human eye (Schmitt 1991). The vulnerability of American bodies to chemical and bio-logical weapons was addressed with chemical protection suits and inoculations that supposedly armored ordinarily fragile human bodies against such threats. The bodies of American warriors thus had a post-human, cyborg-like quality that was often foregrounded in television images of soldiers in chemical suits with masks or in night-vision goggles.

While humans in the Gulf War were invested with mechanical qualities and their bodies were marginalized, machines were invested with human qualities and moved to the visual and thematic center of battle. . . . We were repeatedly told that tanks, missiles, and planes could "see" targets and "make decisions." Meanwhile, although American leaders and many journalists did their best to use euphemistic alternatives to the word "kill" in regard to human casualties in the war, they repeatedly talked about tanks being "killed." In this vein, one ABC News reporter humanized a mass of charred, splintered metal by referring to it as "a cemetery of twisted tanks."[2] . . .

If the dead and mutilated bodies of tanks were recurrent images in the media, the same cannot be said of the dead and mutilated bodies of human beings. These bodies, American as well as Iraqi, largely disappeared. The disappearance of American bodies was partly accomplished by their semantic transformation into "human remains." . . . The Department of Defense, newly sensitive to the potency of broken bodies, changed its traditional rules for war coverage, refusing to allow media coverage of the return and processing of these pouches (Farrell 1991).

But surely the most extraordinary feature of this war was the virtual absence of dead and wounded Iraqi bodies in public representations of a war where probably more than 100,000 Iraqis were killed in close proximity to about a thousand journalists in search of a story. From what little we have so far been allowed to know, it seems fairly clear that, even with smart weapons, one cannot bomb a city on the scale the allies bombed Baghdad and Basra without killing a large number of civilians. . . . If the dead Iraqis were civilians, their bodies were concealed within the term "collateral damage." If they were soldiers, the bodies of Iraqis were collectively referred to as "forces," "units," "assets," and "targets," anything but people with loved ones and feelings. The systematic killing of these soldiers was referred to as "softening up," "pounding," "giving attention to," or "attriting"—as in General Norman Schwarzkopf's remark, reframing mass murder as the completion of a bureaucratic task.[3] . . . The visual backdrop for Schwarzkopf's remark was a map of Iraq where thousands of Iraqi soldiers were represented as a few green rectangles that, when sufficiently "attrited," were removed from the map and placed in one corner, as in a board game. . . .

General Schwarzkopf at his triumphal briefing told a reporter who asked about Iraqi casualties, "We are not in the business of killing." Schwarzkopf was able to make the extraordinary and, on the face of it, absurd contention that he was fighting a war without being in the business of killing largely because of the power of a system of representations that marginalizes the presence of the body in war, fetishizes machines, and personalizes international conflicts while depersonalizing the people who die in them. . . .

Conclusion: Resistance

Antimilitary practices that seek to disrupt the system of representations portraying war as a form of sport or as an international video game often seek to make the disappearing body reappear—by showing the corpses, all the corpses; by connecting people with the fear that is apprehended through bodies; maybe even in civil disobedience by ringing military installations with bodies that refuse to disappear, bodies that insist on deploying their vulnerability as a means toward political power.

Militarism can be undermined by challenging practices that objectify the human body and, instead, restoring an awareness of and connection with the body's subjectivity. The only moment when the American government briefly lost control over the public representation of the Gulf War occurred when an Iraqi air-raid shelter was bombed and the American people saw the destroyed and suffering bodies of Iraqi civilians on television. This incident briefly liberated the resistant power of the body.

If we are to constrain the technologies of destruction our minds have created, it will surely be by balancing our power to objectify bodies with a celebration of their subjectivity. Maybe the ancient Chinese philosopher Lao Tzu put it best when he said:

> He who loves
>   his body
> More than dominion
>   over the empire
> Can be given
>   Custody of the Empire

NOTES

1. *Congressional Record*, August 2, 1989, S9438–439.
2. ABC *World News Tonight*, February 28, 1991.
3. Some of these examples come from White 1991.

THE STRUCTURE OF WAR
The Juxtaposition of Injured Bodies and Unanchored Issues
Elaine Scarry

Torture is such an extreme event that it seems inappropriate to generalize from it to anything else or from anything else to it. Its immorality is so absolute and the pain it brings about so real that there is a reluctance to place it in conversation by the side of other subjects. But this reluctance, and the deep sense of tact in which it originates, increase our vulnerability to power by ensuring that our moral intuitions and impulses, which come forward so readily on behalf of human sentience, do not come forward far enough to be of any help: we are most backward on behalf of the things we believe in most in part because, like ancients hesitant to permit analogies to God, our instincts salute the incommensurability of pain by preventing its entry into worldly discourse. . . .

It is a consequence of the ease with which power can be mixed with almost any other subject that it can be endlessly unfolded, exfoliated, in strategies and theories that—whether compellingly legitimate or transparently absurd—in their very form, in the very fact of occurring in human speech, increase the claim of power, its representation in the world. In contrast, one of two things is true of pain. Either it remains inarticulate or else the moment it first becomes articulate it silences all else: the moment language bodies forth the reality of pain, it makes all further statements and interpretations seem ludicrous and inappropriate, as hollow as the world content that disappears in the head of the person suffering. . . .

War and torture have the same two targets, a people and its civilization (or as they were called earlier, the two realms of sentience and self-extension); the much greater reliance on the symbolic in torture occurs in both spheres. In both war and torture, there is a destruction of "civilization" in its most elemental form. When Berlin is bombed, when Dresden is burned, there is a deconstruction not only of a particular ideology but of the primary evidence of the capacity for self-extension itself: one does not in bombing Berlin destroy only objects, gestures, and thoughts that are culturally stipulated but objects, gestures, and thoughts that are human, not Dresden buildings or German architecture but human shelter. Torture is a parallel act of deconstruction. It imitates the destructive power of war: rather than destroying the concrete physical fact of streets, houses, factories, and schools, it destroys them as they exist in the mind of the prisoner, it destroys them as they exist in the furnishings of a room: to convert a table into a weapon is to set a factory on fire; to hear a confession is to watch from above the explosion of a city block. This same form of substitution occurs in relation to the second target, the sentient source of the first, the human body itself. Whereas the object of war is to kill people, torture usually mimes the killing of people by inflicting pain, the sensory equivalent of death, substituting prolonged mock execution for execution. The numbers involved reinforce this sense of the division between the real and the dramatized. Although the thousands and thousands of political prisoners hurt during the 1970s and 1980s have led Amnesty International to call torture an "epidemic," the numbers of persons hurt are of course vastly larger in war. In torture, the individual stands for "individuals"—huge multiplicity is replaced by close proximity sustained over hours or days or weeks; being in close contact with the victim's hurt provides the sense of "magnitude" achieved in war through large numbers.

But while torture relies much more heavily on overt drama than does war, war, too—as is quietly registered in the language of theaters of battle, international dialogues, scenarios, and stages—has within it a large element of the symbolic and is ultimately, like torture, based on a simple and startling blend of the real and the fictional. In each, the incontestable reality of the body—the body in pain, the body maimed, the body dead and hard to dispose of—is separated from its source and conferred on an ideology or issue or instance of political authority impatient of, or deserted by, benign sources of substantiation. There is no advantage to settling an international dispute by means of war rather than by a song contest or a chess game except that in the moment when the contestants step out of the song contest, it is immediately apparent that the outcome was arrived at by a series of rules that were agreed to and that can now be disagreed to, a series of rules whose force of reality cannot survive the end of the contest because that reality was brought about by human acts of participation and is dispelled when the participation ceases. The rules of war are equally arbitrary and again depend on convention, agreement, and participation; but the legitimacy of the outcome outlives the end of the contest because so many of its participants are frozen in a permanent act of participation: that is, the winning issue or ideology achieves for a time the force and status of material "fact" by the sheer material weight of the multitudes of damaged and opened human bodies. . . .

The essential structure of war, its juxtaposition of the extreme facts of body and voice, resides in the relation between its own largest parts, the relation between the collective casualties that occur *within* war and the verbal issues (freedom, national sovereignty, the right to a disputed ground, the extraterritorial authority of a particular ideology) that stand *outside* war; that are there *before* the act of war begins and *after* it ends; that are understood by warring populations as the motive and justification and will again be recognized after the war as the thing substantiated or (if one is on the losing side) not substantiated by war's activity. The central question that is asked here—What is the relation between the obsessive act of injuring and the issue on behalf of which that act is performed?—is a question about the relation between the interior content of war and what stands outside it. In order to answer that question, however, it is necessary to back up one step and define the relation between two interior facts about war: first, that the immediate activity is injuring; second, that the immediate activity of war is a contest. In participating in war, one participates not simply in an act of injuring, but also in the activity of reciprocal injuring where the goal is to out-injure the opponent. The construction "War is *x*" has, over the centuries, invited an array of predicate nominatives, but there are no two predicate nominatives that have either the accuracy or the definitional totality as the two singled out here, and it is by first understanding precisely how the two qualify each other that it will be possible to arrive at an understanding of the second and more fundamental question about the relation between bodily injury and verbal issues. . . .

I. War Is Injuring

The main purpose and outcome of war is injuring. Although this fact is too self-evident and massive ever to be directly contested, it can be indirectly contested by many means and disappear from view simply by being omitted: one can read many pages of a historical or strategic account of a particular military campaign, or listen to many successive installments in a newscast narrative of events in a contemporary war, without encountering the acknowledgment that the purpose of the event described is to alter (to burn, to blast, to shell, to cut) human tissue, as well as to alter the surface, shape, and deep entirety of the objects that human beings recognize as extensions of themselves. In any given instance, omission may occur out of the sense that this activity is too self-evident to require articulation; it may instead originate in a failure of perception on the part of the describer; again it may arise out of an active desire to misrepresent the central content of war's activity (and this conscious attempt to misrepresent can in its turn be broken down into an array of motives, some malevolent, some relatively benign). . . .

Of all writing—political, strategic, historical, medical—there is probably no work that more successfully holds visible the structural centrality of injuring than Carl von Clausewitz's *On War*. In his description of invasion, for example, he will say, "The immediate object here is neither to conquer the enemy country nor to destroy its army, but simply *to cause general damage*," as he will often elsewhere specify that the object is to "increase the enemy's suffering" (Clausewitz 1976: 91, 93). In battle, for example, the soldier's primary goal is not, as is so often wrongly implied, the protection or "defense" of his comrades (if it were this, he would have led these comrades to another geography); his primary purpose is the injuring of enemy soldiers; to preserve his own forces has the important but only secondary and "negative" purpose of frustrating and exhausting the opponent's achievement of his goal (Clausewitz 1976: 97–98). . . .

War is relentless in taking for its own interior content the interior content of the wounded and open human body.

II. War Is a Contest

Our second premise, that war is a "contest," invokes a predicate nominative that is far less concussive than "injuring" and thus a much less difficult fact to hold steadily visible before one's eyes. Insofar as there is a reluctance to identify war as a contest, the reluctance originates in an impulse almost opposite to that which helps bring about the eclipse of injuring: when the identification is avoided or explicitly rejected, it is so because "contest" is always attended by its near-synonyms of "game" and "play," thus allowing war's conflation not only with peacetime activity but also with that particular form of peacetime activity that is least consequential in content and outcome. . . .

It is . . . seductive but wholly inaccurate to describe the determining activity of the contest in terms of the external issues (the men are not out-freeing one another, or outperforming one another in the act of liberation, or out-proving to one another the legitimacy of their side's historical claim to a certain strip of land), just as it is seductive and inaccurate to describe it in terms of an activity interior to but not central to war. . . . It is, then, once again, the depth, massiveness, intensity, or speed of injuring that is central, and the feat of out-injuring that determines the winner. . . .

If, then, the question, "What it is that differentiates injuring from any other act on which a contest can be based?" is not a question that can be easily answered, neither is it a question that can be easily unasked.

III. What Differentiates Injuring from Other Acts or Attributes
on Which a Contest Can Be Based

A simple element that, perhaps more than any other, complicates the answering of this question is the discrepancy between the small number of participants in most peacetime contests and the massive numbers in war. As will become evident later, the most pervasive error in answering the question may in fact come about by taking as a conceptual model for war the image of single combatants: that is, imagining the determining activity as injuring, but contracting the scale down from an extremely large number of persons to two persons. The inappropriateness of this model will become visible at a later moment, but rather than beginning with the complications that arise from conforming war to the diminutive sale of other contests, it will be helpful to begin with the opposite movement and imagine an ordinary form of contest based on some activity other than injuring now magnified until it conforms to the scale of participation normally occurring in war.

Although the numerical discrepancy is itself an important difference between war and other means of determining a winner and loser, it is not itself the critical differentiating element (and thus does not in and of itself provide a path of substitution for war, though it might in combination with other elements provide a form of substitution). That is, one can imagine a contest based on some relatively benign activity, distributed out over two disputing populations: all members of each civilization—or a large proportion; say, all young adults between the ages of eighteen and thirty-five—could be paired off in a massively extended sequence of chess matches or tennis matches, a sequence of pairings that would take over a thousand days, perhaps two thousand or three thousand, during which the record of wins and losses would be steadily added up, with the cumulative successes and failures announced at frequent but somewhat irregular intervals (three days, ten days, thirty days) so that the two entire populations would be at all times imaginatively engaged in the progress. . . . This extraordinary organizational requirement would, in fact, be one of its benefits, again increasing the depth of engagement of the overall population. The energies of the unconscripted citizens would in large part be absorbed in support activities such as transporting and escorting the contestants or covering their jobs while they were in an intensive period of training for, participating in, or recovering from their specific contests. The massive scale of participation (not only in terms of the number of persons, both conscripted and unconscripted, but in terms of the degree and depth of mental attention that each day and every day over endless days would have to be directed toward this exhausting process) would be critical. It is national rather than individual consciousness that is at stake. . . .

But even if this surrogate contest should *begin* to duplicate the contest of war, it will not *end* by duplicating war, for it is in the nature of its ending that war is remarkable among contests, remarkable in its ability to produce an outcome in one kind of activity (injuring) that is able to translate into a wholly different vocabulary, the right to determine certain territorial and extraterritorial issues. . . .

IV. The End of War: The Laying Edge to Edge of Injured Bodies and Unanchored Issues

The extent to which in ordinary peacetime activity the nation-state resides unnoticed in the intricate recesses of personhood, penetrates the deepest layers of consciousness, and manifests itself in the body itself is hard to assess, for it seems at any given moment "hardly" there, yet seems at many moments, however hardly, *there* in the metabolic mysteries of the body's hunger for culturally stipulated forms of food and drink, the external objects one is willing habitually to put into oneself; *hardly* there but *there* in the learned postures, gestures, gait, the ease or reluctance with which it breaks into a smile; *there* in the regional accent, the disposition of the tongue, mouth, and throat, the elaborate and intricate play of small muscles that may also be echoed and magnified throughout the whole body, as when a man moves across the room, there radiates across his shoulder, head, hips, legs, and arms the history of his early boyhood years of life in Georgia and his young adolescence in Manhattan.

The presence of learned culture in the body is sometimes described as an imposition originating from without: the words "polis" and "polite" are, as Pierre Bourdieu (1977: 95) reminds us, etymologically related, and "the concessions of politeness always contain political concessions." But it must at least in part be seen as originating in the body, attributed to the refusal of the body to disown its own early circumstances, its mute and often beautiful insistence on absorbing into its rhythms and postures the signs that it inhabits a particular space at a particular time. The human animal is in its early years "civilized," learns to stand upright, to walk, to wave and signal, to listen, to speak, and the general "civilizing" process takes place within particular "civil" realms, a particular hemisphere, a particular nation, a particular state, a particular region. Whether the body's loyalty to these political realms is more accurately identified as residing in one fragile gesture or in a thousand, it is likely to be deeply and permanently there, more permanently there, less easily shed, than those disembodied forms of patriotism that exist in verbal habits or in thoughts about one's national identity. The political identity of the body is usually learned unconsciously, effortlessly, and very early—it is said that within a few months of life British infants have learned to hold their eyebrows in a raised position. So, too, it may be the last form of patriotism to be lost; studies of third- and fourth-generation immigrants in the United States show that long after all other cultural habits (language, narratives, celebrations of festival days) have been lost or disowned, culturally stipulated expressions of physical pain remain and differentiate Irish American, Jewish American, and Italian American (Opler 1959; Zborowski 1952)....

The history of the United States' participation in numerous twentieth-century wars may be quietly displayed across the surviving generations of any American family—a grandfather whose distorted feet permanently memorialize the location and landing site of a piece of shrapnel in France, the feet to which there will always cling the narration of a difficult walk over fields of corn stubble; a father whose heart became an unreliable pennywhistle because of the rheumatic fever that swept through an army training camp in 1942, at once exempting him from combat and making him lethally vulnerable to the Asian flu that would kill him several decades later; a cousin whose damaged hip and permanent limp announce in each step the inflection of the word "Vietnam" and, along with the injuries of thousands of his peers, ensures that whether or not it is verbally memorialized, the record of war survives in the bodies, both alive and buried, of the people who were hurt there. If the war involves a country's total population or its terrain, the history may be more widely self-announcing. Berlin, orange and tawny city, bright, modern, architecturally "new," confesses its earlier devastation in the very "newness" necessitated by that devastation and in the temporal discrepancy between its front avenues where it is strikingly "today"—1960, '70, now '85—and the courtyards immediately behind these buildings where time, as though held in place by the still unrepaired bullet holes, seems to have stopped at 1945. Berlin, bombed from above and taken block by block. Or again, Paris, architecturally ancient, silver-white and violet-blue, announces in the very integrity of its old streets and buildings (their stately exteriors undisturbed by war except by the occasional insertion here and there of a plaque to a fallen member of the Resistance) its survival, its capitulation; just as the very different history of World War I, in which two out of every three young Frenchmen either died or lost a limb, is still visible in all the windows of the subway cars—"LES PLACES NUMÉROTÉES SONT RÉSERVÉES PAR PRIORITÉ 1° AU MUTILÉS DE GUERRE ..."—an inscription that each day runs beneath the standing city as though in counterpoint to and partial explanation for that later story recorded earlier.

The physical signs cited here are those that survive the physical activity that produced them by ten years, forty years, sixty years. They only suggest in ghostly outline how deep, how daily, how massive is a population's experience of the residues of war in its immediate aftermath, the first two years, the first four months, when the survivors are immersed, engulfed, in those signs. This immediate period—the war has just been declared over, the designations of "winner" and "loser" have just been received, the terms of peace and the disposition of postwar issues are in the process of being negotiated and accepted and acted on—is what we are here trying to understand. . . .

THE ACTIVITY OF injuring in war has, then, two separable functions. It is the activity by means of which a winner and a loser are arrived at. It also, after the war, provides a record of its own activity. In the first of these two functions, the injuries are referential: it very much matters to which of the two sides injuries and damage occurred, and thus the disputing nations and watching world will attend to the "kill ratios."[1] However, in the second function, the location of the injuries will cease to be dual and will collectively substantiate that the war occurred and is now over. The difference in the direction of referentiality in the two functions can be seen by looking at the different place that casualties have during a conflict and after that conflict. If in the midst of the American Civil War one learns that a battle is occurring in which there are so far twenty thousand casualties, it will very much matter to know whether the North has lost two thousand and the South eighteen thousand, or instead the South has lost two thousand and the North eighteen thousand, or instead that North and South have each lost ten thousand. Such differences will determine who is victorious in the battle, and over the various battles will eventually help to determine which of the two "out-injures" the other and, thus, which of the two is "winner" and which is "loser." But once those final labels are designated and the war is over, it will cease to matter how the casualties in that battle (or in the war as a whole) were distributed, and all twenty thousand, whether originally suffered very unequally or almost equally, will now substantiate the winner and winning issues. . . . Late in the Civil War, a Southern family might say, "The autonomy of the South, the survival of its economic and racial ideas, is crucial to us: 94,000 have died in substantiation of that importance"; or a family in the North might say, "The unity of the country, the supremacy of the industrial North and its beliefs about human justice are crucial: the cost of those beliefs is the lives of 110,000 of our lads." But once the war is over, these verbal constructions will tend to be replaced by one in which the casualties—not now 94,000 and 110,000 but 204,000 (or 534,000 if including death from disease)—collectively substantiate, or are perceived as the cost of, a single outcome: "Racial justice and national unity were to be crucial to the United States as a nation: 534,000 died in the Civil War." . . . Thus, a Southern boy who may have believed himself to be risking and inflicting wounds for a feudal system of agriculture, and until the end of the war will have suffered much hardship and finally death for those beliefs, will once the war is over have died in substantiation of the disappearance of that feudal system and the racial inequality on which it depended.

NOTES

Editors' note: This is a significantly abridged version of the original ninety-seven-page chapter (Scarry 1985: 60–157). Readers are encouraged to refer to the original text for a more thoroughly detailed analysis.

1. For example, in March 1944 Winston Churchill assessed the war in the Pacific as one in which three or four Japanese were being injured for every one Allied soldier (Churchill 1945: 56). The citation of kill ratios is too ubiquitous and familiar to require the recitation of additional instances here.

10.3

THE ENHANCED WARFIGHTER
Kenneth Ford and Clark Glymour

Because of its long-standing support and leverage of advances in the physical sciences, computer science, and engineering, the U.S. military is without peer on the technological front. Many of the military's technical systems have been developed with the aim of improving and extending human performance. Night-vision devices are but one well-known example. Until recently, however, the military has shown limited interest in exploiting biomedical advances that might enhance intrinsic human performance and resilience. This reluctance is starting to wane, but only slowly. . . . New advances in physiology, nutrition, neuroscience, and engineering now offer a significant potential to prevent (or reduce) the degradation of a warfighter's cognitive and physical capabilities during conflict and substantially increase the performance of both combat personnel and the larger systems of which they are part. . . .

Technological approaches to improved human performance such as night-vision goggles are typically not controversial, but biological technologies can stir the public imagination. Action films and television—from *The Six Million Dollar Man* of 1970s TV to the Jason Bourne movie series—have sometimes featured fighters who have been prosthetically or biochemically enhanced by some government agency, licit or illicit. But how and whether actually to enhance the physical, cognitive, and emotional capacities of U.S. military personnel is a serious policy question. . . .

Monitoring the Warfighter

Advances in sensor technology have led to the development of wearable and unobtrusive sensors for a range of biomarkers that can be used to monitor physical and mental states, particularly the psychophysiology, of a warfighter. Next-generation sensors using nanotechnology and flexible conformal materials that provide a "lab on a Band-Aid" could enable even more unobtrusive monitoring systems. This monitoring can be thought of as providing an easy-to-use dashboard or check-engine light for the operator of a weapons system or even for commanders and other senior decision makers working long hours under considerable stress. Recent scientific studies have found molecular targets of opportunity for such physiological sensors. This military interest in monitoring the warfighter connects with the burgeoning quantified-self movement found in the larger civilian community.

Military personnel could in principle be monitored either online in real time or offline periodically, and both types of measurement have been proposed. Such systems could include equipment to monitor sleep patterns, heart rate and variability, respiration, biomarkers for stress or attentiveness, and changes in behavior or self-reported mood; soldiers, sailors, pilots, support personnel, and their supervisors could be given feedback when necessary to improve alertness or other aspects of performance (Blackhurst et al. 2012).

Monitoring and feedback summon the morally troubling image of human beings permanently wired as intermediate cogs in a device that continuously samples and modulates aspects of their biochemistry, their attention, and, in large degree, their action. We, the authors, think that this is at the end of a long slope from present U.S. Defense Department efforts and see little reason to think that end will ever be approached. The military may want to help keep warfighters awake, alert, and healthy, but it is difficult to see any advantage or prospect of creating pharmaceutical cyborgs.

Performance-Enhancing Pharmaceuticals

Advances in neuroscience are slowly but surely yielding a mechanistic understanding of cognition, optimal mental performance, and resilience. Coupled with advances in nutrition and the development of new neuropharmaceuticals, this understanding opens the door to the possibility of enhanced cognitive performance and resilience. One can already observe a rather energetic and large-scale, albeit unconstrained, experiment in pharmaceutical enhancement of cognition well under way on every major college or university campus.

Modafinil and similar alertness or vigilance-support pharmaceuticals have been studied extensively (Caldwell et al. 2000) and have demonstrated utility in several Defense Department operational contexts. Researchers have reported that modafinil improved planning among their test subjects (Turner et al. 2003). More recently, a study of sleep-deprived physicians found that modafinil improved their cognitive flexibility while reducing impulsive behavior (Sugden et al. 2012). Modafinil (and newly emerging successor drugs) could be evaluated to improve performance of senior decision makers and others who must operate at a high level in a sleep-deprived state.

In addition, new pharmaceuticals aimed at mitigating the cognitive losses associated with aging and neurodegenerative diseases are under development. Such substances will likely have application in cognitive enhancement and resilience. It is anticipated that these carefully targeted drugs will more effectively exploit brain plasticity and offer fewer side effects than current drugs such as modafinil. One can reasonably anticipate that some future adversaries will not hesitate to provide their personnel with the latest pharmaceuticals to mitigate the effects of sleep deprivation, to enhance training, or to create other advantages.

The use of performance-enhancing drugs when combined with the possibility of real-time monitoring of biomarkers that reflect operator performance prompts moral concerns, in part because of real worries about long-term health effects, and in part because the image of human beings as permanently wired parts of a military device is abhorrent. The first consideration is serious; pharmaceuticals that enhance alertness or increase strength (in just two of many possibilities) could possibly affect health years later. The second is the end of a conjectural slippery slope that starts with, say, coffee and ends with unlimited access to advanced neuropharmaceuticals. But the truth about slippery slopes is that society starts down a lot of them, and society can, and often does, stop when appropriate.

Loss of Resilience and Its Consequences

Over the past decade, the demands the military places on warfighters have changed in ways that go beyond the strains of the repeated tours of duty common in the Iraq and Afghanistan wars. Modern technological warfare necessitates a level of cognitive ability and discipline unheard of in the history of war, and it does so at every level of command, from the dismounted soldier to the commander in the operations center. In addition, the military population largely reflects the physical condition of the broader civilian population from which it is drawn. A trip to your local Wal-Mart, shopping mall, or airport will illustrate the problem. The U.S. military has a more overburdened and stressed and less healthy and, arguably, less resilient force than in generations past.

In 2011, nearly 110,000 active-duty U.S. Army troops were prescribed antidepressants, narcotics, sedatives, antipsychotics, or antianxiety drugs—reportedly an eightfold increase since 2005 (Murphy 2012). If these numbers are accurate, the dramatic increase in the use of pharmaceuticals must reflect an aggressive attitude toward medication to deal with the consequences of the loss of resilience. Perhaps not entirely coincidentally, suicides across the services have risen sharply. . . .

The causes for suicide are multiple, and the military is making great efforts to reduce the suicide rate among its members. Should effective means be found to reduce the rate of suicide among service members, one can reasonably anticipate that similar benefits would accrue to society as a whole.

Nutrition and Supplementation

One area that can affect the resilience of warfighters and begs for improvement is nutrition and diet supplementation. The quantity and quality of dietary choices and distribution of nutrients throughout the day greatly affect muscle performance, body composition, cognitive performance, and feelings of energy or exhaustion. In addition, a rapidly expanding body of research describes an ever increasing understanding of the link between native gut bacteria and human physical and biochemical characteristics, from increased obesity to cognitive metabolites and immune responses (Burnet 2012). It will be culturally complicated for U.S. military services to make improvements in nutrition, but changes in military diet offer real opportunities for significant increases in performance and resilience.

Military personnel deployed in conflicts eat more or less the usual U.S. diet, but warfighters' nutritional requirements often are, in fact, very unusual. Imagine warfighters as high-performance athletes who are constantly worried about bombs and bullets. One might say that many in our military, as in the broader society, are overfed, overmedicated, and nutritionally undernourished. . . .

In spite of the new performance demands on the modern warfighter, the military has only recently started to focus on ways to exploit the most current research arising from nutrition and performance science to optimize or tailor diets to the nutritional requirements for specific roles and performance. A warfighter's diet roughly mirrors the standard U.S. diet, a regimen that is causally associated with significant prevalence of metabolic syndrome and other problems associated with poor nutrition (e.g. , obesity, diabetes, heart disease, cerebrovascular disease, cancer, and cognitive decline). . . .

At a minimum, improvements to the diet available to warfighters could have an immediate impact on physical and cognitive fitness and a long-term impact on health with respect to common but avoidable maladies such as coronary disease, diabetes, and cancer. Science-based improvements in the efficiency of cellular metabolism, managed through dietary changes and supplementation, could have beneficial impacts on physical, cognitive, and psychological health and resilience, and they certainly warrant further research.

Ethics and the Enhanced Warfighter

One often considers the hazards of supplementation and enhancement, but in the military context the greater moral hazard may be the decision not to enhance warfighters' resilience through feasible and science-based methods that are available. One might also reasonably anticipate research investments in this type of enhancement to have important and beneficial effects in the broader society.

Questions about the health effects of physiological monitoring and feedback, changes in nutrition, and related interventions are not moral hard cases if the effects of the interventions are known and candidly assessed and revealed. . . . A volunteer in the military enters into a contract with the government to take risks that would be allowed for no civilian employee. The government reciprocates by promising, among other things, treatment or compensation if harm results. In doing so, the government must necessarily estimate the benefits and risks to the warfighter, whether the issue is vaccinations, physiological monitoring and feedback, or nutrition, including supplements. . . .

There are human and social costs to any adaptations or augmentations that might have some probability of leaving military personnel disabled, physically or psychologically. Treatment costs may be calculable, but the social costs of losses of human capital are not really estimable. But whatever their total, we are paying those costs already. The augmentations we need are those that improve human performance and, perhaps most important, increase resilience. We should not confuse warfare with sports and deny our military personnel the best science-based enhancements. War will always be hell; we need a more resilient military, humanly resilient.

10.4

SUFFERING CHILD
An Embodiment of War and Its Aftermath in Post-Sandinista Nicaragua
James Quesada

What follows is a story of a ten-year-old boy, Daniel, and his thirty-three-year-old mother, Maria del Carmen, who live in a squatter settlement perched above the city of Matagalpa, Nicaragua. Together they embody the contemporary history of Nicaragua over the past twenty-five years: the Sandinista insurrection and revolution, the Contra war, and the postrevolutionary neoliberal reform era of today. The Department of Matagalpa is located in the northern central highlands of Nicaragua and is the primary coffee-growing region of the country. It was also one of the principal war zones during the U.S.-supported "Contra war" (1981–90). The socioeconomic status of this particular family is the direct outcome of the rapid social and structural changes they have endured over an extended period of time. Unfortunately, violence and poverty are not new to Nicaragua. The late 1980s and early 1990s saw deepening impoverishment and popular unrest in Nicaragua that challenged the daily survival strategies and social networks that people relied on to withstand the grind of poverty and instability.

This article examines a child's lived experience of the far-reaching effects of war and its aftermath, endemic poverty, political instability, and despair. This article, however, is more than just about Daniel; it is about his family, as well. . . . Daniel's family includes his mother, Maria del Carmen; his sole younger brother, Omar, who is eight; and his stepfather Pablo, who is thirty-one. Pablo occasionally resides with them but primarily chooses to stay with his mother, who resides nearby. Maria and Pablo are "historical combatants," individuals who participated in the Sandinista insurrection against the dictator Anastasio Somoza prior to the triumph of the Sandinista revolution in 1979. In the past eighteen years, their daily lives have been affected by insurrection, revolution, war, trade embargoes, economic collapse, an International Monetary Fund–induced shock therapy, hurricanes, homelessness, and unemployment. . . .

Life of War

War is not new to the residents of Matagalpa. It was the site of street fighting and aerial bombardment during the insurrection, and although the threat of direct violence during the Contra war took on a new character, fear and insecurity were endemic. Daniel was born in Matagalpa in 1981, the year the Contra war began in earnest (Sklar 1988). That year, U.S. President Ronald Reagan allocated funds to train an anti-Sandinista military force, popularly known in Nicaragua as "Contras," or counterrevolutionaries, and initiated a devastating economic blockade against Nicaragua. Given its proximity to the Honduran border to the north and the sparsely populated, tropical Atlantic coastal region to the east, Matagalpa became one of the principal military staging grounds during the war. . . .

The city of Matagalpa was spared the direct experience of warfare. Yet Matagalpa did experience combat in the form of military alerts; curfews; restricted travel; and visible evacuations, displacements, and casualties. It also served as a safe haven for rural people fleeing the fighting in the war zones. As a result, from 1979 to 1990, the population of Matagalpa nearly doubled, to around 85,000 inhabitants. When the Contras choked off points along the single route that led from the city to the rest of the country, Matagalpa was periodically cut off from the rest of the country during the war. Although these blockades usually lasted only a few hours, the emotional toll of knowing that the Contras were within striking distance, and that the city was vulnerable, was considerable. . . . For Maria del Carmen's family, the war resulted in repeated separations between parents and children, continuous shortages of food and goods, rampant inflation, faltering infrastructures, limited life options, and a state of chronic uncertainty.

Suffering Child

Often [Maria del Carmen's] boys came to visit me on their way home from school in the early afternoon. They usually arrived shortly after siesta with the excuse of asking for glasses of water. They often left my house with gifts of food, pencils, or other things for which I suspected they had really come. Daniel did the asking. Sometimes I thought he was rather forward and overly aggressive in his attitude. He had a way of asking for things that was more of a demand than a request, and I sometimes became irritated with him. He was always looking for things that I was either not using or throwing away. One afternoon, after I changed the oil in my car, Daniel asked me for the empty oil cans. As he dutifully cleaned them out, I asked him why he wanted them, and he explained, "Oh, I can use them for a lot of things. I can keep water in them, I can make flower pots and make our house look nice. Or I might ask you," he said with a wink, "to keep these in your freezer to make ice." I ended up sharing part of the freezer compartment with Daniel. His younger brother, by contrast, rarely spoke and dutifully followed his older brother's lead. He always had a grin on his face, which I came to regard as a mask that disguised what he really felt. I never got as close to Omar as I did to Daniel.

One afternoon, Daniel and Omar came to visit after school. As was their habit, they asked for water. I offered them a piece of birthday cake, which they gladly accepted. As Daniel accompanied me to the kitchen to get dishes and forks, he mentioned quite matter-of-factly that he felt like dying. I stopped immediately and turned to face him. Daniel displayed neither sadness nor alarm. I asked him to repeat what he had said, and he calmly told me that sometimes he felt like dying. I responded that this was a pretty serious sentiment, and I asked him to explain. We were alone in the kitchen, and Daniel quietly, yet flippantly, told me that everyone would be better off with him dead: "Look at me, I'm all bones, anyway; I'm already dying. I'm too small, and I've stopped growing, and I am another mouth to feed. My mother can't keep taking care of my brother and me, and I can't keep taking care of her. I can't do anything. So it would be better if I just died, since that would help everyone."

His explanation was stated calmly and very reasonably. His concerns were legitimate, and his thinking was relatively clear. Daniel appeared to have arrived at this conclusion quite logically. I asked him whether he had any specific plans to kill himself. He said that he did not, but when the time was right, he would find an appropriate way. I was very distraught yet fought to remain calm. I felt I needed to show some of the same coolness he exhibited but also convey to him that he was a worthy human being who deserved to live and had much to live for. This latter point was a particularly difficult proposition; talking about hope and the future was difficult when so many Nicaraguans experienced so little of either.

Daniel began to describe how he regularly rationed his meals. His family's daily fare was meager, at best. For breakfast they usually had sweetened coffee and tortillas, and the rest of the day they subsisted on *gallo pinto* (mixed rice and beans) with tortilla, which was sometimes accompanied by a piece of *cuajada* (salty dry white cheese). He did not remember the last time he had eaten beef or chicken, although he ate eggs approximately once a week. Daniel explained that he routinely served himself small portions while generously serving his mother and brother, assuring them that he had served them all equal portions. He explained that sometimes he hid his food, and when his mother was bedridden he took his food to her. Daniel gave his brother a tortilla a day because Daniel thought his younger brother was the stronger of the two of them, and he wanted to make sure his brother got enough food. In fact, Omar did appear more robust than his older brother. Daniel said that he was physically exhausted from not sleeping well. He lay awake trying to think of ways to make money such as shoe shining or selling newspapers. He protected his brother from the leaking roof by moving him or holding up a flap of plastic from the wall whenever it rained. Sometimes he stoically allowed himself to get wet, because he did not want to worry his mother or make her get up and go outside to fix the roof. He engaged in daily improvised rituals of sacrifices to contribute in whatever way he could to keep his family from falling apart. Daniel mentioned that he had thought of running away, but to him that would be too cowardly and a betrayal of his mother and brother. So in the end, he thought it would be best to die. He looked at me squarely and said, raising his arm and pinching the skin of his forearm, "Besides, I'm already withering away."

I was caught by surprise by the young age of the person expressing such concerns, the straightforwardness and seemingly accurate appraisal of his ordeal, and, of course, his extreme solution. Here from the "mouth of a babe" came a view of life that captured the pervasive quality of daily difficulties and life's shortcomings. It was rare, it seemed to me, to find one so young so poignantly articulate about the hardships of life. But perhaps more striking was his detached, modulated mode of expression. His general affect and demeanor were very adult and somber. These were very different from the adults I worked with in the mental health clinic, who, when speaking of suffering and sacrifices and hopelessness and demoralization, were either more animated or flat. People's speaking styles hint at the ways in which they respond to their problems. Daniel's manner was matter-of-fact and not designed to elicit pity or despair. Whereas my adult informants' accounts consisted of tales or reasoning that justified their plights as someone else's fault, Daniel's account contained no finger-pointing or blame. He could not or would not fault others. He took responsibility for himself and his family in a way that left him little or no leeway out of his predicament. Hence, in such a context, one can see how he arrived at the conclusion that it was he who was obstructing his family's survival.

Such sophisticated reasoning suggests a heightened sense of responsibility, which, while commendable, indicates how intensely Daniel was trying to shield his family from pain. He was as inseparable from his mother and brother as he was exposed to the contingencies of a harsh environment. Under a leaking plastic roof, at night, on top of a hill, the wind howling, with no electricity, and a dirt floor that quickly turned to mud, Daniel adopted a stoic stance that allowed him to merely withstand and endure. He still strategized to make everything better for his family.

Dying So Others Might Live

Children who are depressed often think they are inadequate or worthless (Cicchetti and Schneider-Rosen 1984). These emotional states are not merely reflections of what children think; they also indicate how they accurately experience themselves in this context. The world appears to them as perpetually frustrating and impossibly demanding. The future appears to promise nothing but failure, suffering, and more hopelessness (Or-Bach 1988). Daniel always struck me as a capable, intelligent boy. Even when he called attention to his malnourished physical body, it was done not in total surrender or despair but in controlled anger. The world was harsh and demanding, yet he seemed to be engaged in an act of valiantly contending with its plural demands, in part by reconstructing his body. He found a new way of accommodating himself bodily to the ever changing nature of the physical and social world. This is his contexture.

Daniel's desire to die could be viewed as his last act of selflessness, aid, and protection for his family. Objectively, Daniel is imperiled simply by living under conditions of scarcity that are particularly difficult for older children (McDonald et al. 1994). These conditions of scarcity were socially produced and were not merely the product of a dysfunctional family or maternal neglect. In a society where more than 50 percent of the population is unemployed, and the state has withdrawn from a commitment to social welfare (Fundación Internacional para el Desafío Economico Global 1992; Walker 1997), the negative consequences of these circumstances have immediate and direct effects on people. Daniel was very conscious of his predicament, of his "skin and bones." Yet although he spoke about his body, his concern was for his family.

He was primarily concerned about his body's relation to his family. His was another mouth to feed in the face of chronic scarcity. Anthony Giddens (1984) has written that "ontological security" is a secure sense of oneself and the world around one, which can be threatened by social ruptures and chaos. Hence, when Daniel's web of meaningful social relationships were threatened by violence, scarcity, rapid change, or uncertainty, his particular knowledge about his body and others' became insecure (Featherstone et al. 1987). This can result in a Manichean way of perceiving (Shneidman 1982). Perhaps Daniel sometimes saw his dilemma as a condition of his physical body versus the family body. His insecurity was real enough, even though his analysis and proposed remedy were amorphous.

Daniel had a heightened sense of responsibility for the well-being of his family. He was well aware that his family had hit a low point, regardless of whether he understood how they had arrived at such a position. He was thus compelled to act as selflessly as possible in an effort to keep his family intact (McLoyd and Wilson 1990: 65). His heightened moral sensibility and awareness of the sets of limitations under which he and his family lived produced a quagmire from which he seemed unable to escape.

Wars produce a continuum of duress. The seeds of Daniel's lived sense of insecurity were sown during a time of war. Although Daniel was never immediately physically threatened, he was the victim of the ripple effects that wars produce. He lived in proximity to combat, and his mother and stepfather were directly engaged in partisan activities that could have cost them their lives. The war in Nicaragua, however, was a physical and psychological war (Klare and Kornbluh 1988; Quesada 1994; Sklar 1988) in which the perpetrators actively sought to produce an atmosphere of insecurity. This insecurity disconnected people from one another and fostered their submission to the dictates of state or local power (Martín-Baró 1988). When the body is bound in webs of interdependencies, death may be an attempt to salvage or re-forge a sense of connectedness, rather than a final act of separation. Herein lies the paradox: one's self-sacrifice permits others to live. I temper this conclusion with the realization that Daniel counted "the body" not only as his own individual body but as the family body of which he was a part. . . . The analysis of Daniel's situation provides an opportunity to read clearly the costs children pay for the actions of war and its devastating aftermath, conditions that are often neglected simply because they are not perceived as a direct mortal threat. The fact is, they are.

FIG 11.0. Technological innovation tends to alter tools and techniques used by military institutions. Over the past century, developments in the fields of physics, chemistry, and computer science have, among other things, led to the creation of new weapons systems that range from nuclear weapons to unmanned aerial vehicles, or drones. This photograph from 2014 depicts U.S. Marines with LS3 (Legged Squad Support System), an experimental robot. Photo by Sarah Dietz/U.S. Marine Corps.

SECTION XI. MILITARISM AND TECHNOLOGY

Compiled by HUGH GUSTERSON

Introduction

The development of military technology and its aesthetic fetishization lie at the core of contemporary militarism. But although narratives of scientific progress are central to Western notions of superiority, it is by no means a foregone conclusion that the side with the most advanced technology wins wars. Thus, despite an overwhelming technological advantage, the United States lost the Vietnam War, where the U.S. technoscientific approach to war was no match for the low-tech improvisation of a determined enemy. (More recently, the United States has similarly been unable to prevail in Iraq and Afghanistan in the face of determined guerrillas armed with Kalashnikovs and improvised explosives.) Meanwhile, the construction of an underground bunker world during the Cold War, documented in this section by Joseph Masco, embodied a state-sponsored fantasy that, with the right technological precautions, nuclear war could be survived.

The lavishly funded development of new military technologies distorts the development of science and constitutes a tacit national industrial policy that favors military corporations (often offered guaranteed profit margins). It also produces what Mary Kaldor (1981) has called "baroque" weapons— complicated, overly designed systems that are often unreliable because they promise too much to divergent constituencies as the price for political viability. For example, the B-2 bomber cost $737 million (in 1997 dollars) per plane and required 119 hours of maintenance per hour of flight.

Technological "progress" often lends a depersonalized quality to the act of killing. Intimate hand-to-hand combat between individuals has given way to new realities: the button presser in an underground control room or the drone operator in a pod in Nevada killing people in Pakistan with the push of a button. Even more removed is the soldier who plants a land mine or drops cluster bombs that may kill or maim a child years later. In this section, H. Patricia Hynes documents the extraordinary damage these low-tech impersonal weapons do to civilians. Alex Edney-Browne argues that, despite the distance from which drone operators kill, they still experience deleterious psychological effects. David H. Price's contribution exposes the blurred boundaries between the National Aeronautics and Space Administration (NASA) and the U.S. military at a time of renewed interest in a militarized "space force."

It is tempting, putting all this together, to see the history of weapons technology as a teleological disaster narrative in which the weapons inevitably become more accurate and destructive even as they also become, psychologically, easier to use with homicidal indifference. But Western leaders, having tried poison gas in World War I, decided to renounce chemical weapons with the Chemical Weapons Convention of 1997 and biological weapons with the Biological Weapons Convention of 1972. Meanwhile, telling a fascinating story that needs to be more widely known, Noel Perrin relates how Japan decided to eliminate guns, reverting to the sword for two hundred years.

The Chemical and Biological Weapons Conventions were largely the work of arms control experts and government bureaucracies, but sometimes weapons are banned in response to mass movements. In 1997, the international grassroots campaign against land mines succeeded in securing the Ottawa Treaty banning land mines, signed by 164 countries (of which the United States is not one). And the Convention on Cluster Munitions entered into force in 2008, after a savvy campaign by international activists, and has now been signed by 108 countries (again, not including the United States).

Scientists themselves have played a key role in these campaigns for arms control and disarmament—campaigns that are, in part, about the ends to which technoscience itself will be put. The final readings in this section are short statements written by scientists calling on their professional colleagues not to work on particular weapons. The first is a pledge signed by more than 3,700 faculty and 2,500 graduate students in physics and engineering to refuse funding to work on the Strategic Defense Initiative (popularly known as "Star Wars"). This pledge was the model for the Network of Concerned Anthropologists' own pledge campaign in 2007–2008 inviting anthropologists to pledge not to work on counterinsurgency in Iraq and Afghanistan.

The final reading is a recent statement by the International Committee for Robot Arms Control (ICRAC) calling for a ban on autonomous robotic weapons systems—weapons that are programmed to take human life without a human in the decision-making loop. The ICRAC fears that recent developments in artificial intelligence, robotics, and information-processing technology make possible autonomous weapons systems that will commit war crimes for which no one can be held accountable. Maybe, following the example of the seventeenth-century Japanese, we can decide that some military technologies are not worth the temporary advantage they confer.

READINGS

11.1 Excerpts from Noel Perrin, *Giving Up the Gun: Japan's Reversion to the Sword, 1543–1879*, by Noel Perrin (New York: David R. Godine, 1988), 33–42.

11.2 Excerpts from Joseph Masco, "Life Underground: Building the American Bunker Society," *Anthropology Now* 1, no. 2 (2009): 13–29.

11.3 Excerpts from David H. Price, "Militarizing Space," *CounterPunch*, online ed., August 10, 2018.

11.4 Excerpts from Alex Edney-Browne, "Embodiment and Affect in a Digital Age: Understanding Mental Illness among Military Drone Personnel," *Krisis* 3 (2016): 1–14.

11.5 Excerpts from H. Patricia Hynes, "Landmines and Cluster Bombs: 'Weapons of Mass Destruction in Slow Motion,'" Truthout.com, September 1, 2011.

11.6 Lisbeth Gronlund and David Wright, "Pledge of Non-Participation," 1986

11.7 International Committee for Robot Arms Control, "The Scientists' Call to Ban Autonomous Lethal Robots," 2013.

11.1

GIVING UP THE GUN
Japan's Reversion to the Sword, 1543–1879
Noel Perrin

There seem to be at least five reasons that explain why Japan . . . could and did turn away from firearms while Europe went rapidly ahead with their development. One—the most obvious—is that for every Blaise de Monluc [*Editors' Note*: Monluc (1502–77) was a French marshal who opposed the development of firearms, which he considered cowardly weapons.] there were a dozen samurai who felt that firearms were getting out of hand. The warrior class in Japan was very much larger than in any European country, amounting to somewhere between 7 percent and 10 percent of the entire population. . . .

A second reason is geopolitical. The Japanese were such formidable fighters, and islands are by nature so hard to invade, that territorial integrity could be maintained even with conventional weapons. Japan was much too small to conquer China . . . but much too fierce for anyone to conquer *her*. The Portuguese never even considered trying; and though the thought seems to have passed through Spanish minds, it was quickly thrust out again. . . .

A third and rather curious reason is that in Japan swords had a symbolic value far greater than they had in Europe. It would therefore have been a greater loss to let them be replaced entirely by guns.

To begin with, the sword was not merely a fighting weapon in Japan; it was the visible form of one's honor—"the soul of the samurai," in the Japanese phrase. So it was in Europe, too: a tap on the shoulder with a sword by the right person and one arose a knight. But in Japan it was the *only* embodiment of honor—or, at least, the only one that formed part of one's costume. . . .

Or, again, swords stood for social importance far more than in feudal Europe. You couldn't even have a family name unless you also had the right to wear a sword. Peasants and merchants in feudal Japan lacked both. . . .

Regular fighting swords doubled as major works of art. . . . Swords are valued as works of art: all over the world, of course, but not with the intensity that the Japanese value them. Probably only in Japan could an incident such as this in a battle in 1582 have occurred. General Hori Hidemasa was besieging Lord Akechi Mitsuhide in his castle of Sakamoto, and this was no siege half in sport, but a fight to the death. Near the end, Lord Akechi sent out this message: "My castle is burning, and soon I shall die. I have many excellent swords which I have treasured all my life, and am loath to have destroyed with me. . . . I will die happy, if you will stop your attack for a short while, so that I can have the swords sent out and presented to you" (Hakusi 1948: 17). General Hori agreed, and fighting ceased while the swords were lowered out of the smoldering castle, wrapped in a mattress. Then it resumed, and the next day the castle fell and Lord Akechi died—presumably happy. . . .

Still another reason is that the de-emphasis of the gun took place as part of a general reaction against outside ideas—particularly Christianity and the Western attitude toward business. Christianity was illegal in Japan after 1616, and the country was closed to foreigners in 1636 principally to keep missionaries from slipping back in. As for businessmen, a seventeenth-century shogun observed that "merchants are fond of gain and given up to greed, and abominable fellows of this kind ought not to escape punishment" (Boxer 1951: 245).

In Europe, of course, guns were not an outside idea. Or if they were, no one realized it. As far as Europeans were concerned, they were something that had simply appeared long ago, back in the fourteenth or maybe the thirteenth century. The devil may have inspired them, but he was whispering in some European's ear when he did.

The fifth reason is the most curious of all. It is purely aesthetic. The symbolic value that swords had in Japan was more or less independent of how one physically handled them in battle. The symbolism could be attached to almost any weapon. It was, for example, to Colt revolvers in the American West. Men felt undressed and almost unsexed without them. ("If you ain't got a gun, why ain't you got a gun?" sneers a character in Stephen Crane's short story "The Bride Comes to Yellow Sky.") Symbolic honor has been attached to spears at various times in Africa, and quite possibly it was to throwing sticks by cavemen.

Quite apart from all that, swords happen to be associated with elegant body movement. A sword simply is a more graceful weapon to use than a gun, in any time or country. This is why an extended scene of swordplay can appear in a contemporary movie and be a kind of danger-laden ballet, while a scene of extended gunplay comes out as raw violence.

This much even an American recognizes. But for the Japanese there was an additional element. In Japanese aesthetic theory, there are some fairly precise rules about how a person of breeding should move his body: how he should stand or sit or kneel. In general, it is desirable that he should have his knees together and, when possible, his hands—the so-called concentration of body, will, and power. Furthermore, it is better if his elbows are not out at awkward angles. In some Japanese circles, these rules still apply in the 1970s, in such ritual occasions as the tea ceremony.

11.2

LIFE UNDERGROUND: BUILDING THE AMERICAN BUNKER SOCIETY
Joseph Masco

One of the first and most powerful effects of the bomb was to transform the United States into a special kind of bunker society, fixated on impending nuclear attack while fantasizing about life within both mental and physical fortresses. Positing life in the bunker as livable (even exciting) was a vital mechanism of militarizing American society in the face of an expanding nuclear threat. It also set the terms for a long-running American fantasy about achieving an absolute and total form of security. . . .

New Fortresses for the Mind and Body

The nuclear state embraced the profound contradictions nuclear weapons posed by normalizing a nuclear state of emergency and then simply calling the result "national security." By the late 1950s, for example, the federal government was not only feverishly building thermonuclear weapons and the means to deliver them around the world; it was also considering a massive investment in fallout shelters across the United States, a program that promised an entirely new national infrastructure, all underground (see figure 11.2.1). For example, the RAND Corporation offered a detailed plan to relocate four million New Yorkers to deep underneath Manhattan:

> The shelters were to be excavated 800 feet below the surface, using conventional excavation and mining techniques. They were to be almost completely isolated from the surface, with air purified and enriched with oxygen as in a submarine, with water tapped from the Delaware Aqueduct system of tunnels and treated (or in an emergency, drawn from internal storage), and with power provided from diesel generators vented to the surface but isolated from the shelter proper. Occupants would be assigned berth in a large dormitory, would receive two cold meals and one hot meal per day, and would draw fresh clothing, take showers, and exercise on a rotational basis. Some 91 entrances were planned and distributed according to population, so that every point in Manhattan was within 5 to 10 minutes walking distance of an entrance. (RAND Corporation 1958: 7) . . .

The civil defense projects of the 1950s formally positioned the bunker as a new American frontier space, populated by a new kind of citizen defined by the constant preparation for nuclear attack. This new Cold War subject was designed to be immune to panic but nonetheless motivated by nuclear fear. Thus, just as Cold War military technologies were being hardened to survive nuclear attack, civil defense efforts sought to engineer a new kind of citizen-soldier, one who was emotionally equipped to support the nuclear state. Hardening both technologies and psychologies against the bomb was a dual project of the early nuclear state, making the nuclear bunker a new site of nation and state building. . . .

GROUP FALLOUT SHELTER
For 240 Persons

FIG. 11.2.1. Federal Civil Defense Administration plans for a group fallout shelter for 240 persons. Image courtesy U.S. National Archives.

As Americans contemplated life underground in the early Cold War period, a new kind of social intimacy with mass death was deeply installed in U.S. national security culture. As the military built multiply redundant technological systems for fighting a nuclear war (including always-on-alert bombers, missiles, and submarines), the civil defense program sought to build a society capable of withstanding the internal pressures of living within a constant state of emergency and facing a new kind of totalizing destructive force. Cold War planners explicitly merged nuclear fear with the ideology of American Exceptionalism. In doing this, they engineered a new kind of militarized society, in which America was depicted as both powerful and vulnerable. This ideology continues to inform U.S. national security culture to this day. . . .

In 1957, the Gaither Committee . . . recommended a crash shelter program that would cost as much as $55 billion over five years. The committee was explicit in the value of the program: the shelter system was designed not only to save lives as the bombs began to fall but also to communicate to the Soviet leadership an American "will to live," and thus win, either a cold or a hot war. Civil defense was theatrical as well as practical, a means of sending signals out into the world from underground bunker spaces, both real and imagined. . . .

Moving Underground

The North American Aerospace Defense Command (NORAD) was the most advanced bunker facility of its time and perfectly illustrates the passions of the Cold War nuclear project. The central facility is buried 2,400 feet deep inside a mountain of almost solid granite and is supported by 1,319 steel springs (each three feet in diameter and weighing more than a thousand pounds), designed to absorb the shock of nearby nuclear detonations. Simultaneously, NORAD was the most isolated and the most connected site in the United States. Secured behind twenty-five-ton blast doors, the facility was both locked down and networked to radar systems, computers, and eventually satellite surveillance systems, assembling enormous data sets of moving objects tracked in real time on a giant central screen (figure 11.2.2). . . .

For citizens, the windowless bunker became a privatized dream space— where time spent waiting for the bombs to fall and the radioactive clouds to clear could be a source of renewal, not ruin. Citizens, however, did not approach the bunker on their own terms or on terms of their own choosing; instead, they were taught how to think about nuclear crisis and their own role in managing it. The project of "civil defense" in the 1950s was less about the protection of citizens and cities than about the emotional training of the populace and the psychological conversion of U.S. citizens into Cold War Warriors.

The Bunker as New American Frontier

At the height of the fallout shelter debate, the Federal Civil Defense Administration (FCDA) produced photographs (see following pages) documenting ordinary Americans in their home bunkers. These images represent the fallout shelter as pure dream space, not only privatized but also part of a pastoral landscape. . . . In each case, the shelter hatch begs to be locked down tight, sealing the inhabitants below in their submarine-like security, locking the inhabitants within a special kind of fantasy space: militarized, privatized, post-nation-state.

FIG. 11.2.2. The representation of the world as data points is among the most profound technological evolutions, but it omits the messy complexity of cultures, politics, and ecosystems. This photo portrays the NORAD Command and Control Center. Photograph courtesy U.S. National Archives.

Figure 11.2.3 presents the arresting image of the suburban home on a seemingly peaceful, sunny day, with a father and daughter slowly descending into a circular hatch cut neatly into the lawn. Framed to enhance the sky and grass, while underscoring the dramatically unhurried nature of the father-daughter descent into the earth, the photograph registers a preternatural calm, belying the context of nuclear war that necessitates this shelter project. Figure 11.2.4 then shows the neatly ordered family space below, complete with air purifier, stove, and bunk beds, already populated by three generations of happy shelter inhabitants. The father can sleep in this image precisely because he has put forth the labor to build a shelter as a personal response to the international nuclear crisis. The grandparents and daughter simply enjoy the time together in this windowless underground space. The canned goods and medical kits become a register of good parenting in this advertisement, which also suggests that time spent in the bunker can be quality family time.

FIG. 11.2.3. Exterior view of a residential family fallout shelter. Photograph courtesy U.S. National Archives.

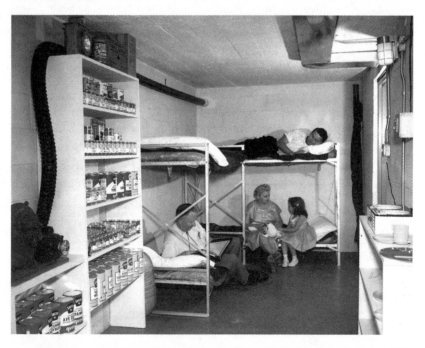

FIG. 11.2.4. Interior view of a residential family fallout shelter. Photograph courtesy U.S. National Archives.

Figures 11.2.5 and 11.2.6 repeat this pictorial structure but with more humor and a repositioning of the shelter as a place to get some peace and quiet, away from the troubles of the world above. In the first image, the smiling male owner pops his head out of the carefully hidden shelter entrance, presenting a covert space surrounded by a thicket of trees and shrubs. On the inside we see him in relaxed pleasure, legs crossed lying on a bunk bed enjoying a magazine, a slight smile on his face, the very picture of contentment. Here the fallout shelter is presented as a privatized retreat, as much bachelor pad as survival kit. . . .

Shelters and consumer capitalism were essential right from the start. President John F. Kennedy asked each American to prepare for nuclear war by finding or building a shelter. He also proposed a $400 million national shelter program one year before the Cuban Missile Crisis, energizing a new industry in store-bought shelters. The FCDA sought to enhance the allure of the shelter by sponsoring a national campaign to design multiuse rooms, good for sitting out a nuclear war or for use in the pre-attack everyday. In the shelter campaign, families were always depicted together, in good health and happy underground when war broke out. These conceptual designs start to explain why families were depicted this way: the FCDA was attempting to relocate the American family to the nuclear bunker—to make the bomb the source of family life rather than the destruction of it.

Despite this effort to romanticize the shelter and to construct it as a dual-use room suited for all kinds of catastrophe, as well as for entertaining guests, most Americans did not—indeed, could not—build nuclear bunkers. Instead, figure 11.2.7 depicts the most wide-ranging response to the bomb: the duck-and-cover drill that every American schoolchild practiced for the forty years of official Cold War. Here, face down, internalized in one's own mind, and completely vulnerable to the world around, is the ultimate Cold War posture: a sightless, private bunker of the most pathos-driven kind.

The FCDA campaigns always offered citizens the best-case scenario for nuclear war—in which the bombs explode well over the horizon—allowing Americans time to get to their shelters and minimize the most destructive effects. The FCDA consequently focused on the middle-class, suburban family living on the periphery of urban centers, creating and reinforcing an image of America as an exclusively white nuclear family. This left unrepresented a vast population of Americans while ignoring the predominantly urban concentration of U.S. populations. . . . Via civil defense, federal authorities promoted an idea of an invulnerable American—able to exist outside of time and space— located within a new mythology of perfect national security.

Scientists and activists almost immediately challenged this denial of death. They critiqued the factual claims of civil defense, helping to foment peace, civil

FIG. 11.2.5. Exterior of a hidden fallout shelter. Photograph courtesy U.S. National Archives.

FIG. 11.2.6. Interior of a hidden fallout shelter. Photograph courtesy U.S. National Archives.

FIG. 11.2.7. Duck-and-cover drill. Photograph courtesy U.S. National Archives

rights, and environmental movements. Perhaps the most devastating critique of the bunker society came in Stanley Kubrick's film *Dr. Strangelove, or How I Learned to Stop Worrying and Love the Bomb* (1963). At the end of the film, as the president and his war council are holed up in the closed world command center known as the "war room," a huge computer screen follows the path of U.S. and Soviet bombers on their final bombing runs, detailing the now un-avoidable outbreak of global nuclear war. Rather than producing despair, how-ever, the president's science adviser, Dr. Strangelove, suggests that the United States can now move a "nucleus of human specimens" to the deepest mine shafts and prepare them (with nuclear reactors for energy and greenhouses to produce food) to wait out the radioactive fallout for a few hundred years. Suggesting a 10:1 ratio of women to men to repopulate the human species, the erotics of the shelter produce immediate desire among the president and his all-male war council, as well as a renewed state of competition with the Soviets, this time to prevent, over the hundreds of years it would take for surface radia-tion to decay, the development of a "mine shaft gap!" The nuclear bunker is revealed here as pure masculine fantasy, participating in an erotics of death that is not subject to self-analysis even as the bombs begin to fall.

MILITARIZING SPACE
David H. Price

Links between the American space program and military have long been one part open secret and one part open question. It has always been difficult to determine just how much of NASA's budget can properly be considered military spending. A few years ago while starting to work on a paper examining Margaret Mead and other anthropologists' work on a 1950s and '60s program designed to measure and shape U.S. public attitudes about space (known as Project Man in Space), I had assumed I would find a basic critical analysis, akin to Gore Vidal's famous essay "The National Security State" (1988), in which Vidal's analysis of mandatory and discretionary spending revealed that the American military's budget was far larger than the meek 37 percent appearing at first glance (when only considering the listed U.S. Department of Defense budget), and once all military-linked projects were counted at agencies such as the Department of Energy, Department of State, and Veterans Administration; foreign arms deal aid packages; and other defense-related projects not included in the Department of Defense budget, could be understood to make up not a minority of the federal budget but approaching 77 percent of the budget. And while I found many excellent contemporary and historical analyses of the links between NASA and military space projects, I could not find straightforward numbers stating how much of the money the U.S. government spends on space goes to military-linked projects.

Links connecting NASA and military projects have been close to the surface since the space administration's origins. Section 305i of NASA's 1958 charter clarified its relationship to the Pentagon, stating, "The Administration shall be considered a defense agency of the United States for the purpose of chapter 17 of title 35 of the United States Code." While nothing is hidden about this, NASA's very public civilian space exploration projects create widespread perceptions that its mission remains essentially one of pure science and exploration.

Beginning in 1957, anthropologists, including Margaret Mead, played a role in formulating the public disassociation of space exploration's direct links to the militarization of space, and the roots of this severance can be traced back to the Project Man in Space program, where Harold Laswell's, Mead's, and Donald Michael's basic narratives championing pioneering elements of space exploration were developed, in part with funding from the Brookings Institution. This work studied and reported on public attitudes about space during the post-Sputnik era and affected policy narratives about the American space program.

A 1983 General Accounting Office report determined that about a quarter of NASA's spending then went to "support military programs." In a 1982 *New York Times* article, John Nobel Wilford reported,

> In a letter on the report, W. H. Sheley Jr., director of the accounting office, said that, based in part on projections that almost half of the space shuttle flights will carry military payloads, more than $1 billion of the requested $3.5 billion for the shuttle in 1983 could be allocated as a military expenditure. Part of the agency's spending for aeronautics and space technology research could also be attributed to military goals, the report said.
>
> By these calculations, Mr. Sheley said, $1.1 billion of NASA's research and development budget of $5.33 billion, or 20.5 percent, should be considered military-related. Another $400 million, or 7.7 percent, was listed under civilian-military support. The space agency's total budget request for 1983 amounts to $6.6 billion. The Pentagon's total direct spending on space activities is not known, but is thought to be equal to or greater than NASA's annual budget" (Wilford 1982).

During the Reagan years, as governmental space exploration and private industry merged in new ways, there were increasing uses of NASA for military and intelligence activities. In the mid-1980s we learned that at least one-third of the space shuttle missions had classified top secret military or intelligence components—many of which ran through the secret National Reconnaissance Office. During the period following the explosion of the *Challenger* shuttle, the significance of these missions became apparent as the Pentagon claimed priority for missions once the shuttles were cleared to fly again following the lifting of the post-*Challenger* moratorium.

The government historian Michael Cassutt, a former policy staff member at the Central Intelligence Agency, the National Reconnaissance Office, and the Office of the Secretary of the Air Force, observed that the space shuttle was so linked to intelligence missions that the National Reconnaissance Office "requirements drove the shuttle design." During the 1980s and '90s, classified payloads became a regular feature of space shuttle missions.

Today, astronauts and NASA are not needed to advance the militarization of space to the next frontier: we have the Pentagon's secret space drone (known as the X-37B) that has circled the Earth with minimal public interest, undertaking secret missions. Well before Donald Trump did his publicity stunt announcing his comic book "Space Force," the Department of Defense built its own space program—benefiting directly from the advances developed by NASA, with a separate space budget comparable to NASA's. The militarized explorations of space today dwarf civilian explorations.

In 2016, under Barack Obama, Defense Secretary Ash Carter pushed for significant increases in the Pentagon's space budget, bluntly arguing that in the past "space was seen as a sanctuary. New and emerging threats make clear that that's not the case anymore and we must be prepared for the possibility of a conflict that extends in space" (Carter 2016: 14). In 2015, U.S. Navy Admiral Cecil D. Haney warned that China and Russia had "advanced directed-energy capabilities that could be used to track or blind satellites, disrupting key operations, and both have demonstrated the ability to perform complex maneuvers in space"(quoted in Duff-Brown 2015). Trump's move to establish a Space Force is little more than a continuation of the Obama administration's effort to militarize space.

While it is simple to separate (or launder) budgetary lines funding civilian space missions designed to orbit the Earth or walk on the moon, there is no simple meaningful way to separate the scientific research needed to launch the *Apollo* astronauts to the moon from the science needed to successfully build intercontinental ballistic missiles designed to carry deadly nuclear payloads to our Soviet enemies. This is the nature of dual-use science, and while the particulars of our culture of science train us to categorically see these as separate enterprises, these developments feed knowledge into a conjoined body of knowledge. Military spy satellites, star wars technology, unknown military tests in space, space weaponry, many innovations now in the public domain—such as early GPS technology—were classified and limited to military applications. This is part of the dual-use nature of militarized science in a capitalist market place.

It remains unknown what role the privately funded space programs of our greatest contemporary malefactors of great wealth, Jeff Bezos and Elon Musk, will play in the development of this new Space Force. Given the ongoing trends of privatized research and development for military and space programs, it is reasonable to assume there will be profits to be shared, even as these elites are acting in ways that appear as if they are preparing the way for their descendants to leave a depleted world behind.

What Trump's formation of an identified Space Force does is to make naked the truth that the American space project, within and outside of NASA, has always been part of a military project wrapped in the public gauze of utopian space-travel fantasies. These fantasies helped channel public understanding of space exploration and its inherent links to the militarization of space, and even while we gained incredible, important scientific knowledge and stunning photos from

[the] Hubble [Space Telescope] and other projects, these were also, at least in part, shiny objects that kept our attention from core military aspects of America's space project. Like most open secrets, little was hidden about this, but the cultural categories we constructed kept the depth of this obvious truth at bay as we entertained visions of utopian space exploration, of a world where developed nations would share satellite data with poor countries as acts of mutual aid, even while NASA's space race with the Soviet Union was a form of warfare. The Mercury and Apollo programs were civilian programs; with some military personnel and project links, the satellite programs, and other NASA-linked projects had significant military links. These military features were frequently highlighted in congressional funding requests, while the public was sold Buck Rogers fantasies.

In very concrete terms, Trump's step toward a Space Force simply connects the dots laid in place by the more polite and articulate administrations that came before him as he moves us into a world where space more openly becomes a warfare platform. But we should expect a culture so deeply embedded in a political economy of warfare and militarization to try to do no less than extend its militarized vision beyond our atmosphere, reaching to militarize the universe.

11.4

EMBODIMENT AND AFFECT IN A DIGITAL AGE
Understanding Mental Illness among Military Drone Personnel
Alex Edney-Browne

The U.S.-led coalition's increasing reliance on drone technology has provoked concern about the "virtualization of violence" (Der Derian 2009: 121). It is feared that technological mediation in drone warfare dehumanizes victims and distances drone personnel, physically and psychologically, from the violent reality of their actions. The human victim of drone surveillance or attack is "reduced to an anonymous simulacrum that flickers across the screen" (Pugliese 2013: 193), while drone personnel perpetrating that violence are "morally disengaged from [their] destructive and lethal actions" (Royakkers and van Est 2010: 289). Discussions about physical and psychological distance are not new to twenty-first-century violence. Hannah Arendt (1964) and Zygmunt Bauman (1989), in their efforts to better understand the Holocaust, pointed to an intrinsic link among technology, distance, and twentieth-century genocide. The Nazis, they argued, relied heavily on technologies and technoscientific discourses to justify, sanitize, and commit mass violence. Perpetrators of violence were distanced from their victims: government bureaucrats and medical professionals became hyper-rational murderers with the help of technoscience's distancing and dehumanizing effects. This was one of Arendt's (1964: 26) famous insights in *Eichmann in Jerusalem: A Report on the Banality of Evil.* . . .

Drone Personnel: Digital Age Soldiers

Drone personnel—the soldiers of the digital age—are often constructed in academic literature as present-day Eichmanns or video-game players. . . . Drone teams may be connected to the battlefield "via a wireless signal or fibre optic cable," but they are not connected "emotionally or psychologically" (Singer 2009: 335). . . . In his report to the United Nations, Special Rapporteur Philip Alston states that "because operators are based thousands of miles away from the battlefield . . . , there is a risk of developing a 'Playstation' mentality to killing" (quoted in Cole et al. 2010: 25). "Rather than seeing human beings," drone personnel "perceive mere blips on screens" (Cole et al. 2010: 4). . . .

The alleged psychological ease with which drone personnel carry out their work is undermined by psychological studies and the handful of available personal testimonies from drone personnel. . . . Psychological studies reveal equal, sometimes higher, prevalence rates of PTSD [post-traumatic stress disorder] in active-duty drone pilots as manned-aircraft pilots, despite drone personnel's complete spatiotemporal removal from the battlespace (Asaro 2013: 217). . . . A comparative psychological study of 670 drone pilots and 751 manned-aircraft pilots found that 5 percent of drone pilots presented with symptoms that placed them at high risk of PTSD (Chappelle et al. 2012: 6). This was higher than their findings for manned-aircraft pilots, of whom only 1 percent were at high risk for PTSD (Chappelle et al. 2012: 6). . . .

The psychological health of drone personnel has become a site of conflict for academic, nongovernmental organization (NGO), and activist critiques of drone warfare. . . . Giving voice to the perpetrator of violence can draw attention away from the victims of violence. . . . A recent review of *Good Kill* (a film about a U.S. Air Force drone pilot) seems motivated by this concern, with its provocative title, "Drone Operators Get PTSD, Civilians Die Nameless" (Gharib 2015). In the case of drone warfare, the mostly Muslim victims of drone strikes are already largely invisible in Western public discourses, where the deaths of white, non-Muslim Westerners are far more likely to be grieved (Butler 2003: 27). . . .

The "radical asymmetry" of drone warfare has become the linchpin of drone warfare criticism, and it is this objection that resonates with the public (Enemark 2013: 367). . . . In *Drone Theory*—to date the most popular theoretical book on drone warfare—Gregoire Chamayou expresses his skepticism towards counter-representations of drone personnel, in particular what he calls the "media picture of empathetic drone operators suffering psychic trauma" (Chamayou 2015: 109). He writes that "whereas the attention drawn to soldiers' psychic wounds was in the past aimed at contesting their conscription by state violence, nowadays it serves to bestow upon this unilateral form of violence an ethico-heroic aura that could otherwise not be procured" (Chamayou 2015: 109)....

It is important, however, that academics who find the U.S. coalition's use of drones objectionable draw on all available resources to mount their critique. This includes taking seriously psychological harm to drone personnel. Pentagon spokespeople and military academics argue that governments have a duty of care to protect their soldiers from unnecessary risk of harm (Plaw 2012; Strawser 2010; Weiner and Sherman 2014). Drone technology's alleged ability to protect soldiers from harm is evoked to justify their use. A key weakness of these arguments is that their conceptions of harm do not account for psychological harm (antisocial behavior, anxiety, depression, and PTSD). As Alison Williams (2011: 387) argues, these commentators "mistakenly assume that it is only the physical body that can be damaged by warfare."...

In the words, tone, and body language of former drone personnel it is often difficult to identify the digital-age Adolf Eichmanns or video-game players evoked by many academics, journalists, NGOs, and politicians.... It is clear from personnel testimonies that drone personnel can ... recognize and empathize with their so-called enemies *as humans*.... These testimonies come from a small group of former drone personnel but offer rich empirical information that may be generalizable to a wider group of active-duty and retired personnel.... In an op-ed for *The Guardian*, the former sensor operator Heather Linebaugh (2013) opens by asking: "How many women and children have you seen incinerated by a Hellfire missile? ... How many men have you seen crawl across a field trying to make it to the nearest compound while bleeding out from severed legs?" She goes onto say, "I watched dozens of military-aged males die in Afghanistan, in empty fields, along riversides, and some outside the compound where their family was waiting for them to return home from the mosque."

Brandon Bryant, a PTSD-suffering former drone pilot, recounts one of his traumatic experiences of killing:

> The smoke clears ... and there's this guy over here, and he's missing his right leg above his knee. He's holding it, and he's rolling around, and the blood is squirting out of his leg, and it's hitting the ground, and it's hot. His blood is hot. But when it hits the ground, it starts to cool off;

the pool cools fast. It took him a long time to die. I just watched him. I watched him become the same colour as the ground he was lying on. (Quoted in Power 2013)

In another description of the same experience, Bryant mentions that he "imagined his [victim's] last moments" as he watched him dying (quoted in *Democracy Now!* 2015). The former drone pilot Matt Martin describes an experience of similar emotional and psychological magnitude in his book *Predator*: his realization that two young boys were in the firing line of a missile he had already deployed. The older boy was riding his bike while the younger boy sat on the handlebars. When the missile struck meters away from the boys, killing them, Martin vividly remembered riding his sister around on the handlebars of his bike as a child. He recalls "smelling her hair" and "hearing her laughter" (Martin 2010: 211). This flashback to childhood suggests Martin had the empathetic realization that *in another reality that could be me. . . .*

To make better sense of technological mediation, recognition, and empathy in drone warfare, it is important to consider the media technology environment of the twenty-first century. High-technology, mediated interaction is part of the fabric of everyday life in today's digital age. This is the environment within which drone personnel live, work, and play. . . . Mark Deuze (2011: 137) writes that media technologies are so pervasive in the twenty-first century that it makes better sense to think of our lives "lived *in* rather than *with* media." Media technologies are imbricated so deeply in our lives—professional, social, and intimate—that "they are becoming invisible": "people in general do not even register their presence" (Deuze 2011: 143). This means an "increasing immateriality of one's experience of reality" whereby the mediated and the unmediated, the "virtual" and the "real," inform each other so closely that it is difficult to tell where one ends and the other begins. In the 1990s, when "Information Age" debates were rife, the Internet was known as "cyberspace": a "coherent place that you could immersively inhabit" that was distinct from "reality" (McCullough 2004: 9). Now the ubiquity of networked media technologies undermines our ability to clearly distinguish between unmediated, non-networked spaces and "cyberspace." It is this pervasive media environment, wherein disembodied interaction is frequent even with the most intimate of contacts, that we must keep in mind as we attempt to understand drone personnel's lived experiences of their work. . . .

Drone personnel are sometimes tasked with surveilling a potential target "for more than eight hours a day" (Asaro 2013: 205). From their surveillance, they can "see and recognise the personal details and daily activities" of the people they are ordered to kill (Asaro 2013: 205). One former pilot writes that "you start to understand people in other countries based on their day-to-day patterns of life. A person wakes up, they do this, they greet their friends this way, etc." (quoted in Bergen and Rothenberg 2014: 115). Brandon Bryant admits to having watched "targets drink tea with friends, play with their children, have sex with their wives on rooftops, writhing under blankets" (Power 2013). Depending on the altitude of the drone and the feed that is watched (surveillance footage, thermal imaging, etc.), drone personnel see their victims from a bird's-eye view as tiny dots, pixelated blobs, or heat signatures. It is clear from their testimonies that this does not prevent them from recognizing—and in some cases, empathizing with—their victims as *humans* engaging in human activities. Imagination is crucial in this regard, but we also need to consider the possibility that humanization occurs because similar visualities are at work in drone surveillance as in horizontal, peer-to-peer surveillance practices. The aerial viewpoint and use of digital signifiers to denote a human's presence is a common visuality in myriad peer-to-peer monitoring interfaces, such as Foursquare, Swarm, Uber, UberEats, Find My Friends, Couple Tracker, MapMyFitness, and Facebook's "nearby friends" feature. . . . It is therefore important to consider how drone personnel's experiences with media technologies outside their work could inform their experiences at work.

DRONE PERSONNEL SUFFERING with psychological illness have likely engaged in alternative readings of drone surveillance's scopic regime—readings that encouraged recognition of and empathy for their victims, or otherwise sowed the seeds of doubt regarding the (im)morality of their work. Ruptures in the scopic regime . . . are evident in Linebaugh's (2013) personal testimony, where she recounts feeling far from omniscient: "The feed is so pixelated, what if it's a shovel, and not a weapon? I felt this confusion constantly, as did my fellow UAV [unmanned aerial vehicle] analysts. We always wondered if we killed the right people, if we endangered the wrong people, if we destroyed an innocent civilian's life all because of a bad image or angle." . . . It already seems clear, from the handful of testimonies cited in this article, that many drone personnel are far less convinced by the mythology of the drone—as an ethical and omniscient technological apparatus—than the public. It is therefore important that their experiences are discovered and communicated. Counterhegemonic potential can be found within drone personnel's testimonies, but that potential is foreclosed when academic and journalistic discourses construct the drone apparatus as invulnerable.

LAND MINES AND CLUSTER BOMBS
"Weapons of Mass Destruction in Slow Motion"
H. Patricia Hynes

Every twenty minutes, a land mine explodes, and fifty to one hundred grams of TNT blast into the victim's foot, leg, and other parts of the body....

The United States devised a class of extremely lightweight antipersonnel (i.e., intended to injure or kill people) mines to block the flow of materials and soldiers from North Vietnam through Laos and Cambodia to South Vietnam during the Vietnam War. Land mines were dropped so routinely and in such high numbers that the U.S. pilots referred to the them as "garbage" (Stover et al. 2000). With land mines supplied by China, the Khmer Rouge subsequently mined rice paddies and country paths used by Cambodian peasants to punish and starve them.

In the 1980s war between Iraq and Iran, thousands of land mines were planted in Iraqi Kurdistan, the region between the two countries, at the rate of three for every inhabitant as the warring countries retreated (Strada 2004). The epidemic of land-mine use in armed conflict was largely ignored until the late 1980s, when relief workers publicized the tragic plight of thousands of limbless land-mine victims in Cambodia, as well as in Afghanistan, where victims were injured from land mines Soviet troops placed in grazing areas, on roads, and in mosques and abandoned houses (Stover et al. 2000).

Land mines were first used widely in World War II and have been used intensively in every conflict since.... Regular armies as well as insurgents used land mines because they are cheap, easily employed, lightweight, durable, and effective in slowing the movement of the enemy and sapping their morale. Sometimes called "the poor man's bomb," land mines and automatic rifles have been the weapons of choice for guerrilla and government armies since the 1970s.

Antipersonnel mines were initially targeted for military defense of encampments and strategic structures and to maim, not kill, enemies to tie up their battlefield resources in saving the wounded. Later, mines were increasingly used as weapons of terror to displace communities and to cause maximum harm to civilians.... In the early twentieth century, 80 percent of land-mine victims were soldiers; by the late twentieth century, 80 percent of the maimed and dead were civilians.

The full scale of global hazard from land mines is difficult to define because so many have been scattered randomly from airplanes in unmapped rural areas, and they lie deadly intact for decades until triggered by a person, vehicle, or animal. Modern mines are small and lightweight, so a combatant can carry and scatter many at a time. Further compounding their deadliness, mines have plastic, camouflaged casings, making metal and visual detection nearly impossible. Land mines pose a major threat to food security, particularly if placed in the breeding areas of insect pests, such as the desert locust. If mines make pest control too dangerous and the desert locusts are able to breed to plague levels, they can ravage crops at the rate of 150–200 kilometers per day. . . .

Socioeconomic Costs to Victims and Communities

Manufacturing antipersonnel mines is relatively easy and inexpensive, at the cost of $3–$30 each. Detecting and neutralizing them is dangerous for the deminer, slow and expensive, at $300–$1,000 per mine destroyed. The United Nations estimates that, at the current rate of removal and cost, it will take 1,100 years to clear all remaining land mines—provided no new ones are used—and cost approximately $33 billion. Many warring groups have not mapped or kept records of where they placed land mines, creating serious difficulties for mine removal and crippling the ability of resettlement, agriculture, and tourism in formerly war-ridden countries. The average total cost of a prosthesis for a survivor of a land-mine explosion (excluding hospital stay) is estimated at $1,000, an amount that would take most typical victims ten years of income to afford. . . .

Unexploded land mines cripple the delivery of aid during war and obstruct redevelopment efforts and recovery from war, thus extending the morbidity of war for decades after hostilities cease. . . . Land-mine victims went into debt and sold assets to pay for their multiple medical treatments. Tens of thousands of domestic animals were killed by land mines, with a minimum loss of $200 per affected household. . . . Thus, acutely disabled land-mine victims further suffer the compounded life crises of food insecurity and hunger, debt, and poverty; loss of agricultural animals; and loss of family relations.

The Plight of Female Land-Mine Victims

Up to twenty-thousand people are maimed or killed each year by these "weapons of mass destruction in slow motion," as land mines have been called by human rights activists. Women and children are the most common casualties in agrarian and subsistence-farming societies, where land mines were deliberately placed in agricultural fields and along routes to water sources and markets to starve a people by killing its farmers (Geiger 2000)....

A vast network of NGOs, coordinated by the International Campaign to Ban Landmines, is working with mine-affected states and has enabled mine clearing to evolve from a military clearance activity to a humanitarian and developmental initiative. Even so, the plight of female amputees is particularly grave. Nearly one-half of land in Cambodia is unsafe for cultivation and human use. As the recovery from war continues, it is likely that an even greater percentage of those injured and killed by land mines will be women and children as they return to peacetime sustenance activities such as collecting firewood and water, tending animals, and farming (Ashford and Huet-Vaughn 2000). Women make up a larger percentage of farmers than men in Asia and Africa and are responsible for up to 80 percent of food produced in many parts of Africa. When maimed, they lose the ability to farm and feed their families, and their husbands often abandon them, leaving them to beg in the streets. While women care for mine-disabled husbands, husbands abandon mine-disabled wives, a phenomenon documented in many countries (Mine Action Service 2001).

Cluster Bombs

Cluster bombs contain several dozen to thousands of bomblets or submunitions capable of injuring and killing people and shattering solid objects. They have been employed through air dropping and ground launching in astoundingly high numbers since the 1970s. Between 5 percent and 30 percent are duds and don't explode; of these unexploded submunitions scattered throughout conflict areas, about 50 percent detonate when jolted (Westing 2002). Cluster bombs, which are used as antipersonnel and antitank weapons; to wreck runway surfaces and destroy electric transmission lines; and for incendiary purposes, are particularly dangerous to civilians because of their wide target area—the size of a football field. Handicap International reported that 98 percent of more than thirteen thousand casualties from cluster munitions recorded with the organization are civilians, of which 27 percent are children returning home after conflict or doing normal daily tasks to survive.

Cluster bombs were initially developed and used by Germany and the Soviet Union during World War II. The United States undertook the first massive use of these munitions during the Vietnam War, inaugurating their extensive use in subsequent armed conflicts. Between 1961 and 1975, the United States dropped 1.5 million cluster bombs with 750 million bomblets in Vietnam,

Laos, and Cambodia, both as antipersonnel weapons and to deny Viet Cong access to areas. By 1975, 294 cluster munitions per square kilometer had been air dropped in Vietnam—approximately two cluster submunitions per person (Handicap International 2007). During the Persian Gulf War of 1991, sixty thousand cluster bombs with thirty million antipersonnel and antitank submunitions were dropped by the United States in Kuwait and Iraq over one month (Handicap International 2007). With flagrant disregard for international humanitarian law, the United States and British forces dropped cluster bombs in urban areas, including Baghdad, Basra, Hillah, Kirkuk, Mosul, and Nasiriyah, during March and April 2003 of the second Gulf War. The British group Landmine Action estimates that at least one million cluster submunitions were dropped by coalition forces in Iraq, leaving fifty thousand live bomblets to maim and kill civilians, assuming a failure rate of 5 percent.

Like land mines, unexploded cluster submunitions make recovery from war much more difficult: farming, herding, forestry, and accessing water sources all become hazardous. Tourism is impossible. Generations are set back in their capacity to pursue economic, human, and community development by the "fatal footprints" of this scourge of war.

Land-Mine and Cluster-Bomb Conventions

International land-mine and cluster-bomb conventions are cited as one of the few successes in curbing one of the worst of modern weapon threats. Of 196 countries, 156 have signed the 1997 UN Convention on the Prohibition of the Use, Stockpiling, Production, and Transfer of Anti-Personnel Mines and on Their Destruction (known as the Ottawa Treaty), and the 2008 UN Convention on Cluster Munitions was signed by 109 countries as of March 2011. The older land-mine convention, the result of immense international NGO organizing through the leadership of the International Campaign to Ban Landmines, has resulted in remarkable consequences. None of the treaty states to the Ottawa Treaty produces land mines; global trade in antipersonnel mines has almost halted; [and] eighty-six countries have completed the destruction of their land-mine stockpiles, effectively destroying more than forty-five million antipersonnel mines. . . .

Despite these remarkable gains, the three countries with the largest militaries—the United States, Russia, and China—as well as those engaged in or threatening hostilities, such as Pakistan and India, North Korea and South Korea, and Israel and Iran, have not signed either convention. . . .

A Mine Free World Foundation: A Mine Free World Foundation provides educational, occupational, and vocational support to land-mine survivors and their families.

Cluster Munitions Coalition: The Cluster Munitions Coalition is an international civil society campaign working to eradicate cluster munitions, prevent further casualties from these weapons, and put an end for all time to the suffering they cause.

International Campaign to Ban Landmines: The International Campaign to Ban Landmines is a global network in more than ninety countries working for a world free of land mines and cluster munitions.

11.6

PLEDGE OF NON-PARTICIPATION
Lisbeth Gronlund and David Wright

We, the undersigned science and engineering faculty, believe that the Strategic Defense Initiative (SDI) program (commonly known as Star Wars) is ill-conceived and dangerous. Antiballistic missile defense of sufficient reliability to defend the population of the United States against a Soviet attack is not technically feasible. A system of more limited capability will only serve to escalate the nuclear arms race by encouraging the development of both additional offensive overkill and an all-out competition in antiballistic missile weapons. The program will jeopardize existing arms control agreements and make arms control negotiation even more difficult than it is at present. The program is a step toward the type of weapons and strategy likely to trigger a nuclear holocaust. For these reasons, we believe that the SDI program represents not an advance toward genuine security, but a major step backward.

The likelihood that SDI funding will restrict academic freedom and blur the distinction between classified and unclassified research is greater than for other sources of funding. The structure of SDI research programs makes it likely that groups doing only unclassified research will be part of a Research Consortium and will therefore work closely with other universities and industries doing *classified* research. Strategic Defense Initiative officials openly concede that any successful unclassified project may *become* classified. Moreover, the potentially sensitive nature of the research may invoke legal restrictions required by the Export Administration Act.

Participation in SDI by individual researchers would lend their institution's name to a program of dubious scientific validity and give legitimacy to this program at a time when the involvement of prestigious research institutions is being sought to increase congressional support. Researchers who oppose the SDI program yet choose to participate in it should therefore recognize that their participation would contribute to the political acceptance of SDI.

Accordingly, as working scientists and engineers, we pledge neither to solicit nor accept SDI funds and encourage others to join us in this refusal. We hope together to persuade the public and Congress not to support this deeply misguided and dangerous program.

11.7

THE SCIENTISTS' CALL TO BAN AUTONOMOUS LETHAL ROBOTS
International Committee for Robot Arms Control

As computer scientists, engineers, artificial intelligence experts, roboticists, and professionals from related disciplines, we call for a ban on the development and deployment of weapon systems in which the decision to apply violent force is made autonomously.

We are concerned about the potential of robots to undermine human responsibility in decisions to use force and to obscure accountability for the consequences. There is already a strong international consensus that not all weapons are acceptable, as illustrated by wide adherence to the prohibitions on biological and chemical weapons, as well as antipersonnel land mines. We hold that fully autonomous robots that can trigger or direct weapons fire without a human effectively in the decision loop are similarly unacceptable.

Demands within the military for increasingly rapid response times and resilience against communications failures, combined with ongoing investments in automated systems, indicate a trend toward fully autonomous robotic weapons. However, in the absence of clear scientific evidence that robot weapons have, or are likely in the foreseeable future to have, the functionality required for accurate target identification, situational awareness, or decisions regarding the proportional use of force, we question whether they could meet the strict legal requirements for the use of force. This is especially true under conditions in which battlefields are not clearly delimited and discrimination among civilians, insurgents, and combatants is increasingly difficult.

Moreover, the proliferation of autonomous robot weapons raises the question of how devices controlled by complex algorithms will interact. Such interactions could create unstable and unpredictable behavior—behavior that could initiate or escalate conflicts or cause unjustifiable harm to civilian populations.

Given the limitations and unknown future risks of autonomous robot weapons technology, we call for a prohibition on their development and deployment. Decisions about the application of violent force must not be delegated to machines.

FIG 12.0. In 1959, in the midst of the Cold War, this sculpture was given to the United Nations by the Soviet Union. The statue, entitled *Let Us Beat Swords into Plowshares*, was created by the well-known Soviet sculptor Yevgeny Vuchetich and can be seen at United Nations headquarters in New York. Photograph by Jean-Pierre Lafont/United Nations.

SECTION XII. ALTERNATIVES TO MILITARIZATION

Compiled by DAVID VINE

Introduction

This section presents diverse approaches to building alternatives to militarization, war, and violence. We conclude the reader this way because we want the book to be a tool not just for classroom learning and scholarly study but also for inspiring readers to help build new alternatives that can lessen the harmful presence of militarization in our world. At the outset, however, we encourage readers to heed the advice of the Buddhist monk Thich Nhat Hanh: he cautions against dividing the world "into two camps—the violent and the nonviolent"—while we stand in one and attack "those we feel are responsible for wars and social injustice." To build peace, he says, we must recognize "the degree of violence in ourselves. We must work on ourselves and also with those we condemn" (Hanh 1993: 65).

Hanh is one example of the rejection of killing, violence, and war found among numerous religious and spiritual traditions worldwide. They include Buddhists, Christians, Hindus, Jains, Jews, Muslims, Quakers, Sikhs, and Taoists, among many others. For Mohandas Gandhi, nonviolence is more than an idea or creed; it is a tool: "Nonviolence is the greatest force at the disposal of [hu]mankind" (Gandhi [1931] 1992). Gandhi used nonviolence to lead a movement that resisted British colonialism and ultimately won Indian independence.

Martin Luther King Jr. and other U.S. civil-rights leaders are among the many globally who have been inspired by and successfully employed Gandhi's model of nonviolence. King's Riverside Church speech in 1967 denouncing the U.S. war in Vietnam provides an alternative vision to a society organized around militarization and war. Beyond opposing a single war, King's speech demands structural change. "We must rapidly begin the shift from a thing-oriented society to a person-oriented society," he argued. Viewing struggles against racism, poverty, and militarism as interconnected, the speech is a touchstone for linking antiracist, anticapitalist, antimilitarist, and related movements. People and the promotion of peoples' well-being must be more important than "machines and computers, profit motives and property rights" to defeat "the giant triplets of racism, extreme materialism, and militarism."[1]

King also provides a vision for transcending boundaries of nationality, race, and class with an "all-embracing and unconditional love" for all human beings. Less widely noted, the Riverside Church speech makes a fundamentally anthropological appeal to amplify the voices of the oppressed and to strive to understand the perspective of supposed enemies. "A more difficult but no less necessary task is to speak for those who have been designated as our enemies," says King:

> Surely we must understand their feelings, even if we do not condone their actions. Surely we must see that the men we supported pressed them to their violence. . . . Here is the true meaning and value of compassion and nonviolence, when it helps us to see the enemy's point of view, to hear [their] questions, to know [their] assessment of ourselves. For from [their] view we may indeed see the basic weaknesses of our own condition, and if we are mature, we may learn and grow and profit from the wisdom of the brothers [and sisters] who are called the opposition. (King 1967)

In contrast to the nearly continuous record of war practiced by the United States and some other nations and empires through history, there are peoples worldwide who have lived without war, as Margaret Mead points out in this section's first excerpt. Her classic article shows how war is a social invention rather than a timeless human universal. Nearly seventy years later, Leslie Sponsel uses decades of anthropological research from cultures in which war and violence are uncommon or unknown to demonstrate that a "nonkilling society" is possible. Archaeological and primatological evidence helps Sponsel debunk the popular idea that humans are naturally violent and war inevitable.

Among anthropologists studying the effects of war and militarization—and envisioning alternatives—Catherine Lutz has long been a leader. Her selection provides a global overview of contemporary social movements concerned about the human and environmental damage inflicted by U.S. and other foreign military bases. The anthropologically inclined Chamoru lawyer and human rights activist Julian Aguon shows how antimilitarist movements are, themselves, a kind of alternative to militarization. "The struggle is long and hard and so often lonely. But there are moments," he says, "wherein we are so remarkably alive. Where we, as part, disappear into the whole for love of it. . . . Down here connection happens."

Anthropologists have also organized themselves to oppose and build alternatives to war and militarization. An excerpt from the Network of Concerned Anthropologists' *Counter-Counterinsurgency Manual* describes the founding of the network (which involved most of this volume's contributors) and efforts to unite anthropologists against recruitment into the "global war on terror."

Finally, Rebecca Solnit describes the power of nonviolent movements in moving the world away from militarization and war, pointing to the oft-overlooked successes of mass resistance struggles. Concluding this section and the book, Solnit embraces hope despite the uncertainty of the future. Solnit echoes Mead's reminder that in the effort to build a less militarized world, "a form of behavior becomes out of date only when something else takes its place." However, as Mead (1940: 405) says, "it is first required to believe that a [new] invention is possible."

READINGS

12.1 Excerpts from Margaret Mead, "Warfare Is Only an Invention—Not a Biological Necessity," *Asia* 40 (1940): 402–5.

12.2 Excerpts from Leslie E. Sponsel, "Reflections on the Possibility of a Nonkilling Society and a Nonkilling Anthropology," in *Toward a Nonkilling Paradigm*, edited by Joám Evans Pim (Honolulu: Center for Global Nonkilling, 2009), 35–45.

12.3 Excerpts from Catherine Lutz, "Bases, Empire, and Global Response," in *Bases of Empire: The Global Struggle against U.S. Military Posts*, edited by Catherine Lutz (New York: New York University Press, 2009), 1–46.

12.4 Excerpts from Julian Aguon, "Down Here," in *Bases of Empire: The Global Struggle against U.S. Military Posts*, edited by Catherine Lutz (New York: New York University Press, 2009), 333–36.

12.5 Excerpts from Roberto J. González, Hugh Gusterson, and David H. Price, "Introduction: War, Culture, and Counterinsurgency," in *The Counter-Counterinsurgency Manual*, edited by Network of Concerned Anthropologists (Chicago: Prickly Paradigm, 2009), 1–20.

12.6 Excerpts from Rebecca Solnit, *Hope in the Dark: Untold Stories, Wild Possibilities*, 3rd ed. (Chicago: Haymarket, 2015).

1. The text and audio of the Martin Luther King, Jr. speech are at https://kinginstitute
.stanford.edu/king-papers/documents/beyond-vietnam. We intended to include an
excerpt from the speech but were unable to secure publishing rights due to licensing
restrictions.

12.1

WAR IS ONLY AN INVENTION—NOT A BIOLOGICAL NECESSITY
Margaret Mead

Is war a biological necessity, a sociological inevitability, or just a bad invention? Those who argue for the first view endow man with such pugnacious instincts that some outlet in aggressive behavior is necessary if man is to reach full human stature. . . . A basic, competitive, aggressive, warring human nature is assumed, and those who wish to outlaw war or outlaw competitiveness merely try to find new and less socially destructive ways in which these biologically given aspects of man's nature can find expression. Then there are those who take the second view: warfare is the inevitable concomitant of the development of the state, the struggle for land and natural resources of class societies springing, not from the nature of man, but from the nature of history. War is nevertheless inevitable unless we change our social system and outlaw classes, the struggle for power, and possessions; and in the event of our success warfare would disappear, as a symptom vanishes when the disease is cured.

One may hold a sort of compromise position between these two extremes; one may claim that all aggression springs from the frustration of man's biologically determined drives and that, since all forms of culture are frustrating, it is certain each new generation will be aggressive and the aggression will find its natural and inevitable expression in race war, class war, nationalistic war, and so on. All three of these positions are very popular today among those who think seriously about the problems of war and its possible prevention, but I wish to urge another point of view, less defeatist perhaps than the first and third, and more accurate than the second: that is, that warfare, by which I mean recognized conflict between two groups as groups, in which each group puts an army (even if the army is only fifteen Pygmies) into the field to fight and kill, if possible, some of the members of the army of the other group—that warfare of this sort is an invention like any other of the inventions in terms of which we order our lives, such as writing, marriage, cooking our food instead of eating it raw, trial by jury, or burial of the dead, and so on. Some of this list anyone will grant are inventions: trial by jury is confined to very limited portions of the globe; we know that there are tribes that do not bury their dead but instead expose or cremate them; and we know that only part of the human race has had the knowledge of writing as its cultural inheritance.

But whenever a way of doing things is found universally, such as the use of fire or the practice of some form of marriage, we tend to think at once that it is not an invention at all but an attribute of humanity itself. And yet even such universals as marriage and the use of fire are inventions like the rest, very basic ones, inventions that were perhaps necessary if human history was to take the turn that it has taken, but nevertheless inventions. At some point in his social development man was undoubtedly without the institution of marriage or the knowledge of the use of fire.

The case for warfare is much clearer because there are peoples even today who have no warfare. Of these the Eskimo are perhaps the most conspicuous examples, but the Lepchas of Sikkim described by Geoffrey Gorer in *Himalayan Village* are as good. Neither of these peoples understands war, not even defensive warfare. The idea of warfare is lacking, and this idea is as essential to really carrying on war as an alphabet or a syllabary is to writing. But whereas the Lepchas are a gentle, unquarrelsome people, and the advocates of other points of view might argue that they are not full human beings or that they had never been frustrated and so had no aggression to expand in warfare, the Eskimo case gives no such possibility of interpretation. The Eskimo are not a mild and meek people; many of them are turbulent and troublesome. Fights, theft of wives, murder, cannibalism occur among them—all outbursts of passionate men goaded by desire or intolerable circumstance. Here are men faced with hunger, men faced with loss of their wives, men faced with the threat of extermination by other men, and here are orphan children, growing up miserably with no one to care for them, mocked and neglected by those about them. The personality necessary for war, the circumstances necessary to goad men to desperation are present, but there is no war. When a traveling Eskimo entered a settlement he might have to fight the strongest man in the settlement to establish his position among them, but this was a test of strength and bravery, not war. The idea of warfare, of one group organizing against another group to maim and wound and kill them, was absent. And without that idea passions might rage but there was no war. . . .

Peoples will all go to war if they have the invention, just as those peoples who have the custom of dueling will have duels and peoples who have the pattern of vendetta will indulge in vendetta. And, conversely, peoples who do not know of dueling will not fight duels, even though their wives are seduced and their daughters ravished; they may on occasion commit murder, but they will not fight duels. Cultures that lack the idea of the vendetta will not meet every quarrel in this way. A people can use only the forms it has. . . .

In many parts of the world, war is a game in which the individual can win counters—counters that bring him prestige in the eyes of his own sex or of the opposite sex; he plays for these counters as he might, in our society, strive for a tennis championship. Warfare is a frame for such prestige seeking merely because it calls for the display of certain skills and certain virtues; all of these skills (riding straight, shooting straight, dodging the missiles of the enemy, and sending one's own straight to the mark) can be equally well exercised in some other framework, and, equally, the virtues (endurance, bravery, loyalty, steadfastness) can be displayed in other contexts. The tie-up between proving oneself a man and proving this by a success in organized killing is due to a definition that many societies have made of manliness. And often, even in those societies that counted success in warfare a proof of human worth, strange turns were given to the idea, as when the Plains Indians gave their highest awards to the man who touched a live enemy rather than to the man who brought in a scalp—from a dead enemy—because the latter was less risky. Warfare is just an invention known to the majority of human societies by which they permit their young men either to accumulate prestige or avenge their honor or acquire loot or wives or slaves or sago lands or cattle or appease the blood lust of their gods or the restless souls of the recently dead. It is just an invention, older and more widespread than the jury system, but nonetheless an invention.

ONCE AN INVENTION is known and accepted, men do not easily relinquish it. The skilled workers may smash the first steam looms that they feel are to be their undoing, but they accept them in the end, and no movement that has insisted on the mere abandonment of usable inventions has ever had much success. Warfare is here, as part of our thought; the deeds of warriors are immortalized in the words of our poets; the toys of our children are modeled on the weapons of the soldier; the frame of reference within which our statesmen and our diplomats work always contains war. If we know that it is not inevitable, that it is due to historical accident that warfare is one of the ways in which we think of behaving, are we given any hope by that? What hope is there of persuading nations to abandon war, nations so thoroughly imbued with the idea that resort to war is, if not actually desirable and noble, at last inevitable whenever certain defined circumstances arise?

In answer to this question I think we might turn to the history of other social inventions and inventions that must once have seemed as firmly entrenched as warfare. Take the methods of trial that preceded the jury system: ordeal and trial by combat. Unfair, capricious, alien as they are to our feeling today, they were once the only methods open to individuals accused of some offense. The invention of trial by jury gradually replaced these methods until only witches, and finally not even witches, had to resort to the ordeal. And for a long time the jury system seemed the one best and finest method of settling legal disputes, but today new inventions, trial before judges only or before commissions, are replacing the jury system. In each case, the old method was replaced by a new social invention. The ordeal did not go out because people thought it unjust or wrong; it went out because a method more congruent with the institutions and feelings of the period was invented. And if we despair over the way in which war seems such an ingrained habit of most of the human race, we can take comfort from the fact that a poor invention will usually give place to a better invention.

For this, two conditions at least are necessary. The people must recognize the defects of the old invention, and someone must make a new one. Propaganda against warfare and documentation of its terrible cost in human suffering and social waste prepare the ground by teaching people to feel that warfare is a defective social institution. There is further needed a belief that social invention is possible and the invention of new methods that will render warfare as outdated as the tractor is making the plow, or the motorcar the horse and buggy. A form of behavior becomes outdated only when something else takes its place, and in order to invent forms of behavior that will make war obsolete, it is first a requirement to believe that an invention is possible.

12.2

REFLECTIONS ON THE POSSIBILITY OF A NONKILLING SOCIETY AND A NONKILLING ANTHROPOLOGY

By Leslie E. Sponsel

Is a nonkilling society possible? Without any hesitation, my answer is affirmative.... Examples of nonkilling and peaceful cultures can be important evidence.... Such sociocultural systems generally accord with Glenn Paige's (2002: 1) definition of a nonkilling society as "characterized by no killing of humans and no threats to kill; no weapons designed to kill humans and no justification for using them; and no conditions of society dependent upon threat or use of killing for maintenance or change."

At the same time, the logic that Paige pursues regarding the frequency of killing by humans is affirmed by anthropology. He argues that women seldom kill other humans and that only a minority of men kill other humans (cf. Levinson 1994). To phrase it another way, the overwhelming majority of humans have not been involved directly in any kind of killing. The Yanomami are an anthropological case in point. They were stereotyped and stigmatized in a derogatory way as "the fierce people" by Napoleon Chagnon ([1968] 1977). However, if one actually scrutinizes his ethnography (description of a culture), then it is apparent that most individuals within Yanomami society do not kill others.

A NONKILLING SOCIETY is not only just a possibility, as Paige theorizes; in reality, many such societies actually exist today. The most famous one is the Semai of the Malaysian forest.... Beyond the Semai, dozens of other nonkilling societies have been extensively documented in the anthropological record.... Bruce Bonta (1993) compiled an annotated bibliography of forty-seven cultures that are generally nonviolent. A wealth of information on these and other aspects of this subject are archived on his encyclopedic Peaceful Societies website (http://www.peacefulsocieties.org)....

Given this extensive documentation of nonkilling and peaceful sociocultural systems, the only way that any author, scholar, or scientist can possibly assert that human nature is inherently murderous and warlike is by ignoring the ample evidence to the contrary from a multitude of diverse sources. Nevertheless, that fact has not prevented many from doing so as apologists for warfare.... Either they have not adequately covered the documentation that is readily available in the published literature, or they just purposefully ignore other arguments and evidence that do not fit their own ideology, theory, arguments, advocacy, and so on. In either of these two instances, their science, scholarship, and writing are seriously deficient and suspect, to say the very least....

Most simple hunter-gatherer bands epitomize Paige's attributes of a nonkilling society (Kelly 2000). They are grounded in an ethos of routine cooperation, reciprocity, and nonviolent conflict resolution, as documented for the San and Mbuti of Africa, Semai of Malaysia, and many others (Bonta 1993; Fry 2007; Kelly 2000). Furthermore, for 99 percent of human existence, from more than two million to roughly ten thousand years ago, humans lived almost exclusively as simple hunter-gatherers (Kelly 2000; Lee and DeVore 1968). Accordingly, although captivating, William Golding's novel *Lord of the Flies* (1954) . . . and the ensuing two movies, are not by any means accurate anthropologically as a reflection on human nature. . . .

The archaeological record does not evidence any regular warfare until relatively late in human prehistory (e.g., Fry 2007; Kelly 2000).

Paige (2002: 101) refers to the twentieth century as "the era of lethality." Anthropology, with its unique combination of temporal depth and spatial breadth offers great hope in this regard, because such widespread lethality is an extremely recent aberration in human nature, judging by evidence from evolution and prehistory accumulated by archaeologists and evidence from the record of some seven thousand cultures in the world (ethnographies) and from cross-cultural comparisons (ethnology). Torture, terrorism, genocide, weapons of mass destruction, and the like are all relatively rare in the vast range of human experience (cf. Levinson 1994). The "era of lethality" endures for decades or so, not millennia or millions of years. However, structural violence in various forms and degrees is coincident with the origin of inequality (social stratification), which emerges most of all with civilization at the state level of sociopolitical organization and complexity (Bodley 2008). Actually, warfare and the institution of the military are relatively recent inventions, as noted long ago by Margaret Mead (1940). There is relatively little evidence of warfare until the Neolithic some ten thousand years ago, depending on the region. The military as a social institution is mostly coincident with the evolution of the state around five thousand years ago, depending on the region (e.g., Bodley 2008; Fry 2007; Kelly 2000).

Moreover, anyone who is a genuine evolutionist realizes that change is inevitable; thus, there is no reason to think that warfare and the institution of the military, not to mention other lethal aspects of humankind or a culture, are inevitable and eternal. Humanity as a whole cannot return to a hunter-gatherer lifestyle—at least at the current level of world population and given economic dependence and preference. . . . However, hunter-gatherers can provide heuristic models of the sociocultural possibilities of a nonkilling society (Fry 2007; Kelly 2000). . . .

It should also be noted that, even within relatively violent societies, most people are nonkilling in their own behavior (cf. Nordstrom 1997). Furthermore, there are individuals, groups, and subcultures that explicitly pursue nonkilling and pacifism, such as the Amish. In addition, even in the midst of wars, such as the recent ones in Afghanistan and Iraq, there are medical doctors and other people who are saving lives and reducing suffering instead of the opposite. . . .

History provides examples of nation-states such as Germany and Japan that have been transformed from a society frequently engaged in war to one pursuing peace. Costa Rica is an instructive example as well. The country abolished the military and instead invested its resources in life-enhancing activities. Cases such as Costa Rica merit much greater recognition, documentation, and analysis by anthropologists and others. . . .

What if the federal government of the United States had not responded to 9/11 by military attack on Afghanistan but, instead, capitalized on world sympathy and advocated concerted action by its leaders through the United Nations, the International Criminal Police Organization (Interpol), and other nonkilling means? Whether or not this would have brought to justice the surviving perpetrators of the 9/11 attacks is uncertain. However, it is certain that U.S. militarism has not achieved that goal in the many years since 2001. Moreover, it is certain that in the interim hundreds of thousands of innocent civilians, including women, children, and elderly, have been killed and injured—so-called collateral damage. Millions have been displaced as refugees internally and beyond their homeland in Afghanistan and Iraq. Billions of dollars have been sacrificed from constructive life-enhancing initiatives to promote nutrition, health, education, economy, and other things in the United States and elsewhere. As Mahatma Gandhi observed, an eye for an eye leads to blindness. . . .

The time is long overdue to open the minds of government leaders and the populace regarding the nonkilling alternatives available for dispute resolution and conflict prevention. . . .

There is also some hope, given historical precedents such as the expulsion of the British colonial empire from India, the dissolution of the apartheid system in South Africa, and the overthrow of the Ferdinand Marcos regime in the Philippines, all generated by the nonviolent actions of courageous and persistent leaders and commoners in the face of overwhelming lethal force. . . .

To go even deeper—into human nature, that is—while many biologists and psychologists might favor nature over nurture as the primary determinant and shaper of aggression, some have revealed strong evidence to the contrary. Of all of the species in the animal kingdom, the closest to humans are the common and pygmy chimpanzees, *Pan troglodytes* and *P. paniscus*, respectively. Only after many years of observation of a few social groups of the common chimpanzee at Gombe Stream Reserve in Tanzania did Jane Goodall and her research associates discover what they described as the rudiments of war (Goodall 1986). However, Margaret Power (1991) and others have argued that this aggression may be influenced by external factors, at least in part, and especially by the primatologists provisioning the chimpanzees with bananas in order to bring them closer for more detailed observation.

In sharp contrast to some groups of the common chimpanzees, independent studies of the pygmy chimpanzees, also called bonobos, have not revealed comparable aggression either in the wild or in captive colonies. In fact, they are just the opposite. They seem to pursue behavior according to the motto "Make Love, Not War." Bonobos use a wide variety of sexual behaviors to avoid or reduce tension within the group on a daily basis. . . . However, the "scientists" who favor the Hobbesian view of human nature apparently have ideological blinders that channel them to emphasize violence to the near-exclusion of nonviolence, stressing the common chimpanzees at Gombe and largely ignoring other common chimpanzee groups elsewhere where such behavior has not been observed. They also downplay the evidence of the peaceful bonobos. . . .

As a heuristic exercise, I marshaled the arguments and evidence for the natural history of peace, pursuing just the opposite position from that of the apologists for war (see Sponsel 1996). The fields of biology, primate ethology, human ethology, human paleontology, prehistoric archaeology, ethnography, and ethnology were surveyed. The basic conclusions were that (1) although conflict is inevitable and common, violence is not; (2) human nature has the psychobiological potential to be either nonviolent/peaceful or violent/warlike; (3) nonviolence and peace appear to have prevailed in many prehistoric and pre-state societies; (4) war is not a cultural universal; and (5) the potential for the development of a more nonviolent and peaceful world is latent in human nature as revealed by the natural history of peace. . . .

[These] studies are an independent and objective confirmation of the assertions in the United Nations Educational, Scientific, and Cultural Organization's "Seville Statement on Violence" of May 16, 1986 ["It is scientifically incorrect to say that war or any other violent behaviour is genetically programmed into our human nature"]. . . .

What is needed more than ever is a collaborative project to research nonviolence and peace in both theory and practice with a commitment, expert personnel, and adequate resources on a scale equivalent to the Manhattan Project of World War II. If that war effort was so important to the world, then why isn't a peace effort even more so? Modern warfare is simply much too expensive in terms of human deaths, injuries, and suffering, as well as money, resources, and the environment. . . .

Is a nonkilling society possible? From my perspective as an anthropologist who has paid some attention to anthropological aspects of peace and nonviolence—and not only war and violence, unlike most colleagues—I find the answer to this question quite simple. A nonkilling society is not only possible to conceive of theoretically, but such societies exist in reality, as revealed by the overwhelming evidence from archaeology, ethnohistory, history, ethnography, and ethnology. Thus, nonkilling is an actuality, not merely a possibility. Nonkilling and peace are scientific facts; the evidence is overwhelming and undeniable, as alluded to in this essay and sustained by the accumulating documentation such as Bonta's website. The time is long overdue to systematically make this explicit and pursue it in every constructive way possible to create a nonviolent and life-enhancing society for the realization of the human potential for freedom, justice, peace, harmony, and creativity. Anthropology has an important role to play in such a noble and vital endeavor, if only more anthropologists can open their minds to the revolutionary possibilities of a nonkilling society and a nonkilling anthropology.

12.3

U.S. BASES, EMPIRE, AND GLOBAL RESPONSE
Catherine Lutz

Deployed from those battle zones in Afghanistan and Iraq to the quiet corners of Curaçao, Korea, and Britain, the U.S. military domain consists of [an estimated eight hundred] sprawling army bases, small listening posts, missile and artillery testing ranges, and berthed aircraft carriers.[1] While the bases are literally barracks and weapons depots and staging areas for war-making and ship repair facilities and golf courses and basketball courts, they are also political claims; spoils of war; arms sales showrooms; toxic industrial sites; laboratories for cultural (mis)communication; and collections of customers for local bars, shops, and prostitution.

The environmental, political, and economic impact of these bases is enormous and, despite Pentagon claims that the bases simply provide security to the regions they are in, most of the world's people feel anything but reassured by this global reach. Some communities pay the highest price: their farmland taken for bases; their children neurologically damaged by military jet fuel in their water supplies; their neighbors imprisoned, tortured, and disappeared by the autocratic regimes that survive on U.S. military and political support given as a form of tacit rent for the bases. Global opposition to U.S. basing has been widespread and growing rapidly, [including] . . . vigorous campaigns to hold the United States accountable for that damage and to reorient their countries' security policies in other, more humane, and truly secure directions.

IN DEFINING THE problem they face, some groups have focused on the base itself, its sheer presence as matter out of place in a world of national borders—that is, they have seen the problem as one of affronts to sovereignty and national pride. Others focus on the purposes the bases serve, which is to stand ready to and sometimes wage war and see the bases as implicating them in the violence projected from them. These objections to war are variously on grounds that are ethical (it is immoral to kill, or modern war necessarily kills civilians and so is unacceptable, or offensive wars are unacceptable), socioeconomic (war drains resources from other, more important social needs and investments), or realist-strategic (current U.S. war-making policy is counterproductive to its and its al-lies' national security). Most also focus on the noxious effects of the bases' daily operations, a high-impact matter given that bases are often the tools of mass in-dustrial warfare, which is a highly toxic, labor-intensive, and violent operation that employs an inordinate number of young men. For years, the movements have logged and described past and current confiscation of land; the health effects from military jet noise and air and water pollution; soldiers' crimes, es-pecially rapes, other assaults, murders, and car crashes, and the impunity they have usually enjoyed; the inequality of the nation-to-nation relationship often undergirded by racism and other forms of disrespect; the culture of militarism that infiltrates local societies and its consequences, including higher rates of enlistment, death, and injury to local youth; the cost to local treasuries in pay-ments to the United States for support of the bases; and the use of the bases for prisoner extradition and torture.

The sense that U.S. bases represent a massive injustice to the community and the nation is an extremely common one in the countries where U.S. bases are most ubiquitous and of longest standing. These are places where people have been able to observe military practice and interstate relations with the United States closely and over a long period of time. In Okinawa, most polls show that 70–80 percent of the island's people want the bases—or, at least, the U.S. Marines—to leave. They want base land back, and they want an end to aviation crash risks, higher rates of prostitution and drug trafficking, and sexual assault and other crimes by U.S. soldiers (see Akibayashi and Takazato 2009; Cheng 2010). . . .

In Korea, the great majority of the population feels that a reduction in U.S. presence would increase national security. Many feel that U.S. bases, while providing nuclear and other deterrence against North Korean attack, have prevented reunification. As well, the U.S. military is seen as disrespectful of Koreans. In recent years, several violent deaths at the hands of U.S. soldiers brought out vast candlelight vigils and other protests across the country. And the original inhabitants of Diego Garcia, evicted from their homes between 1967 and 1973 by the British on behalf of the United States, have organized a concerted campaign for the right to return, bringing legal suit against the British government (see Vine and Jeffery 2009). There is also resistance to the U.S. expansion plans into new areas. In 2007, a number of African nations balked at U.S. attempts at military basing access (Hallinan 2007). In Eastern Europe, despite well-funded campaigns to convince Poles and Czechs of the value of U.S. bases and much sentiment in favor of taking the bases in pursuit of a more Western European identity and of promised economic benefits, vigorous protests including hunger strikes have emerged. . . .

Objections to U.S. bases have been voiced since their inception. The attempt to take the Philippines from Spain in 1898 led to a drawn-out guerrilla war for independence that required 126,000 American occupation troops to stifle. After World War II, there were multiple calls for return of the bases or of the land on which the radically expanded U.S. military presence stood. Voiced both by former colonial rulers like France and Britain, and by the land's original inhabitants, these efforts contributed to the eviction of U.S. bases. . . . Most recently, they were evicted from Panama in 1999, although there are continuing efforts to deal with the failure of the United States to clean up its toxic and explosive remains, including more than 100,000 rounds of unexploded ordnance on firing ranges, despite a Canal Treaty provision for removing such dangers.

WITH THE END of the Cold War, the central pretext used for most U.S. bases evaporated, and calls for their return were renewed. Democratization efforts in Korea, the Philippines, and elsewhere had meanwhile succeeded, and would allow for more energetic calls for redress of grievances against the U.S. military. So, as Roland Simbulan (2009) describes, the Philippine movement to oust the bases was successful in 1991, based first in the charter provided by a new post-Marcos constitution that declared, "Foreign military bases, troops or facilities shall not be allowed in the Philippines except under a treaty duly concurred in by the Senate and, when the Congress so requires, ratified by a majority of the votes cast by the people in a national referendum held for that purpose."

SUSTAINED CAMPAIGNS OF direct action and political lobbying resulted in the 2003 removal of the U.S. Navy from Vieques, Puerto Rico. As Katherine McCaffrey (2002) notes . . . , the success of this anti-base campaign where others had failed hinged in part on use of arguments about the environmental and health damage of the military's activities. . . .

An unprecedented global mobilization of peace movements arose in the wake of the terror attacks and counterattacks from 2001 forward. . . . The work to expel overseas U.S. military bases is considered by many, including an international body that met in Indonesia in 2003, to be one of the four pivotal goals of the global peace movement.

NOTE

1. The major current concentrations of U.S. sites outside those war zones are in South Korea, with 106 sites and 29,000 troops; Japan, with 130 sites and 49,000 troops, most concentrated in Okinawa; and Germany, with 287 sites and 64,000 troops. Guam, with twenty-eight facilities covering a third of the island's land area, has nearly 6,600 airmen and soldiers and is slated to radically expand over the next several years.

12.4

DOWN HERE
Julian Aguon

Stories of ordinary people fighting extraordinary battles against military colonialism are to be cherished as much for their pure wealth of information as for their subtle announcements of the presence of beauty where it has survived brutality.

I've been thinking about beauty so much lately. About folks being robbed of it, folks fading for want of it, folks rushing to embrace only ghosts of it. This is the point: Empire is eating Everybody. All of us. The whole wide array of ancient narratives of what it means to be human on this planet—snack. Chomp, chomp.

Our world today is desperate—for us to get out into it. Throw our arms around it. See it. See Other People. Places and ruins and rocks and landscapes. Horses and the sun. Rising in different lands, over different people, with different—and the same—dreams. We need to get back to the dirt. We could use some fresh air. Those who don't know firsthand what kinds of cancer come with the presence of U.S. military bases, or how it feels to always be coming back from burying the dead, need to travel to see—not take from—the world. So that awe may repair their eyes. So that the word "solidarity" would mean something. Something more. People cannot rush to the rescue of a world whose magic they haven't seen. They don't even know what the bombs are falling on. They don't know the people, haven't heard us tell our own stories. Haven't stood in our rivers or danced with us to our music. Moved for a while to our groove. Those at the top of the world cannot read about this magic.

At the time of this writing my own people, the indigenous Chamoru of Guahan (Guam), have both our hands up and are holding the line as best we can. Fighting a war that no one thinks we can win. Facing down death. Mostly losing. U.S. military realignment in the Asia Pacific region, particularly the pending explosion of the U.S. military personnel population now set at 35,000, is rushing an endangered folk, colonized by Spain, Japan, and the United States since the 1500s, toward full-blown extinction. The boys and the bombers are coming. So are the nukes, the subs, the brand-new bowling alleys and movie theaters and gas stations for the soldiers on now expanding bases. Ruby Tuesday also. Home Depot. Walmart. All of it crammed onto the thirty-mile island of which the United States already occupies a third. . . . Activists know too well that Empire comes with a bang. Back home, that banging by now is so loud that folks can't hear one another, are getting so tired shouting over the noise to reach one another, simultaneously so outraged and so sad, that many of our finest warriors have simply gone home and shut the door. To cry. Cook. Be with their children.

NOBODY DOUBTS THAT the way forward is solidarity. But how bruised has the word become? Or, bigger, what weight do our words carry in these topsy-turvy times where war is, you know, peace. U.S. National Defense, the Global Commitment. Folks on the ground, for the most part, are wonderfully gifted in this regard. In this Age of Flippery, they remain the untricked ones. . . .

So what do we do? Where do we look? And if our arms are heavy already, where should we, really, cast our net of hope? My own small suggestion is that we do some serious inversion. If we're living in times of Bigger Is Better (e.g., the rationale of Empire, global capitalism, and spreading militarization)—and we all agree these are dark days—then we do well to draw in our gaze. Forsake the horizon, at least for a while, for the hue. Yes, Empire is big. Obviously bad. And the struggle is long and hard and so often lonely. But there are moments in the struggle, as anyone on the ground knows, wherein we are so remarkably alive. Where we, as part, disappear into the whole for love of it. Down here, we are rescued in moments. Down here connection happens. I've seen it. I've been sustained by it. In Guam. In Hawaii. And I know from other friends that the same happens elsewhere. In the other hot spots. We who fight daily for our homelands, our cousins, our loved ones' imaginations, our right to die from something other than cancer are fighting for each other. We fight so that the sky doesn't fall down on our sister. That is love. In the time of cholera and everything else. . . .

We [the indigenous peoples of Micronesia] are folks whose survival will depend on an ability to recognize a quiet fact: we are heirs to civilizations born up to two thousand years before Jesus. We've survived this long for a reason. And despite what they say, we don't have to do what we're told, and die. . . .

So I cannot help but reserve a last word for my sisters and brothers in the struggle. No one ever need tell us to keep on keeping on. That's our MO.

One activist to another, I lay flowers at your feet. I can only think how tired they must be.

12.5

WAR, CULTURE, AND COUNTERINSURGENCY
Roberto J. González, Hugh Gusterson, and David H. Price

The Network of Concerned Anthropologists was formed in the summer of 2007 when eleven like-minded anthropologists began corresponding and searching for ways to express concerns over recent efforts to militarize anthropology. We decided to take collective action and produce a statement of our objections to developing trends in the militarization of anthropology. This statement was loosely modeled on a document circulated by physicists, computer scientists, and engineers in the mid-1980s opposing Ronald Reagan's Strategic Defense Initiative and pledging to decline funding to participate in it. The two physicists who originated that statement, Lisbeth Gronlund and David Wright, went on to work for the Union of Concerned Scientists; hence, the name we chose for ourselves. Our own statement, worked out over a period of weeks through intense email exchanges, clarified our shared objections to military and intelligence agencies' uses of anthropology in the present political context. We circulated the statement among colleagues and posted it on our website, collecting more than one thousand signatures from like-minded anthropologists and other scholars. (The website was mysteriously taken down on the final day of the 2007 American Anthropological Association [AAA] meetings but was soon restored). Like other historical movements within American anthropology (such as the Anthropologists for Radical Political Action of the early 1970s), we work for change within professional organizations such as the AAA and the American Association of University Professors.

Not all members of the network have the same critiques of military uses of anthropology. Some members of the network are opposed to all forms of military employment by anthropologists, while others limit their critiques to specific relationships, particularly those involving secrecy or those that risk betraying standard relationships that emerge when we do ethnography. These differences and our ability to make common cause over larger issues is a fundamental strength of the network.

The network generates public critiques of new developments and policy proposals. We do not oppose engagement with military and civilian policy makers; we want to expand public debates to include informed critiques that use scholarship and political and ethical critiques to move toward better policies and practices. We strive for a form of public anthropology that engages the public and policy makers on topics that include the ethics and efficacy of the Human Terrain System, the Minerva Consortium, counterinsurgency, and abuses of anthropological research. . . .

We encourage our readers . . . to join with us and to seek their own ways, as anthropologists and as citizens, in which to undo the damage done to Iraq and Afghanistan by U.S. military intervention and to join us in the struggle to contest the militarization of anthropology.

12.6

HOPE IN THE DARK
Untold Histories, Wild Possibilities
Rebecca Solnit

On January 18, 1915, six months into World War I, as all Europe was convulsed by killing and dying, Virginia Woolf wrote in her journal, "The future is dark, which is on the whole, the best thing the future can be, I think." Dark, she seems to say, as in inscrutable, not as in terrible. We often mistake the one for the other. Or we transform the future's unknowability into something certain, the fulfillment of all our dread, the place beyond which there is no way forward. But again and again, far stranger things happen than the end of the world. . . . Who, four decades ago, could have conceived of the changed status of all who are nonwhite, non-male, or non-straight, the wide-open conversations about power, nature, economies, and ecologies?

There are times when it seems as though not only the future but the present is dark: few recognize what a radically transformed world we live in, one that has been transformed not only by such nightmares as global warming and global capital but by dreams of freedom, of justice, and transformed by things we could not have dreamed of. We adjust to changes without measuring them; we forget how much the culture changed.... What accretion of incremental, imperceptible changes made them possible, and how did they come about? ...

Some years ago, scientists attempted to create a long-range weather forecasting program. It turned out that the most minute variations, even the undetectable things, the things they could perhaps not even yet imagine as data, could cause entirely different weather to emerge from almost identical initial conditions. This was famously summed up as the saying about the flap of a butterfly's wings on one continent that can change the weather on another. History is like weather, not like checkers. (And you, if you're lucky and seize the day, are like that butterfly.) ...

IN 1785, NO one in Britain was thinking about slavery, except slaves, ex-slaves, and a few Quakers and soft-hearted evangelicals. In his book *Bury the Chains* (2005), Adam Hochschild tells the story of how the dozen or so original activists gathered at a London printer's shop at 2 George Yard, near what is now the Bank tube stop. From that point onward, this handful of hopefuls created a movement that in half a century abolished slavery in the British Empire and helped spark the abolition movement that ended slavery in the United States a quarter-century or so later. Part of the story is about the imagination and determination of a few key figures. But part of it is about a change of heart whereby enough people came to believe that slavery was an intolerable cruelty to bring its day to an end, despite the profitability of the institution to the powerful who defended it. It was arguments, sermons, editorials, pamphlets, conversations that changed the mind of the public: stories, for the decisions were mostly made in London (encouraged by witnesses and slave revolts abroad). The atrocities were mostly out of sight of the audience. It required imagination, empathy, and information to make abolition a cause and then a victory. In those five decades, antislavery sentiments went from being radical to being the status quo.

Stories move faster in our own time. It has taken less than forty years for homosexuality to go from being classified as a crime and a mental disorder to being widely accepted as part of the variety of ordinary, everyday life—and though there is a backlash, backlashes for all their viciousness cannot turn back the clock or put the genie back in his lamp. Polls suggest that homophobia is more a property of the old than the young, that society will gradually shed it, is shedding it, as the generations pass. Like views of slavery, the change comes so incrementally it can only be measured in court decisions and opinion polls, but it did not come as naturally as a change in the weather. It was made, by activists, but also by artists, writers, comedians, and filmmakers who asserted other versions of sexuality, other kinds of family, by all those parade organizers and marchers, by millions of ordinary individuals living openly as gay or lesbian, out to their families and communities, by people leaving behind their fears and animosities. Along similar lines, shifts in thought that led to activism and then shifts in law have radically revised the life and rights of the disabled. . . .

IT'S IMPORTANT TO say what hope is not: it is not the belief that everything was, is, or will be fine. The evidence is all around us of tremendous suffering and tremendous destruction. The hope I'm interested in is about broad perspectives with specific possibilities, ones that invite or demand that we act. It's also not a sunny everything-is-getting-better narrative, though it may be a counter to the everything-is-getting-worse narrative. You could call it an account of complexities and uncertainties, with openings. "Critical thinking without hope is cynicism, but hope without critical thinking is naïveté," the Bulgarian writer Maria Popova recently remarked. And Patrisse Cullors, one of the founders of Black Lives Matter, early on described the movement's mission as to "provide hope and inspiration for collective action to build collective power to achieve collective transformation, rooted in grief and rage but pointed toward vision and dreams." It's a statement that acknowledges that grief and hope can coexist. The tremendous human rights achievements—not only in gaining rights but in redefining race, gender, sexuality, embodiment, spirituality, and the idea of the good life—of the past half-century have flowered during a time of unprecedented ecological destruction and the rise of innovative new means of exploitation. And the rise of new forms of resistance, including resistance enabled by an elegant understanding of that ecology and new ways for people to communicate and organize, and new and exhilarating alliances across distance and difference. Hope locates itself in the premises that we don't know what will happen and that in the spaciousness of uncertainty is room to act. When you recognize uncertainty, you recognize that you may be able to influence the outcomes—you alone or you in concert with a few dozen or several million others. Hope is an embrace of the unknown and the unknowable, an alternative to the certainty of both optimists and pessimists. . . . But it's important to emphasize that hope is only a beginning; it's not a substitute for action, only a basis for it. . . .

[The historian Howard] Zinn [writes], "The struggle for justice should never be abandoned because of the apparent overwhelming power of those who have the guns and the money and who seem invisible in their determination to hold onto it. That apparent power has, again and again, proved vulnerable to moral fervor, determination, unity, organization, sacrifice, wit, ingenuity, courage, patience." . . .

People in official institutions devoutly believe they hold the power that matters, though the power we grant them can often be taken back; the violence commanded by governments and militaries often fails, and nonviolent direct-action campaigns often succeed. The sleeping giant is one name for the public: when it wakes up, when we wake up, we are no longer only the public; we are civil society, the superpower whose nonviolent means are sometimes, for a shining moment, more powerful than violence, more powerful than regimes and armies. We write history with our feet and with our presence and our collective voice and vision. And yet, and of course, everything in the mainstream media suggests that popular resistance is ridiculous, pointless, or criminal, unless it is far away, was long ago, or, ideally, both. These are the forces that prefer the giant remain asleep. Together we are very powerful, and we have a seldom told, seldom remembered history of victories and transformations that can give us confidence that yes, we can change the world because we have many times before.

Abdullah, Ibrahim. 2002. "Youth Culture and Rebellion: Understanding Sierra Leone's Wasted Decade." *Critical Arts* 16, no. 2: 19–37.

Abdullah, Ibrahim. 2004. "Bush Path to Destruction: The Origin and Character of the Revolutionary United Front." In *Between Democracy and Terror: The Sierra Leone Civil War*, edited by Ibrahim Abdullah, 41–65. Dakar: Council for the Development of Social Science Research in Africa.

Abélès, Marc. 2006. *Politique de la survie*. Paris: Flammarion.

Adams, Richard. 1970. *Crucifixion by Power: Essays on Guatemalan National Social Structure, 1944–1966*. Austin: University of Texas Press.

Adams, Thomas. 1999. "The New Mercenaries and the Privatization of Conflict." *Parameters*, Summer, 103–16.

Agamben, Giorgio. [1995] 1998. *Homo Sacer: Sovereign Power and Bare Life*. Stanford, CA: Stanford University Press.

Agamben, Giorgio. [1995] 2000. *Means without Ends: Notes on Politics*. Translated by Vincenzo Binetti. Minneapolis: University of Minnesota Press.

Agamben, Giorgio. [2003] 2005. *State of Exception*. Translated by Kevin Attel. Chicago: University of Chicago Press.

Agier, Michel. 2002. *Au bords du monde, les réfugiés*. Paris: Flammarion.

Aguilar-Moreno, M. 2007. *Handbook to Life in the Aztec World*. Oxford: Oxford University Press.

Aguon, Julian. 2009. "Down Here." In *Bases of Empire: The Global Struggle against U.S. Military Posts*, edited by Catherine Lutz, 333–36. New York: New York University Press.

Ahmed, Akbar. 2013. *The Thistle and the Drone: How America's War on Terror Became a Global War on Tribal Islam*. New York: Brookings Institution.

Akibayashi, Kozue, and Suzuyo Takazato. 2009. "Okinawa: Women's Struggle for Demilitarization." In *Bases of Empire: The Global Struggle against U.S. Military Posts*, edited by Catherine Lutz, 246–69. New York: New York University Press.

Al-Ali, Nadje. 2007. *Iraqi Women: Untold Stories from 1948 to the Present*. London: Zed.

Altinay, Ayse Gul. 2004. *The Myth of the Military-Nation: Militarism, Gender, and Education in Turkey*. London: Palgrave Macmillan.

Amano, Denchu. 1995. "Shika Hōyō" [Shika Hōyō Ritual in Buddhism]. *Kokushi Daijiten* 6:682.

Amemiya, Kozy. 2002. *Reinventing Population Problems in Okinawa: Emigration as a Tool of American Occupation*. Working Paper no. 90. Oakland, CA: Japan Policy Research Institute.

American Anthropological Association. 1971. "Principles of Professional Responsibility." http://www.americananthro.org/ParticipateAndAdvocate/Content.aspx ?ItemNumber=1656.

American Anthropological Association. 2007. "Statement on H[uman] T[errain] S[ystem]," November 8. http://s3.amazonaws.com/rdcms-aaa/files/production/public /FileDownloads/pdfs/pdf/EB_Resolution_110807.pdf.

Americas Watch. 1986. "Civil Patrols in Guatemala." *Americas Watch Report*, August.

Anderson, Elijah. 1999. *Code of the Street: Decency, Violence, and the Moral Life of the Inner City*. New York: Norton.

Appadurai, Arjun. 1996. *Modernity at Large: Cultural Dimensions of Globalization*. Minneapolis: University of Minnesota Press.

Arendt, Hannah. 1963. *Eichmann in Jerusalem: A Report on the Banality of Evil*. New York: Viking.

Arextaga, Begoña. 1997. *Shattering Silence: Women, Nationalism and Political Subjectivity in Northern Ireland*. Princeton: Princeton University Press.

Asad, Talal. 1983. "Notes on Body, Pain, and Truth in Medieval Christian Ritual." *Economy and Society* 12, no. 3: 287–327.

Asad, Talal. 2003. *Formations of the Secular: Christianity, Islam, Modernity*. Stanford, CA: Stanford University Press.

Asaro, Peter M. 2013. "The Labor of Surveillance and Bureaucratized Killing: New Subjectivities of Military Drone Operators." *Social Semiotics* 23, no. 2: 196–224.

Ashford, Mary-Wynne, and Yolanda Huet-Vaughn. 2000. "The Impact of War on Women." In *War and Public Health*, edited by Barry S. Levy and Victor W. Sidel, 193–206. Washington, DC: American Public Health Association.

Astore, William. 2018. "Make Sports, Not War." *TomDispatch.com*, August 19. http:// www.tomdispatch.com/blog/176459/tomgram%3A_william_astore%2C_make _sports%2C_not_war.

Atran, Scott. 2010. *Talking to the Enemy: Faith, Brotherhood, and the (Un)making of Terrorists*. New York: HarperCollins.

Axworthy, Lloyd. 2004. "A New Scientific Field and Policy Lens." *Security Dialogue* 35, no. 3: 348–49.

Aziz, Barbara Nimri. 2007. *Swimming Up the Tigris: Real Life Encounters with Iraq*. Gainesville: University Press of Florida.

Bacevich, Andrew. 2005. *The New American Militarism: How Americans Are Seduced by War*. New York: Oxford University Press.

Badaró, Máximo. 2015. "One of the Guys: Military Women and the Argentine Army." *American Anthropologist* 117, no. 1: 86–99.

Bailey, Beth. 2007. "The Army in the Marketplace: Recruiting an All-Volunteer Force." *Journal of American History* 94, no. 1: 47–74.

Bailey, Beth. 2014. "Soldiering as Work: The All-Volunteer Force in the United States." In *Fighting for a Living: A Comparative Study of Military Labour*, edited by Erik-Jan Zürcher, 581–612. Amsterdam: Amsterdam University Press.

Baran, Paul A., and Paul M. Sweezy. 1966. *Monopoly Capital: An Essay on the American Economic and Social Order*. New York: Monthly Review.

Barker, Holly. 2003. *Bravo for the Marshallese: Regaining Control in a Post-nuclear, Post-colonial World*. Belmont, CA: Wadsworth/Thomson.

Barnard, Clinton. 1948. Letter to William Donovan, October 28. William Donovan Papers, U.S. Army War College, Carlisle, PA, Box 73a.

Barnett, Michael. 2011. "Armed for Humanity." In *Empire of Humanity: A History of Humanitarianism*, by Michael Barnett, 171–94. Ithaca: Cornell University Press.

Bauman, Zygmunt. 1989. *Modernity and the Holocaust*. Cambridge: Polity.

Beals, Ralph L. 1967. "Background Information on Problems of Anthropological Research and Ethics." *American Anthropological Association Fellow Newsletter* 8, no. 1: 9–13.

Bederman, Gail. 1996. *Manliness and Civilization: A Cultural History of Gender and Race in the United States, 1880–1917*. Chicago: University of Chicago Press.

Benedict, Ruth. [1946] 1989. *The Chrysanthemum and the Sword*. 2nd ed. Boston: Houghton Mifflin.

Benjamin, Walter. 1969. "Theses on the Philosophy of History." In *Illuminations: Essays and Reflections*. Edited by Hannah Arendt. Translated by Harry Zohn. New York: Schocken.

Bergen, Peter L., and Daniel Rothenberg. 2014. *Drone Wars: Transforming Conflict, Law and Policy*. Cambridge: Cambridge University Press.

Berreman, Gerald. 1968. "Is Anthropology Alive? Social Responsibility in Anthropology." *Current Anthropology* 9:391–96.

Besteman, Catherine. 1996. "Violent Politics and the Politics of Violence: The Dissolution of the Somali Nation-State." *American Ethnologist* 23:579–96.

Bhan, Mona. 2013. *Counterinsurgency, Democracy, and the Politics of Identity in India: From Warfare to Welfare?* New York: Routledge.

Bickford, Andrew. 2011. *Fallen Elites: The Military Other in Post-Unification Germany*. Stanford, CA: Stanford University Press.

Binford, L. 1996. *The El Mozote Massacre: Anthropology and Human Rights*. Tucson: University of Arizona Press.

Bishara, Amal. 2012. *Back Stories: U.S. News Production and Palestinian Politics*. Stanford, CA: Stanford University Press.

Blacker, Coit, and Gloria Duffy, eds. 1976. *International Arms Control: Issues and Agreements*. Stanford, CA: Stanford University Press.

Blackhurst, Jack, Jennifer Gresham, and Morley O. Stone. 2012. "The Quantified Warrior: How [the Defense Department] Should Lead Human Performance Augmentation." *Armed Forces Journal* (December). http://armedforcesjournal.com/the-quantified-warrior.

Bodley, John. 2008. *Anthropology and Contemporary Human Problems*. Lanham, MD: AltaMira.

Bongioanni, Carlos. 2003. "As Okinawa Landfill Space Dwindles, Recycling Is Urged." *Stars and Stripes*, February 6.

Bonta, Bruce. 1993. *Peaceful Peoples: An Annotated Bibliography*. New York: Scarecrow.

Booth, Ken. 1991. "Security in Anarchy: Utopian Realism in Theory and Practice." *International Affairs* 67, no. 3: 527–45.

Borneman, John. 1995. "American Anthropology as Foreign Policy." *American Anthropologist* 97, no. 4: 663–72.

Bourdieu, Pierre. 1977. *Outline of a Theory of Practice*. Translated by Richard Nice. Cambridge: Cambridge University Press.

Bourgois, Philippe. 1995. *In Search of Respect: Selling Crack in El Barrio*. Cambridge: Cambridge University Press.

Boxer, Charles. 1951. *The Christian Century in Japan, 1549–1650*. Berkeley: University of California Press.

Branigin, William, and William Claiborne. 2001. "Allies Say Artillery Fire on Iraqis Is Heaviest Yet; Barrage Seen as 'Preparing Battlefield.'" *Washington Post*, February 22, A1.

Brauer, Jurgen. 2007. "United States Military Expenditure." In *Arms, War, and Terrorism in the Global Economy Today*, edited by Wolfram Elsner, 973–1015. Hamburg: LIT.

Brennan, Denise. 2004. *What's Love Got to Do with It? Transnational Desires and Sexism in the Dominican Republic*. Durham, NC: Duke University Press.

Bringa, Tone. 1996. *Being Muslim the Bosnian Way: Identity and Community in a Central Bosnian Village*. Princeton: Princeton University Press.

Broyles, William, Jr. 1986. *Brothers in Arms*. New York: Knopf.

Bryant, Brandon. 2013. "A Drone Warrior's Torment: Ex–Air Force Pilot Brandon Bryant on His Trauma from Remote Killing" (interview by Amy Goodman). *DemocracyNow!* October 25. https://www.democracynow.org/2013/10/25/a_drone_warriors_torment _ex_air.

Burke, Edmund. 1901. *A Philosophical Inquiry into the Origin of Our Ideas of the Sublime and Beautiful*. Boston: Little, Brown.

Burnet, Philip W. J. 2012. "Gut Bacteria and Brain Function: The Challenges of a Growing Field." *Proceedings of the National Academy of Sciences of the United States of America* 109, no. 4: E175–76.

Burrell, Jennifer L. 2014. *Maya after War: Conflict, Power, and Politics in Guatemala*. Austin: University of Texas Press.

Butler, Judith. 2003. "Violence, Mourning, Politics." *Studies in Gender and Sexuality* 4, no. 1: 9–37.

Buzan, Barry. 1991. *People, States and Fear: An Agenda for International Security Studies in the Post–Cold War Era*. 2nd ed. London: Longman.

Caldwell, J. A., J. L. Caldwell, N. K. Smythe, and K. K. Hall. 2000. "A Double-Blind, Placebo-Controlled Investigation of the Efficacy of Modafinil for Sustaining the Alertness and Performance of Aviators: A Helicopter Simulator Study." *Psychopharmacology* 150, no. 3: 272–82.

Campbell, Howard. 2009. *Drug War Zone*. Austin: University of Texas Press.

Campbell, Timothy. 2008. "Bios, Immunity, Life: The Thought of Robert Esposito." In *Bios: Biopolitics and Philosophy*, edited by Robert Esposito, translated by Timothy Campbell, vii–xlii. Minneapolis: University of Minnesota Press.

Camus, Albert. 1955. *The Myth of Sisyphus and Other Essays*. New York: Vintage.

Carlsson, Ingvar. 1995. *Our Global Neighbourhood: The Report of the Commission on Global Governance*. Oxford: Oxford University Press.

Carr, Marilyn, and Martha Chen. 2004. *Globalization, Social Exclusions and Work with Special Reference to Informal Employment and Gender.* Policy Integration Department Working Paper no. 20. Geneva: International Labour Organization.

Carter, Ash. 2016. "Statement to the U.S. House of Representatives Appropriations Committee." February 25. https://docs.house.gov/meetings/AP/AP02/20160225 /104483/HHRG-114-AP02-Wstate-CarterA-20160225.pdf.

Chagnon, Napoleon. [1968] 1977. *Yanomamo: The Fierce People.* New York: Holt, Rinehart, and Winston.

Chagnon, Napoleon. 1988. "Life Histories, Blood Revenge, and Warfare in a Tribal Population." *Science* 239:985–92.

Chamayou, Gregoire. 2015. *Drone Theory.* London: Penguin.

Chant, Sylvia, and Carolyn Pedwell. 2008. *Women, Gender and the Informal Economy: An Assessment of ILO Research and Suggested Ways Forward.* Geneva: International Labour Organization.

Chappelle, Wayne, Kent McDonald, Billy Thompson, and Julie Swearengen. 2012. "Prevalence of High Emotional Distress and Symptoms of Post-Traumatic Stress Disorder in U.S. Air Force Active Duty Remotely Piloted Aircraft Operators." 2010 U.S. Air Force School of Aerospace Medicine Survey Results. Air Force Research Laboratory final report AFRL-SA-WP-TR-2013-0002. Wright-Patterson Air Force Base, OH.

Cheng, Sealing. 2010. *On the Move for Love: Migrant Entertainers and the U.S. Military in South Korea.* Philadelphia: University of Pennsylvania Press.

Chilean House of Representatives, Special Investigation Committee. 1965. *A Report from the Special Investigation Committee. Santiago, Chile.* https://www.bcn.cl /laborparlamentaria/wsgi/consulta/verDiarioDeSesion.py?id=619131.

Churchill, Winston. 1945. *The Dawn of Liberation.* London: Cassell.

Cicchetti, Dante, and Karen Schneider-Rosen, eds. 1984. *Childhood Depression.* San Francisco: Jossey-Bass.

Clausewitz, Carl von. 1976. *On War.* Translated by Michael Howard and Peter Paret. Princeton: Princeton University Press.

Cockburn, Cynthia. 2001. "The Gendered Dynamics of Armed Conflict and Political Violence." In *Victims, Perpetrators or Actors? Gender, Armed Conflict and Political Violence,* edited by C. O. N. Moser and F. Clark, 13–29. London: Zed Books.

Cohen, Ronald. 1984. "Warfare and State Formation: Wars Make States and States Make Wars." In *Warfare, Culture and Environment,* edited by R. Brian Ferguson, 329–59. Cambridge, MA: Academic Press.

Cohen, Ronald, and Elman Service, eds. 1978. *Origins of the State: The Anthropology of Political Evolution.* Philadelphia: Institute for the Study of Human Issues.

Cohn, Carol. 1987. "Sex and Death in the Rational World of Defense Intellectuals." *Signs* 12, no. 4: 687–718.

Cole, Chris, Mary Dobbing, and Amy Hailwood. 2010. *Convenient Killing: Armed Drones and the "Playstation" Mentality.* Oxford: Fellowship of Reconciliation.

Comaroff, Jean, and John L. Comaroff. 1999. "Occult Economies and the Violence of Abstraction: Notes from the South African Postcolony." *American Ethnologist* 26, no. 2: 279–303.

Connell, Evan. 1984. *Son of the Morning Star*. San Francisco: North Point.

Connerton, Paul. 1989. *How Societies Remember*. Cambridge: Cambridge University Press.

Cook, Fred J. 1964. "The Warfare State." *Annals of the American Academy of Political and Social Science* 351, no. 1: 102–9.

Copetas, Craig. 1999. "It's Off to War Again for Big U.S. Contractor." *Wall Street Journal*, April 14, A21.

Crocker, Chester A., Fen Hampson, and Pamela R. Aall. 1996. *Managing Global Chaos: Sources of and Responses to International Conflict*. Washington, DC: U.S. Institute of Peace.

Cullen, Patrick. 2000. "Keeping the New Dogs of War on a Tight Leash." *Conflict Trends* 6:36–39.

Cumings, Bruce. 1999. "Boundary Displacement: The State, the Foundations, and International and Area Studies during and after the Cold War." In *Parallax Visions: Making Sense of American–East Asian Relations*, 173–204. Durham, NC: Duke University Press.

Cypher, James M. 2007. "From Military Keynesianism to Global-Neoliberal Militarism." *Monthly Review* 59, no. 2 (June 2007): 37–55.

Danner, Mark. 1993. "The Truth of El Mozote." *New Yorker*, December 6, 50–133.

Darley, John G. 1952. "Contract Support of Research in Psychology." *American Psychologist* 7, no. 12: 719–20.

Darley, John G. 1957. "Psychology and the Office of Naval Research: A Decade of Development." *American Psychologist* 12, no. 6: 305–22.

Daulitzai, A. 2006. "Acknowledging Afghanistan: Notes and Queries on an Occupation." *Cultural Dynamics* 18, no. 3: 293–311.

Davis, R., A. Taylor, and E. Murphy. 2014. "Gender, Conscription and Protection, and the War in Syria." *Forced Migration Review* 47:35–38.

Dean, Robert D. 2001. *Imperial Brotherhood: Gender and the Making of Cold War Foreign Policy*. Amherst: University of Massachusetts Press.

De León, Jason. 2018. "The Border Wall Is a Metaphor" (interview with Micheline Aharanian Marcom). New American Story Project. https://newamericanstoryproject.org.

Deleuze, Gilles. 1995. *Negotiations: 1972–1990: European Perspectives*. Edited by Lawrence D. Kritzman. Translated by Martin Joughin. New York: Columbia University Press.

DeMain, Paul. 1991. "Troops on Their Way Home." *News from Indian Country* 5, no. 3: 1.

de Waal, Alex. 1998. *Famine Crimes: Politics and the Disaster Relief Industry in Africa*. Bloomington: Indiana University Press.

de Waal, Alex, ed. 2002. *Demilitarizing the Mind: African Agendas for Peace and Security*. Trenton, NJ: Africa World.

Der Derian, James. 2009. *Virtuous War: Mapping the Military-Industrial-Media-Entertainment Network*. New York: Routledge.

Derrida, Jacques. 1987. *The Post Card: From Socrates to Freud and Beyond*. Translated by Alan Bass. Chicago: University of Chicago Press.

Deuze, Mark. 2011. "Media Life." *Media, Culture and Society* 33, no. 1: 137–48.

Diamond, Sigmund. 1992. *Compromised Campus: The Collaboration of Universities with the Intelligence Community, 1945–1955*. Oxford: Oxford University Press.

Diken, Bulent, and Carsten Bagge Lausten. 2005. "Becoming Abject: Rape as a Weapon of War." *Body and Society* 11, no. 1: 111–28.

Douglas, Mary. 2002. *Purity and Danger: An Analysis of the Concepts of Pollution and Taboo*. London: Taylor.

Douglas, Mary, and Aaron Wildavsky. 1982. *Risk and Culture*. Berkeley: University of California Press.

Dowden, Richard, and Robert Fisk. 1991. "Crisis in the Gulf: Wild Jubilation Follows the Chaotic Rout." *The Independent*, February 28.

Du Bois, Cora. 1949 *Social Forces in Southeast Asia*. Minneapolis: University of Minnesota Press.

Duff-Brown, Beth. 2015. "The Final Frontier Has Become Congested and Contested." *Stanford University Center for International Security and Cooperation News*, March 4. https://cisac.fsi.stanford.edu/news/security-space-0.

Duffield, Mark. 2001. *Global Governance and the New Wars: The Merging of Development and Security*. London: Zed.

Duffield, Mark. 2004. *Carry on Killing: Global Governance, Humanitarianism, and Terror*. Copenhagen: Danish Institute for International Studies.

Dunbar-Ortiz, Roxanne. 2004. "Annihilation until Unconditional Surrender: Indian Country." *CounterPunch*, October 11.

Duschinski, Haley. 2009. "Destiny Effects: Militarization, State Power, and Punitive Containment in Kashmir Valley." *Anthropological Quarterly* 82, no. 3: 691–717.

Eden, Lynn. 2004. *Whole World on Fire: Organization, Knowledge, and Nuclear Weapons Devastation*. Ithaca: Cornell University Press.

Editor's Report. 2004. "Terrorism as 'Indian Country' Is Wrongful Assumption." *Indian Country Today*, October 5. http://www.indiancountry.com/content.cfm?id=1096409627.

Edney-Browne, Alex. 2016. "Embodiment and Affect in a Digital Age: Understanding Mental Illness among Military Drone Personnel." *Krisis* 3:1–14.

Eisenhower, Dwight D. 1961. Farewell Address, January 17. Papers of Dwight D. Eisenhower as President of the United States, 1953–61, Speech Series, Box 38, Dwight D. Eisenhower Presidential Library, Abilene, KS.

Elliott, Michael A. 2007. *Custerology: The Enduring Legacy of the Indian Wars and George Armstrong Custer*. Chicago: University of Chicago Press.

Elshtain, Jean Bethke. 1995. "The Compassionate Warrior: Wartime Sacrifice." In *Women and War*, edited by Jean Bethke Elshtain, 205–10. Chicago: University of Chicago Press.

Enemark, Christian. 2013. *Armed Drones and the Ethics of War: Military Drones in a Post-Heroic Age*. London: Routledge.

Engelhardt, Tom. 2007. *The End of Victory Culture: Cold War America and the Disillusioning of a Generation*. 2nd ed. Amherst: University of Massachusetts Press.

Enloe, Cynthia. 1983. *Does Khaki Become You? The Militarization of Women's Lives*. Boston: South End.

Enloe, Cynthia. 1988. *Does Khaki Become You? The Militarization of Women's Lives*. Rev. ed. London: Pandora.

Enloe, Cynthia. 2007. *Globalization and Militarism: Feminists Make the Link*. Lanham, MD: Rowman and Littlefield.

Enloe, Cynthia. 2010. *Nimo's War, Emma's War: Making Feminist Sense of the Iraq War*. Berkeley: University of California Press.

Evans, Gareth. 2006. "From Humanitarian Intervention to the Responsibility to Protect." Speech delivered at the Symposium on Humanitarian Intervention, University of Wisconsin, Madison, March 31. http://reinhardmeyers.uni-muenster.de/docs/evans.pdf.

Evans, Thomas W. 1993. The All-Volunteer Army after Twenty Years: Recruiting in the Modern Era. *Army History* 27:40–46.

Falconí, Carola, and José Carlos Agüero. 2003. "Violaciones sexuales en las comunidades campesinas de Ayacucho." In *Violaciones sexuales a mujeres durante la violencia política en el Perú*, edited by Comisión de Derechos Humanos, 23–48. Lima: Comisión de Derechos Humanos.

Falla, Ricardo. 1999. *Massacres in the Jungle: Ixcan, Guatemala, 1975–1982*. Boulder, CO: Westview.

Farrell, John. 1991. "Where We Shroud Our Heroes." *Boston Globe*, February 27, 57–64.

Fassin, Didier. 2007. "Humanitarianism as a Politics of Life." *Public Culture* 19, no. 3: 499–520.

Fassin, Didier, and Mariella Pandolfi, eds. 2010. *Contemporary States of Emergency: The Politics of Military and Humanitarian Interventions*. Brooklyn, NY: Zone.

Fassin, Didier, and Paula Vasquez. 2005. "Humanitarian Exception as the Rule: The Political Theology of the 1999 Tragedia in Venezuela." *American Ethnologist* 32, no. 3: 389–405.

Featherstone, Michel, David Jary, and Alan Tomlinson. 1987. "Leisure, Symbolic Power and the Life Course." In *Sport, Leisure and Social Relations*, edited by John Horne, 113–38. London: Routledge.

Feigenbaum, Harvey, and Jeffrey Henig. 1997. "Privatization and Political Theory." *Journal of International Affairs* 50, no. 2: 338–55.

Feldman, Allen. 1991. *Formations of Violence: The Narrative of the Body and Political Terror in Northern Ireland*. Chicago: University of Chicago Press.

Feldman, Jonathan. 1989. *Universities in the Business of Repression*. Boston: South End.

Fenrick, W. J. 2001. "Targeting and Proportionality during the NATO Bombing Campaign against Yugoslavia." *European Journal of International Law* 12, no. 3: 489–502.

Fenton, William Nelson. 1947. *Area Studies in American Universities: For the Commission on Implications of Armed Services Educational Programs*. Washington, DC: American Council on Education.

Ferguson, R. Brian. 2008. "Ten Points on War." *Social Analysis* 52, no. 2: 33–34.

Ferrándiz, Francisco. 2013. "Exhuming the Defeated: Civil War Mass Graves in 21st-Century Spain." *American Ethnologist* 40, no. 1: 38–54.

Finnström, Sverker. 2008. *Living with Bad Surroundings: War, History, and Everyday Moments in Northern Uganda*. Durham, NC: Duke University Press.

Finnström, Sverker, and Neil Whitehead, eds. 2013. *Virtual War and Magical Death: Technologies and Imaginaries for Terror and Killing*. Durham, NC: Duke University Press.

Fithen, David. 1999. "Diamonds and War in Sierra Leone." Ph.D. diss., University College of London.

Fleischer, Jeff. 2004. "Operation Hollywood: Interview with David Robb." *Mother Jones*, September 20. https://www.motherjones.com/politics/2004/09/operation-hollywood/.

Foley, Conor. 2010. *The Thin Blue Line: How Humanitarianism Went to War*. London: Verso.

Foot, Rosemary. 1990. *A Substitute for Victory: The Politics of Peacekeeping at the Korean Armistice Talks*. Ithaca: Cornell University Press.

Ford, Kenneth, and Clark Glymour. 2014. "The Enhanced Warfighter." *Bulletin of the Atomic Scientists* 70, no. 1: 43–53.

Forester, Cindy. 1992. "Conscript's Testimony: Inside the Guatemalan Army." *Report on Guatemala* 13, no. 2: 6, 14.

Forte, Maximilian, ed. 2014. *Good Intentions: Norms and Practices of Imperial Humanitarianism*. Montreal: Alert.

Foster, John Bellamy, Hannah Holleman, and Robert W. McChesney. 2008. "The U.S. Imperial Triangle and Military Spending." *Monthly Review* 60, no. 5: 1–19.

Foucault, Michel. 1961. *Madness and Civilization: A History of Insanity in the Age of Reason*. London: Tavistock.

Foucault, Michel. 1979. *Discipline and Punish: The Birth of the Prison*. New York: Vintage.

Foucault, Michel. 1980. *History of Sexuality*. Volume 1, *An Introduction*. New York: Vintage.

Fried, Morton. 1969. *The Evolution of Political Society*. New York: Random House.

Fried, Morton, Marvin Harris, and Robert Murphy, eds. 1968. *War: The Anthropology of Armed Conflict and Aggression*. New York: Natural History.

Frühstück, Sabine. 2007. *Uneasy Warriors: Gender, Memory, and Popular Culture in the Japanese Army*. Berkeley: University of California Press.

Fry, Douglas. 2007. *Beyond War: The Human Potential for Peace*. New York: Oxford University Press.

Fundación Internacional para el Desafío Economico Global. 1992. *El impacto diferenciado de género de las políticas de ajuste sobre las condiciones de vida en el área rural y concentraciones urbanas intermedias*. Managua: Norad.

Galloway, Joseph L. 1991. "The Point of the Spear." *U.S. News and World Report*, March 11, 32.

Galtung, Johan. 1967. "Scientific Colonialism." *Transition* 30 (April–May): 10–15.

Gandhi, Mohandas K. 1992. "Ahimsa, or the Way of Nonviolence." In *A Peace Reader*, edited by Joseph J. Fahey and Richard Armstrong, 171–74. New York: Paulist.

Gans, Herbert. 1980. *Deciding What's News*. New York: Vintage.

Garrett-Peltier, Heidi. 2014. "The Job Opportunity Cost of War." *Truthout.com*, December 10. https://truthout.org/articles/cost-of-war.

Gberie, Lansana. 2005. *A Dirty War in West Africa: The RUF and the Destruction of Sierra Leone*. Bloomington: Indiana University Press.

Geiger, Jack. 2000. "The Impact of War on Human Rights." In *War and Public Health*, edited by Barry S. Levy and Victor W. Sidel, 39–50. Washington, DC: American Public Health Association.

Geldard, Frank A. 1953. "Military Psychology: Science or Technology?" *American Journal of Psychology* 66: 335–48.

Gharib, Ali. 2015. "'Good Kill': Drone Pilots Get PTSD, Civilians Die Nameless." *The Nation*, June 29. https://www.thenation.com/article/good-kill-drone-pilots-get-ptsd -civilians-die-nameless.

Gibson, James William. 1994. *Warrior Dreams: Violence and Manhood in Post-Vietnam America*. New York: Hill and Wang.

Gibson, James William. 2000. *The Perfect War: Technowar in Vietnam*. New York: Grove.

Giddens, Anthony. 1979. *Central Problems in Social Theory*. Berkeley: University of California Press.

Giddens, Anthony. 1984. *The Constitution of Society*. Cambridge: Polity.

Giffords, Gabrielle. 2014. "The Lessons of Physical Therapy." *New York Times*, January 8, A23.

Gilgen, Albert R. 1982. *American Psychology since World War II: A Profile of the Discipline*. Westport, CT: Greenwood.

Gill, Lesley. 1997. "Creating Citizens, Making Men: The Military and Masculinity in Bolivia." *Cultural Anthropology* 12, no. 4: 527–50.

Gill, Lesley. 2004. *School of the Americas: Military Training and Political Violence in the Americas*. Durham, NC: Duke University Press.

Gillem, Mark L. 2004. *America Town: Building the Outposts of Empire*. Minneapolis: University of Minnesota Press.

Gillen, Jarrles. 1997. *Violence: Reflections on a National Epidemic*. New York: Random House.

Gilligan, Andrew. 1998. "Inside Lt. Col. Spicer's New Model Army." *Sunday Telegraph*, November 22, A1.

Gittler, Juliana. 2004. "Illegal Dumping a Big Mess for Bases." *Stars and Stripes*, August 8. https://www.stripes.com/news/illegal-dumping-a-big-mess-for-bases-1.22517.

Glasius, Marlies, and Mary Kaldor. 2009. *A Human Security Doctrine for Europe: Project, Principles, Practicalities*. London: Routledge.

Glasstone, Samuel, and Philip J. Dolan. 1977. *The Effects of Nuclear Weapons*. 3rd ed. Warren, MI: Knowledge.

Goedde, Petra. 2003. *GIs and Germans: Culture, Gender and Foreign Relations 1945–1949*. New Haven: Yale University Press.

Goffman, Erving. 1961. *Asylums: Essays on the Social Situation of Mental Patients and Other Inmates*. Garden City, NY: Anchor.

Golden, Mark. 2003. "Childhood in Ancient Greece." In *Coming of Age in Ancient Greece*, edited by Jenifer Neils and John H. Oakley, 13–30. New Haven: Yale University Press.

Gombrich, Richard. 1988. *Theravada Buddhism: A Social History from Ancient Benares to Modern Colombo*. London: Routledge and Kegan Paul.

González, Roberto J. 2009. *American Counterinsurgency: Human Science and the Human Terrain*. Chicago: Prickly Paradigm.

González, Roberto J. 2010. *Militarizing Culture: Essays on the Warfare State*. Walnut Creek, CA: Left Coast.

González, Roberto J., Hugh Gusterson, and David Price. 2009. "Introduction: War, Culture, and Counterinsurgency." In *The Counter-Counterinsurgency Manual*, edited by Network of Concerned Anthropologists, 1–20. Chicago: Prickly Paradigm.

Goodall, Jane. 1986. *The Chimpanzees of Gombe*. Cambridge: Cambridge University Press.

Goodman, Amy. 2009. "Pentagon Pundits: Interview with David Barstow." *Democracy Now!* May 8.

Goodwin, Christopher. 1997. "Mexican Drug Barons Sign Up Renegades from Green Berets." *Sunday Times,* August 24, A1.

Gough, Kathleen. 1968. "Anthropology and Imperialism." *Monthly Review* 19, no. 11: 2–27.

Graves, Robert. 1929. *Good-Bye to All That.* New York: Cape and Smith.

Gray, Colin S., and Keith Payne. 1980. "Victory Is Possible." *Foreign Policy* 39 (Summer): 14–27.

Gray, J. Glenn. 1959. *The Warriors: Reflections on Men in Battle.* New York: Harcourt Brace.

Green, Linda. 1994. "Fear as a Way of Life." *Cultural Anthropology* 9, no. 2: 227–56.

Green, Linda. 1999. *Fear as a Way of Life: Mayan Widows in Rural Guatemala.* New York: Columbia University Press.

Greenberg, Michael, and David Schneider. 1994. "Violence in American Cities: Young Black Males Is the Answer, but What Was the Question?" *Social Science and Medicine* 39, no. 2: 179–87.

Grossman, Dave, and Gloria DeGaetano. 1998. *Stop Teaching Our Kids to Kill.* New York: Crown.

Guatemalan Bishops Conference. 1988. *Cry for Land: Pastoral Letter.* Guatemala City: Guatemala Bishops Conference.

Gupta, Akhil. 1998. *Postcolonial Developments.* Durham, NC: Duke University Press.

Gusterson, Hugh. 1991. "Nuclear War, the Gulf War, and the Disappearing Body." *Journal of Urban and Cultural Studies* 2, no. 1: 45–55.

Gusterson, Hugh. 1996. *Nuclear Rites: A Weapons Laboratory at the End of the Cold War.* Berkeley: University of California Press.

Gusterson, Hugh. 1999a. "Feminist Militarism." *PoLAR: Political and Legal Anthropology Review* 22, no. 2: 17–26.

Gusterson, Hugh. 1999b. "Nuclear Weapons and the Other in the Western Imagination." *Cultural Anthropology* 14, no. 1: 111–43.

Gusterson, Hugh. 2007. "Anthropology and Militarism." *Annual Review of Anthropology* 36:155–75.

Gusterson, Hugh. 2016. *Drone: Remote Control Warfare.* Cambridge: MIT Press.

Gutmann, Matthew, and Catherine Lutz. 2010. *Breaking Ranks: Iraq Veterans Speak Out against the War.* Berkeley: University of California Press.

Haas, Jonathan, ed. 1990. *The Anthropology of War.* Cambridge: Cambridge University Press.

Hakusi, Inami. 1948. *Nippon-To: The Japanese Sword.* Tokyo: Cosmo.

Hallinan, Conn. 2007. "Into Africa." *Foreign Policy in Focus,* March 15. http://www.fpif.org/fpiftxt/4079.

Hamilton, W. 2003. "Toying with War." *The Age,* May 4. http://www.theage.com.au/articles/2003/05/03/1051876901536.html.

Hammond, Phil. 2007. *Media, War and Postmodernity.* New York: Routledge.

Handicap International. 2007. *Circle of Impact: The Fatal Footprint of Cluster Munitions on People and Communities.* May 1. https://reliefweb.int/report/world/circle-impact-fatal-footprint-cluster-munitions-people-and-communities.

Hanh, Thich Nhat. 1993. *Love in Action: Writings on Nonviolent Social Change*. 3rd ed. Berkeley, CA: Parallax.

Hannerz, Ulf, and Anthony T. Carter. 2004. *Foreign News: Exploring the World of Foreign Correspondents*. Chicago: University of Chicago Press.

Hardt, Michael, and Antonio Negri. 2000. *Empire*. Cambridge: Cambridge University Press.

Hardt, Michael, and Antonio Negri. 2004. *Multitude: War and Democracy in the Age of Empire*. New York: Penguin.

Hautzinger, Sarah, and Jean Scanlan. 2013. *Beyond Post-Traumatic Stress: Homefront Struggles with the War on Terror*. Walnut Creek, CA: Left Coast.

Hayden, Robert. 1996. "Imagined Communities and Real Victims: Self-Determination and Ethnic Cleansing in Yugoslavia." *American Ethnologist* 23, no. 4: 783–801.

Heider, Karl G. 1979. *Grand Valley Dani: Peaceful Warriors*. New York: Holt, Rinehart, and Winston.

Herman, Ellen. 1995. "The Career of Cold War Psychology." In *The Romance of American Psychology*, 126–30. Berkeley: University of California Press.

Hertsgaard, Mark. 1988. *On Bended Knee: The Press and the Reagan Presidency*. New York: Schocken.

Higate, Paul. 2012. "The Private Militarized and Security Contractor as Geocorporeal Actor." *International Political Sociology* 6, no. 4: 355–72.

Hochschild, Adam. 2005. *Bury the Chains: Prophets and Rebels in the Fight to Free an Empire's Slaves*. Boston: Mariner.

Hoffman, Daniel. 2007. "The City as Barracks: Freetown, Monrovia, and the Organization of Violence in Postcolonial African Cities." *Cultural Anthropology* 22, no. 3: 400–428.

Hoffman, Daniel. 2008. *Living with Bad Surroundings: War, History, and Everyday Moments in Northern Uganda*. Durham, NC: Duke University Press.

Hoffman, Daniel. 2010. "The Sub-Contractors: Counterinsurgency, Militias and the New Common Ground in Social and Military Science." In *Dangerous Liaisons: Anthropologists and the National Security State*, edited by Laura McNamara and Robert Rubenstein, 3–24. Santa Fe, NM: School for Advanced Research Press.

Hoffman, Daniel. 2011. "Violence, Just in Time: War and Work in Contemporary West Africa." *Cultural Anthropology* 26, no. 1: 34–57.

Hofstadter, Richard. 1966. *Anti-Intellectualism in American Life*. New York: Vintage.

Hoganson, Kristin L. 1998. *Fighting for American Manhood: How Gender Politics Provoked the Spanish-American and Philippine-American Wars*. New Haven: Yale University Press.

Holm, Tom. 1992. "Patriots and Pawns: State Use of American Indians in the Military and the Process of Nativization in the United States." In *The State of Native America: Genocide, Colonization, and Resistance*, edited by M. Annette Jaimes, 213–23. Boston: South End.

Holman, Kimberly. 2009. "Yo, Joe! Guard Adds Real-Life Heroes to G.I. Movie." *Grizzly: Official News Magazine of the California National Guard*, September.

Holmes, Richard. 1985. *Acts of War*. New York: Free Press.

Hosaka, Masayasu. 1985. *Haisen Zengo* [Before and after the Defeat in the War]. Asahi, Japan: Shinbunsha.

Hoyt, Mike. 1993. "The Mozote Massacre." *Columbia Journalism Review*, January–February, 31–34.

Human Rights Watch. 2003. *International Humanitarian Law Issues in a Potential War in Iraq*. Human Rights Watch Briefing Paper, February 20. http://www.hrw.org /backgrounder/arms/iraq0202003.htm#5.

Hunt, Michael H. 1987. *Ideology and U.S. Foreign Policy*. New Haven: Yale University Press.

Hynes, H. Patricia. 2011. "Landmines and Cluster Bombs: 'Weapons of Mass Destruction in Slow Motion.'" *Truthout.com*, September 1. https://truthout.org/articles/landmines -and-cluster-bombs-weapons-of-mass-destruction-in-slow-motion/.

Ignatieff, Michael. 1997. *The Warrior's Honor: Ethnic War and the Modern Conscience*. New York: Holt.

International Commission on Intervention and State Sovereignty. 2001. *The Responsibility to Protect*. Ottawa: International Development Research Centre. http://www.iciss.ca /pdf/Commission-Report.pdf.

International Committee for Robot Arms Control. 2013. "The Scientists' Call to Ban Autonomous Lethal Robots." https://www.stopkillerrobots.org/2013/10/scientists-call/.

Ivie, Robert L. 2005. "Savagery in Democracy's Empire." *Third World Quarterly* 26, no. 1: 55–65.

Jackson, Robert H. 1990. *Quasi-States: Sovereignty, International Relations, and the Third World*. Cambridge: Cambridge University Press.

Jeffords, Susan. 1989. *The Remasculinization of America: Gender and the Vietnam War*. Bloomington: Indiana University Press.

Jerryson, Michael, and Mark Juergensmeyer, eds. 2010. *Buddhist Warfare*. Oxford: Oxford University Press.

Johnson, Chalmers. 2004. *The Sorrows of Empire: Militarism, Secrecy, and the End of the Republic*. New York: Metropolitan.

Johnson, Sheila K. 2001. *Of Sex, Okinawa, and American Foreign Policy*. Occasional Paper no. 23. Oakland, CA: Japan Policy Research Institute.

Johnston, Barbara Rose, ed. 2007. *Half-Lives and Half-Truths: Confronting the Radioactive Legacies of the Cold War*. Santa Fe, NM: School of American Research Press.

Johnston, Barbara Rose. 2012. "Nuclear Savages." *CounterPunch* (online ed.), June 1.

Johnston, Barbara Rose, and Holly Barker. 2008. *Consequential Damages of Nuclear War: The Rongelap Report*. Walnut Creek, CA: Left Coast.

Jorgensen, Joseph, and Eric Wolf. 1970. "Anthropology on the Warpath in Thailand." *New York Review of Books*, November 19, 26–35.

Joseph, Paul. 2011. *Soft Counterinsurgency: Human Terrain Teams and U.S. Military Strategy in Iraq and Afghanistan*. London: Palgrave Macmillan.

Junger, Ernst. 1975. *The Storm of Steel*. New York: Fertig.

Kabeer, Naila. 2008. *Mainstreaming Gender in Social Protection for the Informal Economy*. London: Commonwealth Secretariat.

Kaldor, Mary. 1981. *The Baroque Arsenal*. New York: Hill and Wang.

Kaldor, Mary, and Alan Johnson. 2007. *New Wars and Human Security: An Interview with Mary Kaldor*. London: Foreign Policy Centre.

Kalecki, Michal. 1972. *The Last Phase in the Transformation of Capitalism*. New York: Monthly Review Press.

Kapferer, Bruce. 1988. *Legends of People, Myths of State: Violence, Intolerance, and Political Culture in Sri Lanka and Australia*. Washington, DC: Smithsonian Institution Press.

Kaplan, Robert. 2004. "Indian Country." *Wall Street Journal*, September 21, A22.

Kaplan, Robert. 2005. *Imperial Grunts: The American Military on the Ground*. New York: Random House.

Katō, Hidetoshi. 1965. "Bidan no Genkei" [The Prototype of the Heroic Stories]. *Asahi Janaru*, April, 74–78.

Keegan, John. 1978. *The Face of Battle*. New York: Penguin.

Keen, David. 2005. *Conflict and Collusion in Sierra Leone*. New York: Palgrave.

Kelly, John, Beatrice Jauregui, Sean T. Mitchell, and Jeremy Walton, eds. 2010. *Anthropology and Global Counterinsurgency*. Chicago: University of Chicago Press.

Kelly, Raymond. 2000. *Warless Societies and the Origin of War*. Ann Arbor: University of Michigan Press.

Keyes, Charles F. 1987. *Thailand: Buddhist Kingdom as Modern Nation-State*. Boulder, CO: Westview.

Khalidi, Rashid. 2004. *Resurrecting Empire: Western Footprints and America's Perilous Path in the Middle East*. Boston: Beacon.

Kim, Ji-ho. 2003. "GIs Chalk Up $32 Billion Won in Damages." *Korea Herald*, January 31.

King, Martin Luther, Jr. 1967. "Beyond Vietnam: A Time to Break Silence, Declaration of Independence from the War in Vietnam." Speech delivered at Riverside Church, New York, April 4. https://kinginstitute.stanford.edu/king-papers/documents/beyond-vietnam.

Klare, Michael. 1995. *Rogue States and Nuclear Outlaws: America's Search for a New Foreign Policy*. New York: Hill and Wang.

Klare, Michael. 1999. "The Kalishnikov Age." *Bulletin of the Atomic Scientists* 55, no. 1: 18–22.

Klare, Michael, and Peter Kornbluh, eds. 1988. *Low Intensity Warfare: Counterinsurgency, Proinsurgency, and Antiterrorism in the Eighties*. New York: Pantheon.

Kohn, Richard H. 2009. "The Danger of Militarization in an Endless 'War' on Terrorism." *Journal of Military History* 73, no. 1: 177–208.

Kohrt, Brandon, and Robert Koenig. 2009. "Child Soldiers after War." *Anthropology News* 50, no. 5: 27.

Koppes, Clayton R., and Gregory D. Black. 1990. *Hollywood Goes to War: How Politics, Profits and Propaganda Shaped World War II Movies*. Berkeley: University of California Press.

Krasniewicz, Louise. 1992. *Nuclear Summer: The Clash of Communities at the Seneca Women's Peace Encampment*. Ithaca: Cornell University Press.

Kratoska, Paul H., ed. 2005. *Asian Labor in the Wartime Japanese Empire: Unknown Histories*. London: Routledge.

Kuletz, Valerie. 1998. *The Tainted Desert: Environmental and Social Ruin in the American Southwest*. New York: Routledge.

Kuran, Peter. 2006. *How to Photograph an Atomic Bomb*. Santa Clara, CA: VCE.

Lafontaine, Annie. 2002. "Réfugié ou 'Local Staff'? Changement de statut et enjeux de pouvoir au Kosovo d'après-guerre." *Anthropologie et Sociétés* 26, no. 1: 89–106.

Lakoff, Andrew. 2008. "The Genetic Biothreat, or, How We Became Unprepared." *Cultural Anthropology* 23, no. 3: 399–428.

Lakoff, George, and Mark Johnson. 1980. *Metaphors We Live By*. Chicago: University of Chicago Press.

Latham, Michael E. 2000. *Modernization as Ideology: American Social Science and Nation Building in the Kennedy Era*. Chapel Hill: University of North Carolina Press.

Lazarus-Black, Mindie. 2001. "Law and the Pragmatics of Inclusion: Governing Domestic Violence in Trinidad and Tobago." *American Ethnologist* 28, no. 2: 388–416.

Lee, Jae-hee. 2002. "Seoul City to Investigate Contaminated Spring Water near U.S. Military Base." *Korea Herald*, July 6.

Lee, Richard, and Irven DeVore, eds. 1968. *Man the Hunter*. Chicago: Aldine.

Lerner, Daniel, and Dwight Lasswell, eds. 1951. *The Policy Sciences: Recent Developments in Scope and Method*. Stanford, CA: Stanford University Press.

Levinson, David. 1994. *Aggression and Conflict: A Cross-Cultural Encyclopedia*. Santa Barbara, CA: ABC-CLIO.

Li, Darryl. 2010. *A Universal Enemy?: "Foreign Fighters" and Legal Regimes of Exclusion and Exemption under the "Global War on Terror."* Rochester, NY: Social Science Research Network.

Li, Darryl. 2015a. *Jihad in a World of Sovereigns: Law, Violence, and Islam in the Bosnia Crisis*. Rochester, NY: Social Science Research Network.

Li, Darryl. 2015b. "Offshoring the Army: Migrant Workers and the U.S. Military." *University of California, Los Angeles, Law Review* 124:126–74.

Liebenow, J. Gus. 1987 *Liberia: The Quest for Democracy*. Bloomington: Indiana University Press.

Lifton, Robert Jay. 1973. *Home from the War: Learning from Vietnam Veterans*. New York: Simon and Schuster.

Lifton, Robert Jay. 1999. "Evil, the Self, and Survival" (interview with Harry Kreisler). November 2. Institute for International Studies, University of California, Berkeley.

Linard, André. 1998. "Mercenaires S.A." *Le Monde Diplomatique*, August, 31.

Lindenbaum, Shirley. 1974. *Kuru Sorcery Disease and Danger in the New Guinea Highlands*. Palo Alto, CA: Mayfield.

Linebaugh, Heather. 2013. "I Worked on the U.S. Drone Program." *The Guardian*, December 29. https://www.theguardian.com/commentisfree/2013/dec/29/drones-us -military.

Linenthal, Edward T., and Tom Engelhardt, eds. 1996. *History Wars: The Enola Gay and Other Battles for the American Past*. New York: Holt Paperbacks.

Lira, Elizabeth, and Maria Isabel Castillo. 1991. *Psicología de la amenaza política y del miedo Santiago*. Santiago: Chile y América (Centro de Estudios Sociales).

Lloyd, John. 2006. "Cry, the Benighted Continent." *Financial Times*, August 4. https:// www.ft.com/content/1243bcc8–22b7–11db-91c7–0000779e2340.

Lock, Peter. 1998. "Military Downsizing and Growth in the Security Industry in Sub-Saharan Africa." *Strategic Analysis* 22, no. 9: 1393–1426.

Lococo, Edmond. 2007. "Lockheed, Sikorsky Grab Villain's Roles in Film 'Transformers.'" Bloomberg News Service, July 3.

Lubkemann, Stephen. 2008. *Culture in Chaos: An Anthropology of the Social Condition in War*. Chicago: University of Chicago Press.

Luke, Timothy W. 1989. "What's Wrong with Deterrence? A Semiotic Interpretation of National Security Policy." In *International/Intertextual Relations: Postmodern Readings of World Politics*, edited by Michael J. Shapiro and James Der Derian, 207–29. Lexington, MA: Lexington Books.

Lutz, Catherine. 1999. "Ethnography at the War Century's End." *Journal of Contemporary Ethnography* 28:610–19.

Lutz, Catherine. 2001. *Homefront: A Military City and the American Twentieth Century*. Boston: Beacon.

Lutz, Catherine, ed. 2009a. *Bases of Empire: The Global Struggle against U.S. Military Posts*. New York: New York University Press.

Lutz, Catherine. 2009b. "The Military Normal: Feeling at Home with Counterinsurgency in the United States." In *The Counter-Counterinsurgency Manual*, edited by Network of Concerned Anthropologists. Chicago: Prickly Paradigm.

Lutz, Catherine, and Jane L. Collins. 1993. *Reading National Geographic*. Chicago: University of Chicago Press.

Măcek, Ivana. 2011. *Sarajevo under Siege: Anthropology in Wartime*. Philadelphia: University of Pennsylvania Press.

Makaremi, Chowra. 2010. "Utopias of Power: From Human Security to the Responsibility to Protect." In *Contemporary States of Emergency: The Politics of Military and Humanitarian Interventions*, edited by Didier Fassin and Mariella Pandolfi, 107–27. New York: Zone.

Malkki, Lisa. 1995. *Purity and Exile: Violence, Memory, and National Cosmology among Hutu Refugees in Tanzania*. Chicago: University of Chicago Press.

Mamdani, Mahmood. 2001. *When Victims Become Killers: Colonialism, Nativism, and the Genocide in Rwanda*. Princeton: Princeton University Press.

Mamdani, Mahmood. 2010. "Responsibility to Protect or Right to Punish?" *Journal of Intervention and Statebuilding*, 4, no. 1: 53–67.

Manchester, William. 1979. *Good-Bye, Darkness: A Memoir of the Pacific War*. 2nd ed. Boston: Little, Brown.

Manz, Beatriz. 1998. *Refugees of a Hidden War: The Aftermath of Counterinsurgency in Guatemala*. Albany: State University of New York Press.

Manz, Beatriz. 2004. *Paradise in Ashes: A Guatemalan Journey of Courage, Terror, and Hope*. Berkeley: University of California Press.

Marks, John. 1979. *The Search for the "Manchurian Candidate": The CIA and Mind Control*. New York: Times Books.

Marks, John, and Patricia Greenfield. 1987. "How the CIA Assess Weakness: The Gittinger Personality Assessment System." In *The Power of Psychology*, edited by David Cohen, 13–31. London: Croom Helm.

Marshall, S. L. A. 1947. *Men against Fire: The Problem of Battle Command in Future War*. Washington, DC: Combat Forces Press.

Martin, Matt. 2010. *Predator: The Remote-Control Air War over Iraq and Afghanistan: A Pilot's Story*. Minneapolis: Zenith.

Martín-Baró, Ignacio. 1988. "From Dirty War to Psychological War: The Case in El Salvador." In *Flight, Exile and Return: Mental Health and the Refugee*, edited by Adrianne Aron, 2–22. San Francisco: Committee for Health Rights in Central America.

Martín-Baró, Ignacio. 1989. "La institucionalización de la guerra." Paper presented at the 12th International Psychology Conference, Buenos Aires, Argentina, June 25.

Masco, Joseph. 2004. "Nuclear Technoaesthetics: Sensory Politics from Trinity to the Virtual Bomb in Los Alamos." *American Ethnologist* 31, no. 3: 349–73.

Masco, Joseph. 2006. *The Nuclear Borderlands: The Manhattan Project in Post–Cold War New Mexico*. Princeton: Princeton University Press.

Masco, Joseph. 2008. "Target Audience: The Emotional Impact of U.S. Government Films on Nuclear Testing." *Bulletin of the Atomic Scientists* 64, no. 3: 23–31.

Masco, Joseph. 2009. "Life Underground: Building the American Bunker Society." *Anthropology Now* 1, no. 2: 13–29.

Masco, Joseph. 2014. *The Theater of Operations: National Security Affect from the Cold War to the War on Terror*. Durham, NC: Duke University Press.

Matsui, Kakushin. 1994. *Gakuto Shutsujin Goju-nen* [Fifty Years after the Drafting of Students]. Asahi, Japan: Sonorama.

McCaffrey, Katherine T. 2002. *Military Power and Popular Protest: The U.S. Navy in Vieques, Puerto Rico*. New Brunswick, NJ: Rutgers University Press.

McCullough, Malcolm. 2004. *Digital Ground: Architecture, Pervasive Computing, and Environmental Knowing*. Cambridge: MIT Press.

McDonald, Mary Alice, Marian Sigman, Michael P. Espinosa, and Charlotte G. Neumann. 1994. "Impact of a Temporary Food Shortage on Children and Their Mothers." *Child Development* 65, no. 2: 404–15.

McLeish, Kenneth. 2015. *Making War at Fort Hood: Life and Uncertainty in a Military City*. Princeton: Princeton University Press.

McLoyd, Vonnie C., and Leon Wilson. 1990. "Maternal Behavior, Social Support, and Economic Conditions as Predictors of Distress in Children." *New Directions for Child and Adolescent Development* 46:49–69.

McNamara, Laura. 2001. "Ways of Knowing about Nuclear Weapons." Ph.D. diss., University of New Mexico.

McNamara, Laura, and Robert Rubenstein. 2011. *Dangerous Liaisons: Anthropologists and the National Security State*. Santa Fe, NM: School for Advanced Research Press.

Mead, Margaret. 1940. "Warfare Is Only an Invention—Not a Biological Necessity." *Asia* 40:402–5.

Melman, Seymour. 1985. *The Permanent War Economy: American Capitalism in Decline*. New York: Simon and Schuster.

Melton, Arthur W. 1952. "Military Requirements for the Systematic Study of Psychological Variables." In *Psychology in the World Emergency*, edited by John C. Flanagan, 117–36. Pittsburgh: University of Pittsburgh Press.

Merry, Sally. 1995. "Resistance and the Cultural Power of Law." *Law and Society Review* 29, no. 1: 11–26.

Metz, Stephen. 2000. "Armed Conflict in the Twenty-First Century: The Information Revolution and Postmodern Warfare." Strategic Studies Institute report, U.S. Army War College, Carlisle, PA.

Meyers, Barton. N.d. "The Effects of Funding on Psychology in the United States after World War II." Unpublished paper.

Miller, Creighton. 1984. *Benevolent Assimilation: The American Conquest of the Philippines, 1899–1903*. New Haven: Yale University Press.

Miller, Richard L. 1986. *Under the Cloud: The Decades of Nuclear Testing*. New York: Free Press.

Mills, C. Wright. 1956. *The Power Elite*. New York: Oxford University Press.

Mine Action Service, United Nations Department for Disarmament Affairs and Department of Peacekeeping Operations. 2001. *Gender Perspectives on Landmines*. Geneva: United Nations.

Minear, Larry, T. van Baarda, and M. Sommers. 2000. *NATO and Humanitarian Action in the Kosovo Crisis*. Providence, RI: Institute for International Studies, Brown University.

Ministerio de Defensa de la Argentina. 2010. *Informe sobre la integración de la mujer en las fuerzas armadas*. Buenos Aires: Ministerio de Defensa.

Mitsuru, Yoshida. 1985. *Requiem for Battleship Yamato*. Translated by Richard H. Minear. Seattle: University of Washington Press.

Mochizuki, Shinkō. 1958. "Sange" [Buddhist Ritual]. *Mochizuki Bukkyō Daijiten* 2:1495–96.

Montejo, Victor. 1987 *Testimony: Death of a Guatemalan Village*. Willimantic, CT: Curbstone.

Moodie, Ellen. 2012. *El Salvador in the Aftermath of Peace: Crime, Uncertainty, and the Transition to Democracy*. Philadelphia: University of Pennsylvania Press.

Morris, Nicholas. 1999. "UNHCR and Kosovo: A Personal View from within UNHCR." *Forced Migration Review* 5:14–17.

Muehlmann, Shaylih. 2014. *When I Wear My Alligator Boots: Narco-Culture in the U.S.-Mexico Borderlands*. Berkeley: University of California Press.

Murakami, Shigeyoshi. 1970. *Kokka Shintō* [State Shintoism]. Tokyo: Iwanami Shoten.

Murphy, Kim. 2012. "A Fog of Drugs and War." *Los Angeles Times*, April 7. http://articles.latimes.com/2012/apr/07/nation/la-na-army-medication-20120408.

Nader, Laura. 1997. "The Phantom Factor: Impact of the Cold War on Anthropology." In *The Cold War and the University: Toward an Intellectual History of the Postwar Years*, edited Noam Chomsky and Ira Katznelson, 107–46. New York: New Press.

Naim, Moises. 2006. *Illicit: How Smugglers, Traffickers, and Copycats Are Hijacking the Global Economy*. New York: Anchor.

National Science Foundation. 1951. *Federal Funds for Science, 1950–51*. Washington, DC: U.S. Government Printing Office.

National Science Foundation. 1952. *Federal Funds for Science, 1951–52*. Washington, DC: U.S. Government Printing Office.

Naylor, R. T. 2005. *Wages of Crime: Black Markets, Illegal Finance, and the Underworld Economy*. Ithaca: Cornell University Press.

Neal, Richard. 1991. "U.S. Centcom Briefcom from Riyadh, Saudi Arabia." Federal News Service, U.S. Defense Department Briefing, February 19.

Nelson, Diane M. 2015. *Who Counts: The Mathematics of Life and Death after Genocide.* Durham, NC: Duke University Press.

Network of Concerned Anthropologists, ed. 2009. *The Counter-Counterinsurgency Manual.* Chicago: Prickly Paradigm.

Nickerson, Colin. 1991. "Watch on the Line: Marking Time in No Man's Land." *Boston Globe*, February 26.

Nordstrom, Carolyn. 1997. *A Different Kind of War Story.* Philadelphia: University of Pennsylvania Press.

Nordstrom, Carolyn. 2003. "Public Bad, Public Good(s) and Private Realities." In *Political Transition: Politics and Cultures*, edited by Paul Gready, 212–24. London: Pluto.

Nordstrom, Carolyn. 2004. *Shadows of War: Violence, Power, and International Profiteering in the Twenty-First Century.* Berkeley: University of California Press.

Nordstrom, Carolyn. 2007. *Global Outlaws: Crime, Money, and Power in the Contemporary World.* Berkeley: University of California Press.

Nordstrom, Carolyn. 2010. "Women, Economy, War." *International Review of the Red Cross* 92, no. 877: 161–76.

Nordstrom, Carolyn, and JoAnn Martin, eds. 1992. *The Paths to Domination, Resistance, and Terror.* Berkeley: University of California Press.

Nordstrom, Carolyn, and Antonius Robben, eds. 1995. *Fieldwork under Fire: Contemporary Studies of Violence and Survival.* Berkeley: University of California Press.

Oakes, Guy. 1994. *The Imaginary War: Civil Defense and American Cold War Culture.* New York: Oxford University Press.

Oakes, Maude. 1951. *Two Crosses of Todos Santos.* Princeton: Princeton University Press.

O'Brien, Kevin. 1998. "Military-Advisory Groups and African Security: Privatized Peacekeeping." *International Peacekeeping* 5, no. 3: 78–105.

Ogata, Sadako. 2005. *The Turbulent Decade: Confronting the Refugee Crises of the 1990s.* New York: Norton.

Ohnuki-Tierney, Emiko. 1987. *The Monkey as Mirror: Symbolic Transformations in Japanese History and Ritual.* Princeton: Princeton University Press.

Ohnuki-Tierney, Emiko. 1993. *Rice as Self: Japanese Identities through Time.* Princeton: Princeton University Press.

Ohnuki-Tierney, Emiko. 2002. *Kamikaze, Cherry Blossoms, and Nationalisms: The Militarization of Aesthetics in Japanese History.* Chicago: University of Chicago Press.

Opler, Morris. 1959. *Culture and Mental Health.* New York: Macmillan.

Or-Bach, Israel. 1988. *Children Who Don't Want to Live.* San Francisco: Jossey-Bass.

Orbinski, James. 2008. *An Imperfect Offering: Humanitarian Action for the 21st Century.* New York: Walker.

Orford, Anne. 2010. "The Passions of Protection: Sovereign Authority and Humanitarian War." In *Contemporary States of Emergency,* edited by Didier Fassin and Mariella Pandolfi, 335–56. New York: Zone.

O'Sullivan, John, and Alan Meckler. 1974. *The Draft and Its Enemies: A Documentary History.* Chicago: University of Illinois Press.

Ota, Masahide. 1996. "Governor of Okinawa at the Supreme Court of Japan." *Ryukyuanist* 35:1–7.

Otterbein, Keith. 2009. *The Anthropology of War*. Long Grove, IL: Waveland.

Paige, Glenn D. 2002. *Nonkilling Global Political Science*. Hawaii: Center for Global Nonkilling.

Pandolfi, Mariella. 2000. "Une souveraineté mouvante et supracoloniale." *Multitudes* 3, no. 3: 97–105.

Pandolfi, Mariella. 2006. "La zone grise des guerres humanitaires." *Anthropologica* 48, no. 1: 43–58.

Pandolfi, Mariella. 2008. "Laboratory of Intervention: The Humanitarian Governance of the Postcommunist Balkan Territories." In *Postcolonial Disorders*, edited by Mary-Jo DelVecchio Good, Sandra Teresa Hyde, Sarah Pinto, and Byron J. Good, 157–86. Berkeley: University of California Press.

Pandolfi, Mariella, and Marc Abélès. 2012. "Présentation: Politiques jeux d'espaces." *Anthropologie et Sociétés* 26, no. 1: 5–9.

Panofsky, Wolfgang K. H. 1998. "Dismantling the Concept of 'Weapons of Mass Destruction.'" *Arms Control Today*, February, 3–8.

Parenti, Michael. 1986. *Inventing Reality: The Politics of the Mass Media*. New York: St. Martin's.

Parsons, Talcott. 1986. "Social Science: A Basic National Resource." In *The Nationalization of the Social Sciences*, edited by Samuel Z. Klausner and Victor M. Lidz, 41–112. Philadelphia: University of Pennsylvania Press.

Paul, Benjamin, and William Demarest. 1988. "The Operation of a Death Squad in San Pedro La Laguna." In *Harvest of Violence*, edited by Robert Carmack, 19–154. Norman: University of Oklahoma Press.

Pawson, Lara. 2007. "Reporting Africa's Unknown Wars." In *Communicating War: Memory, Media and Military*, edited by Sarah Maltby and Richard Keebler, 42–54. Bury St. Edmonds, UK: Arena.

Pedelty, Mark. 1995. *War Stories: The Culture of Foreign Correspondents*. New York: Routledge.

Perrin, Noel. 1988. *Giving Up the Gun: Japan's Reversion to the Sword, 1543–1879*. Boston: Godine.

Peteet, Julie. 1991. *Gender in Crisis: Women and the Palestinian Resistance Movement*. New York: Columbia University Press.

Peteet, Julie. 2009. "The War on Terror, Dismantling, and the Construction of Place: An Ethnographic Perspective from Palestine." In *Iraq at a Distance: What Anthropologists Can Tell Us about the War*, edited by Antonius C. G. M. Robben, 80–105. Philadelphia: University of Pennsylvania Press.

Philippine Overseas Employment Agency. 2004. "Stock Estimate of Overseas Filipinos (as of December 2004)." http://www.poea.gov.ph/html/statistics.html.

Plaw, Avery. 2012. "Drone Strikes Save Lives, American and Other." *New York Times*, November 14.

Polychroniou, Chronis. 2008. "Rethinking the Promise of Critical Education: Interview with Henry Giroux." *OpEdNews.com*, December 3.

Porter, Toby. 2000. "The Partiality of Humanitarian Assistance: Kosovo in Comparative Perspective." *Journal of Humanitarian Assistance*, June. https://sites.tufts.edu/jha/archives/150.

Power, Margaret. 1991. *The Egalitarians—Human and Chimpanzee*. New York: Cambridge University Press.

Power, Matthew. 2013. "Confessions of a Drone Warrior." *GQ*, October 22. https://www .gq.com/story/drone-uav-pilot-assassination.

Prendergast, John. 1997. *Crisis Response: Humanitarian Band-Aids in Sudan and Somalia*. London: Pluto.

Price, David H. 2008. *Anthropological Intelligence: The Deployment and Neglect of American Anthropology in the Second World War*. Durham, NC: Duke University Press.

Price, David H. 2011. *Weaponizing Anthropology: Social Science in Service of the Militarized State*. Petrolia, CA: CounterPunch.

Price, David H. 2018. "Militarizing Space: Starship Troopers Same as It Ever Was." *CounterPunch*, August 10. https://www.counterpunch.org/2018/08/10/militarizing -space-starship-troopers-same-as-it-ever-was/.

Pugliese, Joseph. 2013. *State Violence and the Execution of the Law: Biopolitical Caesurae of Torture, Black Sites, Drones*. New York: Routledge.

Quesada, James. 1994. "Contested Lives, Contested Territories: An Ethnography of Polarization, Distress, and Suffering in Post-Sandinista Nicaragua." Ph.D. diss., University of California, San Francisco.

Quesada, James. 1998. "Suffering Child: An Embodiment of War and Its Aftermath in Post-Sandinista Nicaragua." *Medical Anthropology Quarterly* 12, no. 1: 51–73.

RAND Corporation. 1958. *Report on a Study of Non-Military Defense*. Santa Monica, CA: RAND. https://www.rand.org/content/dam/rand/pubs/reports/2008/R322.pdf.

Rasul, Shafiq, Asif Iqbal, and Rhuhel Ahmed. 2004. "Detention in Afghanistan and Guantánamo Bay." Unpublished report posted by the Center for Constitutional Rights. http://ccrjustice.org/files/report_tiptonThree.pdf.

Remarque, Erich Maria. 1975 [1929]. *All Quiet on the Western Front*. Translated by A. W. Wheen. New York: Little, Brown.

Reynolds, Craig. 2006. *Seditious Histories: Contesting Thai and Southeast Asian Pasts*. Seattle: University of Washington Press.

Richards, Paul, ed. 2004. *No Peace, No War: An Anthropology of Contemporary Armed Conflicts*. Athens: Ohio University Press.

Richter, Matthew. 2006. "Free Fire Zones? We Called It Indian Country: America's Vietnamese Killing Fields." *American Comments*. http://www.iwchildren.org/veterans /goodeadindian.htm.

Riecken, Henry W. 1962. "National Resources in the Social Sciences." In *Symposium Proceedings: The U.S. Army's Limited-War Mission and Social Science Research*, edited by William A. Lybrand, 26–28. Washington, DC: Special Operations Research Office.

Rieff, David. 2002. *A Bed for the Night: Humanitarianism in Crisis*. New York: Simon and Schuster.

Robben, Antonius C. G. M., ed. 2010. *Iraq at a Distance: What Anthropologists Can Teach Us about the War*. Philadelphia: University of Pennsylvania Press.

Rogers, A. P. V. 2004. *Law on the Battlefield*. 2nd ed. Manchester, UK: Manchester University Press.

Roggo, Béatrice Mégevand. 2000. "After the Kosovo Conflict, a Genuine Humanitarian Space: A Utopian Concept or an Essential Requirement?" *International Review of the Red Cross* 82, no. 837: 31–47.

Rosaldo, Renato. 1989. *Culture and Truth*. Boston: Beacon.

Ross, Fiona. 2002. *Bearing Witness: Women and the Truth and Reconciliation Commission in South Africa*. London: Pluto.

Rotter, Andrew Jon. 2000. *Comrades at Odds: The United States and India, 1947–1964*. Ithaca: Cornell University Press.

Royakkers, Lambèr, and Rinie Van Est. 2010. "The Cubicle Warrior: The Marionette of Digitalized Warfare." *Ethics and Information Technology* 12, no. 3: 289–96.

Rutherford, Kenneth. 2008. *Humanitarianism under Fire: The U.S. and UN Intervention in Somalia*. Bloomfield, CT: Kumarian.

Said, Edward. 1978. *Orientalism*. New York: Pantheon.

Sanford, Victoria. 2003. *Buried Secrets: Truth and Human Rights in Guatemala*. New York: Palgrave.

Sasson-Levy, Orna. 2003. "Feminism and Military Gender Practices: Israeli Women Soldiers in 'Masculine' Roles." *Sociological Inquiry* 73, no. 3: 440–65.

Sassoon, Siegfried. 1931. *Memoirs of an Infantry Officer*. New York: Coward McCann.

Scarry, Elaine. 1985. *The Body in Pain: The Making and Unmaking of the World*. New York: Oxford University Press.

Scheper-Hughes, Nancy. 1992. *Death without Weeping: The Violence of Everyday Life in Brazil*. Berkeley: University of California Press.

Scheper-Hughes, Nancy. 1994. "The Last White Christmas: The Heidelberg Pub Massacre." *American Anthropologist* 96, no. 4: 805–17.

Scheper-Hughes, Nancy. 2006. "Dangerous and Endangered Youth." In *Inclusion and Exclusion in the Global Arena*, edited by Max Kirsch, 287–315. New York: Routledge.

Scheper-Hughes, Nancy. 2014. "Militarization and the Madness of Everyday Life." *South Atlantic Quarterly* 113, no. 3: 640–55.

Scheper-Hughes, Nancy, and Philippe I. Bourgois. 2004. *Violence in War and Peace*. Malden, MA: Blackwell.

Schmitt, Eric. 1991. "Racing through the Darkness in Pursuit of Scuds." *New York Times*, February 24, A17.

Schmookler, Andrew Bard. 1994. *The Parable of the Tribes: The Problem of Power in Social Evolution*. Albany: State University of New York Press.

Scott, Joan W. 1986. "Gender: A Useful Category of Historical Analysis." *American Historical Review* 91, no. 5: 1053–75.

Scull, Andrew. 1984. *Decarceration: Community Treatment and the Deviant—A Radical View*. Oxford: Polity.

Shannon, Kelly. 2010. "Veiled Intentions: Islam, Global Feminism, and U.S. Foreign Policy since the Late 1970s." Ph.D. diss., Temple University, Philadelphia.

Shapiro, Arnold, dir. 1985. *Return to Iwo Jima*. Documentary film. North Hollywood, CA: ARP Videos.

Shapiro, H. A. 2003. "Fathers and Sons, Men and Boys." In *Coming of Age in Ancient Greece*, edited by Jennifer Neils and John H. Oakley. New Haven: Yale University Press.

Sheftick, Gary, and Grafton Pritchartt. 2009. "Face of Defense: Soldiers Bring Life to 'G.I. Joe.'" *American Forces Press Service*, August 11. http://archive.defense.gov/news/newsarticle.aspx?id=55441.

Sheppard, Simon. 1999. "Soldiers for Hire." *Contemporary Review*, August, 66–69.

Shibusawa, Naoko. 2010. *America's Geisha Ally: Reimagining the Japanese Enemy.* Cambridge: Harvard University Press.

Shibusawa, Naoko. 2013. "Ideology, Culture, and the Cold War." In *The Oxford Handbook of the Cold War*, edited by Richard Immerman and Petra Goedde, 34–39. Oxford: Oxford University Press.

Shils, E. A. 1949. "Social Science and Social Policy." *Philosophy of Science* 16, no. 3: 219–42.

Shimada, Kinji. 1995. "Hirose Takeo." *Kokushi Daijiten* 11:1096.

Shneidman, Edwin. 1982. *Voices of Death.* New York: Harper and Row.

Sider, Gerald. 1993. *Lumbee Indian Histories: Race, Ethnicity, and Indian Identity in the Southern United States.* Cambridge: Cambridge University Press.

Sigal, Leon. 1986. "Sources Make the News." In *Reading the News*, edited by Robert Karl Manoff and Michael Schudson, 9–37. New York: Pantheon.

Silliman, Stephen W. 2008. "The 'Old West' in the Middle East: U.S. Military Metaphors in Real and Imagined Indian Country." *American Anthropologist* 110, no. 2: 237–47.

Simbulan, Roland G. 2009. "Peoples Movement Responses to Evolving U.S. Military Activities in the Philippines." In *Bases of Empire: The Global Struggle against U.S. Military Posts*, edited by Catherine Lutz, 145–80. New York: New York University Press.

Simma, Bruno. 1999. "NATO, the UN and the Use of Force: Legal Aspects." *European Journal of International Law* 10, no. 1: 1–22.

Simone, AbdouMaliq. 2002. "The Visible and the Invisible: Remaking Cities in Africa." In *Under Siege: Four African Cities: Freetown, Johannesburg, Kinshasa, Lagos*, edited by Okwui Enwezor, 23–43. Ostfildern-Ruit, Germany: Hatje Cantz.

Simpson, Christopher. 1993. "U.S. Mass Communication Research, Counterinsurgency, and Scientific 'Reality.'" In *Ruthless Criticism: New Perspectives in U.S. Communication History*, edited by William Solomon and Robert W. McChesney, 313–48. Minneapolis: University of Minnesota Press.

Sims, Calvin. 2000. "A Hard Life for Amerasian Children." *New York Times*, July 23, I10.

Singer, Max, and Aaron Wildavsky. 1993. *The Real World Order: Zones of Peace/Zones of Turmoil.* Chatham, MA: Chatham House.

Singer, P. W. 2001–2. "Corporate Warriors: The Rise of the Privatized Military Industry." *International Security* 26, no. 3 (Winter): 186–220.

Singer, P. W. 2004. *Corporate Warriors: The Rise of the Privatized Military Industry.* Ithaca: Cornell University Press.

Singer, P. W. 2005. *Children at War.* New York: Pantheon.

Singer, P. W. 2009. *Wired for War: The Robotics Revolution and Conflict in the Twenty-First Century.* New York: Penguin.

Sklar, Holly. 1988. *Washington's War on Nicaragua.* Boston: South End.

Sloyan, Patrick. 1998. "U.S. Has Policy Allowing Nuclear Attack on Iraq." *Irish Times*, February 3.

Sluka, Jeffrey. 1989. *Hearts and Minds, Water and Fish: Support for the IRA and INLA in a Northern Irish Ghetto*. Greenwich, CT: JAI.

Sluka, Jeffrey, ed. 2000. *Death Squad: The Anthropology of State Terror*. Philadelphia: University of Pennsylvania Press.

Sluka, Jeffrey. 2011. "Death from Above: UAVs and Losing Hearts and Minds." *Military Review*, May–June, 70–76.

Smillie, Ian, Lansana Gberie, and Ralph Hazelton. 2000. *The Heart of the Matter: Sierra Leone, Diamonds and Human Security*. Ottawa: Partnership Africa Canada.

Solnit, Rebecca. 2016. *Hope in the Dark: Untold Histories, Wild Possibilities*. 3rd ed. Chicago: Haymarket.

Solomon, Norman. 2005. "The Military-Industrial-Media Complex." *Extra!*, July–August. https://fair.org/extra/the-military-industrial-media-complex.

Specht, Wayne. 2001. "Misawa F-16 Drops Tanks, Training Missiles on Farm." *Stars and Stripes*, November 10.

Sponsel, Leslie E. 1996. "The Natural History of Peace: A Positive View of Human Nature and Its Potential." In *The Natural History of Peace*, edited by Thomas Gregor, 95–125. Nashville: Vanderbilt University Press.

Sponsel, Leslie E. 2009. "Reflections on the Possibility of a Nonkilling Society and a Nonkilling Anthropology." In *Toward a Nonkilling Paradigm*, edited by Joám Evans Pim, 35–45. Honolulu: Center for Global Nonkilling.

Stannard, David. 1992. *American Holocaust*. Oxford: Oxford University Press.

Starn, Orin. 1986. "Engineering Internment: Anthropologists and the War Relocation Authority." *American Ethnologist* 13, no. 4: 700–720.

Starr, Scott. 2007. "Indian Country: Beyond the Green Zone in Iraq." *Z Magazine*, August 24. http://www.zmag.org/content/showarticle.cfm?ItemID=13623.

Stiglitz, Joseph E. 2002. *Globalization and Its Discontents*. London: Lane.

Stockholm International Peace Research Institute. 2008. *SIPRI Yearbook 2008: Armaments, Disarmament, and International Security*. Oxford: Oxford University Press.

Stoll, David. 1992. "Between Two Fires: Dual Violence and the Reassertion of Civil Society in Nebaj, Guatemala." Ph.D. diss., Stanford University.

Stover, Eric, James C. Cobey, and Jonathan Fine. 2000. "The Public Health Effects of Land Mines: Long-Term Consequences for Civilians." In *War and Public Health*, edited by Barry S. Levy and Victor W. Sidel, 137–48. Washington, DC: American Public Health Association.

Strada, Gino. 2004. *Green Parrots: A War Surgeon's Diary*. Milan: Charta.

Strawser, Bradley Jay. 2010. "Moral Predators: The Duty to Employ Uninhabited Aerial Vehicles." *Journal of Military Ethics* 9, no. 4: 342–68.

Stroeken, Koen, ed. 2012. *War, Technology, Anthropology*. New York: Berghahn.

Sturdevant, Saundra Pollack, and Brenda Stoltzfus. 1993. *Let the Good Times Roll: Prostitution and the U.S. Military in Asia*. New York: New Press.

Suarez-Orozco, Marcelo. 1990. "Speaking of the Unspeakable: Toward a Psycho-Social Understanding of Responses to Terror." *Ethos* 18, no. 3: 353–83.

Sudworth, John. 2008. "New Dawn for US-S. Korea Military Ties." *BBC News*, March 8.

Sugden, Colin, Charlotte R. Housden, Rajesh Aggarwal, Barbara J. Sahakian, and Ara Darzi. 2012. "Effect of Pharmacological Enhancement on the Cognitive and Clinical Psychomotor Performance of Sleep-Deprived Doctors." *Annals of Surgery* 255, no. 2: 222–27.

Suhrke, Astri, M. Barutciski, P. Sandison, and P. Garlock. 2000. *The Kosovo Refugee Crisis: An Evaluation of UNHCR's Emergency Preparedness and Response.* unkt.org/wp-content/uploads/2016/08/Refugee-Crisis-PDF.pdf.

Szasz, Thomas. 1997. *The Manufacture of Madness: A Comparative Study of the Inquisition and the Mental Health Movement.* Syracuse, NY: Syracuse University Press.

Takahashi, Nobuo. 1994a. "Gunkoku Bidan" [Heroic Stories of a Military Nation]. In *Taishū bunka jiten*, edited by Ishikawa Hiroyoshi, 224–25. Tokyo: Kōbundō.

Takahashi, Nobuo. 1994b. "Gunshin" [War-Deities]. In *Taishū bunka jiten*, edited by Ishikawa Hiroyoshi, 226. Tokyo: Kōbundō.

Takahashi, Nobuo. 1994c. "Gyoukusai" [Scattering of a Shattered Crystal]. In *Taishū bunka jiten*, edited by Ishikawa Hiroyoshi, 204. Tokyo: Kōbundō.

Tambiah, Stanley. 1986. *Sri Lanka: Ethnic Fratricide and the Dismantling of Democracy.* Chicago: University of Chicago Press.

Taussig, Michael. 1986. *Shamanism, Colonialism, and the Wild Man: A Study in Terror and Healing.* Chicago: University of Chicago Press.

Taussig, Michael. 1992. *The Nervous System.* London: Routledge.

Taussig, Michael. 1999. *Defacement: Public Secrecy and the Labor of the Negative.* Stanford, CA: Stanford University Press.

Tate, Winifred. 2015. *Drugs, Thugs, and Diplomats: U.S. Policymaking in Colombia.* Stanford, CA: Stanford University Press.

Theidon, Kimberly. 2003. "Disarming the Subject: Remembering War and Imagining Citizenship in Peru." *Cultural Critique* 54: 67–87.

Theidon, Kimberly. 2007. "Gender in Transition: Common Sense, Women and War." *Journal of Human Rights* 6:453–78.

Tilly, Charles. 1975. *The Formation of National States in Western Europe.* Princeton: Princeton University Press.

Tilly, Charles. 1992. *Coercion, Capital, and European States, A.D. 900–1992.* New York: Wiley-Blackwell.

Tilly, Charles, Gabriel Ardant, and Social Science Research Council (U.S.) Committee on Comparative Politics. 1975. *The Formation of National States in Western Europe.* Princeton: Princeton University Press.

Tilly, Chris, and Charles Tilly. 1997. *Life under Capitalism.* Boulder, CO: Westview.

Tishkov, Valery. 2004. *Chechnya: Life in a War-Torn Society.* Berkeley: University of California Press.

Treat, John Whittier. 1997. "The *Enola Gay* on Display." *Positions* 5, no. 3: 863–78.

Truth and Reconciliation Commission. 2003. *Final Report.* Lima: Truth and Reconciliation Commission.

Tuchman, Gaye. 1978. *Making News.* New York: Free Press.

Turnbull, Stephen. 2003. *Mongol Warrior 1200–1350.* London: Osprey.

Turner, Danielle C., Trevor W. Robbins, Luke Clark, Adam R. Aron, Jonathan Dowson, and Barbara J. Sahakian. 2003. "Cognitive Enhancing Effects of Modafinil in Healthy Volunteers." *Psychopharmacology* 165, no. 3: 260–69.

Turner, Fred. 1996. *Echoes of Combat: The Vietnam War in American Memory*. New York: Anchor.

Turse, Nick. 2008. *The Complex: How the Military Invades Our Everyday Lives*. New York: Metropolitan.

U.S. Congress, House Armed Services Committee. 1955. *Report of a Special Subcommittee of the Armed Services Committee*. http://www.niraikanai.wwma.net/pages/archive/price.html.

United Nations Security Council. 1947. *Trusteeship of Strategic Areas (Security Council Resolution 21)*. April 2. http://www.un.org/en/ga/search/view_doc.asp?symbol=S/RES/21(1947).

Vallaeys, Anne. 2004. *Médecins sans Frontières: La biographie*. Paris: Fayard.

Van Buren, Peter. 2015. "War Porn: Hollywood and War, from World War II to *American Sniper*." *Truthout.com*, February 19. https://truthout.org/articles/war-porn-hollywood-and-war-from-world-war-ii-to-american-sniper/.

van Schendel, Willem, and Abraham Itty, eds. 2005. *Illicit Flows and Criminal Things: States, Borders, and the Other Side of Globalization*. Bloomington: Indiana University Press.

Vaux, Tony. 2001. *The Selfish Altruist*. London: Earthscan.

Verdery, Katherine. 1991. *National Identity under Socialism: Identity and Cultural Politics in Ceausescu's Romania*. Berkeley: University of California Press.

Vidal, Gore. 1988. "The National Security State." *The Nation*, June, 782–86.

Vine, David. 2011. *Island of Shame: The Secret History of the U.S. Military Base on Diego Garcia*. Princeton: Princeton University Press.

Vine, David. 2015. *Base Nation: How U.S. Military Bases Abroad Harm America and the World*. New York: Metropolitan.

Vine, David, and Laura Jeffery. 2009. "'Give Us Back Diego Garcia': Unity and Division among Activists in the Indian Ocean." In *Bases of Empire: The Global Struggle against U.S. Military Posts*, edited by Catherine Lutz, 181–217. New York: New York University Press.

Virno, Paolo. 2004. *A Grammar of the Multitude: For an Analysis of Contemporary Forms of Life*. New York: Semiotext(e).

Visweswaran, Kamala, ed. 2013. *Everyday Occupations: Experiencing Militarism in South Asia and the Middle East*. Philadelphia: University of Pennsylvania Press.

Wagner, Sarah. 2008. *To Know Where He Lies: DNA Technology and the Search for Srebrenica's Missing*. Berkeley: University of California Press.

Walker, Thomas, ed. 1997. *Nicaragua without Illusions: Regime Transition and Structural Adjustment in the 1990s*. Wilmington, DE: Scholarly Resources.

Wall, Robert. 2000. "Army Leases Eyes to Watch Balkans." *Aviation Week and Space Technology*, October 30, 68.

Wallace, Anthony F. C. 1970. *The Death and Rebirth of the Seneca*. New York: Knopf.

Waterston, Alisse, ed. 2009. *An Anthropology of War: Views from the Frontline*. London: Berghahn.

Weber, Cynthia. 2006. *Imagining America at War: Morality, Politics, and Film*. New York: Routledge.

Weiner, Robert, and Tom Sherman. 2014. "Drones Spare Troops, Have Powerful Impact." *San Diego Union-Tribune*, October 9.

Westing, Arthur. 2002. "Conventional Warfare and the Human Environment." In *War or Health: A Reader*, edited by Illka Taipale, 407–15. London: Zed.

White, David M. 1950. "The 'Gatekeeper': A Case Study in the Selection of News." *Journalism Quarterly* 27:383–90.

White, Diane. 1991. "Everyday Uses for Gulfspeak." *Boston Globe*, February 27.

Wilford, John Noble. 1982. "Military Said to Get about 25% of NASA's 1983 Research Budget." *New York Times*, May 3. https://www.nytimes.com/1982/05/03/us/military -said-to-get-about-25-of-nasa-s-1983-research-budget.html.

Williams, Alison J. 2011. "Enabling Persistent Presence? Performing the Embodied Geopolitics of the Unmanned Aerial Vehicle Assemblage." *Political Geography* 30, no. 7: 381–90.

Wills, Gary. 2010. *Bomb Power: The Modern Presidency and the National Security State*. New York: Penguin.

Wilson, Charles E. 1944. "For the Common Defense." *Army Ordnance* 26, no. 143: 285–88.

Wolf, Eric R. 1957. *Sons of the Shaking Earth*. Chicago: University of Chicago Press.

Wool, Zoe. 2015. *The Weight of Life at Walter Reed*. Durham, NC: Duke University Press.

Woolf, Virginia. 1938. *The Three Guineas*. London: Hogarth.

"WPB Aide Urges U.S. to Keep War Set-Up." 1944. *New York Times*, January 20, 1. https://www.nytimes.com/1944/01/20/archives/wpb-aide-urges-us-to-keep-war -setup-wilson-calls-on-industry-and.html.

Yukio, Hayashi. 2003. *Practical Buddhism among the Thai-Lao: Religion in the Making of a Region*. Kyoto: Kyoto University Press.

Zborowski, Mark. 1952. "Cultural Components in Response to Pain." *Journal of Social Issues* 8:16–30.

Zeitlin, Maurice, K. A. Lutteman, and J. W. Russell. 1973. "Death in Vietnam: Class, Poverty, and the Risks of War." *Politics and Society* 3, no. 3: 313–28.

Zilberg, Elana. 2011. *Space of Detention: The Making of a Transnational Gang Crisis between Los Angeles and San Salvador*. Durham, NC: Duke University Press.

Zogby, John. 2009. "War, Peace, and Politics." *The Way We'll Be*, September 26. http:// www.zogby.com/blog2/index.php/category/war.

EDITORS

CATHERINE BESTEMAN is the Francis F. Bartlett and Ruth K. Bartlett Professor of Anthropology at Colby College. Her research addresses border security regimes, displacement, political subjectivity, and race and has focused most particularly on Somalia, South Africa, and the US. She is past president of the Association of Political and Legal Anthropology and a Guggenheim Fellow.

ANDREW BICKFORD is an assistant professor of anthropology at Georgetown University. He conducts research on war, militarization, health, biotechnology, bioethics, and the state in the United States and Germany. His current research examines biotechnology research in the U.S. military and the bioethics of the military's efforts to develop and make "super-soldiers." He was selected as a 2014–15 Residential Fellow at the Woodrow Wilson International Center for Scholars in Washington, DC.

ROBERTO J. GONZÁLEZ is the chair of the Anthropology Department at San José State University. His areas of interest include science, technology, and society; militarism and culture; environmental anthropology; and anthropological ethics. He has written and edited several books on these topics, including *Militarizing Culture: Essays on the Warfare State*. He has conducted ethnographic research in Latin America and the United States. His most recent research project focuses on the uses of big data by military and intelligence agencies.

HUGH GUSTERSON is a professor of international affairs and anthropology at George Washington University. He is a past president of the American Ethnological Society, and his academic work addresses the political culture of nuclear weapons, counterinsurgency, drone warfare, and security culture. He has written numerous books and academic articles. In addition, he writes a regular column for the *Bulletin of Atomic Scientists* and has written for the *Washington Post*, the *Los Angeles Times*, the *Boston Globe*, and *Nature* magazine.

GUSTAAF HOUTMAN is the editor of the journal *Anthropology Today* at the Royal Anthropological Institute (London) and specializes in the anthropology of Burmese Buddhism. He has taught at various universities and is currently teaching at the University of Mandalay and the University of Yangon.

CATHERINE LUTZ is the Thomas J. Watson Jr. Family Professor of Anthropology and International Studies at Brown University. She is the author of *Homefront: A Military City and the American 20th Century* and editor of *The Bases of Empire* and other works on security and militarization, gender violence, education, and transportation. She has also consulted with the United Nations Department of Peacekeeping Operations and the government of Guam. She is past president of the American Ethnological Society and was selected as a Guggenheim Fellow and a Radcliffe Fellow.

KATHERINE T. MCCAFFREY is an associate professor of anthropology at Montclair State University. Her research interests focus on social inequality and violence, its consequences, and resistance to it in Latin America and the United States. She has examined a multi-decade-long movement to evict the U.S. Navy from Vieques, Puerto Rico, and the ongoing military legacies on that island. More recently, she has been conducting participatory action field research among new immigrants and refugees in New Jersey. She is the former general editor of *Anthropology Now*.

AUSTIN MILLER is a fellow at the Graduate Center of the City University of New York, where he has conducted research on embodiment and technology. He has taught urban anthropology at Queens College and Brooklyn College. As a member of the *Anthropology Now* Findings Collective, he co-publishes review articles triennially. His ongoing doctoral research focuses on the politics of HIV prevention in Barcelona. He has also published both original and translated poetry.

DAVID H. PRICE is a professor of anthropology and sociology at St. Martin's University. He has conducted cultural anthropological and archaeological field work in Egypt and elsewhere in the Near East. His primary research area is the history of anthropology, along with various interactions between anthropologists and military/intelligence agencies. Much of his historical and contemporary writing focuses on the ethical and political context of anthropological practice in relation to the security state.

DAVID VINE is a professor of anthropology at American University. His work focuses on issues that include war, U.S. foreign and military policy, military bases, forced displacement, and human rights. His books include *Base Nation: How U.S. Military Bases Abroad Harm America and the World* and *Island of Shame: The Secret History of the U.S. Military Base on Diego Garcia*.

AUTHORS

JULIAN AGUON is a human rights lawyer and founder of Blue Ocean Law, a progressive law firm that specializes in advancing self-determination for native Pacific Islanders.

WILLIAM ASTORE is a retired U.S. Air Force lieutenant-colonel who has taught at the Air Force Academy, the Naval Postgraduate School, and the Pennsylvania College of Technology.

MÁXIMO BADARÓ is a professor of social anthropology at the Universidad Nacional de San Martín in Buenos Aires.

BETH BAILEY is the Foundation Distinguished Professor of History and director of the Center for Military, War, and Society Studies at the University of Kansas.

MICHAEL BARNETT is a professor of international affairs and political science at George Washington University's Elliot School of International Affairs.

DAVID BARSTOW is a senior writer at the *New York Times* and the winner of three Pulitzer Prizes.

RALPH L. BEALS (1901–85) was a professor of anthropology at the University of California, Los Angeles.

SEALING CHENG is an associate professor of anthropology at the Chinese University of Hong Kong.

BRUCE CUMINGS is the Gustavus F. and Ann M. Swift Distinguished Service Professor in the Department of History at the University of Chicago.

JASON DE LEÓN is an associate professor of anthropology at the University of Michigan and director of the Undocumented Migration Project.

ALEX EDNEY-BROWNE is a doctoral candidate in the Politics and International Relations Department at the University of Melbourne.

DWIGHT D. EISENHOWER (1890–1969) was a U.S. Army general and the thirty-fourth President of the United States.

JEAN BETHKE ELSHTAIN (1941–2013) was the Laura Spelman Rockefeller Professor of Social and Political Ethics at the University of Chicago Divinity School.

KENNETH FORD is a computer scientist and founder and director of the Florida Institute for Human and Machine Cognition.

JOHN BELLAMY FOSTER is the editor of the journal *Monthly Review* and a professor of sociology at the University of Oregon.

JOHAN GALTUNG is a Norwegian sociologist and the president of the Galtung Institute for Peace Theory and Peace Practice.

LESLEY GILL is a professor of anthropology at Vanderbilt University.

MARK L. GILLEM is a professor of architecture at the University of Oregon.

HENRY A. GIROUX is the director of the Centre for Research in the Public Interest at McMaster University.

CLARK GLYMOUR is Alumni University Professor in the Department of Philosophy at Carnegie Mellon University.

LINDA GREEN is a professor of anthropology at the University of Arizona.

LISBETH GRONLUND is a physicist and co-director of the Union of Concerned Scientists Global Security Program.

ELLEN HERMAN is a professor of history at the University of Oregon.

DANIEL HOFFMAN is a professor of anthropology at the University of Washington.

HANNAH HOLLEMAN is an assistant professor of anthropology and sociology at Amherst College.

H. PATRICIA HYNES retired as a professor of environmental health at Boston University's School of Public Health and is director of the Traprock Center for Peace and Justice.

MICHAEL JERRYSON is an associate professor of religious studies at Youngstown State University.

BARBARA ROSE JOHNSTON is an environmental anthropologist and senior research fellow at the Center for Political Ecology.

ROBERT KOENIG is a documentary film director, producer, writer, and editor.

BRANDON KOHRT is an adjunct assistant professor of cultural anthropology at Duke University.

PAUL H. KRATOSKA is a historian and the publishing director at NUS Press of the National University of Singapore.

ROBERT JAY LIFTON is a lecturer in psychiatry at Harvard Medical School and Distinguished Professor Emeritus of Psychiatry and Psychology at the City University of New York.

CHOWRA MAKAREMI is a tenured researcher at the French National Center for Scientific Research, École des Hautes Études en Sciences Sociales in Paris.

MAHMOOD MAMDANI is a professor of anthropology, political science, and African studies at Columbia University and the director of the Makerere Institute of Social Research in Uganda.

JOSEPH MASCO is a professor of anthropology at the University of Chicago.

ROBERT W. MCCHESNEY is the Gutgsell Endowed Professor in the Department of Communication at the University of Illinois, Urbana-Champaign.

MARGARET MEAD (1901–78) was an anthropologist who taught at the New School and Columbia University and served as a curator at the American Museum of Natural History.

CAROLYN NORDSTROM is a professor emerita of anthropology at the University of Notre Dame.

EMIKO OHNUKI-TIERNEY is the William F. Vilas Professor of Anthropology at the University of Wisconsin, Madison.

ANNE ORFORD is the Redmond Barry Distinguished Professor and Michael D. Kirby Professor of International Law at the University of Melbourne.

MARIELLA PANDOLFI is a professor of anthropology at the University of Montreal.

MARK PEDELTY is a professor of communication studies and an affiliate professor of anthropology at the University of Minnesota.

NOEL PERRIN (1927–2004) was an essayist and a professor of English at Dartmouth College.

JULIE PETEET is a professor of anthropology at the University of Louisville.

JAMES QUESADA is a professor of anthropology at San Francisco State University.

DAVID L. ROBB is a freelance journalist and Hollywood reporter who has been nominated three times for a Pulitzer Prize.

ELAINE SCARRY is the Walter M. Cabot Professor of Aesthetics and General Theory of Value in the Department of English at Harvard University.

NANCY SCHEPER-HUGHES is a professor of anthropology and the director of the medical anthropology program at the University of California, Berkeley.

NAOKO SHIBUSAWA is an associate professor of history and American studies at Brown University.

STEPHEN W. SILLIMAN is a professor and the chair of the Department of Anthropology at the University of Massachusetts, Boston.

P. W. SINGER is a political scientist and international relations scholar who is a strategist for the New America Foundation.

REBECCA SOLNIT is a writer, activist, and historian and a contributing editor at *Harper's Magazine*.

LESLIE E. SPONSEL is a professor emeritus of anthropology at the University of Hawai'i, Mānoa.

KIMBERLY THEIDON is the Henry J. Leir Professor of International Humanitarian Studies at the Fletcher School of International Affairs at Tufts University.

JOHN WHITTIER TREAT is a professor of East Asian languages and literature at Yale University.

PETER VAN BUREN is a writer and a former U.S. Foreign Service Officer who spent a year in Iraq serving as a team leader from two Provincial Reconstruction Teams.

DAVID WRIGHT is a physicist and the co-director of the Union of Concerned Scientists' Global Security Program.

Page numbers in italics refer to illustrations.

Aall, Pamela R., 221
abolition movement, 351
Abu Ghraib, 112, 160, 230
academic freedom, 272–73, 329
academics, 24, 160, 249–50, 253–54, 270, 321
Accuracy in Media, 238
Advisory Commission on Human Radiation, 177
aesthetics, 23–24, 109, 143, 146, 242
Afghanistan, 1, 56, 81n4, 82, 191, 227–29, 350;
  drone warfare, 322; humanitarian aid, 219;
  as "Indian Country," 149–50; land mines,
  324U.S. military occupation, 20–21, 294,
  344; U.S. military spending, 33–34; war, 17,
  23, 141, 156–58, 160, 162, 200, 303, 341–42
Africa, 269, 307, 346; colonialism, 15–16;
  humanitarian aid, 205, 212–14, 216–17; land
  mines, 326; military-commercial complex,
  148–49; military intervention, 208; nonviolent conflict resolution in, 340; self-rule,
  154–55; war crimes in, 218n2; West, 28. *See
  also specific cities and countries*
African Americans, 60, 172
African studies, 262
African Union, 216
Agamben, Giorgio, 201
agency, 62, 213–14
Age of Enlightenment, 154
aggression, 12, 16, 23, 52–53, 83, 112, 336–37,
  342–43. *See also* violence
Agreement for the Promotion of Investment,
  66–67
Agüero, José Carlos, 88
Aidid, Mohamed Farrah, 204–5
Air Force Association, 174n3
Albania, 81n4, 206–7
Alliance for Progress, 122
Allied Land Forces, South East Asia
  (ALFSEA), 75

All People's Congress, 43
All-Volunteer Force (AVF), 41, 59–60,
  61–62, 162
Almond, Gabriel, 258
Almond, Peter, 232
al-Qaeda, 151–52
Alston, Philip, 320
Amaya, Rufino, 98–99
American Anthropological Association, 15, 16,
  20, 349–50
American Association for the Advancement of
  Science, 125
American Association of Universities, 270
American Association of University Professors,
  350
American exceptionalism, 141, 157, 161, 309
American Newspaper Publishers Association, 31
American Psychological Association, 257
American Sniper (film), 39, 243–46
American University: Special Operations
  Research, 259
Amish, 341
Amnesty International, 284
Angola, 52, 54, 77, 81n3
Annan, Kofi, 206
Anthropologists for Radical Political Action,
  350
anthropology, 163, 174; foreign research proj-
  ects, 266–69; globalization, 18; humanitarian
  intervention, 199, 202; militarization of, 8,
  349–50; and militarism, 14, 16–17, 19, 21; and
  peace, 334–35; public, 350; and war, 14–16,
  20, 340–41
apartheid, 49, 86, 117, 342; nuclear, 163–64
Apollo (space program), 318, 319
Appadurai, Arjun, 62
area studies, 251–52
Arendt, Hannah, 203, 273, 320

Cantril, Hadley, 258
capitalism, 182, 184; consumer, 61, 312; evolution of, 28, 32, 221; global, 348; and militarism, 22; and military spending, 30–33. *See also* post-Fordism
Capus, Steve, 227
Carnegie Corporation, 252–53
Carter, Ashton, 318
Cassutt, Michael, 318
Castle test series, 137, 139
censorship, 121, 118, 160, 232
Center for a New American Security, 157
Central America, 15, 95, 120, 174, 194–95, 268–69. *See also specific cities and countries*
Central Intelligence Agency (CIA), 249, 252–53, 258, 259n4, 267–69, 271, 318
Chagnon, Napoleon, 12–13, 340
Chamoru of Guahan, 348
Chamayou, Gregoire, 321
Chechnya, 17
Chemical Weapons Convention, 304
Cheney, Dick, 160
Chernobyl, 175
children, 7, 52, 104, 111–13, 128–29, 189, 348; Aztec, 11; education of, 158, 172; Greek, 9; and land mines, 326–27; as "little savages," 156–57; military, in pop culture, 233, 331; and military service, 162; minority, 115; in Mongolia, 10–11; in Nicaragua, 296–301; in Nepal, 71; "price of freedom," 185; and radiation, 176, 183; as soldiers, 57–58, 71–73; in Sparta, 9–10; and toys modeled on weapons, 3–5, 338; and violence, 114; and war, 54, 145, 238, 300–301, 321–23, 337, 342, 344
Chile, 162, 260, 263
China, 22, 151, 163, 168, 306; area studies, 252–54, 266; Buddhism in, 68; Japanese expansion into, 73–75; land mines, 324, 328; Tang dynasty, 146; weapons capability, 318
Chomsky, Noam, 223
Christianity, 147, 306
The Chronicle of Beiqi, 146
The Chrysanthemum and the Sword (Benedict), 15
Churchill, Winston, 291n1
citizenship, 96, 98–99, 213, 215, 272–73
Civil Defense Forces (CDF), 45, 48
Clarke, Torie, 225–26
Clausewitz, Carl von, 286

Clinton, Bill, 113, 164, 206, 226, 240
cluster bombs, 326–28
CNN, 225
Cohn, Carol, 121
Cold War, 25n8, 51n4, 58–59, 131, 139n2, 217, 332, 346; anthropology and, 15–17; censorship, 242; economics, 30; and *gijichon*, 63, 67; humanitarian order, 213; ideologies, 33, 154–56, 198, 204–5; militarism and, 7; nuclear fallout shelters, 303, 308–10, 313; nuclear militarism, 178; and Okinawa, 182; post–Cold War period, 76–78, 200, 219–20; scientific research, 248, 250, 252–53, 255–57, 259; Western discourses, 164
Colegio Militar de Nacion (CMN), 101, 103–4
collateral damage, 210, 281, 342
Collins, Jane L. 164
Colombia, 80, 81n3, 150
colonialism and colonization, 16, 152–53, 156, 192, 214
Colorado, 139
Columbia University, 252, 253
Columbine, 113, 115
Conant, James B., 253
Condiff, Cole, 39–40
Congo-Brazzaville, 77
Conneh, Ayesha, 46
Conneh, Sekou, 46
Connell, Evan, 94
Connerton, Paul, 126n1
conscription, 18, 59, 321
contamination, 180, 182; environmental, 19, 177–78; nuclear, 137–39, 168, 175; of trash, 185–86
Conté, Lansana, 46
Convention on Cluster Munitions, 304
Convention on the Prohibition of the Use, Stockpiling, Production, and Transfer of Anti-Personnel Mines and on Their Destruction, 304, 327–28
Cooper, Bradley, 39
Cooperative for Assistance and Relief Everywhere (CARE), 205
corporate warriors, 58
corporations, 43; and military-industrial complex, 5, 303; and military spending, 28, 30, 32, 37, 40–41; private military, 48–49, 76–81
Correctional Services Act, 117

Costa Rica, 342

Costner, Kevin, 232

Council on Gender Policy, 104–6

Counterinsurgency Field Manual, 160–61

Crane, Stephen, 307

crime: crimes against humanity, 200, 216; and
genocide, 215, 218n2; hate crimes, 113; homosexuality as, 351–52; humanitarian crimes,
198, 203; and incarceration, 117; on military
bases, 170, 180, 182, 184–86; organized, 80,
253; public, 126; by soldiers, 184–86, 345;
war crimes, 111–12, 125, 149, 231–32, 305

Croatia, 77

Crocker, Chester C., 221

Cry for Land (pastoral letter), 125

Cuba, 121, 262

Cuban Missile Crisis, 232, 312

Cullors, Patrisse, 352

Curaçao, 344

Custer, George Armstrong, 94, 151

cyberspace, 323

cyborgs, 292

Daigo Fukuryu Maru (No. 5 Lucky Dragon), 175

Dani, 277

Darfur (Sudan), 208, 215–16, 217–18n1

Davies, John Paton, 252

Dawkins, Pete, 61

The Day after Trinity (documentary), 280

decarceration, 117

decolonization, 212–13

defense contractors, 2, 226–28

Deleuze, Gilles, 50

DeMain, Paul, 150

democracy, 47, 121, 191; and colonialism, 213;
defense industry as threat to, 2; and education, 273; and humanitarian intervention,
217; and war, 181

Democratic Republic of Congo, 13, 80, 207

deterrence theory, 174

Detroit (Michigan), 112

Deuze, Mark, 322

Devine, John, 113

de Waal, Alex, 197

Diamond, Sigmund, 252–53

Diego Garcia, 346

Diken, Bulent, 88

Disney Corporation, 7

Djibouti, 168

Dominican Republic, 159

Donovan, William, 252

Doob, Leonard, 255

Douglas, Mary, 54

dreg, 50

Dresden (Germany), 283

drones, 319–24, 329–30

Drone Theory (Chamayou), 321

*Dr. Strangelove, or How I Learned to Stop Worry-
ing and Love the Bomb* (film), 314

drugs, 118, 293

dual-use science, *248*, 318

DuBois, Cora, 251

Duffield, Mark, 201

DynCorp, 227

East Germany. *See* Germany

Eastwood, Clint, 231

Economic Community of West African States
Monitoring Group (ECOMOS), 49

economy: extra-legal, 52, 54–55

Eden, Lynn, 139n2

The Effects of Nuclear Weapons (Pentagon), 279

Egypt, 22

Eichmann, Adolf, 320–21

Eisenhower, Dwight D., 2, 5, 28, 32, 36–38,
41, 264

El Mozote massacre, 238

El Salvador, 121, 123–24, 161, 223, 235, 238–39

Elshtain, Jean Bethke, 84

emotion, 23, 36, 260; children and, 156, 183, 300;
Cold Warriors and, 131, 310; drone teams and,
320, 322; emotional abuse, 95; and gender,
102, 156; and emotionality, 155; and fear,
109–10, 119–25; and guilt, 88; heightened,
94; and nuclear war, 134–35, 137, 139; and
shame, 89; soldiers and, 292; war films and,
244–46; war on terror and, 131, 133

employment 31, 250; intelligence agencies, 267;
military labor, 57, 350; military service and,
95, 97; military spending and, 28–29, 32, 34,
42–43; and unemployment, 115, 170, 182, 261,
297; urban violence and, 115; warfare state
and, 270; youth and, 50

Engelhardt, Tom, 159

England. *See* Great Britain

Enloe, Cynthia, 58, 84

Mexico, 11, 81n3, 118, 168, 193–95

Michael, Donald, 317

The Mickey Mouse Club (television program), 233

Micronesia, 349

Middle East, 74–75, 208; colonial cartography, 168, 186, 192; colonialism in, 15; and humanitarian aid, 210, 212–14; as "Indian Country," 151–52; and Orientalism, 164; stereotypes of, 142, 148–49; wars in, 21, 116, 153. *See also specific cities and countries*

militarism: alternatives to, 333–35; and American society, 12; and anthropology, 14, 16–17, 19, 21; and cinema, 230–34, 243–46; defined, 6; economics and, 48; and fear, 109–10; as ideology, 8–9, 282; as human invention, 24; and masculinity, *82*, 83–84; and military spending, 30; nuclear, 175; patriotism and, 41; and physical and cultural landscapes, 167; political economy of, 27; and popular culture, 224; rhetoric of, 141–42; and technology, 24, 303; in United States, 342; and universities, 328–29; and war, 22–23

militarization: defined, 6

military bases, 8, 19, 167–68, 170, 344–48. *See also specific bases*

military colonialism, 347

military-industrial complex, 2, 5, 28, 33, 37, 41, 223, 264

military labor, 57–58

military monks, 58, 67–70

military normal, 5, 158–62. *See also* public relations

military psychology, 255–58

military spending, 12, 19, 27–34, 158–59, 257, 315–17

Mills, C. Wright, 30

Milošević, Slobodan, 206

Minerva Consortium, 350

Mitsuru, Yoshida, 93

modafinil (drug), 293

modernization, 154

Mongol Empire, 11

Mongolia, 10, 151

Monluc, Blaise de, 305–6

Monrovia (Liberia), 45–46

Montt, Efraín Rios, *108*

Moon, Katharine, 64

Morgan, Matt, 234

Mosul (Iraq), 327

Mothers of Plaza de Mayo, 125

Mountbatten, Louis, 74

movies, 230–34, 243–46

Mozambique, 52

MSNBC, 225

Mullen, Mike, 157

museums, 239–43

Musk, Elon, 318

Mutual Defense Treaty, 63

Myanmar, 22

My Lai massacre, 149

Myrdal, Gunnar, 265

Myung-Bak, Lee, 63–64

Nagasaki, 110, 131, 137, 182, 243, 278–79

Nagl, John, 157

Nasiriyah, 327

National Aeronautics and Space Administration (NASA), *248*, 304, 315–18, 319

National Air and Space Museum, 239, 241–42

National Archives, 239

National Campaign against Youth Violence, 113

National Geographic (magazine), 164

National Institute of Mental Health (NIMH), 256

National Institutes of Health (NIH), 265

nationalism, 215

National Mental Health Act, 256

National Museum of American History, 239, 241

National Museum of Iraq, 186

National Patriotic Front of Liberia, 47

National Reconnaissance Office, 317–18

National Rifle Association (NRA), 114

National Science Foundation (NSF), 256, 263, 265

national security, 219–20; in post–World War II era, 6–7; and civil defense, 308–9; and militarism, 12; and militarized academy, 270–71, 273; national security state, 14, 21; rhetoric of, 313–14; and U.S. bases, 345–46

"The National Security State" (Vidal), 316

nation-states, 4, 17, 79, 215, 288, 342

Native Americans, 149–53, 218n2

"natural rights of man," 154–55

Nazis, 30, 174, 320

Neal, Richard, 150

Negri, Antonio, 44–45, 200–201
neoliberalism, 80
Neolithic Revolution, 13
Nepal, 57, 58, 64, 71–73
Network of Concerned Anthropologists, 304, 335, 349
Nevada, 131, *132*, 133–34, 137, 175, 304
Newark (New Jersey), 115
New Guinea, 277
New Humanitarian Order, 198
new wars theory, 220, 221
New York, 308
Ngo Ngoc Tuan, 94
Nicaragua, 121, 296–97, 301
Nigeria, 22
Nixon, Richard M., 61, 63
Nogales (Mexico), 193
nonkilling society, 339–41, 344
Non-Proliferation Treaty, 163–64
nonviolence, 333–34, 343–44
Norman, Hinga, 47
North American Aerospace Defense Command (NORAD), 77, 310, *311*
North Atlantic Treaty Organization (NATO), 17, *56*, 77, 84, 206–9, 221
North Carolina, 170
Northern Ireland, 16, 18, 124
North Korea, 63, 180, 328, 346. *See also* South Korea; Korean War
North Vietnam. *See* Vietnam
Norway, 219
nuclear testing, 163, 175–78
nuclear war, 110, 134, 137, 139n2, 314; and American Exceptionalism, 309
nuclear weapons, 130–31, 139; chromium-51, 177; civil defense, 308, 310, 314; effects on human body, 278–80; and militarism, 19; national security, 308; proliferation of, 164, 165; racialized terms toward, 163; Western discourse of, 163–64
Nuremberg Code, 176
Nuttini, Hugo, 263

Oakes, Guy, 135
Obama, Barack, 318
Occupied Territories, 18, *166*. *See also* Israel; Palestine
Office of Naval Research (ONR), 257–58

Office of Strategic Services (OSS), 249–53
Office of Veteran Affairs, *26*
Ogata, Sadako, 207
Okinawa (Japan), 145–46, 181–85, 345, 347n1
On War (Clausewitz), 286
Operation Cue, 131, 135, *136*, 137
Operation Hollywood (Robb), 230
Orbinski, James, 204
Organization for Security and Cooperation in Europe, 199
Orientalism, 164–65
Oshkosh Defense, *26*
Ottawa Treaty, 304, 327–28
Ottoman Empire, 214
Oxfam, 208
Ozick, Cynthia, 243

Pacific Islanders, 19
pacifism, 341, 343–44, 347
Paige, Glenn, 339–41
Pakistan, 22, 163, 165, 304, 328
Palestine, 18, *166*, 168, 186–92
Panama, 159, 346
Paramount Pictures, 3–4
Paris (France), 289
Parsons, Talcott, 256
patriotism, 39, 41, 146, 288–89
Peaceful Societies (website), 340
Pearl Harbor, 145
Peleliu, 92
Penados del Barrio, Próspero, 125
People's Liberation Army (PLA), 71
People's Movement for Democratic Change, 45
Pericles, 10
Persian Gulf, 174. *See also* Gulf Wars
Peru, 83, 85–86, 88, 90n2, 95
Peterson, Val, 135
Petraeus, David, 160
pharmaceuticals, 293
Philadelphia (Pennsylvania), 112
Philippines, 63–67, 150, 156, *196*, 277, 342, 346
Pitt, Brad, 245
Plains Indians, 338
Plutarch, 9
Poland, 260
polis, 288
political economy, 27, 31–32, 44, 49, 50. *See also* capitalism

Polynesia, 168
Popova, Maria, 352
popular culture, 20, 23, 223, 224
Porter Corps, 75
post-Fordism, 43–45, 47, 49, 51n3. *See also*
   capitalism
post-traumatic stress disorder (PTSD), 24, 115,
   320–22
Power, Margaret, 342–43
Predator (Martin), 322
Presidential Academic Advisory Board, 113
President's Commission on an All-Volunteer
   Armed Force, 61
President's Defense Science Board, 256
prisons, 115–17, 171
private military companies (PMCS), 48–49, 76–81
privatization, 28, 77, 80, 271
privatized military firms (PMFS), 76–78
Proctor & Gamble, 7
Project Camelot, 250, 256, 259–65
Project CLEAR, 258
Project 4.1 (study), 176
Project Man in Space program, 315–17
propaganda, 29, 71, 238; Hollywood films, 244,
   246; nuclear testing films, 110, 130–31; and
   militarism, 169; U.S. military, 142, 161,
   234, 246
prostitution, 58, 167; and military bases, 63, 65,
   180, 185, 344–45
psychological research, 254–55
Psychological Strategy Board, 258
PTSD, 24, 115, 320–22
public relations, 142, 159–61, 206. *See also*
   military normal
Pygmies, 336
Pyle, Ernie, 93

Rabi, I. I., 280
Rand Corporation, 308
recapitulation theory, 156–57
race and racism, 123, 153, 155–56, 173, 334, 345
rape, 88–90
Reagan, Ronald, 238, 297, 317, 349
Remarque, Erich Maria, 91–94
Republic of the Philippines–Korea Economic
   and Technical Cooperation Agreement, 66
Reserve Officer Training Corps (ROTC), 77
Reynolds, Craig, 70

rhetoric: of gender, 83; of generosity, 201; of
   maturity, 156; of memory, 243; militarism
   and, 141–42; of national security, 181
The Right Stuff (film), 233
Robb, David, 223, 230–34
Rockefeller Foundation, 252–53
rogue states, 163–64
Romania, 25n8, 178
Ronderos (rural patrols), 88
Rosenthal, Abe, 238
Ross, Fiona, 86
Rosser, Thomas "Tex," 94
Rumsfeld, Donald, 225
Russia, 64–65, 328. *See also* Soviet Union
Rwanda, 203, 214–15, 219

sacrifice: Aztecs and, 11–12; in combat, 84, 91,
   92–93, 140, 144–47, 210, 212, 224, 244, 301;
   glorification of, *82;* maternal, 87; and patrio-
   tism, 36; zones of, 167
Sadao, Araki, 145
Said, Edward, 155, 164
Saipan, 146
Sandinistas, 296
Sands of Iwo Jima (film), 244
Sandy Hook Elementary School massacre, 113
San people, 340
Sassoon, Siegfried, 92–93
Saudi Arabia, 22, 76–77
Saving Private Ryan (film), 6
Scarry, Elaine, 126n4, 159, 275–77
Schmookler, Andrew Bard, 14
Schneider, David, 115
School of the Americas, 18
Schurmann, Franz, 254
Schwarzkopf, Norman, 281–82
scientific colonialism, 261–62, 264
scientific militarism, 277
Scott, Joan, 155
Scull, Andy, 117
Seiberling, John, 149
Semai people, 13, 340
Senderistas, 88
Seoul (South Korea), 63, 180, 184
September 11 attacks: and "the homeland," 193;
   and "war on terror," 159, 225–26, 342; and
   militarism, 20, 38, 40; and "real Americans,"
   151–52